Erika Szyszczak
Adam Cygan

# Understanding
# EU Law

*Second Edition*

LONDON
SWEET & MAXWELL
2008

Published in 2008 by
Sweet & Maxwell Limited of 100 Avenue Road,
*http://www.sweetandmaxwell.co.uk*

First edition      (2005) Szyszczak, Cygan
Second edition      (2008) Szyszczak, Cygan

Copyright ©
Erika Szyszczak and Adam Cygan assert the moral right to be
identified as the authors of this work

No natural forests were destroyed to make this product;
only farmed timber was used and re-planted.

Typeset by J&L Composition Ltd, Filey, North Yorkshire
Printed and bound by
Krips, Meppel, the Netherlands

British Library Cataloguing in Publication Data

A CIP catalogue record for this book
is available from the British Library

ISBN 978–1–84703–279–9

UNDERSTANDING LAW
Editor: Roger Brownsword

*Understanding Contract Law*
John N. Adams and Roger Brownsword

*Understanding Law*
John N. Adams and Roger Brownsword

*Understanding Criminal Law*
C.M.V. Clarkson

*Understanding Public Law*
Gabriele Ganz

*Understanding Equity and Trusts*
Jeffrey Hackney

*Understanding Tort Law*
Carol Harlow

*Understanding Property Law*
Tim Murphy, Simon Roberts and Tatiana Flessas

*Understanding EU Law*
Erika Szyszczak and Adam Cygan

*Understanding Environmental Law*
Mark Stallworthy

# Preface

In 2005 our aim in writing the first edition of this book was to provide an accessible and modern understanding of European Union law, based upon an analysis of the principles which have under-pinned EU integration. The year of this second edition, 2008, is a watershed in the history of the EU. It is a time for nostalgic reflection and a chance to glimpse the future. We celebrate the golden anniversary of the first EEC Treaty coming into force[1] with an affirmation from the three dominant EU Institutions that ". . . we know that Europe is our common future".[2] Paradoxically, at the same time, the EU has undergone a radical makeover: as a result of the signing of the Treaty of Lisbon on December 17, 2007, it has a change of name (to the Union), a consolidation of the basic Treaty Treaties into two texts (a new *Treaty on European Union* and a *Treaty on the Functioning of the Union*) and with this, the challenge of learning yet a new set of numbers for the basic Treaty provisions. We have tentatively assumed that the Treaty of Lisbon will be ratified by the Member States and have therefore discussed the changes the Treaty will make to EU integration. But, . . . just in case, and to avoid too much confusion . . . we have used italics to cite the new numbering of the Treaty Articles.

We thank our colleagues and students who over the years have refined our own understanding of EU Law. A special thanks to the "guinea pigs" for the first edition who gave constructive feedback. The University of Leicester provided us with a study leave which enabled us to write a second edition. Finally, our thanks to our families—Basia, Agnieszka, Richard, Jamie, Larissa and William—for their patience and forbearance in allowing us to write this book.

Leicester
April 2008

---

[1] The Treaty of Rome (EEC) was signed on March 25, 1957 and came into force on January 1, 1958.

[2] European Parliament, Council of the European, Commission of the European Communities, Declaration on the Occasion of the 50th Anniversary of the Signature of the Treaties of Rome, March 25, 2007.

# Contents

# Alphabetical Table of Cases

# Numerical Table of Cases

## European Court of Justice

## Court of First Instance

# Table of Cases Before UK Courts

# 1: Institutional, Economic and Political Integration in the European Union

## SUMMARY

## 1.1 Introduction

European history in the first half of the 20th century is dominated by military conflict. Peace and stability in Europe through economic and political consensus have been the primary achievements of European integration which began in the aftermath of World War II. This integration, which commenced in the early 1950s, had at its core reconciliation between France and Germany and putting an end to a recurring cycle of wars. Subsequent co-operation has been based upon a voluntary observance of legally binding Treaty provisions and secondary legislation which are guaranteed by a supra-national court. In 1951 six Member States[1] signed the Treaty of Paris and created the European Coal and Steel Community. The principles of shared sovereignty and supra-national co-operation which underpinned this first Treaty remain relevant to European integration over 50 years later.

Today the European Union (EU) dominates the geopolitical area of the continent of Europe and following the 2007 enlargement

---

[1] In addition to France and Germany, Italy, the Netherlands, Belgium and Luxembourg were signatories.

consists of 27 Member States with a population estimated at over 490 million citizens. This makes the EU the world's largest trading bloc in terms of population and an important international economic player. The geographic land mass of the EU spans from the Arctic Circle in Finland to the Azores in the Atlantic Ocean, yet even following the 2007 enlargement, many European countries remain outside the process of EU integration. One consequence of the 2004 and 2007 enlargements is that the centre of gravity of the EU has shifted eastwards and its surface area has increased by over a quarter. From 2004 the EU shares a border with countries of the former Soviet Union.

The EU does not constitute the entire continent of Europe which can be divided in to those countries inside the EU and those situated on its periphery. For some, such as Norway and Switzerland, referenda have confirmed their intention to remain outside. Others, for example, Croatia and Macedonia, are engaged in a process of accession leading to EU membership in 2010. Turkey, the only non-Christian country to seek EU membership, is unlikely to complete accession negotiations before 2015 and several Member States remain openly hostile to Turkish accession. Countries such as the Ukraine, which shares the EU's eastern border, remain outside the formal accession process, but nonetheless cannot ignore the consequences of having the world's most populous single economic and political zone as its neighbour. The day-to-day decision-making of the EU's neighbours is influenced by the spill over of the EU's policy objectives. In addition to economic policies, EU norms also influence environmental policies and increasingly immigration and human rights strategies.

EU integration has created what Harding refers to as a "European legal space" (2000:130). Despite the rejection of the Constitutional Treaty in 2005, which would have provided the EU with a single Constitutional document the existing Treaty framework has enabled 50 years of economic, social and political integration. This has led to the creation of the Internal Market and allowed the EU to pursue political integration through inter-governmental co-operation which was initiated by the Treaty of Maastricht Treaty in 1992. Linked to this internal integration is the relationship which the EU enjoys with the wider world through the Common Commercial Policy (CCP) and Common Foreign and Security Policy (CFSP). These policies seek to provide a uniform voice for the EU in economic and foreign affairs.

The primary objective of the Internal Market was the removal of internal barriers to trade and the creation of a corresponding common policy towards third countries. Article 133 EC regulates the import of products from third countries and is the Treaty base for the EU's Common Commercial Policy (CCP). To protect the integrity of the Internal Market in goods it has been necessary to employ controls, both physical and fiscal, which regulate access in to the Internal Market from third countries. Today the trading relationship which the EU enjoys with third countries is influenced by an external set of rules arising from the World Trade Organisation (WTO) in which the Member States are, in certain circumstances, represented by the EU as a single trading bloc. This will occur where the Member States have granted exclusive competence to the EU through the Treaty. The European Court of Justice (ECJ) confirmed this in *Opinion 1/94*,[2] but also held that in the absence of exclusive EU competence, Member States retain the right to regulate certain aspects of the WTO.

Following the Maastricht Treaty, the focus of Internal Market regulation has shifted away from goods and has become more orientated towards the free movement of persons and EU citizenship.[3] Additionally, the influx of economic migrants in to the EU, following the collapse of the Berlin Wall, required a coherent policy towards third country nationals entering the EU. The strategic policy has been part of a broader package of measures which have sought to ease internal movement for EU nationals while simultaneously improving security and tackling illegal immigration and organised crime. The incorporation of the Schengen *acquis* in to the EU has been a central part of this strategy. Within the enlarged EU wide discrepancies exist in the pace of economic development between the 27 Member States, and these discrepancies are even greater when compared with the EU's neighbours. The challenge for the EU is to facilitate economic migration and individual mobility for EU nationals, while maintaining effective barriers towards third country nationals (Cygan, 2004:251).

The process of internal integration influences the development of the EU's external policies. Post enlargement the EU's relationship with its neighbours is a paramount consideration and includes a degree of quasi-integration which did not exist between the EU and its neighbours throughout the Cold War period. While pressing for its neighbours to improve their economic and social polices, and

---

[2] *Opinion 1/94 (Competence of the Community to Conclude International Agreements Concerning Services and the Protection of Intellectual Property)* [1994] E.C.R. I-5267.
[3] See Case C-85/96 *Martínez Sala v Freistaat Bayern* [1998] E.C.R. I-2691.

providing financial assistance for this, the EU has correspondingly restricted access to its territory for nationals from the neighbouring states. The EU is attempting to control migration and labour markets within its own borders and seeks to influence the migration policies and practice of its neighbours. Free movement of persons in the EU requires a common policy with regard to the removal of internal borders and close co-operation with its neighbours to manage movement across the EU's external borders. EU polices such at the Neighbourhood Strategy[4] have recognised that the external aspect of the Schengen *acquis* can only be achieved with the co-operation of its neighbours. The incentive offered to North African countries and the Ukraine was nearly €1 billion euros between 2004–2006 in technical assistance for improved border controls and economic regeneration.[5]

Despite 50 years of integration the EU lacks homogeneity with regard to many of the political aspirations it seeks to achieve. The Laeken Declaration[6] identified that EU citizens felt disconnected with the integration project and the rejection of the Constitutional Treaty by the Heads of State confirms this, at least in part. Furthermore, the *acquis communitaire*, the whole breadth of laws and policies which make up the EU, have not guaranteed uniformity of action. For example, co-operation in the area of foreign and security policy, first introduced at Maastricht 1991, and broadened at Amsterdam 1997, has not led to uniform responses to political crises which have concerned the EU since 1992.

The lack of a coherent policy towards the break up of Yugoslavia, witnessed recently in EU disagreement on the status of an independent Kosovo and the fragmented approach to the Iraq War in 2003, demonstrate that full political integration remains illusive

The process of EU integration, whether economic or political, cannot be understood without considering both the internal aspects of integration, and the EU's external relations policy. EU integration is a multi-faceted package of legislation and policies which binds the Member States together, yet the reach and impact of this law and policy goes beyond the borders of the EU. The standpoint of this book is that in order to understand EU law it is necessary to understand *how* EU integration has developed internally, how it is posi-

---

[4] COM(2003) 104 final. Communication from the Commission to the Council and the European Parliament Wider Europe—Neighbourhood: A New Framework for Relations With Our Eastern and Southern Neighbours.

[5] COM (2004) 373 final.

[6] Laeken European Council December, 15, 2001.

tioned within the geopolitical context of the continent of Europe, and how the outside world views the EU.

## 1.2 The Historical Context of European Integration

European integration is not a post-war 20th century concept. European history up to the mid-20th century is categorised by military expansionists from the Romans to Napoleon and Hitler, who have pursued aggressive campaigns attempting to unify the continent (Chalmers, 1998:2). These attempts were based on the assumption that military superiority would create and maintain an empire. As the history books illustrate forced integration sooner or later, ends in failure. Consequently, post World War II European integration has been pursued through creating a consensus amongst political elites and economically active individuals with the objective of creating shared European values.

The roots of the EU lie in the Second World War. Since 1945 European co-operation and integration has taken place at various levels and is characterised by a desire to avoid conflict. Jean Monnet, described as the architect of European integration, argued that only a federal Europe could avoid future military conflict (Monnet, 1978). The Council of Europe in 1948 was the first formal co-operation in post war Europe. The genesis of the Council of Europe can be traced back to Winston Churchill's Zurich University speech in 1946. Here he spoke of a "common European home" and "united states of Europe" which required Franco-German reconciliation. The most notable and enduring achievement of the Council of Europe has been the European Convention on the Protection of Human Rights and Fundamental Freedoms (ECHR) 1950. The jurisprudence of the European Court of Human Rights, which has interpreted the principles of the ECHR has provided uniform minimum standards of human rights norms for all signatories.

The process of reconciliation began with the French Foreign Minister Robert Schuman advocating the eponymous Schuman Plan on May 9, 1950. In this post-war period, Europe was still reliant upon the Marshall Aid programme which the US had provided since 1945 to assist European regeneration. Schuman was advocating that Marshall Aid be replaced with a distinct European renaissance. At the core was a belief that economic integration would deliver prosperity for individuals. The plan would require nation states to work within a formal supra-national institutional framework. Schuman viewed his plan as a blueprint for economic, political and military co-operation in Europe. But from 1950 to the early 1990s the Cold War would dominate European politics and provide a diversion and barrier to wider European integration.

A feature of European co-operation in the early 1950s is that it lacked trust and commitment from those involved. France remained cautious of Germany and was unenthusiastic about military co-operation. The French Parliament refused to ratify the European Defence Community Treaty in 1952 and though some military co-operation existed in the form of the Western European Union, the North Atlantic Treaty Organisation (NATO) signed in 1949 overshadowed this informal co-operation. Ironically, despite the desire for an independent European identity, NATO has remained dominated by the US and suggests that military co-operation requires a strong transatlantic relationship. The Western European Union did evolve in the 1980s and was formally absorbed in to the EU under the CFSP.

The UK was a reluctant participant in the early years of European integration, primarily because it remained distrustful of political co-operation with France. The UK participated in NATO and was closer to the US and its strategic aims rather than to France or Germany. This tense relationship with its European neighbours would see the UK outside the formal framework of European integration until 1973.

## The European Coal and Steel Community

At the heart of the Schuman Plan was the proposal to place Franco-German coal and steel production under the control of supra-national institutions. The reasons for this were two-fold. Firstly, the plan recognised that coal and steel had been used as the raw materials of war. If production of these basic commodities were placed beyond the exclusive control of nation states, this could prevent their use for aggressive military purposes. Secondly, Schuman recognised that to be independent of US economic assistance, there would need to be economies of scale in the production of coal and steel. This required that production of these raw materials would be managed centrally by supra-national institutions. The result was the European Coal and Steel Community (ECSC), which came in to force in 1952 and expired in 2002. This Treaty is significant because it transferred competence in decision-making, albeit in the limited sphere of coal and steel, to supra-national institutions. Italy and the Benelux countries joined France and Germany in the ECSC while the UK watched suspiciously from the sidelines.

The formal economic co-operation of the ECSC was a marked progress in European integration from the Council of Europe (Craig and De Búrca, 2007:5). The co-operation was founded on economic collaboration and free trade in coal and steel. In addition to the decision-making institutions, the Treaty established a Court of Justice that would guarantee implementation of the Treaty and secondary legislation and arbitrate between Member States. These distinct features of the European integration, which seemed radical at the time, are now the accepted norms of European integration.

The ECSC had spill over effects that went beyond economic integration. It undoubtedly contained elements of political integration through transfer of decision-making power to the supra-national institutions. These were a High Authority under the control of a President which was the most powerful body, a Council of Ministers, and an Assembly composed of representatives from national parliaments. While the Council of Europe remained a forum for discussion, the ECSC created a formal decision-making structure, which unlike other international agreements required the surrender of sovereign policy-making and legal powers. Crucially, the ECSC required solidarity between the Member States. The prevailing objective was that by acting together the benefits derived by the Member States would be greater than if they acted individually. Accordingly, if a Member State did not abide by the rules of the ECSC Treaty, the Court of Justice would ensure that the objectives of the Treaty were enforced. In this lies the beginning of the principle of supremacy which is the foundation of European Community (EC) law and through which the sophisticated economic integration of the Internal Market has been achieved.

## The EEC and Euratom Treaties

The failure of a European defence policy and limited progress on political integration suggested that in the early 1950s European integration lacked clear and tangible objectives. The relative success of the ECSC provided those six Member States with a structure within which to operate. The 1955 Messina Conference culminated in the production of the *Spaak Report*.[7] The conclusions of the Spaak inquiry were presented to an inter-governmental meeting of the Six and led to the establishment of the European Economic Community (EEC) and the European Atomic Energy Community (Euratom).

---

[7] Named after the then Dutch Foreign Minister Paul Henri Spaak.

The Treaties of Rome signed in 1957 established both Communities and came in to force in 1958. The EEC and Euratom followed the institutional structure of the ECSC. Two new institutions were established for the EEC and Euratom, namely a Commission and Council of Ministers, with the Court of Justice and Assembly serving all three Communities. The economic integration process which began with these Treaties is often described as being functionalist because it focussed on delivering tangible economic benefits through sectoral management of economic activity by a technocratic elite (Craig, 1999:2).

For those countries outside the Treaties the European Free Trade Association (EFTA) was established in 1960 as an alternative means for economic co-operation. The UK took the lead in EFTA demonstrating its reluctance to join a Franco-German dominated EEC. Most of the EFTA countries have now joined the EU, with the exception of Switzerland and Norway. Both countries enjoy strong economic links with the EU Member States and have adopted many. Internal Market principles with respect to their own external trade policies. This reinforces the proposition that EU law and policy has spill over effects and that even prosperous European countries cannot ignore the norms of the Internal Market.

The creation of three separate Treaties was inefficient in terms of administration. In 1965 the Merger Treaty was signed and this came in to force in 1967. The effect of this was to merge the High Authority of the ECSC with the two Commissions in to one body which is still known as the European Commission. Furthermore, the Merger Treaty provided that there would only be one Council of Ministers, which is the primary decision making body. Other institutional changes included the creation of a European Assembly which elected its MEPs for the first time in 1979. The Single European Act (SEA) 1987 officially changed the name to the European Parliament. The change of name prompted the European Parliament to seek an increased role as co-legislator with the Council of Ministers. The question of how to increase the powers of the European Parliament has been a central issue in Treaty changes that have taken place since 1986. One reason for this was that the EEC was described as undemocratic and lacking a system of checks and balances. According to Westlake (1998: 433) and Shackleton (2000:334), the phased increase of legislative powers for the European Parliament has proved the most effective way in which to remedy this so called "democratic deficit" in the political process.

## The Single European Act (SEA) 1986

Since the 1950s economic integration has passed through many phases. The 1960s and 1970s were categorised by "Eurosclerosis" when integration was slow primarily because of national self-interest (Nichol, 1984:36). During this period the ECJ ensured that the foundations for an economic constitution were laid. Following the 1985 White Paper on the Completion of the Internal Market[8] which was accepted by the Intergovernmental Conference (IGC), economic integration achieved a new impetus. Pescatore, sceptical about this development, argued that significant progress towards economic integration had already been achieved by 1985 and the SEA did no more than reaffirm existing provisions of the EEC Treaty (Pescatore, 1987:11).

The SEA is characterised by its single market objective and the usage of different governance techniques which are discussed throughout this book. In a procedural context it restricted the national veto, the primary reason for Eurosclerosis and replaced it with qualified majority voting (QMV). This created a communitaire method of economic integration, based upon majoritarian principles. The SEA also included a fixed deadline of December 31, 1992, for completion of the Internal Market. Taken together these developments were important for several reasons. Firstly, they focussed the Member States to achieve the objectives of the White Paper within a given timescale. Secondly, this task was made easier through the White Paper utilising the principle of mutual recognition, which came from the Court's 1979 *Cassis de Dijon* judgment,[9] as the guiding principle for economic integration. In practice this meant a move away from highly technical, complex and maximum standard sectoral legislation, to the introduction of legislation based upon minimum standard harmonisation. Thirdly, the completion of economic integration was identified as a necessary precursor to more ambitious political integration initiated by the Maastricht Treaty. This latter point represents a neofunctionalist interpretation of integration which suggests that economic integration will have spill over effects that lead to integration in other, more sensitive, policy areas (Craig, 1999:3).

The objectives of the White Paper were broadly successful and in 1989 the European Council held two inter-governmental conferences which were intended to examine the next steps for European

---

[8] (COM (85) 220).
[9] Case 120/78 *Cassis de Dijon* [1979] E.C.R. 649.

integration. In the first IGC the Member States considered how to move forward with Economic and Monetary Union (EMU). The adoption of a single European currency was viewed as the next logical step to follow the completion of the Internal Market. In 1999 the Euro became the single European currency for all transactions involving financial institutions in 12 out of 15 Member States, with notes and coins entering circulation in 2002.

The second IGC considered the controversial issue of political integration. For some Member States, most notably the UK, closer political integration has presented problems. The primary effect of closer integration is the transfer of sovereignty and the power of political decision-making to the European level. Policies such as immigration, defence and foreign affairs, which were considered to be the exclusive domain of Member States, were brought within the competence of the EU. The outcome of the two IGC's was brought together in the Maastricht Treaty.

## The Treaty of Maastricht 1993

The Maastricht Treaty introduced inter-governmental co-operation between the Member States in two new pillars of foreign policy and justice and home affairs. These inter-governmental pillars, based on political co-operation were distinct from the economic co-operation of the Internal Market and did not utilise the same decision-making procedures. Furthermore, decisions taken under the pillars were not subject to automatic review by the ECJ. Consequently the development of political co-operation at the European level created the European Union (EU), the umbrella term for all EU activity. The change of name to the EU was intended to reflect more accurately the depth of co-operation and the desire expressed in the Maastricht Treaty for "ever closer integration". The two new pillars were in addition to the central pillar of economic co-operation, the European Community (EC) pillar. The central pillar itself had changed its name from the EEC to the EC with the word 'Economic' having been dropped. This reflected the new competence of the EC in social policy and environmental matters which while flanking economic integration, also have broader social objectives. The UK was sceptical of this "social Europe" and secured an opt-out from the Social Chapter of the Maastricht Treaty which led to criticism that an a la carte Europe undermined integration (Szyszczak 1994:313).

In the early 1990s European politics was dominated by the effects of the collapse of the Soviet Union and the democratisation of

Eastern Europe running alongside a move to market economics. One immediate impact of this was the determination of the new democracies (such as Poland and Hungary) to become integrated in to the EU. The Maastricht Treaty came too early for any significant development towards this proposed enlargement. Several Member States questioned whether such an enlargement was prudent while the EU was pursuing deeper political integration and monetary union. The post-Maastricht debate was dominated by discussions of whether widening membership, or deepening integration of the existing Member States, should be the priority. The result was to try and do both and the 1996 IGC was established to consider how eastward enlargement and deeper integration could be assimilated.

## The Treaty of Amsterdam 1997

The 1996 IGC resulted in the Amsterdam Treaty which proved a mixed success with regard to preparing for enlargement (Langrish, 1998:18). The crucial questions of the institutional structure and decision-making post enlargement were deferred to a further IGC in 2000, but a commitment to enlargement, sooner rather than later, was given. The Member States agreed March 1998 as the date for the formal opening of talks with those countries selected for enlargement, though no final commitment to a completion date for accession negotiations was given.

With regard to the objective of deeper integration the Amsterdam Treaty consolidated many of the Maastricht developments. The UK, with a new Labour government signed the Social Chapter first introduced at The Treaty of Maastricht. One significant development in EU competence brought about by the Treaty of Amsterdam came in the area of immigration policy. The Schengen Agreement, hitherto outside of the scope of the EU was incorporated in to Title IV the EC pillar[10] reflecting the "communitarisation" of immigration policy. The Schengen Agreement had allowed for free movement of nationals from Schengen countries across all Schengen borders, and for third country nationals to move freely once they have entered the Schengen area. The UK, which had always remained outside the Schengen Agreement, secured an opt-out from the Schengen *acquis*.[11]

---

[10] Title IV Visas, Asylum and Immigration and Other Policies Related to Free Movement of Persons.

[11] Art.69 EC and Protocol on the Integration of the Schengen *Acquis* into the Framework of the European Union, Protocol on the Application of Certain Aspects of Article 14 EC of the Treaty Establishing the European Community to

Additionally, some aspects of immigration policy moved from pillar three to Title IV of the EC pillar with the UK again securing an opt-out, but reserving the right to participate when it was in the national interest. This move of immigration policy in to the EC pillar is significant. The primary effect is that these aspects of border control and immigration policy are now subject to different decision-making procedures where the veto is less prominent. Furthermore, such legislation is subject to judicial review by the Court of Justice.

## The Treaty of Nice 2001

The lack of political consensus concerning the question of institutional reform in preparation for enlargement defined the Treaty of Amsterdam. The prospect of enlargement posed several challenges for the EU. The Treaty of Nice was intended to reform the Institutions in preparation for enlargement but was agreed against a backdrop of popular disenchantment with the EU and a feeling of disconnection between the citizens and the EU integration project. Criticisms of over-intrusive and prescriptive legislation, an absence of relevance in the daily lives of citizens and disagreement between Member States on the scope of integration required a change of direction for the integration process.

The rejection of the Nice Treaty by Irish citizens in the 2001 referendum embodied the feeling of mistrust which many citizens felt towards the EU. The Irish gave their consent to the Treaty in a second referendum and the Treaty entered in to force on February 1, 2003. Within the Treaty a Declaration was attached expressing the need to "re-connect" the citizen with the political process of integration. Consequently, in July 2001, the Commission published a *White Paper on the Future Governance of the EU* setting out various options for Institutional reform.[12] The issue of citizen disengagement dominated the EU before the Treaty of Nice, this despite the citizen being the recipient of EU rights in areas such as social and employment policy. The strategy post-Nice has been to place the individual at the heart of the integration process and can be considered as recognition of the role of the citizen to achieving economic prosperity.

the United Kingdom and Northern Ireland and Protocol on the position of the United Kingdom and Ireland.

[12] COM(2001) 428 *European Governance—A White Paper*.

## *The Constitutional Treaty 2004 and the Treaty of Lisbon 2007*

Three years of discussion in the Constitutional Convention culminated in the Constitutional Treaty in 2004 which was rejected by both France and Spain in referenda in 2005. This failure to ratify what was considered to be an EU Constitution forced the EU to "pause for reflection" in relation to further Treaty reform. Following two years of 'reflection' the German Presidency in the first half of 2007 pushed for agreement of a new Treaty which was accepted by the Member States at the European Council in June 2007. The Presidency Conclusions[13] provided for the convening of an Intergovernmental Conference (IGC) which was to draft a new Treaty the objective of which was to "enhance the efficiency and democratic legitimacy of the enlarged Union, as well as the coherence of its external action".[14]

Following the IGC negotiations the Member States agreed what is known as the Treaty of Lisbon 2007. Unlike the Constitutional Treaty, which consisted of repealing all other Treaties and replacing them with a single document called a "Constitution", the Treaty of Lisbon abandons this approach. Once ratified by all Member States the Treaty of Lisbon will introduce in to the existing Treaty framework a number of reforms, many of which were first included in the Constitutional Treaty.

The Treaty of Lisbon contains two substantive clauses amending respectively the Treaty on the European Union (TEU) and the EC Treaty. The TEU retains its existing name and the EC Treaty will be called Treaty on the Functioning of the Union TFEU), with the Union having a single legal personality. The word 'Community' is replaced by the word 'Union' throughout and it is stated that the two Treaties constitute the Treaties on which the Union is founded and that the Union replaces and succeeds the Community. The Presidency Conclusions stated that the new Treaty does not have a "constitutional" character. The terminology used throughout the Treaties seeks to reflect this change with the term 'Constitution' omitted. The use of the term 'Constitution' together with the creation of the posts of the Union Minister for Foreign Affairs were but two inclusions in the Constitutional Treaty which caused concern for some Member States. Such developments were viewed as creating an EU "superstate".

---

[13] Brussels European Council June 2007 21–22, 11177/1/07 REV 1.
[14] Brussels European Council June 2007 21–22, 11177/1/07 REV 1, p.15.

The Treaty of Lisbon was formally signed by the Member States in December 2007. The target date for ratification of the Treaty of Lisbon Treaty is January 1, 2009 which will allow for the new institutional arrangements to be put in place before the European Parliament elections in June 2009.

The amendments introduced by the Treaty of Lisbon has led to a new Consolidated Treaty of the European Union which includes both the TEU and TFEU. The consequence of this consolidation is that the Treaty numbers have changed from those in the existing TEU and EC Treaties. Where relevant the new Treaty provisions have been included in this book.

## Creating a European Polity?

The new Treaty framework constitutes the EU's primary legislation providing a Constitutional foundation. Treaty development in the EU has been a slow process, but since 1986 there have been four new Treaties that have been ratified by the Member States. With each new Treaty new competences have been added and individual rights increased. The challenge since 1957 has been to guarantee the rights contained within the Treaty and it is the ECJ which has ensured Treaty rights take precedence over domestic laws. Since 1957 the principle of supremacy has developed through the ECJ constitutionalising the Treaty in judgments such as *Van Gend en Loos*.[15] The ECJ's judgments have consistently held that the Treaties have established a new legal order with its own institutions and enforcement mechanism in which "Member States have limited their sovereign rights in ever wider fields and the subjects of which comprise not only the Member States but also their nationals".[16]

The shared characteristic of all Treaty developments has been the incremental extension of individual rights whether economic or social, for example the introduction of art.13 EC by the Treaty of Amsterdam. This provision extends the principle of non-discrimination seen in art.12 EC which is limited to discrimination on grounds of nationality. Article 13 EC provides for non-discrimination on grounds of race, gender, sexual orientation and religious belief and has provided a Treaty base for introduction of directives such as dir.2004/43/EC on the principle of equal treatment between persons

---

[15] Case 26/62 *Van Gend en Loos v Nederlanse Administratie der Belastingen* [1963] E.C.R. 1.

[16] *Opinion 1/91* [1991] E.C.R. 6102, *ibid, Van Gend en Loos* at 12–13.

irrespective of racial or ethnic origin.[17] The directive permits, under art.5, for positive action to prevent or compensate for disadvantages resulting from a racial or ethnic origin. To undertake positive action, disadvantages must first be established and the means to eliminate them must be proportionate and positive action is precluded as soon as the disadvantageous situation has disappeared. The provision is similar to art.2 (4) of the 1976 Equal Treatment Directive[18] which provides that "provisions contrary to the principle of equal treatment, when the concern that originally inspired them is no longer well-founded, shall be revised".[19] In *Kalanke*[20] the case concerned the decision to offer employment to a female applicant over a male applicant in circumstances where both were equally qualified. The decision was based upon a German law requiring that female candidates receive preference, all other criteria being equal, in sectors in which women were under-represented. The law defined under-representation as occurring when women constitute less than half of the employees.

The Court held that since art.2 (4) was an exception to the right to equal treatment, it must therefore be interpreted strictly and consequently struck down the rule providing that priority must be given to women, as long as they were under-represented, among equally qualified candidates for promotion. The narrow interpretation by the Court is not surprising but the Court does not exclude the possibility of positive action and consequently, provisions such as art.5 of dir.2004/43/EC have been included in specific legislation intended to promote greater equality in the workplace.

The inclusion of art.13 EC in the Amsterdam Treaty was based upon 40 years of jurisprudence and policy that gradually extended the scope of non-discrimination from the traditional concept of nationality in art.12 EC to provide increased protection against discrimination to individuals in the workplace. In this context, what factors can be identified that have enabled EU law to provide individuals with a diverse and comprehensive set of rights enforceable before national courts? This increased protection has occurred *despite* the absence of a single EU Constitution.

---

[17] Council dir.2000/43/EC of June 29, 2000 implementing the principle of equal treatment between persons irrespective of racial or ethnic origin, O.J. L 180, July 19, 2000, p. 22–26.

[18] Council dir.1976/207/EEC of February 9, 1976 on the implementation of the principle of equal treatment for men and women as regards access to employment, vocational training and promotion, and working conditions, (1976) O. J. L 39, p.40.

[19] Arts 3(2)(c) and 5(2)(c) Council dir.1976/207/EEC.

[20] Case C-450/93 *Kalanke v Freie Hansestadt Bremen* (1995) E.C.R. I-3051.

Agreement between the Member States to create the Treaties has its roots in supra-national co-operation using classical diplomatic techniques between sovereign nation states (Hartley, 2001:238). The Treaties, being a form of international law, have required a commitment by the Member States to a principle of solidarity, contained in art.10 EC, that they will uphold the objectives of the Treaties. In the absence of an explicit supremacy provision in the Treaties, it has been left to the ECJ to ensure, through techniques such as direct effect and state liability,[21] that individuals can enforce their Treaty rights.

The role of the ECJ is to ensure compliance with the Treaties and the secondary legislation, the latter of which expands upon the basic Treaty principle. The Treaties, written by the Member States, are a statement of EU competence and provide the legal base for further action. Questions relating to EU competence to introduce secondary legislation have regularly been considered by the Court. Where competence exists the Court has sought to maximise the protection individuals receive under the legislation. In the absence of specific Treaty provisions granting competence, for example, in areas such as health or education, the Court has refrained from re-writing the Treaties and bringing such policies within EU competence. The only exception to this is where the activity is incidental to exercise the specific rights granted by the Treaty, for example in relation to rights of free movement.[22] In these situations, the objective of the Court has been to maximise the circumstances where Community rights are available, rather than rewrite the Treaty to extend competence. Similarly, in circumstances where the Member States have introduced secondary legislation which is beyond the competence of the Treaty, the Court of Justice has declared that this is ultra vires,[23] thereby confirming that the Treaties define the parameters of EU action.

The absence of one single constitutional document should not necessarily be considered as a weakness or a restriction to integration. The Court has ensured that, where the EU has competence the rights contained within the Treaty are guaranteed. The Treaty structure can be explained as an expression of what sovereign nation states have wanted to achieve at a given moment. Integration has

---

[21] See for example Case 6/64 *Costa v ENEL* [1964] E.C.R. 585 and Joined Cases C-6 and 9/90 *Francovich and Bonifaci v Italian State* [1991] E.C.R. I-5357.

[22] See for example Cases 296/82 and 26/83 *Luisi and Carbone v Minister del Toro* [1984] E.C.R. 377.

[23] Case C-376/98 *Germany v Council (Tobacco Advertising)* [2000] E.C.R. I-8419.

been incremental which is characteristic of the supra-national structure of the EU. It remains for the Court to act as both guarantor of Treaty rights and guardian of legal competence. Consequently, the success or otherwise of European integration should be judged upon the basis of achieving the expressly stated Treaty objectives.

Wyatt et al contend that European integration has been achieved incrementally through several Treaty amendments with further competencies being added on each occasion (Wyatt and Dashwood, 2007:83). This observation has been challenged by other commentators who have contended that the Court of Justice is an activist judicial institution (Rasmussen, 1988:29). Through judgments such as *Defrenne*,[24] where the Court acknowledged the social objectives of art.141 EC to eliminate discrimination between men and women in employment, has the Court pushed forward the process of integration beyond the intentions of the Member States? Have the Court's judgments interpreted Community rights more broadly than that which the Member States set out in the Treaty? If so, has the Court acted as an integrationist and quasi-constitutional court which has invented new rights, or extended existing ones? Alternatively, has the Court of Justice merely fulfilled its remit under art.220 EC? The answer to these issues lies partly within the Treaty itself and partly through the case law of the Court.

Since 1957 the objective of the Treaty has been the creation of an 'ever closer union'. The construction of an Internal Market was likewise a clear Treaty objective and the Court has used judgments such as *Cassis* de *Dijon* and *Bosman*[25] to move forward the process of economic integration and create an "economic constitution" (Maduro, 1998:98; Szyszczak, 2007). The Court, mindful of the ambivalence of Member States to pursue economic integration in the 1960s and 1970s, took it upon itself to keep momentum in the integration process when the political will was absent.

The Court's teleological, or purposive, interpretation of the Treaties can be identified as the central element through which an economic constitution has been created (Weiler, 1999:42). The legal integration promulgated by the Court is part of the wider objective of integration and governance which is the responsibility of all Institutions. Though the EU does not have a government, it possesses clear governance structures and legislative procedures which are based on institutional interaction and the use of clearly

---

[24] Case 149/77 *Defrenne v Sabena* [1978] E.C.R. 1365.
[25] Case C-415/93 *Union Royal Belges de Sociétés de Football Association v Jean-Marc Bosman* [1995] E.C.R. I-4921.

defined powers. The Court has regularly acted as arbiter of the relationship between the political institutions, and its primary role has been to ensure that the legislative powers given to the Institutions by the Treaties can be fully exercised. It is these legislative procedures and institutional structure which will now be considered in more detail.

## 1.3 The Issue of Legal Base

EU competence arises from the Treaty which provides a legal foundation for all EU action. As the EU has a multi-level governance structure this requires that competencies are allocated between the various levels. In some instances the EU has exclusive competence to act, whereas in others it shares competence with the Member States. In such circumstances, according to the principle of subsidiarity in art.5 EC, the Community should only act if the Member States acting independently could not achieve the result. Though the presumption for action would, under art.5 EC, appear to lie with the Member States, it can be argued that the principle of subsidiarity conflicts with the objective an "ever closer union" which presupposes action at the EU level to achieve integration. The Amsterdam Protocol on Subsidiarity contains rules relating to the application of subsidiarity against which the Commission benchmarks legislative proposals. According to Chalmers (1998:223) the Commission should only act if a failure to do so would conflict with the Treaty requirements. The Court, perceived as integrationist institution has through its judgments applied a narrow interpretation of subsidiarity and viewed it as a restriction to further integration.[26]

Subsidiarity is a political concept because it concerns the choice of legislative actor and, in part, explains *why* the Court is reluctant to review legislation. Article 5 EC also contains the closely related principle of proportionality, which is a legal concept. This principle, developed by the Court in judgments such as *Cassis de Dijon*, requires legislative action to not go beyond that which is absolutely necessary to achieve the desired objective. It reflects a criticism which many citizens share about EU legislation, that it is too prescriptive and detailed. The Amsterdam Protocol on Subsidiarity

---

[26] Case C-84/94 *United Kingdom v Council* (*Working Time Directive*) [1996] E.C.R. I-5755.

also extends to the principle of proportionality and requires Institutional justification for the contents of the legislative proposal. The choice of legal base for legislation is crucial, as this will determine which legislative process is used, and in turn defines the extent of institutional participation. Legal base questions raise a number of horizontal issues concerning the relationship between the Institutions. Treaty amendments have introduced new legislative procedures and it remains in the hands of the Commission to decide which Treaty base is the most appropriate. The choice of Treaty base has proved controversial on occasion because this has led to the exclusion of the European Parliament from the decision-making process. In the *Commission v Council (Titanium Dioxide)*[27] the Court stated that the choice of legal basis for a Community legal act must rest on objective factors which are amenable to judicial review, including in particular the aim and content of the act.[28] In this case the legislative measure at issue concerned the setting of titanium dioxide levels. The purpose of the directive was twofold. Firstly, it promoted a high level of environmental protection, and secondly, it sought to increase competition in the titanium dioxide market. Environmental matters are covered by art.175 EC and require unanimity by the Council but under this legal base only required consultation with the European Parliament. By contrast, the issue of competition being an Internal Market measure required the use of qualified majority voting in Council and application of the co-operation procedure under art.95 EC. This Treaty base gives Parliament the power to propose amendments to the legislation which is not possible under the consultation process. The Commission selected art.95 EC as the base but the Council substituted it for art.175 EC.

The Court considered the objective of the measure and held the primary purpose was to promote the Internal Market and that environmental considerations were of secondary concern, making art.95 EC the appropriate Treaty base. The Court was mindful of the need to guarantee Parliament's rights under the Treaty to participate in

---

[27] Case C-300/89 *Commission v Council (Titanium Dioxide)* [1991] E.C.R. I-2867.
[28] Case C-300/89 *Commission v Council (Titanium Dioxide)* [1991] E.C.R. I-2867, para.10. See also Case C-84/94 *United Kingdom v Council* [1996] E.C.R. I-5755, para.25; Joined Cases C-164/97 and C-165/97 *Parliament v Council* [1999] E.C.R. I-1139, para.12; Case C-269/97 *Commission v Council* [2000] E.C.R. I-2257, para.43; Case C-336/00 *Huber* [2002] E.C.R. I-7699, para.30; Case C-491/01 *British American Tobacco* [2002] E.C.R. I-11453, para.93; Case C-338/01 *Commission v Council* [2004] E.C.R. I-4829, para.54; Case C-110/03 *Belgium v Commission* [2005] E.C.R. I-5425, para.78; and Case C-347/03 *Regione autonoma Friuli-Venezia Giulia* [2005] E.C.R. I-3785, para.72.

the legislative process and this is part of the Court's strategy to review choice of Treaty base and promote institutional balance within the EU.[29]

Treaty base is central to the concept of vires and the objective of the Court is to ensure the legality of decision-making. Without this, EU law would be devoid of its democratic legitimacy. Any system of public law requires a rule of law, which includes governance according to the law. In the absence of a specific Treaty base art.308 EC permits Community action if this is necessary to promote the operation of the Internal Market. Article 308 EC requires the Council to act unanimously and merely to consult the Parliament. The Court is unenthusiastic about art.308 EC as a Treaty base primarily because of the limited role which it affords to the European Parliament and has in certain circumstances, annulled the legislation.[30] The Court has in specific circumstances accepted art.308 EC a Treaty base, for example in relation to a directive which was intended to prohibit discrimination in access to vocational training. The Court stated the primary purpose of the measure was to prohibit discrimination on grounds of nationality and held that this was an implied power of the Council and accordingly it could use art.308 EC to ensure effective remedial action was taken.[31]

The EU has no inherent powers and the Treaties define the scope of action. In *Germany v Parliament and Council* (*Tobacco Advertising Directive*) the Court acknowledged the boundary of EC competence and rejected the argument that economic integration per se is a justification for legislative action. In this case the Member States introduced a directive which banned all forms of tobacco advertising, except for minimal promotion of tobacco products at the point of sale. The Commission used arts 47 (2), 55 and 95 EC as the legal base and argued this was an Internal Market measure which sought to create a uniform market in tobacco products by prohibiting all forms of advertising. The Court agreed with the German government that the measure went beyond the scope of the Treaty base. The measure, banning all forms of tobacco advertising, had broader impact than the Internal Market and in particular had a public health objective which was beyond the scope of the Treaty and this included art.308 EC.

---

[29] Case C-70/88 *European Parliament v Council* (*Chernobyl*) [1990] E.C.R. I-2041.

[30] Case C-21/94 *European Parliament v Council* (*Road Taxes*) [1995] E.C.R. I-1827.

[31] Case C-295/90 *European Parliament v Council* (*Students Rights of Residence*) [1992] E.C.R.-I 4193.

The Treaty of Lisbon will introduce new legal bases for the EU to acquire competence in the protection intellectual property rights (*art.118 TFEU*), the regulation of sport (*art.6 TEU, art.165 TFEU*), space exploration (*art.4 TEU, art.13 TFEU*), tourism (*art.6 TEU, art.195 TFEU*), civil protection (*art.6 TEU, art.196 TFEU*) and administrative co-operation (*art.6 TEU, art.74 TFEU*). Commentators such as Weatherill have been critical of the EU extending its competence in to areas such as sport and have argued that EU regulation does not necessarily improve the administration or organisation of, for example, sport (Weatherill: 2007, 56).

The Treaty of Lisbon by extending competence in to areas, which could be viewed as lying on the periphery of EU integration, is seeking to increase the profile of the EU and engage more directly with citizens.

## *Enhanced Co-operation*

The Amsterdam Treaty included a Chapter that provided the framework for closer co-operation between Member States. This flexibility recognises that EU integration had developed a heterogeneous nature. Flexibility allows Member States to pursue an array of policies with different procedural and Institutional arrangements and several reasons may be identified for the inclusion of the closer co-operation provisions. Firstly enlargement would create a more diverse EU and flexibility would be an essential tool to maintain the dynamic integration of an EU consisting of 25 Member States. Secondly, both the Maastricht and Amsterdam Treaties were characterised by dissidence and intransigence by Member States, for example the UK and Denmark. Flexibility would avoid blockage by one Member State where the majority wished to pursue integration. Thirdly, flexibility would avoid the creation of an à la carte Europe outside the Institutional framework, for example as seen with the creation of the Schengen Convention in 1985 and which the Amsterdam Treaty incorporated in to the EC Treaty.

Article 11 EC sets out the conditions under which closer co-operation between Member States may be pursued. To avoid disintegration within the Internal Market closer co-operation is only possible in areas that are not subject to exclusive EU competence. Furthermore, it cannot concern citizenship, distort competition or discriminate between nationals of Member States. Article 40 TEU also provides for closer co-operation in third pillar activity if it "would enable the EU to develop more rapidly an area of freedom security and justice". Under art.17 TEU, there is some scope for flexibility in the operation of the CFSP, but this is on a case-by-case basis. This recognises that lack of foreign policy consensus that exists, and reflects the lack of political agreement that existed within the EU.

The Treaty also provides for what is referred to as pre-determined flexibility and through which the UK and Ireland have secured the right to remain outside integration in the area of Asylum and Immigration. Both countries have secured the right to opt-in to those provisions of Title IV where it would be beneficial. This opt-in is in practice a more positive response to EU integration than the opt-out of the Social Chapter secured by the UK at Maastricht and both the UK and Ireland have regularly participated in initiatives introduced under Title IV.

The Treaty of Nice amended and clarified the conditions under which closer co-operation operates. Article 43 TEU states the conditions under which such co-operation may be pursued and specifically provides that it can only operate as a last resort. Article 43 TEU has also reduced the number of Member States required for enhanced co-operation from a majority, to only eight Member States. Article 11 EC has removed the right of veto for a Member State and requires that they appeal to the European Council if they have concerns relating to the enhanced co-operation. The European Council can still approve the proposal by a qualified majority and the European Parliament must also assent if the measure would normally be subject to co-decision.

Following the Treaty of Lisbon 2007 there are new provisions for enhanced co-operation both in the TEU and TFEU. *Article 20 TEU* states that enhanced co-operation will be possible where it protects and reinforces the integration process and Member States pursuing enhanced co-operation may make full use of the EU Institutions.[32] *Articles 326–334 TFEU* provides the legal framework for enhanced co-operation including the role of the Council[33] and the use of qualified majority voting where appropriate.[34] Acts adopted in the framework of enhanced co-operation shall bind only on participating Member States and shall not be regarded as part of the *acquis*.

[32] Arts 20 (1)–(2) TEU.
[33] Art.330 TFEU.
[34] Art.330 TFEU.

## 1.4 The Status of Primary and Secondary Legislation

The Treaties, which are the primary legislation of the EU, provide for the introduction of secondary legislation to achieve the objectives of integration. Article 249 EC provides that EC secondary legislation comes in the form of Regulations, Directives, Decisions, Recommendations and Opinions. Regulations and Directives have general legal application and are aimed at the Member States. By contrast, Decisions are binding only upon the party to which they are addressed. Consequently, individuals can ordinarily only challenge a decision through the judicial review process under art.230 EC. Recommendations and Opinions are not legally binding but are important because the Court has stated that national courts must consider them when interpreting EC law.[35]

Regulations are defined by art.249 EC as being of general application and are directly applicable. Direct applicability means that the provision will apply directly in the legal order of the Member States without the need for incorporation in to national legislation.[36] By contrast directives, which art.249 EC defines as binding as to their effect, do require domestic implementation. Member States can choose the form of implementation, but cannot alter the content of the directive itself. Crucially, Member States must implement the directive by the final date stated within it. Questions relating to Member States' implementation have given rise to numerous cases before the Court. Firstly there are instances of incorrect implementation, as in *Factortame*[37] where the UK's incorporation of Common Fisheries Policies Directives via the Merchant Shipping Act 1988 did not give effect to the EC measure. Alternatively, Member States may fail to implement the legislation altogether as occurred in *Francovich*[38] In this case, the Italian government failed to implement a directive which provided for minimum state compensation for employees in the case of employer insolvency.

One issue relating to both primary and secondary legislation is whether the provision has direct effect. Direct effect is a constitutional principle of EC law, developed by the Court of Justice. Legislation and the rights contained within it can be used by an

---

[35] Case 322/88 *Grimaldi v Fondes des Maladies Professionnelles* [1989] E.C.R. 4407.

[36] In Case 39/72 *Commission v Italy* [1973] E.C.R. 101 the Court stated that subjecting regulations to domestic implementation will endanger the uniform application of EC law.

[37] C-213/89 *R v Secretary State of Transport Ex p. Factortame Ltd* [1990] E.C.R. I-2433.

[38] Joined Cases C-6 and 9/90 *Francovich v Italian State* [1991] E.C.R. I-5357.

individual before his or her national court. In *Van Gend en Loos* the Court stated that Treaty articles will have direct effect if they satisfy the following criteria:

- they must be clear and precise;
- unconditional; and
- not subject to further implementation.

Not all Treaty provisions will fulfil these criteria but crucially the Court has extended the principle to the fundamental provisions of the Internal Market such as arts 12, 28, 39, 43 and 49 EC. The Court has also acknowledged the direct effect of art.81 and 82 EC which regulate competition law. The effect of these judgments has been to facilitate integration by providing Communitarian interpretations of fundamental objectives, thereby making Treaty rights accessible to individuals.

With regard to secondary legislation, regulations do not have automatic direct effect. The Court has applied the same conditions for regulations as for Treaty provisions to determine whether they have direct effect. With regard to directives the question of direct effect is more complicated. Member States under art.249 EC must implement the measure by the date contained within the directive. The Court in *Van Duyn v Home Office*[39] confirmed the direct effect of directives. It stated:

"[i]t would be incompatible with the binding effect attributed to a directive by Article [249] to exclude, in principle, the possibility that the obligation which it imposes may be invoked by those concerned.

... [t]he useful effect of such an act would be weakened if individuals were prevented from relying on it before their national courts and if the latter were prevented from taking it into consideration as an element of Community law."

In this case dir.64/221/EEC, which was adopted to implement art.48 EC (now art.39 EC), allows Member States to derogate from the free movement of workers on grounds of public policy, public security or public health. It is not subject to any condition nor does it require any further action by the Member State.

---

[39] Case 41/74 *Van Duyn v Home Office* [1974] E.C.R. 1337.

Directives cannot fulfil the same criteria for direct effect, as do Treaty provisions, because the third condition of no further implementation cannot, by its very nature, be fulfilled. In *Van Duyn* the Court held that for directives the following criteria would need to be satisfied to establish direct effect. The measure must be:

- clear and precise;
- unconditional; and
- the time limit for implementation has expired.

In *Ministero del Publico v Ratti*[40] the Court reaffirmed *van Duyn* and stated further that a Member State which had not implemented a directive within the prescribed period:

"[c]annot rely, as against individuals, on its own failure to perform the obligations of the directive. . ."

Direct effect is therefore an important constitutionalising technique developed by the Court, to ensure the uniform application of EC law, and guarantee individual rights granted by the EC Treaty (Pescatore, 1983:158). The application of direct effect by ECJ as a tool of integration will be examined in more detail in Chapter 2.

## 1.5 The Legislative Procedures

### The "Community Method" of Decision Making

The "Community Method" is the general term describing how European legislation is adopted.[41] The European Commission has the right of initiative (i.e. it is the sole body that may submit a legislative proposal). The legislative proposals are examined by the European Parliament and the Council of the European Union, and finally adopted by either the Council or both European Parliament and Council. The Court of Justice guarantees respect for the rule of law: legal acts may be challenged by Member States, the three institutions or, under certain circumstances third parties.

---

[40] Case 148/78 *Ministero del Publico v Ratti* [1979] E.C.R. 1629.
[41] See COM (2001) 428 final White Paper on European Governance.

The complicated legislative procedures and their incremental development reflect the supra-national structure of the EU. The Member States participate in the decision-making process through the Council together with the other political institutions. Each actor is acutely aware of the others presence and each Institution seeks to play its full part in the legislative process. The EU's desire to reconnect with the citizen has led to other non-governmental actors and civil society being brought within the consultation stage of the legislative process. This is part of a broader attempt, going back to the SEA 1986, to democratise decision-making and to make legislation more acceptable to the citizen. There are several decision-making procedures and their use depends upon the Treaty base for the legislative measure as seen in the *Titanium Dioxide* case. The most important and widely used procedure is the co-decision procedure. The defining feature of co-decision is that it brings together the Council and European Parliament in a process of joint decision-making.

One other, though rarely used procedure is the consultation procedure, the original decision-making procedure within the Treaty of Rome. This process, utilised under art.308 EC, only involves the Council and Commission. The Parliament will be consulted, but its opinions have no binding qualities, except that Consultation is an "essential procedural requirement". The Court has acknowledged that though Parliament's views are not binding it does have the procedural right to give an opinion and will annul an act where this does not occur.[42] Even where the input of the Parliament is peripheral, the Court has protected its interests and promoted institutional balance and procedural propriety in the decision-making process.

## The Co-decision Procedure: Article 251 EC

The Maastricht Treaty introduced the co-decision procedure. This was a development from the co-operation procedure introduced in the SEA 1986. The purpose of the co-operation procedure was twofold. Firstly, it introduced the process of qualified majority voting (QMV), which replaced unanimity and limited the national veto, thereby making decision-making in Council easier. Secondly, the co-operation procedure brought the European Parliament within the decision-making process and gave it the power to propose amendments. The objective of this was to enhance the democratic quality

---

[42] Case 138/79 *Roquette Frères v Council* [1980] E.C.R. 3333.

of legislation. The power of amendment was limited because the Council retained the right to reject amendments and adopt the legislative proposal in its original form.

The Maastricht co-decision procedure remedied some of the defects of the co-operation procedure by protecting the power to propose amendments. The co-decision procedure introduced a new stage, a so-called 'third reading', whereby a new joint body called a Conciliation Committee would be convened if the Parliament and Council failed to agree an amended proposal. This Conciliation Committee seeks to agree, within six weeks of being convened, an amended legislative proposal which both Institutions can support. Though an improvement over the co-operation procedure, co-decision was still subject to drawbacks, not least that the Council could still adopt the original proposal by unanimity if the Conciliation Committee could not agree a joint text.

The co-decision procedure finally became *real* joint decision-making through changes introduced by the Amsterdam Treaty 1997 (Shackleton, 2000:326). The crucial development introduced at Amsterdam comes at the stage when the Conciliation Committee is convened (see diagram below). Under the Maastricht Treaty, art.251 EC stated that if the Council and Parliament failed to agree on the content of a measure in the Conciliation Committee then the Council could, using unanimity agree its original common position. Significantly, under the post Amsterdam version of art.251 EC such unilateral Council action is prohibited. The effect of the Amsterdam amendments was to shift the centre of gravity, within the co-decision procedure, in favour of the European Parliament and this was a definitive attempt by the Member States to address the democratic deficit. Co-decision is now the common legislative procedure for Internal Market measures introduced under art.95 EC.

The Treaty of Nice 2001 extended the scope of art.251 EC to cover additional policy areas and the Treaty of Lisbon continues the trend with 40 additional areas moving from unanimity to QMV. This includes the whole of justice and interior affairs. Only the most sensitive areas remain subject to unanimity. These are tax, social security, citizens' rights, languages, seats of the Institutions and the main lines of common foreign, security and defence policies. In some of these areas, such as anti-discrimination measures, the European Parliament has gained the right of consent (*art.19 TFEU*).

Under the Treaty of Lisbon co-decision between the Council and Parliament is substantially extended (as foreseen by the Constitutional Treaty) and becomes known as the "ordinary legislative procedure" (*art.289 TFEU*). Particularly important is the extension of co-decision into agriculture, fisheries, transport and structural funds in addition to the whole of the current "third pillar" of justice and interior affairs. The European Parliament now becomes the co-equal legislator for almost all European laws. The new budgetary procedure ensures full parity between Parliament and Council for approval of the whole annual budget with the current distinction between compulsory and non-compulsory expenditure abolished.

### *The Co-decision procedure post Amsterdam—art.251 EC (art.294 TFEU The Ordinary Legislative Procedure)*

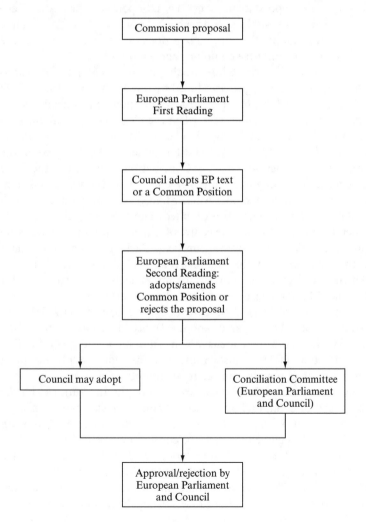

*The Assent Procedure—art.250 EC*

The assent procedure was used by the SEA 1986 and extended by the Maastricht Treaty 1991. It is used in a limited number of cases such as when voting on the decision to admit new Member States under art.49 TEU or to sign Association Agreements. In this procedure, the proposal can only be adopted following a positive vote by both the Parliament and the Council.

## 1.6 The Assent Procedure—art.250 EC

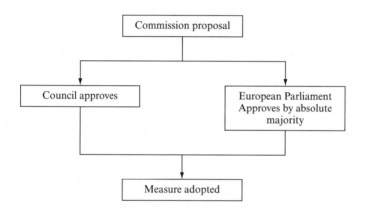

## 1.7 The Institutional Structure of the EU

*Institutional dynamics*

Any system of governance requires an institutional structure and capacity to fulfil the tasks of administration and the EU is no different in this respect. For example, in the legislative process the political Institutions have clearly defined roles and the ECJ ensures that there is no concentration of legislative power in the hands of one institution. Article 7 EC states that the tasks entrusted to the Community shall be carried out by the following Institutions:

- a European Parliament;
- a Council;
- a Commission;
- a Court of Justice; and
- a Court of Auditors.

Two advisory Committees in the form of the Economic and Social Committee and Committee of the Regions advise the Commission and Council in relation to policy development, but they are not formal Institutions and their opinions are not binding. With the exception of the Court of Justice and the Court of Auditors, which conducts a financial review of the EU budget, the remaining institutions are all political.

Article 7 EC states that the each Institution shall act within the limits of the powers conferred upon it. The Treaty defines the scope of institutional activity and as within all systems of democratic governance requires the institutions to act inter vires. Treaty base is the determinant of institutional action. The requirement to act within the limit of powers conferred by the Treaty is intended to ensure that each political institution participates fully in the governance process and that power is not concentrated in the hands of one body.

The maintenance of institutional balance in the legislative process is a task which is entrusted to the Court of Justice and requires the Court to review the choice of Treaty base for secondary legislation.[43] Accordingly, the Treaty base will determine the scope of participation in legislative decision-making by the institutions, and in particular the European Parliament. For example, art.95 EC, the provision through which Internal Market measures are introduced, requires legislation to be introduced through the co-decision procedure of art.251 EC.

The legislative process does not only involve the legislative procedures as described in the Treaties. Many practical and organisational aspects are left to the Institutions to agree among themselves through inter-institutional agreements which lay down specific procedures which are followed during the legislative or policy making process. Article 10 EC provides for a principle of genuine

---

[43] See for example the *Chernobyl* (fn.29) and Students *Rights of Residence* (fn.31) judgments.

and mutual "loyal" co-operation between Member States and the EU which the ECJ has held also applies to dealings between the Institutions. In *European Parliament v Council of the European Union*,[44] the Court held that:

". . .the dialogue between institutions, on which the consultation procedure in particular is based, is subject to the same mutual duties of genuine cooperation as those which govern relations between Member States and the Community institutions".[45]

The Court has consistently taken the view that where a legislative procedure grants the Parliament a right of participation, then Parliament should be able to enforce this right. In the *Chernobyl* judgment,[46] the Court stated that by allowing Parliament to protect these rights it was upholding the institutional balance of the Community. The Court applied teleological reasoning with regard to two Treaty provisions. Firstly, the Court gave a purposive meaning to art.7 EC. Each institution having to act within the limits of its powers implies that each institution can utilise *fully* the powers which it has been given by the Treaty.

Secondly, the Court examined the operation of art.230 EC which permits judicial review of EC legislation by institutions and individuals. Post-Nice all Institutions and the Member States are categorised as privileged applicants who can bring an action as of right. Individuals are classified as non-privileged applicants, who must first fulfil the narrow criteria of art.230 EC[47] which require an applicant to demonstrate that a measure has "direct and individual concern". Prior to Maastricht, the European Parliament was categorised as a non-privileged applicant and could not bring an action as of right. In *Chernobyl*, the Council had introduced legislation using art.175 EC as the Treaty base, resulting in the Parliament having a limited consultative role. The Parliament argued that the legislation should have been introduced through art.95 EC, which pre-Maastricht would have triggered the co-operation

---

[44] Case C-65/93 [1995] E.C.R. I-643.
[45] Case C-65/93 [1995] E.C.R. I-643, para.23.
[46] See fn.29 above.
[47] See Case 25/62 *Plaumann v Commission* [1963] E.C.R. 95 and Case C-50/00 *Unión de Pequeños Agricultores v Council* [2002] E.C.R. 1-6677.

procedure, resulting in an increased role for the Parliament to propose amendments.

The Court agreed with the Parliament and stated that, despite the absence of automatic locus standi under art.230 EC, the judicial review action would be permitted in the interests of the "institutional balance" of the Community. The Court reasoned that Parliament was given a right of participation in the legislative process and the measure should have been introduced under art.95 EC. Accordingly, a corollary of this right to involvement was a right to protect and enforce the guaranteed Treaty rights before the Court. In this case, as Parliament was challenging the Commission and Council it could not rely upon either Institution to bring an action upon its behalf. To avoid a democratic deficit, the Court held that the Parliament must be able to challenge the measure itself. The Court therefore stands as arbiter and protector not only of individual rights but also as guarantor of institutional participation in the political decision-making process.

The decision-making procedures of the EU are complex and contribute to the institutional dynamics and tension that exist in the relationship between the Institutions. The complexity arises from the fact that decision-making is supra-national and not based upon a traditional parliamentary procedure that exists in nation states. To fully understand the role of each institution within the structures of EU governance it is necessary to consider the participation by each in the decision-making process and the political relationship that exists between them.

## The Commission

The Commission consists of 27 Commissioners, one each from the Member States. The Commissioners, though appointed by their national governments, do not represent their Member State and operate under a principle of collective responsibility. The Treaty of Lisbon 2007 provides that the size of the European Commission will be reduced after 2014, corresponding to two thirds of the number of Member States, unless the European Council decides (unanimously) otherwise (*art.17 (4) TEU*). The members of the Commission will be chosen according to a system based on equal rotation among the Member States decided by the Nice Treaty (*art.244 TFEU*). Furthermore, the Treaty of Lisbon requires that the President of the Commission will be elected by the European Parliament. The candidate will be proposed to MEPs by the European Council, nominated by QMV, taking into account the results of the parliamentary elections (*art.17 (7) TEU*). The European Parliament will also invest the whole Commission, including the High Representative for Foreign Affairs, who will also be Vice-President of the Commission.

The Commission has on several occassions been criticised for its failure to ensure internal propriety. Under current Treaty arrangements the European Parliament has the power to approve the appointment of Commissioners and dismiss the entire Commission.[48] In 1999, following allegation of fraud and mismanagement against the Santer Commission a committee of the European Parliament and the Court of Auditors inquired in to the alleged fraud. The Report led to the resignation of the entire Commission, which would have been dismissed by the Parliament had in not resigned. The Report stated that "it is difficult to find anyone who has even the slightest sense of responsibility".[49] This review of Commission activity demonstrates the presence of institutional checks and balances within the Treaty which provide a degree of democratic accountability of the un-elected Commission. The aftermath of this affair led to the appointment of a new Commission under Romano Prodi and precipitated a more general discussion on EU constitutional reform (Tomkins 1999:758). The subsequent developments originating in the Commission's White Paper on EU Governance, the Laeken Declaration and the Convention on the Future of Europe have their roots in the Commission's resignation and shared the objective of reconnecting with sceptical EU citizens who distrust *all* EU Institutions. In 2004 the Commission was again subject to review by the European Parliament, when it objected to the proposed appointment of the Italian nominee Rocco Buttiglione for the Freedom, Security and Justice portfolio in the Barosso Commission. The Parliament considered Buttiglione's personal opinions conflicted with his function as Commissioner with prime responsibility for fundamental rights. Following Parliament's rejection of the entire Commission, Buttiglione was replaced and his nomination withdrawn by Italian government.

The European Commission is often described as the Executive of the EU, but its role is more than that of a civil service. Article 211 EC requires the Commission to ensure the proper functioning of the Internal Market by ensuring application of the Treaty and secondary

---

[48] Art.201 EC.
[49] Committee of Independent Experts: *Fraud and Mismanagement in the Commission* para.9.4.25.

legislation and it will initiate infringement actions before the ECJ under art.226 EC against any Member State which breaches the Treaty. The Commission's enforcement role also extends to issuing fines against Member States for non-compliance with an ECJ judgment under art.228 EC.[50] Until May 2004 the Commission also had sole responsibility for enforcement of competition law under arts 81, 82 and 85 EC, though reg.1/2003 has transferred primary competence for this to National Competition Authorities in the Member States.

To ensure the proper functioning of the Internal Market the Treaty has also given the Commission a legislative role. The Commission is the primary initiator of legislation and is arguably the political driving force behind the integration process. The Commission also possesses its own legislative powers under the comitology process through which legislative acts are agreed in specialist committees composed of technocrat representatives from Member States and chaired by a Commission official.[51] This power conferred upon it by art.202 EC involves the creation of highly technical and complex legislative measures. These expert committees are a technocratic form of government, and though concerned with technical measures, the process is often criticised for lacking transparency and accountability (Craig, 1999:47). There are several types of procedures and corresponding committees, depending on the type of legislation at issue. It depends equally on the procedure and committee chosen to what extent the Commission may derogate from what the Committee advises.

Comitology has been challenged by individuals and other institutional actors under art.230 EC. In *Köster*[52] the Court confirmed that the Council had legitimately delegated powers to the Commission under art.202 EC. The most criticised aspect of the comitology process is the absence of participation by the European Parliament. Since the SEA 1986 the European Parliament has, through successive Treaty developments, gained additional decision-making powers, except in the area of comitology where it remains, by comparison, a bystander. The Parliament challenged this in *European Parliament v*

---

[50] See Case C-45/91 *Commission v Greece* [2000] E.C.R. I-5047.
[51] The criteria, committees and procedures are laid down in a Council Decision ("comitology decision") of June 28, 1999, OJ 1999, L 184/23.
[52] Case 25/70 *Einfuhr-und-Vorratsstelle für Getreide und Futternittel v Köster* [1970] E.C.R.

*Council* (*Comitology*).[53] The Parliament sought standing under art.230 EC to challenge a legislative measure which was introduced through comitology, arguing that the co-operation procedure was more appropriate. Parliament's argument focussed on the need to maintain institutional balance within the EU. The Court's judgment in *Comitology*, delivered one year before the *Chernobyl* judgment, rejected this argument by stating that art.202 EC specifically excludes the Parliament from comitology and places it within the domain of the Commission and Council. Accordingly, the Court held that the Parliament had no automatic right to participate when art.202 EC was the Treaty base. This distinguishes the judgment from *Chernobyl* where the Court accepted an alternative Treaty base of art.95 EC was appropriate because the measure had an Internal Market objective and as such required Parliament's input.

The role of the European Parliament in the comitology process remains uneasy. As co-legislator through the co-decision procedure, it is difficult for the European Parliament to accept implementing measures to be decided in a Council-Commission setting only. After long negotiations, the Institutions have arrived at a compromise on a procedure referred to as the "regulatory procedure with scrutiny". This enables the European Parliament to oppose the adoption of a Commission decision prepared in Committee where it is felt that the matter should be dealt with through co-decision.[54]

Douglas-Scott (2002:135) defines comitology as one of the "necessary evils of EU governance". The breadth of competence and the need for swift action in certain circumstances, for example as with the BSE crisis, requires executive action and the Commission is the most appropriate Institution for this. The preoccupation with transparency and greater accountability of EU activity suggests that the opaque comitology process should be restricted to merely technical measures. Delegated legislation is part of all systems of governance, for example UK ministers are awarded powers of delegated legislation under the Statutory Instrument procedure and its use in the EU should not be criticised per se.

The Commission plays a central role in the integration process but is still dogged by questions of democratic accountability, despite the check provided by the European Parliament. It has both pre and

---

[53] Case 302/87 *European Parliament v Council* (*Comitology*) [1988] E.C.R. 5615.
[54] Decision 2006/4512/EC, OJ 2006, L 200/11. Consolidated version published in OJ 2006, C-255/4. See also the Joint Statement (EP, Council, Commission) published in OJ 2006, C-255/1.

post-legislative function and provides a degree of political continuity while the composition of the Council and Parliament may change. The workload of the Commission has increased dramatically as the EU has acquired increased competence and through the reforms required for the 2004 enlargement. Commission personnel and resources have lagged behind these developments with the result that EU political governance has adopted the practice of outsourcing the monitoring of certain policies to specific agencies such as the European Environment Agency (EEA) and European Food Standards Agency (EFSA). These agencies provide expert evidence to the Commission, for example EFSA has taken a lead role in advising the Commission in relation to the access of Genetically Modified Organisms (GMOs) in to the Internal Market. They also provide expert advice when the Commission formulates policy, are part of the comitology process and advise on best practice for implementing policy under the OMC. The use of such agencies is part of a strategy to modernise EU governance and improve the delivery of policy objectives.

## The Council

The Council is the legislative arm of the EU, though the legislative function is now shared with the Parliament when the co-decision procedure is being used. Under art.203 EC the Council is composed of ministers who are authorised to commit the government of their Member State. The composition of the Council is not fixed and varies according to the policy area under discussion. On some occasions this will include politicians from regional, devolved or federal institutions. The Council has a Presidency which rotates every six months to a different Member State. A degree of continuity in Council activities is maintained through the so-called "Troika" of the immediately preceding, the present and the future Council President co-ordinating policy priorities. The Council also has its own civil service in the Committee of Permanent Representatives (COREPER) which is composed of the Ambassadors of each Member State. COREPER provides information on technical aspects of legislative proposals and keeps the minister informed of any political problems which may arise in the course of the decision-making process.

The task of the Council is to take the final decision on proposals submitted to it by the Commission under the EC Treaty and to act on an inter-governmental basis when considering matters under pillars two and three. The primary difference between decision-making under the TEU and the EC Treaty is that unanimity is the norm for inter-governmental decisions, whereas QMV is used under the EC pillar. This was first introduced in the SEA 1986 and has been extended to cover all measures introduced under art.95 EC. The effect of QMV has been to rationalise decision-making by restricting the national veto. Under the QMV process Member States are allotted votes according to population with currently a total of 321 votes allotted to the 25 Member States. For a qualified majority to be agreed, and a measure passed, it must receive 232 votes. The allocated votes are important and reflect the fact that the Council is dominated by political relationships. All Member States seek to maximise their influence in decision-making and use their votes to, where necessary, form alliances and create blocking minorities.

The Treaty of Lisbon 2007 proposes a new voting system in the Council but this will not come into force until 2014 and will still be subject, until 2017, to being blocked by recourse to the voting rules established in the Treaty of Nice (*art.16 (4) TEU*). In addition, a new mechanism based on the "Ioannina compromise"[55] was agreed which will allow 55 per cent of States forming 65 per cent of the population of the Union to ask for a delay and reconsideration of a draft law before its adoption.[56] A Protocol negotiated in the last hours of the IGC, at the request of Poland, states that the Council can only amend or repeal the "Ioannina" clause by consensus.[57]

The relationship the Council shares with the European Parliament differs depending upon whether decision-making is under the EC Pillar or inter-governmental. Under pillars two and three the European Parliament is only consulted on broader questions of

[55] The Ioannina compromise took its name from an informal meeting of foreign ministers in the Greek city of Ioannina on March 29, 1994. Among the decisions taken at the meeting was a Council decision concerning the specific question of qualified majority voting in an enlarged 16-member Community. The decision was later adjusted in the light of Norway's decision not to join. The resulting compromise lays down that if members of the Council representing between 23 votes (the old blocking minority threshold) and 26 votes (the new threshold) express their intention of opposing the taking of a decision by the Council by qualified majority, the Council will do all within its power, within a reasonable space of time, to reach a satisfactory solution that can be adopted by at least 68 votes out of 87. Following the re-weighting of votes in the Council of Ministers, the Treaty of Nice put an end to the Ioannina compromise.
[56] Art.16 (4) TEU.
[57] Protocol on the Decision of the Council relating to the implementation of art.16 (4) TEU and art.205(2) TFEU between November 1, 2014 and March 31, 2017 on the one hand, and as from April 1, 2017 on the other.

policy rather than specific legislative decisions. By contrast, the Commission is integrated in to decision-making in all three pillars, raising questions relating to a democratic deficit that the un-elected institution has pre-eminence over the elected Parliament.

The political accountability of the Council is an important issue. Though there exists a degree of Council responsibility to the European Parliament arising out of the co-decision procedure, no corresponding accountability exists with regard to pillars two and three. Though Council members are politically accountable to their national parliaments the Council is not accountable as a single body in the same way that the Commission is to the European Parliament. Council meetings are characterised as lacking transparency, with deliberations conducted in private and this contributes to the perception of a democratic deficit. Some changes have been made to the Council's Rules of Procedure to address these criticisms. For example, in 1993 the Council agreed to publish voting records under the co-decision and co-operation procedures. The Treaty of Amsterdam 1997 added art.255 EC which is a commitment to institutional transparency and access to documentation for the EU citizen. The right to documents is not absolute and subject to grounds of public policy and public security, but the Court has stated that the Council must establish clear reasons for non-disclosure.[58]

The European Parliament has no corresponding powers to seek the removal of the Council as it can with the Commission under art.201 EC. The Council, like the Parliament is composed of elected representatives from the Member States, and the relationship between them is one based on political dialogue. The two Institutions serve different constituencies, the Council represents the national government and the Parliament the citizens of the EU who have elected it. This relationship, perhaps more than any other, defines the supranational structure of the EU.

## The European Council

The practice of heads of government summit meetings has taken place since 1969 but was only given legal recognition by the SEA 1986. The heads of government meet at least twice during each Presidency and provide the guidance for EU policy under the CFSP. Article 4 TEU provides for a more formal structure and states that the:

---

[58] Case T-174/95 *Svenska Journalistförbundet v Council* [1998] E.C.R. II-2289.

"European Council shall provide the Union with the necessary impetus for development and shall define the general policy guidelines thereof".

Though not a formal institution the European Council does provide a political focus and direction for the EU (Craig and de Búrca, 2007:56). The European Council operates without any formal rules, rarely publishes agendas or minutes of meetings and though it is the highest legislative body in the EU it lacks a formal Treaty base. Arguably the European Council fills the political vacuum left by the absence of any form of EU government, but the existence of the European Council without a formal Treaty base, would seem to conflict with the objective of cosntitutionalising the Treaty through institutional balance.

The Treaty of Lisbon 2007 will formalise the status of the European Council with the creation of a new 'permanent' President of the European Council who will be elected for two and a half years. Article 15 TEU states that the Council will provide the Union with the necessary impetus for its development and shall define the general political directions and priorities thereof. The European Council will not exercise any legislative functions. The role of the permanent President will be to chair and drive forward the work of the European Council and focus on key strategic and policy initiatives. The President will have overall responsibility of the European Council agenda and the meeting and is required to report to Parliament afterwards (*art.15 (2) TEU*). The European Council becomes a fully fledged Institution of the EU which will be subject to supervision by the ECJ (*art.265 TFEU*).

## *The European Parliament*

The European Parliament has been elected by universal suffrage since 1979, though is not a parliament in the traditional sense. The Parliament shares legislative competence with the Council, but unlike the Council cannot pass legislation independently of the other. In the context of Pillars two and three, the Parliament only has a consultative role. Nonetheless the European Parliament is an important political institution. Through representative democracy it provides the EU with a degree of democratic legitimacy and together with national parliaments has contributed to the 'parliamentarisation' of the EU. This parliamentarisation occurs through scrutiny of Council activities by national parliaments, and through the European Parliament drawing on principles of parliamentary practice and procedure when it participates in the legislative process. The purpose, which both national parliaments and the European Parliament share, is the accountability of decision-makers.

The European Parliament contributes to a more democratic EU by fulfilling a broad supervisory role. In addition to providing a check upon Council action in the legislative process, the Parliament reviews the activities of other Institutions. For example, under art.193 EC it can establish temporary committees of inquiry. The 1999 Committee of Independent Experts in to Fraud and Mismanagement in the Commission is one such Committee. This was part of a broader scrutiny of Commission activity which allows for a censure motion against the Commission under art.201 EC. Article 197 EC permits the Parliament to submit oral questions to the Commission and the Council. As part of its supervisory role, the European Parliament has one key power under art.272 EC, namely the ability to veto Commission proposals for non-compulsory expenditure. It can also, under art.272 (8) EC, veto the entire budget for 'important reasons'. In the 1999 Commission crisis the Parliament used the threat of this power as leverage over the Commission to force its resignation.

The relationship of the Parliament with the EU citizen is central, as it remains his or her primary contact point with the EU Institutions. Under art.195 EC the European Parliament can appoint an Ombudsman who provides citizens with a direct opportunity of informing about institutional maladministration which he/she may have suffered. The creation of an EU Ombudsman reflects administrative practice in many Member States where they form a part of the process of ensuring good government. The establishment of the Ombudsman is yet another way in which the EU has tried to bridge the democracy gap to the citizen.

The above procedures have created a perception of a democratic EU accountable to its citizens but in practice the impact is minimal. For example, the Ombudsman while providing for a cheap and quick form of review lacks any corresponding power of enforcement (Douglas-Scott, 2002:107). The Laeken Declaration and Convention suggested that EU citizens remain distant from the EU. While the Parliament provides an internal institutional balance, it remains questionable whether on its own it can overcome the wider problem of citizen disconnection. The European Parliament has only had minimal success in bridging the democracy gap with the citizen. For example, though art.255 EC extends the transparency principle to Parliamentary documents, this has not made a significant impact upon EU democratisation.

Despite its position as a political institution the Parliament has also been an effective litigator. The Parliament has regularly intervened in cases, for example, *Roquette Frères* and has also utilised art.230 EC to initiate actions in its own name. The Court has through judgments such as *Chernobyl*, recognised Parliament's rights to protect its own prerogatives by granting locus standi under art.230 EC. The Court's judgment reinforced the concept institutional balance. Furthermore, the Maastricht Treaty added the language of the ECJ to art.230 EC which in its revised form stated that Parliament could initiate judicial review proceedings of a measure where it was seeking to "protect its own prerogatives". This judgment is part of an incremental development in Parliament's status as a political institution which the Treaty amendments have also acknowledged through the extension of its role in the decision-making process. These gradual developments can be considered as a movement towards a constitutional structure based upon institutional balance and the separation of powers (Westlake, 1998:434). The Nice Treaty 2001 reinforced the argument of gradual constitutionality based upon increasing democratic legitimacy by awarding the European Parliament the status of privileged applicant for the purposes of art.230 EC. This has placed it on a par with the other institutions and Member States and it is now open to the Parliament to challenge the validity of any legislative proposal and not just one which affects its prerogatives.

Despite the Treaty developments the impact upon the citizen of Parliament's increased role remains unclear. The Treaty of Lisbon recognises the central role of the European Parliament to provide democratic legitimacy in the EU but this has yet to be appreciated by EU citizens who are less enthusiastic at election time. Politically it vies for power with the other Institutions, yet any extension to its powers can only come at the expense of the other Institutions and with their consent. In these circumstances, the assessment of Dehousse (1998:595) may be most appropriate analysis of the institutional arrangements. Dehousse argues that the EU's institutional development resembles a federal structure in which the legislative function will be shared between two branches, which represent the EU's population and the States.

The Treaty of Lisbon strengthens the role of the European Parliament, primarily by increasing the number of policy areas within to co-decision. The new Treaty applies co-decision to all areas where European laws are adopted under the ordinary legislative procedure, unless an explicit provision to the contrary is made. This, it will be recalled, has transferred a number of policy areas to co-decision such as the Common Agricultural Policy (CAP) and asylum and immigration.

The Treaty of Lisbon introduces the principle of regressive proportionality for the apportionment of seats in the European Parliament. Paradoxically, this principle was immediately broken by the IGC, which gave one more seat to Italy for the term 2009–2014, asserting that the Parliament will now be composed of 750 members plus its President (*art.2 TEU*). The largest state (Germany) will have 96 MEPs; the smallest (Malta and Luxembourg) six. MEPs will henceforth represent "the Union's citizens" rather than "the peoples of the States" as the EC Treaty currently provides for.[59] This change is intended to be more than a symbolic recognition of the European Parliament's representative role of the citizen in decision-making. It remains unclear how much impact, if any, this change of wording will have with voters within the Member States.

---

[59] Art.189 EC.

# 2: The European Court of Justice

## 2.1 Introduction

The European Court of Justice (ECJ) at Luxembourg has grown in to one of the most important and influential judicial institutions in the world. Through the elaboration of concepts such as the supremacy of Community law, direct effect and state liability the Court has played a major role in the constitutional evolution of the EU (Arnull, 2006:3). Since the 1960s the Court of Justice has obliged Member States to take their commitments seriously and has consistently insisted on effective protection of the rights granted to individuals and companies under EU law. Through the preliminary reference procedure under art.234 EC, the Court engages in an ongoing dialogue with national courts and seeks to assist them in their role as front-line enforcers of Community law. In 1989, a Court of First Instance (CFI) was attached to the European Court of Justice to help deal with a rapidly increasing workload. Without the vital and often groundbreaking contributions of both Courts it is doubtful whether so many of the EU's objectives could have been so successfully achieved.

In recent years, concerns have been expressed about the capacity of this judicial system, originally designed for a Community of six Member States with limited competences. In 2008 it must function effectively in the context of an enlarged EU consisting of 27

Member States. In order to address these concerns, the reform of the judicial architecture was included on the agenda of the Inter-governmental Conference which led to adoption of the Treaty of Nice 2000. This Treaty, introduced a number of amendments to the EC Treaty as it relates to the Community's judicial system. The reforms provided for in the Treaty of Nice, have, by and large been implemented, most notably with the establishment of a European Union Civil Service Tribunal perhaps being the most radical. Moreover, it is likely that a Community Patent Court will also be established in due course.[1]

## 2.2 Historical development of the Community Courts

*Origins*

The European Coal and Steel Community (ECSC) was established with its own judicial authority in 1952. The success of the ECSC led to the establishment at the end of the 1950s of a European Economic Community (EEC) and a European Atomic Energy Community (Euratom). The ECSC, EC and Euratom together came to constitute the three "European Communities". A single "Court of Justice of the European Communities" in Luxembourg served the needs of all three Communities. The EEC was subsequently renamed the European Community (EC)[2] and in practice the EC Treaty proved to be by far the most important of the three treaties.[3] The vast majority of cases which come before the Court of Justice concern interpretation of the EC Treaty and secondary legislation adopted under it, and it has become common to refer to the law of all three treaties simply as "Community" law. Through its case-law, the Court of Justice has promoted Community law as an innovative and uniquely effective "new legal order" of international law, the subjects of which comprise not only the Member States but also their nationals.[4]

---

[1] See Commission Proposal for a Council Decision conferring jurisdiction on the Court of Justice in disputes relating to the Community patent (COM (2003) 827 final) art.229A EC.

[2] By art.G (A)(1) of the Treaty on European Union.

[3] The ECSC Treaty, which was concluded for a limited period of 50 years, expired in 2002.

[4] See the line of authority beginning with Case 26/62 *Van Gend en Loos* [1963] E.C.R. 1.

## *National courts as courts of Community law*

The doctrines of direct effect and supremacy of Community law, as developed in the early case-law of the Court, had profound implications for national courts (Weiler, 1999). With individuals entitled to rely on Community rights directly before national courts and with the national judge empowered to strike down domestic rules infringing the higher Community law, national courts were "co-opted" into the Community system of judicial protection and became the front-line enforcers of Community law. The vast majority of cases involving issues of Community law are handled by domestic courts within the Member States rather than by the Court of Justice. A relationship of close co-operation between national courts and the Court of Justice, which is founded on the preliminary reference procedure provided for in art.234 EC, ensures a large degree of consistency of interpretation and uniform application of the Treaty rules despite the different legal traditions. Laenarts argues that that the judicial system of the EU must be viewed in a broader context of its relationship with domestic legal orders and that there is an interlocking system of jurisdiction of the Community courts and the national courts (Laenarts 2007, 1652). At the heart of this is the objective of all Courts to protect the rule of law and guarantee Community law rights.

The two-way dialogue between the Court of Justice and national judiciaries, which the preliminary reference procedure facilitates, is perhaps the most interesting and essential feature of the entire Community judicial system. The development of the art.234 EC procedure and its increasing use over the past 50 years by the national judiciary is generally regarded as a success. For example, the principles of direct effect and supremacy and the general principles of Community law such as non-discrimination have penetrated in to national legal systems, and Community law has become a reality in the day-to-day case law of national courts (Timmermans, 2004:399).

## *Establishment of the Court of First Instance*

The Single European Act 1986 amended the EC Treaty so as to include provision for the attachment of a new "Court of First Instance of the European Communities" to the existing ECJ.[5] At the time, it was felt that a second court was needed to relieve the Court of Justice of certain classes of less important cases which were

---

[5] Art.11 of the Single European Act 1986.

taking up too much of its time. For example, there was general consensus that jurisdiction over cases brought by employees of the Community institutions against their employers ("staff cases") should be transferred to the Court of First Instance.[6] While such cases are of considerable importance to the individual applicant, staff cases are of little significance for the overall development of Community law. The new Court of First Instance was formally established by Council Decision 88/591[7] and began its work alongside the ECJ in 1989. Initially, jurisdiction over quite limited classes of action was transferred to the Court of First Instance on an experimental basis. Having demonstrated an ability to cope effectively with the areas of responsibility transferred to it, the Court of First Instance was granted more extensive jurisdiction by a series of decisions adopted by the Council during the course of the 1990s.[8] The status of the Court of First Instance was further enhanced by the Treaty of Nice, which repealed Council Decision 88/591[9] and instead gave the Court of First Instance an explicit basis in the EC Treaty.[10] Today, the Court of First Instance is responsible for hearing at first instance all actions brought under the EC Treaty by individuals and companies.[11]

## The Treaty on European Union

The EU Treaty makes provision for further inter-governmental co-operation in the areas of foreign and security policy (the "second pillar") and justice and home affairs (the "third pillar"). Acts adopted under these inter-governmental pillars of the EU Treaty do not have the same legal effects as acts of Community law, resembling rather instruments of traditional international law. In general, the Court of Justice is excluded from any role in the second and third

---

[6] More recently jurisdiction over this category of cases has been transferred entirely to the new EU Civil Service Tribunal.

[7] OJ 1988 L 319/1.

[8] See Council Decision 93/350 (OJ 1993 L 144/21); Council Decision 94/149 (OJ 1994 L 66/29); art.17 of the Act of Accession of 1994 in the version set out in art.10 of the Decision of the Council of January 1, 1995 (OJ 1995 L 1/1); and Council Decision 1999/291 (OJ 1999 L 114/52).

[9] Art.10 of the Treaty of Nice.

[10] In the revised art.220 EC.

[11] Limited jurisdiction in direct actions brought by Member States was also transferred to the Court of First Instance by Council Decision 2004/407/EC of April 26, 2004, which amended art.51 of the Statute of the Court to provide that the Court of First Instance shall have jurisdiction for direct actions brought by Member States challenging, inter alia, Council anti-dumping regulations and certain implementing measures.

pillars, although several Conventions which the Council has adopted under the third pillar in relation to matters of justice and home affairs do provide for the Court of Justice to have jurisdiction over their interpretation. The Treaty of Amsterdam 1997, which entered into force on May 1, 1999, amended the EC and EU Treaties so as to extend further the jurisdiction of the Court of Justice in the area of justice and home affairs.[12] In particular, art.35 TEU now allows Member States to "opt-in" to the preliminary reference procedure in relation to third pillar measures. The first references from national courts under art.35 TEU have only recently come before the Court of Justice.[13] However, not all Member States have opted-in under art.35 TEU and so the national courts of Belgium and Italy, for example, can make references to Luxembourg on the interpretation of acts adopted under the third pillar, while the national courts of the UK and Ireland cannot.

## *The increasing workload of the Community Courts*

In 1999, the ECJ and CFI published a joint policy paper entitled "The Future of the Judicial System of the European Union".[14] This paper highlighted the difficulties the two Courts were experiencing as a result of the ever-increasing number of cases coming before them. In particular, the paper pointed out that the number of references for preliminary rulings coming before the Court of Justice increased by 85 per cent between 1990 and 1998. An inability to cope with this workload was leading to unacceptable delays in the processing of cases (Rasmussen, 2000:1073). A number of developments were likely to further increase this workload, including the entry into force of legislation concerning the new single currency, the extension of the Court's jurisdiction by the Treaty of Amsterdam to cover sensitive domains such as visas, asylum and immigration, and the creation of new areas of jurisdiction under various third pillar

---

[12] The Treaty of Amsterdam also transferred many matters of justice and home affairs from the third pillar into the first "Community" pillar, and renamed the third pillar "police and judicial cooperation in criminal matters".

[13] See in particular the judgments in Joined Cases C-187/01 and C-385/01 *Gözütok and Brugge* [2003] E.C.R. I-5689, Case C-469/03 *Filomeno Mario Miraglia* [2005] E.C.R. I-2009, and Case C-436/04 *Van Esbroeck* [2006] E.C.R. I-2333, all concerning interpretation of art.56 of the Convention Implementing the Schengen Agreement, and Case C-105/03 *Pupino* [2005] E.C.R. I-5285, concerning the interpretation of Framework Decision 2001/220/JHA on the standing of victims in criminal proceedings.

[14] Available on the website of the Court of Justice at *www.curia.eu.int*. [Accessed April 8, 2008].

Conventions. At the Court of First Instance, meanwhile, a flood of new cases could be expected in the areas of trade marks, access to documents of the Community institutions and staff cases coming from newly established EU bodies such as the European Central Bank, Europol and decentralised agencies such as the Office for Harmonisation of the Internal Market. Furthermore, an increase in the workload of the CFI would inevitably lead to an increase in the number of appeals coming before the Court of Justice. Enlargement of the EU would compound this crisis even further by increasing the number of potential litigants and the number of national courts entitled to make preliminary references. In recognition of this crisis of capacity at the Community Courts, the Member State governments agreed to include the issue of reform of the Community's judicial system on the agenda of the Intergovernmental Conference which ran throughout the year 2000.

## The Nice Treaty 2001 and the Treaty establishing a Constitution for Europe

In December 2000, the Heads of State and Government meeting at Nice agreed the terms of the Treaty of Nice. The main objective of the Treaty of Nice was to prepare the European institutions for enlargement of the EU (Arnull, 1999:516). In the case of the Community Courts, the objective of reforming the judicial system so that it could cope with the ever-worsening workload crisis was another important concern (Rasmussen, 2000:1078). The reforms to the EU's judicial architecture adopted at Nice were pragmatic rather than radical and their entry into force resulted in little immediate change to the way the Community Courts operate. Perhaps the most striking development was the introduction of provision for the establishment of specialist "judicial panels" which would be attached to the CFI. Judicial panels would constitute a third tier of Community jurisdiction below the Court of Justice and the CFI. As with most of the Nice amendments, however, the Treaty did not itself establish these tribunals, but rather provided a legal basis for subsequent implementing action by the Council. Consequently, the full impact of the Nice reforms would only be felt over a period of years.

## Establishment of the EU Civil Service Tribunal

The EU Civil Service Tribunal was the first judicial panel to be created pursuant to the new provisions of the EC Treaty introduced at Nice. The Tribunal was formally established by Council Decision in 2004.[15] Declaration No.16 to the Treaty of Nice requested the Court of Justice and the Commission to prepare as swiftly as possible, after the Treaty entered into force, a draft decision establishing a judicial panel with jurisdiction to deliver judgments at first instance on disputes between the Community and its servants. The seven judges and the registrar of the new Tribunal were sworn in towards the end of 2005 and the Tribunal held its first hearing on March 28, 2006. The establishment of this third Community Court has contributed to the improved operation of the Community courts system (Timmermans, 2004:401), if for no other reason that staff cases are more efficiently dealt with, and constitutes an important precedent for the creation of future judicial panels (Lavranos, 2005:264).

## 2.3 The Legal Framework Governing the Community Courts

*The EC Treaty*

The fundamental legal basis of the Community Courts is found in art.220 EC. This article, as amended by the Treaty of Nice, provides that "[t]he Court of Justice and the Court of First Instance, each within its jurisdiction, shall ensure that in the interpretation and application of this Treaty, the law is observed". Article 220 EC goes on to provide that "judicial panels may be attached to the Court of First Instance . . . in order to exercise, in certain specific areas, the judicial competence laid down in this Treaty." Articles 221 to 245 EC then go on to set out the most fundamental principles relating to the composition and jurisdiction of the Court of Justice and the Court of First Instance.

Prior to the Treaty of Nice this article simply provided for a Court of Justice which "shall ensure that in the interpretation and application of this Treaty the law is observed." The legal basis of the CFI was then found in a piece of secondary legislation and the CFI was merely "attached" to the Court of Justice. By giving the CFI an express Treaty basis alongside the Court of Justice in art.220 EC, the Nice Treaty placed the CFI on a firmer constitutional footing and therefore put it in a better position to take on more general jurisdiction over more important matters of Community law. It is noteworthy

---

[15] Council Decision 2004/752/EC/Euratom of November 2, 2004.

that art.220 EC now provides that any judicial panels which may be established by the Council will be "attached" to the Court of First Instance. It is worth recalling that not so long ago, it was the Court of First Instance which was "attached" to another court, the Court of Justice.

The revised art.220 EC opened up the way for an important evolution in the Community's courts system. Previously, the Court of Justice had always been the biggest and most important element of the whole judicial system. After Nice, the transfer of even more significant competences to the Court of First Instance was possible, to the extent that the Court of First Instance could become the biggest and busiest court at the centre of the Community's judicial apparatus. A smaller Court of Justice would then operate as a supreme court of appeal, with responsibility only for cases concerning fundamental constitutional issues and appeals raising questions of the unity and coherence of Community law. A third level of judicial authority, the judicial panels, will exercise first instance jurisdiction in specialist areas such as staff cases and trade marks. The amendments to the EC Treaty adopted at Nice do not in themselves create such a three-tier courts structure, but the revised Treaty framework opens the way for an evolution in this direction over the years ahead. The recent establishment of the European Union Civil Service Tribunal marks an important and tangible milestone in this evolution.

## The Statute of the Court of Justice

After the EC Treaty, the next most important legal instrument governing the Community Courts is the Statute of the Court of Justice. The Statute is laid down in a Protocol to the Treaty and sets out the most important rules governing the practical functioning of the Community Courts. The Statute lays down rules on, inter alia, the organisation of chambers of the Courts, the categories of lawyer entitled to plead before the Courts, written and oral procedure before the Courts, the delivery of judgments by the Courts and the procedure for appealing a decision of the Court of First Instance to the Court of Justice. A completely revised Statute was introduced by the Treaty of Nice.[16]

---

[16] Annex I of the Statute was added by Council Decision 2004/752 establishing the EU Civil Service Tribunal and sets out detailed rules governing the jurisdiction, composition, organisation and procedure of that Tribunal.

As a Protocol to the EC Treaty, the Statute has the status of primary Community law and so in principle any changes to it can only be brought about by a full Treaty revision. However, art.245 EC has always allowed for the amendment of certain provisions of the Statute by unanimous decision of the Council. The Treaty of Nice extended the scope of Statute provisions which may be amended by the Council without any need for a Treaty revision. Under the revised art.245 EC, virtually all provisions of the Statute can now be amended by a unanimous vote of the Council at any time. This is an important development as the Statute can now be changed more easily when circumstances so require. This will allow for greater flexibility in adapting the Court to the needs of a rapidly evolving and expanding EU.[17]

## The Rules of Procedure of the Court of Justice and the Court of First Instance

After the Statute, more detailed rules governing the practical day-to-day functioning of the Courts are laid down in the two Courts' Rules of Procedure. These Rules contain very thorough guidelines on the internal organisation and procedure of the Courts. Matters dealt with include, inter alia, the rights and obligations of lawyers appearing before the Courts, procedures for summoning and examining witnesses, rules on costs, legal aid, service of documents and, importantly, time-limits. The Rules of Procedure were initially drawn up by the Court of Justice itself, but required the unanimous approval of the Council before coming into force. Until recently, any alterations to the Rules of Procedure also required the unanimous approval of the Council. This led to long delays in making even the most minor amendments and greatly restricted the ability of the Courts to amend their procedures where appropriate for the efficient processing of cases. In its submissions to the Nice Intergovernmental Conference, the Court of Justice pleaded for a power to amend its Rules of Procedure internally, without having to refer to the Council at all.[18] The Member State governments could not accept this proposal, but they did agree to a compromise whereby the Rules of Procedure can now be amended by a mere qualified majority vote of the Council. The purpose of this is to make it easier to obtain

---

[17] The Lisbon Treaty goes further in allowing for amendment of the Statute by qualified majority vote.

[18] This is a right which is enjoyed by the European Court of Human Rights at Strasbourg.

approval for amendments in the future and should thus make the overall courts system slightly more flexible. The Rules of Procedure of both Courts were last amended in October 2005 with a view to enhancing the efficiency of proceedings.[19] The Decision establishing the EU Civil Service Tribunal provides that until the entry into force of its own Rules of Procedure, that Tribunal should apply the Rules of Procedure of the Court of First Instance, except for the provisions concerning a single judge.[20]

## 2.4 Composition and Formations

### Numbers of judges and Advocates General

Article 221 EC provides that the Court of Justice "shall consist of one judge per Member State". This article was the subject of much debate during the Nice Inter-governmental Conference. Many feared that after enlargement a Court of Justice consisting of 27 or more judges would come to resemble little more than a deliberative assembly rather than a collegiate judicial body. There were even suggestions that the number of judges should be limited to a fixed number, as is the case on the US Supreme Court. Politically, however, it would have been very difficult to achieve agreement on such a move. In any event, there was broad consensus at Nice that a judge representing every national legal order should sit on the Court of Justice. This is seen as enhancing the legitimacy of the Court and allows every national legal tradition to contribute to the development of the common body of Community law. Ten new judges therefore joined the Court when the EU enlarged on May 1, 2004 and two more from Romania and Bulgaria on January 1, 2007, bringing the total number of judges to 27. Under *art.254 TFEU* the number of judges in the Court "shall be determined by the Statute of the Court of Justice of the European Union".

Article 222 EC provides that the Court of Justice is to be assisted by eight Advocates General.[21] The role of the Advocate General is to

---

[19] See Amendments to the Rules of Procedure of the Court of Justice of October 18, 2005 (OJ 2005 L 288/51) and Amendments to the Rules of Procedure of the Court of First Instance of October 12, 2005 (OJ 2005 L 298/1).

[20] Art.3(4) of Council Decision 2004/752/EC/Euratom.

[21] Under art.254 TFEU the number of Advocates General assisting the Court may be increased to more than eight.

assist the Court by delivering a reasoned submission after the case has been heard but before the Court deliberates. In the majority of cases, the judgment of the Court follows the Opinion expressed by the Advocate General. Allocation of the eight Advocate General positions between the Member States is a complex matter. Under the rules currently in force,[22] the five largest Member States are always entitled to appoint one Advocate General each. The remaining three Advocate General positions are filled by representatives of the other Member States in accordance with a system of rotation. The Council may, acting unanimously, increase the number of Advocates General if the Court so requests.[23] Following the entry into force of the Treaty of Nice it is now possible to dispense with the need for an Advocate General's Opinion in absolutely every case.[24] This should make the work of the Court more efficient as there are certain categories of cases, such as uncontested infringement actions against a Member State, where the Advocate General's Opinion was a purely formal requirement and contributed little of substance to the determination of the case.

As regards the CFI, art.224 EC provides that the Court of First Instance shall comprise "*at least* one judge per Member State" (emphasis added). This Article was completely revised by the Treaty of Nice and the insertion of the phrase "at least" is very significant. In contrast to the ECJ, this allows for membership of the CFI to expand *beyond* a number of one judge per Member State. The exact number of judges to sit on the CFI is to be determined by the Statute of the Court of Justice and the Council may therefore increase the number of judges simply by amending the Statute. The revised art.224 EC now also allows the Council to amend the Statute so as to provide for the Court of First Instance to be assisted by Advocates General.[25] Up to now, the CFI has not had any Advocates General, although there was always a procedure under which one

---

[22] As set out in the Joint Declaration on art.31 of the Decision adjusting the instruments concerning the accession of the new Member States to the EU (OJ 1995 L 1/221).

[23] Art.222 EC. The number of Advocates General remained unchanged after enlargement on May 1, 2004.

[24] The revised art.222 EC provides that the Advocate General shall be required to deliver an opinion only in those cases which "in accordance with the Statute of the Court of Justice, require his involvement". Paragraph 5 of the new art.20 of the Statute of the Court, meanwhile, provides: "Where it considers that the case raises no new point of law, the Court may decide, after hearing the Advocate General, that the case shall be determined without a submission from the Advocate General."

[25] This is maintained by *art.254 TFEU*.

member of the CFI could be nominated by the other judges to act as Advocate General for a particular case.[26]

The Preamble to Council Decision 2004/752 establishing the EU Civil Service Tribunal provides that the number of judges of this judicial panel should match its caseload.[27] The exact number of judges is laid down in the new Annex I to the Statute of the Court of Justice, which in its art.2 provides that the Civil Service Tribunal shall consist of seven judges. Should the ECJ so request, the Council, acting by a qualified majority, may increase the number of judges. The Civil Service Tribunal does not have any Advocates General.

## Appointment of Judges and Advocates General

Article 223 EC provides that the Judges and Advocates General of the Court of Justice "shall be chosen from persons whose independence is beyond doubt and who possess the qualifications required for appointment to the highest judicial offices in their respective countries or who are jurisconsults of recognised competence." They are to be appointed by common accord of the governments of the Member States for a term of six years. There is to be a partial replacement of the Judges and Advocates General every three years. Article 224 EC provides that the members of the Court of First Instance are to be chosen from persons "whose independence is beyond doubt and who possess the ability required for appointment to high judicial office." Again, they are appointed by common accord of the governments of the Member States for a term of six years and membership is partially renewed every three years. In all cases, retiring judges and Advocates General are eligible for re-appointment. The members of both Courts elect a President from among their number for a term of three years. He or she may also be re-elected at the end of this period. According to art.226 EC, members of judicial panels are to be appointed from persons "who possess the ability required for appointment to judicial office". They are to be appointed by unanimous decision of the Council.

The Treaty of Lisbon 2007 makes provision for an important change to the procedure for appointing judges and Advocates General. First proposed by the Constitutional Treaty[28] *art.255*

---

[26] Under art.2 (3) of the old Council Decision 88/591, now reflected in art.49 of the Statute of the Court of Justice. Detailed rules on how this nomination should take place in practice are laid down in the Rules of Procedure of the Court of First Instance.

[27] Recital 6 of the Decision.

[28] Art.III-357 of the Treaty establishing a Constitution for Europe.

*TFEU* provides for the establishment of an advisory panel which would deliver opinions on the suitability of candidates for positions of Judges and Advocates General on the Community Courts. This panel would comprise seven persons chosen from among former members of the Court of Justice and the General Court,[29] members of national supreme courts and lawyers of recognised competence, one of whom would be proposed by the European Parliament. This procedure would certainly introduce more transparency and accountability in the area of judicial appointments in the EU. In fact, a variant of such a procedure has already been employed in the selection the members of the EU Civil Service Tribunal. In accordance with the Council Decision establishing the Tribunal,[30] the members of the Civil Service Tribunal were appointed by the Council from a shortlist of recommended candidates drawn up by an Advisory Committee of "wise men" composed of former judges and Advocates Generals and other European jurists of recognised competence. This Committee was required to give an opinion on candidates' suitability to perform the duties of judge of the Tribunal and to append to its opinion a list of candiates having the most suitable high-level experience. This list had to contain the names of at least twice as many candiates as there were judges to be appointed. When appointing judges from this list, the Council was obliged to ensure a balanced composition of the Tribunal both in terms of geographical representation and in terms of the national legal systems represented.[31]

## *Formations in which the Courts deliberate*

Article 221 EC provides that the Court of Justice shall sit in chambers or in a Grand Chamber, in accordance with rules laid down in the Statute. The Court may also sit as a Full Court where the Statute so provides. Article 16 of the Statute goes on to provide that the chambers in which the Court sits may be made up of three or five judges. Currently there are eight chambers at the Court of Justice, which sit in formations of three or five judges. The judges of the Court elect the Presidents of Chambers from among their number. The Presidents of Chambers are elected for periods of three years and may be re-elected once. The Grand Chamber consists of 13

---

[29] The Court of First Instance being renamed the 'General Court' by art.256 TFEU.
[30] Art.3 of Annex I to the Statute of the Court of Justice, as introduced by Decision 2004/752.
[31] Art.3(1) of Annex I to the Statute of the Court of Justice.

judges, with a quorum of nine, and is composed of the President of the Court, the Presidents of the chambers and other judges who are appointed in accordance with conditions laid down in the Rules of Procedure.[32] The Court will sit in a Grand Chamber for the most important cases and when a Member State or an EU institution which is a party to the proceedings so requests.

The Grand Chamber formation was a new concept introduced by the Treaty of Nice 2001. Previously, the majority of important cases were heard by an ad hoc "Petit Plenum" of nine judges which was constituted by the President of the Court in a relatively informal manner when the need arose. With the Court of Justice growing to 27 members, it was felt that a more formal arrangement was required to determine which judges should hear the most important cases. Some critics at the time of the Nice negotiations expressed a fear that the Grand Chamber arrangement would lead to a hierarchical division between an elite group of judges who sit on the Grand Chamber over a long period of time and the other judges who are excluded. Traditionally, there has been no sense of hierarchy among the judges of the Court and it is generally accepted that the protection of national interests is not a significant factor in the deliberations of individual members. The risk with the Grand Chamber was that a hierarchy would be introduced and that governments, especially those of the larger Member States, would try to exert political pressure to ensure that 'their' judge is a member of the Grand Chamber. However, in introducing an objective system of appointment based on seniority in office, the amendments to the Court's Rules of Procedure adopted on April 8, 2003 and on October 18, 2005[33] to implement the new system appear to allay those fears of political influence in the process of constituting the Grand Chamber.

The CFI also functions largely in chambers of three or five judges, and art.50 of the Statute provides that the CFI may also sit in Grand Chamber where the Rules of Procedure so provide. This Article also allows for the CFI to be constituted by a single judge in certain cases. The Civil Service Tribunal itself sits in chambers of three judges, but

---

[32] These conditions, which are based on the seniority in office of the members of the Court, were specified in amendments to the Rules of Procedure adopted on April 8, 2003 (OJ 2003 L 147/17) and further clarified in amendments to the Rules of Procedure adopted on October 18, 2005 (OJ 2005 L 288/1).

[33] These conditions, which are based on the seniority in office of the members of the Court, were specified in amendments to the Rules of Procedure adopted on April 8, 2003 (OJ 2003 L 147/17) and further clarified in amendments to the Rules of Procedure adopted on October 18, 2005 (OJ 2005 L 288/1).

may in certain cases determined by its Rules of Procedure sit in Full Court or in a chamber of five judges or of a single judge.[34]

## 2.5 The Court as Constitutional Guarantor

Article 220 EC requires the Court to ensure that the Treaty objectives are fulfilled. According to O'Neill (1994), the Court has taken a broad interpretation of this provision. Most importantly the Court guarantees the supremacy of Community law in the Member States in the absence of a written Treaty provision. The emphasis upon integration by the Court has been to maximise individual rights, but this has lead to criticisms of judicial activism (Shapiro, 1999:321). Judgments of the Court provide communitarian interpretations of fundamental Treaty principles, for example, the concept "worker" under art.39 EC,[35] or abuse of a dominant position under art.82 EC.[36] The judgments have guaranteed the uniform application of EC law and promoted the cause of economic integration.

Weiler (1999) has suggested that the Court of Justice displays the characteristics of a constitutional court. In the absence of a formal written Constitution[37] judgments such as *Konstantinidis*[38] and *Johnson*,[39] have constitutionalised certain Treaty provisions because the Court has referred to them as "fundamental rights or principles". In *Konstantinidis* the applicant challenged the manner in which his Greek surname had been transliterated in to German, arguing that the incorrect spelling amounted to discrimination under art.12 EC. Consequently, this infringed his rights under art.43 EC. Advocate General Jacobs argued that Konstantinidis' right to free movement under the Treaty, which was a "fundamental right", had been infringed because he suffered discrimination arising from an incorrect spelling of his name which could not be objectively justified. The Advocate General further stated that the fundamental right

---

[34] Art.4(2) of Annex I to the Statute of the Court of Justice.
[35] Case 53/81 *Levin v Staatssecretaris van Justitie* [1982] E.C.R. 1035.
[36] Case 27/76 *United Brands v Commission* [1978] E.C.R. 207.
[37] The rejected Constitutional Treaty is the closest the EU has come to formal document that was titled a "constitution". Though the Treaty of Lisbon includes many of the provisions found in the Constitutional Treaty, the Treaty of Lisbon itself is considered to be an amending Treaty rather than a single document which provides for a constitutional settlement.
[38] Case 168/91 *Konstantinidis v Stadt Altensieg, Standesamt, and Landramsamt Colw, Ordnungsamt* [1993] E.C.R. I-1191.
[39] Case 222/84 *Johnson v Chief Constable RUC* [1986] E.C.R. 1651.

to human dignity had also been infringed and this violation would interfere with the exercise of his Community law rights. The right to human dignity was a higher legal norm that is protected by domestic human rights provisions and the ECHR.

The Court, while coming to the same conclusion, did not share the human rights reasoning of the Advocate General. The Court held that the discrimination suffered infringed his fundamental economic right of free movement under art.43 EC because the incorrect spelling of his name could lead to confusion for potential clients. The Court described art.43 EC as "one of the fundamental legal provisions of the Community". The reasoning of the Court's judgment was intended to promote economic integration while circumventing relevant, but difficult, questions of human rights protection in Community law (Coppell and O'Neill, 1992:671). In *Johnson* the Court considered fundamental rights in Community law within the context of the protection afforded by the ECHR. The case concerned the application of dir.76/207/EEC, the Equal Treatment Directive, in circumstances where a female police officer in Northern Ireland was prevented, by ministerial action, from performing armed duties. The Court held that the applicant was entitled to "effective judicial protection", which would include review of the Ministers' decision by a judicial body and whether the decision was compatible with the aims of the directive. The Court's judgment referred to arts 6 and 13 ECHR that provide for the right to effective judicial protection. Article 6 of the directive, which provides for access to judicial procedures for employees in the event of a dispute, should, according to the Court, be read within the context of arts 6 and 13 of the ECHR.

To guarantee both institutional participation and individual rights the Treaty provides several procedures through which the fundamental rights and principles of Community law can be protected. The common feature of these procedures is that they seek to ensure compliance with EC law, and two Treaty provisions stand out. Firstly, under art.230 EC the Institutions and individuals can seek judicial review of a Community act with a view to obtaining its annulment. Access by individuals to art.230 EC has, for many years, raised questions of whether fundamental rights are being adequately protected, in the light of the restrictive criteria for locus standi under art.230 EC. Secondly, through art.234 EC national courts are given a pivotal role to protect individual rights, reinforcing the concept that Community law has become an integral part of the domestic legal order. The Court's statement in *Van Gend en Loos* that Community law is a "new legal order" defines the integrationist stance taken by the Court. Direct effect and state liability developed by the Court have become the techniques through which the fundamental principles of Community law, such as the principle of non-discrimination, are enforced within the domestic courts and will be considered in more detail in Chapter 3. The remainder of this chapter will consider the procedures through which the Court guarantees Treaty rights.

## 2.6 The Division of Jurisdiction

Under arts 226 EC, the Court of Justice has jurisdiction over direct actions brought by the Commission against Member States for failure to fulfil their obligations under the Treaty. The Court also has jurisdiction for actions brought by one Member State against another Member State for failure to fulfil its obligations (art.227 EC). Actions for judicial review of Community acts which are brought by Member States or Community institutions under art.230 EC are also heard by the Court of Justice. The jurisdiction of the Court of First Instance in the area of direct actions has been progressively extended over the past decade and the Court of First Instance now has jurisdiction over all actions brought under the Treaty by individuals and companies. This includes actions for annulment of Community acts brought by individuals under art.230, actions for damages under art.235 EC and, up until the establishment of the new EU Civil Service Tribunal, staff cases brought under art.236 EC.

In line with the overall trend towards transforming the Court of First Instance into the Community's main court of first instance jurisdiction, the provisions of the Treaty of Nice dealing with direct actions before the Community Courts strengthened further the position of the Court of First Instance. In particular, the revised art.225 (1) EC now sets out explicitly the areas over which the Court of First Instance has jurisdiction. Significantly, this article has been revised so as to state that the Court of First Instance has jurisdiction over all direct actions except those reserved in the Statute for the Court of Justice. Council Decision 2004/407/EC of April 26, 2004 has since amended art.51 of the Statute of the Court of Justice so as to clarify the exact areas of direct action jurisdiction that are now reserved to the Court of Justice. As a result of this Decision, certain limited categories of actions taken by Member States, such as direct actions brought by Member States challenging, inter alia, Council anti-dumping regulations and certain implementing measures, are now also to be heard by the Court of First Instance.[40] These developments would appear to suggest that in time responsibility for all direct actions, whether brought by Member States, institutions or individuals, may be transferred to the Court of First Instance.

## Direct actions

### (i) Article 226 EC and 228 EC: Enforcement actions

In fulfilling its task of enforcing Community law the Commission can seek recourse to the judicial procedure under art.226 EC which permits the Commission to bring infringement proceedings against a Member State for breaching its obligations under EC law. This enforcement is a crucial task for the Commission and the impact of art.226 EC cannot be understated. It is triggered by a Member State's failure to comply with a Treaty obligation. The procedure involves giving the State an opportunity to submit observations before the Commission delivers a reasoned opinion. If the State fails to comply with the opinion, proceedings are commenced before the Court.

A significant proportion of proceedings are settled before reaching the Court and art.226 EC works effectively when Member States cooperate with the Commission. One problem is the question of enforcement of a judgment against the Member State. Until the Maastricht Treaty there was an absence of sanctions should the Court's ruling be ignored. Under art.228(2) EC the Commission can impose a financial sanction on further application to the Court in the vent of a failure by a State to comply with the ruling.[41] In *Commission v France* A.G. Geelhoed emphasised that the purpose of art.228 EC is to ensure Member State compliance with Community law.[42] In this respect the sanctions provided for in that Article serve a twofold purpose. Firstly they should have a dissuasive preventive effect by making it economically unattractive for a Member State to infringe Community law. Secondly the sanction has a specific persuasive effect by allowing sufficient pressure to be brought to bear on a Member State to ensure compliance with Community law after an infringement has been determined by the Court. Moreover the Advocate General stressed that these sanctions are particular to

---

[40] See revised art.51 of the Statute of the Court.
[41] See for example Case C-387/97 *Commission v Greece* [2000] E.C.R. I-5047.
[42] Case 304/02 *Commission v France* [2005] E.C.R. I-6263.

the Community legal order and cannot be compared to existing sanction mechanisms at the national level.

The Advocate General stated that the Court should be permitted to impose a lump sum fine in addition to a periodic payment for breach of Community law. The Advocate General's reasoning is that when determining whether the Court can impose both a lump sum and a periodic penalty payment, the objective and rational of art.228 EC is decisive. Advocate General Geelhoed considered the purpose of this Article is to ensure that Member States fulfill their obligations under Community law. By their nature the lump sum and the periodic penalty payment serve different purposes, the first being dissuasive and the latter persuasive. Accordingly in the Opinion of the Advocate General it must be open for the Court to impose both sanctions simultaneously.

*(ii) Article 230 EC: Actions for annulment*

Under art.230 EC, an applicant seeks the annulment of a measure adopted by an Institution. An action for annulment may be commenced by a privileged applicant which, under art.230 EC, are the Member States or Community institutions. Individuals, whether legal or natural, are categorised as non-privileged applicants and can challenge a measure if it can be shown to be of "direct and individual concern". Accordingly, individuals are generally restricted to challenging decisions as they are addressed at specific parties. The Court has in specific circumstances permitted challenges to regulations but this has occurred where the measure exhibits the characteristic of a decision, for example, if identifies particular undertakings. The Court has stated in *Calpak v Commission*[43] that, judicial review will be permitted on such occasions because of the substance and nature of the measure. Judicial review will not be denied merely by virtue of the nomenclature which the Commission has applied to a measure.

The granting of locus standi by the Court to individuals has, since the judgment in *Plaumann v Commission*,[44] only been permitted within very narrow criteria. Occasionally, the Court has relaxed the conditions, for example in *Cordoniu*[45] and *Extramet*,[46] where the

---

[43] Case 789/79 *Calpak SpA v Commission* [1980] E.C.R. 1949.
[44] Case 25/62 *Plaumann v Commission* [1963] E.C.R. 95.
[45] Case C-309/89 *Cordoniu v Commission* [1994] ECR-I 1853.
[46] Case C-358/89 *Extramet Industrie SA v Council* [1991] E.C.R. I-2501.

Court demonstrated a broader willingness to protect specific commercial interest as part of a wider policy of promoting economic integration (Maduro, 1998:25; Arnull, 2001:7). Since *Plaumann*, the Court has consistently stated that locus standi to individuals will only be granted if the measure being challenged is of direct and individual concern. In *Plaumann* the Court stated this requires the applicant to demonstrate that:

> "[b]y reason of certain attributes which are peculiar to them or by reason of circumstances in which they are differentiated from all other persons."

Individual applicants have tended to be successful in cases involving decisions rather than general legislative measures. In *Nold v Commission*[47] the Commission introduced new trading procedures in the coal industry which resulted in the applicant losing its status as a direct wholesaler, and consequently, a direct supplier of coal. Nold argued that the new rules jeopardised profitability to the extent of undermining the entire business. This infringed the right to property and freedom to trade which are guaranteed by the German constitution. Nold satisfied the criteria of direct and individual concern because the measure was addressed directly at coal producers and did not require intervening action by a Member State. The decision was of individual concern because Nold, as an individual, constituted a finite group of potential applicants that are more commonly referred to as a "closed class".[48] This identification through the Commission decision individualised the party from other applicants.

For an individual applicant to be successful then he/she must differentiate his/herself from all other potential applicants. In competition cases, or other cases where an economic right is involved, it has proved factually easier for an applicant to demonstrate the impact which the decision has. For example, an applicant can demonstrate that a legitimate expectation has been infringed and that this has led to the applicant suffering a financial loss. This was the position in both *Nold* and *Cordoniu*. In cases involving general legislative measures such as a regulation or directive, or if the measure affects all applicants uniformly a challenge under art.230 EC is less likely to succeed. Such cases, which tend to involve non-

---

[47] Case 4/73 *Nold v Commission* [1974] E.C.R. 491.
[48] Case 11/82 *Piriaki-Patraiki v Commission* [1985] E.C.R. 207.

economic rights have broader impact, and the irony of the art.230 EC requirement of individual concern is that the greater the number of individuals that are affected by a measure, the less likely that the Court will grant locus standi (Cygan, 2003:1004).

The restricted application of art.230 EC by the Court has had the effect of preventing proxy or group actions by individuals who collectively are affected by a measure in the same way.[49] Harlow (2002) criticises this approach as restricting the development of popular justice in the EU and reinforcing the notion of a democratic deficit by preventing judicial review of a legislative act when a large group of citizens share the same concerns. In *Greenpeace* the applicants sought judicial review of Commission funding for two powers stations which were to be built on the Canary Islands. The building work commenced without an Environmental Impact Assessment (EIA) under dir.85/337/EEC being carried out. The Island's residents initiated proceedings in the national court and sought a reference under art.234 EC. This domestic action for judicial review of the Commission's Decision was rejected by the Spanish Administrative Court which stated that it did not have jurisdiction to grant a remedy against the Commission. Greenpeace subsequently commenced a proxy action on behalf of the residents under art.230 EC where they sought compliance with the EIA Directive. The ECJ, rejecting their claim, stated that Greenpeace could not be individually concerned because the EIA Directive was aimed at Member States and was a general legislative measure. In such circumstances any challenge relating to application of the EIA Directive should be commenced before the national court.

The effect of the ECJ's judgment was to exclude *any* challenge to the Commission's funding of the project. The Court argued that Greenpeace was not in any special position vis-à-vis the Commission's decision, even if they represented a significant proportion of the Islanders. The directive was a general legislative measure and consequently Greenpeace could not under the *Plaumann* formula be individualised. The Court's reasoning recognises that Greenpeace was not part of the decision-making process, and as such, was not contemplated by the Commission when it made the decision.

Cygan (2003) criticises this decision and contrasts the Court's approach in *Greenpeace* with that of judicial review in the Member States, where national courts have viewed group actions as efficient

---

[49] See Case C-321/95 *Stichting Greenpeace v Commission* [1998] E.C.R. I-1651; Case C-50/00 *Unión de Pequeños Agricultores v Council* [2002] E.C.R. 1-6677.

mechanisms for the protection of individual. Furthermore, he cites an inconsistent approach to protecting effective remedies under Community law, with actions against Community Institutions being less successful than those which involve Member States. The ECJ has based its objections to widening the grounds of locus standi on a floodgates policy, whereby any relaxation of the rules would lead to opportunistic litigants initiating challenges which may undermine the decision-making process. In the Opinion of A.G. Jacobs in *Unión de Pequeños Agricultores (UPA)*[50] the floodgates argument was rejected as a justification for not extending locus standi. The Advocate General argues that the problem is not insurmountable and could be addressed through adequate procedural measures The Court's judgment in *UPA* rejected this view and stated that any reform of art.230 EC is a matter exclusively for the Treaty makers and added that the narrow criteria for *locus standi* should not be mitigated through use of the Court's Rules of Procedure.

The Opinion of A.G. Jacobs is largely based on a fundamental rights argument. The Advocate General contends that access to an effective remedy through art.230 EC is a fundamental right and one which *all* courts have a duty to protect. This view was shared by the CFI in the *Jégo-Quéré* judgment. In addition to referring to arts 6 and 13 ECHR in support of his views, the Advocate General refers to art.47 of the Charter of Fundamental Rights which protects the right to an effective remedy. Advocate General Jacobs stated:[51]

"That principle [of an effective remedy] is, as the Court has repeatedly stated, grounded in the constitutional traditions common to the Member States and in Articles 6 and 13 of the European Convention on Human Rights. Moreover, the Charter of fundamental rights of the European Union, while itself not legally binding, proclaims a generally recognised principle in stating in Article 47 that 'everyone whose rights and freedoms guaranteed by the law of the Union are violated has the right to an effective remedy before a tribunal.'"

For both the Advocate General and the CFI there is no compelling reason to read in to the notion of individual concern, a requirement

---

[50] See Case C-321/95 *Stichting Greenpeace v Commission* [1998] E.C.R. I-1651; Case C-50/00 *Unión de Pequeños Agricultores v Council* [2002] E.C.R. 1-6677 at para.101.
[51] See Case C-321/95 *Stichting Greenpeace v Commission* [1998] E.C.R. I-1651; Case C-50/00 *Unión de Pequeños Agricultores v Council* [2002] E.C.R. 1-6677 at para.39.

that an individual applicant seeking to challenge a measure must be differentiated from all others affected by it. The overriding question should be the protection of fundamental rights, which in this case is a right to an effective remedy, which the Court has acknowledged in *Johnson*. In *UPA*, as in *Konstantinidis*, A.G. Jacobs adopts a higher legal norms argument with regard to access to an effective remedy, the denial of which cannot be justified, even in the application of Community law.

The ECJ rejected the arguments advanced by the Advocate General. Furthermore the ECJ subsequently overturned on appeal the CFI's judgment in *Jégo-Quéré*.[52] In neither of these judgments did the Court apply art.47 of the Charter, instead relying on the principles of arts 6 and 13 of ECHR which it acknowledged in judgments such as *Johnson*. The Court argued that in cases such as *UPA*, the applicant could seek an effective remedy in the domestic courts, and apply arts 6 and 13 ECHR. It will be remembered that in *Johnson* the right to judicial review of the ministerial decision was a right to be exercised in the national court and not before the ECJ. Cygan (2003) and Usher (2003) criticise the judgment in *UPA* as being inconsistent with the Court's general approach to protecting individual rights. It will be recalled that in the *Chernobyl* case, the pre-Maastricht version of art.230 EC did not permit the European Parliament to protect its prerogatives, yet through teleological reasoning the Court afforded Parliament this right. The Court's justification was the need to maintain institutional balance within the legislative procedure, but it is equally important that individuals have access to effective judicial protection when their rights are infringed. In *UPA* the Court stated it would not re-draft art.230 EC to extend locus standi for individual applicants suggesting this was a task for the Treaty makers. The ECJ argued that it is for individuals to seek effective remedies in their domestic courts but Greenpeace demonstrates that this will not always be possible.

*(iii) Article 288 EC: The Non-contractual liability of EU Institutions*

Under art.288 EC, which is based on a principle of non-contractual liability, individuals may apply for compensation from an Institution for damage which he/she has suffered. The damage must have arisen

---

[52] Case 263/02P *Commission v Jégo-Quéré* [2004] E.C.R. 1-3425.

out of the acts or omissions of the Institution and is a possible alternative to the lack of a remedy under art.230 EC. Article 288 EC can be seen within the context of the administrative and legislative activities of the Institutions and falls within a general principle of governance and sound and efficient administration. It is therefore necessary to consider the damage arising out of the conduct complained of and according to Lasok and Bridge (1991) it is "unthinkable that every damage should be made good and every misconduct could lead to compensation".

The Court's judgments have stated that for an individual to be successful he/she must demonstrate:

(a)   actual damage to the plaintiff;

(b)   a causal link between the damage claimed and the conduct alleged against the institution; and

(c)   the illegality of this conduct (i.e. a wrongful act or omission on the part of the institution, or its servants).

On the question of wrongful act the Court stated in *Zuckerfabrik Schöppenstedt*[53] that where general legislative measures are concerned then an applicant must satisfy two criteria. Firstly, the applicant must establish that there is a breach of a superior rule of law, for example the principle of non-discrimination or proportionality.[54] Secondly the applicant must demonstrate that the breach is sufficiently serious. This requires that the breach to be manifest and grave. In *Mulder v Council and Commission*[55] the Court held that individuals must show that both the scale of loss and the degree of the Community's breach of the rule of law are both sufficiently serious to warrant the award of damages.

In *Zuckerfabrik Schöppenstedt* the ECJ has restricted the application of art.288 EC when the nature of the Community's liability in damages is in respect of "legislative action involving measures of economic policy". According to the Court, such legislation involves "choices of economic policy", leaving a large degree of discretion in the hands of the Institution which presumably will seek to act in the public interest. This continues the trend, which is apparent when individuals seek remedies against the EU Institutions, that the Court

---

[53] Case 5/71 *Zuckerfabrik Schöppenstedt v Council* [1971] E.C.R. 975.
[54] Case 83/76 *Bayerische HNL v Council and Commission* [1978] E.C.R. 1209.
[55] Joined Cases C-104/89 and C-37/90 *Mulder v Council and Commission* [1992] E.C.R. I-3061.

is reluctant to award any remedy without a high degree of culpability. The remedy under art.288 EC is independent of any action which an individual may bring under art.230 EC. If an individual applicant has failed to be granted locus standi under art.230 EC it is unlikely they will be any more successful in an action for damages under art.288 EC.

## *Article 234 EC: References for a preliminary ruling*

The preliminary reference procedure of art.234 EC plays a critical role in the development of Community law. Where a question arises in proceedings before a national court on the interpretation or validity of a provision of Community law, the national court may— or in certain cases, must—stay its proceedings and refer the question of Community law to the Court of Justice. The Court of Justice will hear the arguments of the parties and will then provide the national court with a definitive answer to its question. Having received this answer, the national court will continue hearing the national proceedings and will ultimately apply this definitive interpretation of Community law to the facts of the case before it. Traditionally, it was only the Court of Justice which had jurisdiction to deliver preliminary rulings. However, an enormous increase in the number of references being sent to the Court over the past decade has made it necessary to consider shifting some of this preliminary reference responsibility to the Court of First Instance.

Article 225 (3) EC, as revised by the Treaty of Nice, now provides that the CFI shall have jurisdiction to hear and determine questions referred for a preliminary ruling under art.234, but only "in specific areas laid down by the Statute". The difficult issue involved in the transfer of preliminary reference jurisdiction to the CFI is the question of when and how appeals to the Court of Justice should be allowed against a preliminary ruling of the CFI. Such an appeal procedure could lead to even further delay in a reference process that is already considered to be far too long. After Nice, the revised art.225(3) EC provides that an appeal against a preliminary ruling of the CFI should be possible, but only in exceptional circumstances "where there is a serious risk of the unity or consistency of Community law being affected".[56] The CFI may also refer the case to the Court of Justice at the very outset of the procedure where it

---

[56] Further details on how this review procedure could work in practice are set out in arts 62 and 62b of the revised Statute of the Court of Justice. Here it is provided that "where the First Advocate General considers that there is a serious risk of the

considers that the case "requires a decision of principle likely to affect the unity or consistency of Community law". Given this uncertainty about how an appeal procedure would work in practice, it is likely that at the beginning only a very limited preliminary reference jurisdiction will be transferred to the CFI on an experimental basis. At the moment, there are no concrete proposals to transfer any preliminary reference jurisdiction to the CFI.

References for a preliminary ruling are specific to Community law. The Court is the supreme guardian of Community legality, but is not the only judicial body empowered to apply Community law. National courts have a key role to play inasmuch as they retain jurisdiction to review the administrative implementation of Community law by the Member State. Treaty provisions and secondary legislation directly confer rights upon EU citizens, which national courts must uphold. To ensure the effective and uniform application of Community legislation and to prevent divergent interpretations, art.234 EC provides for a preliminary ruling procedure. Under art.234 EC, where a national court seeks a preliminary ruling on the application of a legislative act, the ECJ will clarify the interpretation of Community law in order to ascertain whether the national legislation or administrative action comply with Community law.

The national court and not the parties to the action decide if a preliminary reference is required and the preliminary reference must ask clear, unambiguous and relevant question questions to the ECJ. These should relate to the Community measure at issue and its application in national law.[57] The ECJ's reply is not merely an opinion, but takes the form of a judgment. The ECJ does not decide the domestic action, which is left to the national court, but the ECJ's preliminary ruling will provide a clear explanation of the Community law issue. In *Arsenal Football Club v Reed*[58] the English High Court made a reference to the ECJ seeking clarification on the application of dir.89/104/EEC on the Community Trademark. When the preliminary ruling was received, Laddie J. rejected the judgment stating that the ECJ had decided the factual issues of

---

unity or consistency of Community law being affected, he may propose that the Court of Justice review the decision of the Court of First Instance". This proposal is to be made within one month of delivery of the decision by the Court of First Instance and the Court of Justice then has one further month to decide whether or not the decision should be reviewed. Furthermore, in a declaration attached to the Treaty of Nice (Declaration 15), the Member States call upon the Court of Justice to act under an emergency procedure when reviewing a decision of the Court of First Instance on a question referred for a preliminary ruling.

[57] Case 104/ 79 *Foglia v Novello (1)* [1980] E.C.R. 745.

[58] Case C-206/01 *Arsenal Football Club v Reed* [2002] E.C.R. I-273.

the case and therefore exceeded its jurisdiction. Laddie J. did not consider himself bound by the preliminary ruling, but this action is outside the spirit, let alone the requirement, of art.234 EC. The Court of Appeal subsequently overturned the High Court judgment and applied the preliminary ruling, finding in favour of the applicant that their trademark had been infringed.

The fundamental question relating to preliminary rulings is in what circumstances should they be made? Article 234 EC states that when a matter is before a national court against which there is no further judicial remedy, then the national court is under an obligation to make a reference. Where the case is before any other court against whose judgment an appeal is possible then a discretion is retained. Even in these circumstances national courts are encouraged to make a reference to ensure that Community law rights are available and consistently applied.

Courts from which an appeal is possible may apply the doctrine of acte clair. This principle arises from French administrative law and as applied in Community law does not require national courts to make a reference if the legal issue in question has been decided by a previous court ruling. In *CILFIT*[59] the ECJ stated that acte clair could be used in circumstances where there was "no scope for reasonable doubt as to the manner in which the question raised is to be resolved." Acte clair is therefore a useful principle as it helps prevent the ECJ from being overwhelmed by references on established points of law. National courts must apply Community law correctly and should not use acte clair unless, according to Court of Appeal in *R v Stock Exchange Ex p. Else*,[60] the national court is "completely confident" that it can resolve the issue itself. If any doubt exists then a reference should ordinarily be made.

The statement of the Court of Appeal in *Else* is a workable application of acte clair for all lower courts. It preserves their discretion to refer, but encourages them to do so if there is any doubt. For those courts from which there is no appeal, the doctrine of acte clair would seem to be of minimal assistance, though the ECJ has acknowledged that such courts do not need to make a reference if a matter has been clearly decided.[61] On a literal interpretation art.234 EC places a positive obligation upon courts of last instance to refer, and this

---

[59] Case 283/81 *CILFIT* [1982] E.C.R. 3415.

[60] *R v International Stock Exchange of the UK and the Republic of Ireland Ex p. Else* [1993] 1 All E.R. 420.

[61] Case 28-30/62 *Da Costa en Schaake v Nederlandse Belastingadministratie* [1963] E.C.R. 31.

requirement has been reinforced through the Court's judgment in *Köbler*.[62] In this judgment the Court appears to reject the view that acte clair can be applied by courts of last instance and takes a pragmatic approach to art.234 EC. The Court stated:

> "Moreover, it is, in particular, in order to prevent rights conferred on individuals by Community law from being infringed that under the third paragraph of Article 234 EC a court against whose decisions there is no judicial remedy under national law is required to make a reference to the Court of Justice." (para.34)

> "The [Austrian] court (was not entitled to take the view that resolution of the point of law at issue was clear from the settled case-law of the Court or left no room for any reasonable doubt (Case 283/81 *CILFIT and Others* [1982] ECR 3415, paragraphs 14 and 16). It was therefore obliged under the third paragraph of Article 234 of the Treaty to maintain its request for a preliminary ruling." (para.118)

In *Köbler* the applicant was a university professor, who applied for a length-of-service increment provided for by Austrian law. He was refused on the ground that he had not completed 15 years' service as a professor at Austrian universities. Köbler claimed that service at universities elsewhere in the EU should be included. The Austrian Supreme Administrative Court made a reference to the ECJ seeking clarification whether the Austrian law infringed art.39 EC. But after the Court's judgment the Austrian Court withdrew the reference and dismissed the applicant's claim arguing that the increment was a loyalty bonus and not part of his salary. This Austrian court based its decision on the acte clair doctrine stating that the question of loyalty bonuses in such circumstances had been decided by the ECJ in *Schöning-Kougebetopoulou*.[63] Köbler, through this action, sought compensation from the Austrian government under the state liability principle. His primary argument was that through the national court's judgment, which failed to account in to account the preliminary ruling, he had suffered a financial loss.

The Court stated that it had not expressed a view in *Schöning-Kougebetopoulou* on whether, and if so under what conditions, the

---

[62] Case C-224/01 *Köbler v Republik Österreich* [2003] E.C.R. I-239.
[63] C-15/96 *Schöning-Kougebetopoulou v Freie und Hansestadt Hamburg* [1998] E.C.R. I-4730.

obstacle to freedom of movement for workers constituted by a loyalty bonus could be justified. The inferences drawn by the Austrian court were incorrect and it was not entitled to take the view that the matter was acte claire. While the ECJ held that the Austrian court had failed to follow the requirements of art.234 EC it concluded that Community law did not expressly cover the point at issue in relation to the loyalty bonus. Consequently, having regard to all the circumstances, the infringement could not be regarded as being sufficiently serious to give rise to State liability.

The Court's judgment was explicit on the point that as a court of last instance, the Austrian Administrative Court *must* make a reference and accept the preliminary ruling once provided. *Köbler* is an interesting judgment because it was delivered at a time when the future of the preliminary rulings procedure is the subject of much debate both judicially and academically (Tridimas, 2003:9). In 2004 the average waiting time for a preliminary ruling, even before the impact of enlargement was fully felt, was 18 months. While it is crucial to maintain the uniformity of Community law, this must be balanced against the need to ensure that the judicial process remains efficient. Significant delay can undermine the principle of an effective remedy[64] which the Court places so much emphasis upon. If placed in to its chronological context, the *Köbler* judgment may be interpreted as the Court sending out a message to the Member States, and particularly the 2004 Accession States, reminding them of their obligations when applying Community law. The Court stated that incorrect application of Community law by national courts can give rise to State liability and this may be interpreted as a warning of the consequences of the failure to adequately protect individual rights. *Köbler* may be considered as the Court making a value judgment in which it is prepared to sacrifice a degree of expediency for uniform application and effective protection of individual rights in an enlarged EU.

The obligations of courts of last instance under art.234 EC was considered in *Traghetti del Mediterraneo*[65] where the Court built upon its findings in *Köbler*. The *Traghetti* case concerned a commercial dispute between two Italian ferry companies, Traghetti and its competitor Tirrenia di Navigazione (Tirrenia), which operated services between mainland Italy, Sardinia and Sicily. Tirrenia

---

[64] See for Case C-66/95 *R v Secretary of State for Social Security Ex p. Sutton* [1997] E.C.R. I-2163.

[65] Case C-173/03 *Traghetti del Mediterraneo SpA v Italy* [2006] E.C.R. I-5177.

received subsidies from the Italian public authorities, which Traghetti alleged were used by Tirrenia to offer below cost ferry services and therefore constituted an abuse of Tirrenia's dominant position. Traghetti also alleged that the public subsidies breached EC rules on state aid and art.86 EC. Traghetti was unsuccessful in its action and went into liquidation during the course of the proceedings which were finally dismissed by the Italian Court of Cassation in 1996, some 15 years after the action first started. Traghetti considered that in dismissing its action, the Italian Court of Cassation, the court of last instance in this case, had both misinterpreted the Community law on which Traghetti relied and had breached its obligation contained in the final paragraph article of art.234 EC to refer relevant questions to the Court of Justice. Therefore, Traghetti brought an action for damages against the Italian state at the Tribunale di Genova for damages caused by the Italian Court of Cassation's erroneous interpretation of provisions of EC law relevant to the dispute.

*Traghetti* was a dispute which concerned the application of EC competition law the application of which was decentralised from May 1, 2004. As a result, there is an even greater need to ensure consistency of interpretation and application of EC competition law. When this is combined with obligation on national courts on the basis of *Traghetti* liability (which is discussed in Chapter 3) one potential consequence of the judgment may be that national courts of last resort will be more inclined to refer questions of interpretation of competition law to the Court of Justice. This movement towards increased use of the art.234 EC procedure by national courts of last resort in competition cases is also likely because the shift to a more effects-based system has resulted in more uncertainty. The scope for an increased number of art.234 EC references exists across the board in competition law, but some particular examples of uncertainty do spring to mind. The Commission's interpretation of Community courts' case law on art.81(3) EC in its guidelines[66] is not wholly consistent with the Court's case law, and therefore national courts may well find themselves in a position of needing assistance from the Court on questions of interpretation. The evolving state of the law concerning abuse of a dominant position pursuant to art.82 EC is another example of an area which seems likely to trigger art.234 EC requests from national courts.

---

[66] Commission Notice on the co-operation between the Commission and the courts of the EU Member States in the application of arts 81 and 82 EC, (1994) OJ C101/5.

The Court's judgment in *Traghetti* will have an impact on how national courts, in particular national courts of last resort, deal with complex competition cases. In most cases involving courts of last resort, it will be the interpretation of Community law to a particular set of facts (as found by the lower courts) which will be at issue, as courts of last resort generally deal with appeals on points of law only. Although art.234 (3) EC contains an obligation on courts of last resort to refer any questions on the interpretation of Community law the Court has accepted the acte clair doctrine. The question this raises is how do the acte clair doctrine and the *Traghetti* principle sit together? In many ways they are complementary, because although *CILFIT* principle enables national courts not to refer questions of interpretation of Community law to the Court the *CILFIT* conditions are in fact very difficult to fulfil. Furthermore, the Court was clear in *Traghetti* that a failure to refer a question to the Court in the case of questions of interpretation where the answer is in some doubt may be classified as a manifest infringement of Community law, which may in turn give rise to Member State liability. The Court remained silent on whether all such failures will amount to manifest infringement (Nassimpian, 2007:827)

## *The relationship between art.230 EC and art.234 EC*

Actions under art.230 EC are commenced directly before the ECJ, whereas to employ art.234 EC an action must first be commenced before the national court. The two Treaty provisions have different objectives and use different procedures. The restricted locus standi for applicants under art.230 EC has led litigants to commence actions before national courts with the expectation that the court will make a reference to clarify the issue of Community law. There are limitations to this, most notably the limited remedies which a national court may offer by comparison to those under art.230 EC where an applicant will be seeking annulment of the offending measure. The *Greenpeace* case illustrates how applicants may be denied access to an effective remedy both before their national court and before the ECJ.

It will be recalled that the Spanish court dismissed the domestic action and this was supported by the Opinion of A.G. Cosmas.[67] The Advocate General stated that such a challenge would not be

---

[67] Para.74.

permitted in national courts on the grounds that an indirect challenge to a Commission decision cannot be sought through art.234 EC. The Spanish court could control domestic administrative action and whether an EIA had been carried out. However, it lacked the competence to provide a remedy on the substantive issue of the challenge in relation to the Commission decision to finance the project in the absence of an EIA.

In *UPA* A.G. Jacobs examined the relationship between arts 230 and 234 EC and in particular whether through art.234 EC an individual could obtain an effective remedy. Advocate General Jacobs argued[68] that proceedings brought directly before the ECJ are more appropriate for determining issues of validity than proceedings pursuant to art.234 EC and they are less liable to cause legal uncertainty for individuals and the Community Institutions. In addition to those points, the Advocate General was of the view that the Court's restrictive attitude towards individual applicants is anomalous in the light of its case-law on other aspects of judicial review and recent developments in the administrative laws of the Member States.

Focussing on the principle of an effective remedy the Advocate General was sceptical as to the suitability of art.234 EC. The principle of effective judicial protection requires that applicants have access to a court which is competent to grant remedies capable of protecting them against the effects of unlawful measures. Access to the ECJ via art.234 EC is not a remedy available to individual applicants as a matter of right. National courts may refuse to refer questions, and although courts of last instance are obliged to refer under art.234 EC, appeals within the national judicial systems are liable to entail long delays. Such delays may themselves be incompatible with the principle of effective judicial protection and the need for legal certainty. The Advocate General concluded that proceedings before the ECJ under art.230 EC are generally more appropriate for determining issues of validity than reference proceedings under art.234 EC. This is because the Institution which adopted the measure is challenged directly and is a party to the proceedings from the beginning.

The Court rejected the reasoning of the Advocate General, though it accepted that the right to an effective remedy for individuals is part of Community law and protected by arts 6 and 13 of the ECHR. The Court referred to the judgment in *Johnson* and stated

[68] Para.37.

that individuals can obtain effective remedies in their domestic legal system when they do not fit within the criteria for standing under art.230 EC by seeking a reference under art.234 EC. The remedy though will only be effective where the defendant is the Member State as the national court cannot review acts of the Institutions or annul a Community measure. For Harlow (2002) and Cygan (2003) this position remains unsatisfactory because it leaves a legal vacuum in the EU system of protecting individual rights that the Treaty of Lisbon 2007 does not adequately fill.

## *Appeals*

Appeals against decisions of the Court of First Instance account for an increasing proportion of the cases coming before the Court of Justice. As the jurisdiction of the Court of First Instance grows in the years ahead, it is likely that the number of appeals coming before the Court of Justice will also increase. Article 225 (1) EC provides that decisions given by the Court of First Instance may be subject to a right of appeal to the Court of Justice "on points of law only". The Court of Justice will therefore not review the facts as found by the Court of First Instance. This is consistent with the likely evolution of the role of the Court of Justice along the lines of a supreme court which deals only with fundamental constitutional issues and questions concerning the unity and coherence of Community law.

In accordance with the provisions of reg.40/94 on the Community trade mark[69] and reg.6/2002 on Community designs,[70] the Court of First Instance already hears appeals against decisions of the Boards of Appeal of the Office for Harmonisation in the Internal Market (OHIM) in Alicante, Spain. OHIM is the body responsible for administration of the Community trade mark and designs regime, and a flood of appeals to the Court of First Instance are expected in the coming years against decisions of these Boards of Appeal. Decisions given by new judicial panels established in accordance with the procedures laid down in art.225a EC may also be subject to a right of appeal to the Court of First Instance on points of law.[71] Article 9 of Annex I to the Statute of the Court, as introduced by Council Decision 2004/752 establishing the EU Civil Service Tribunal, provides for just such an appeal. An appeal would also lie

---

[69] OJ 1994 L 11/1.

[70] OJ 2002 L 3/1.

[71] Art.225a also states that an appeal may be allowed also on matters of fact where the Council decision setting up the panel so provides.

from decisions of any future Community Patent Court that may be set up.[72] It is possible that in time the Boards of Appeal of the OHIM may themselves be transformed formally into judicial panels within the meaning of art.220 EC.[73]

## 2.7 Future Perspectives

### The Treaty of Lisbon 2007

The Constitutional Treaty proposed the abolition of the Union's three pillar structure which consequently would have extended the jurisdiction of the Community Courts to cover third pillar matters. By contrast, though the Treaty of Lisbon maintained the three pillar structure it does retain the incorporation of a legally binding EU Charter of Fundamental Rights first included in the Constitutional Treaty. The Court has hitherto been reluctant to consider the Charter within its judgments,[74] but this proposed extension of jurisdiction could result in an enormous wave of new litigation concerning the protection of individuals' fundamental rights in an EU context. The Court of Justice could thus find itself in the position of ultimate defender of a bill of rights applying to millions of EU citizens.

Under the Treaty of Lisbon (*art.19 TEU*) the Court retains its role of ensuring observance of EU law by the Member States but there are several important changes to the organisation of the Court. The significant change is that the Court of Justice of the European Community will now be referred to as the Court of Justice of the European Union (*art.19 (1) TEU*). Not only does this acknowledge the renaming of all laws as EU law, but it also recognises that the Court will have increased jurisdiction over the inter-governmental pillars, which the Lisbon Treaty maintains, and in particular pillar three.[75]

---

[72] COM (2003) 828 final.

[73] In a declaration to the Treaty of Nice, Luxembourg, the seat of the Community Courts, undertakes not to claim the seat of the Boards of Appeal should they be transformed into judicial panels.

[74] To date references have been made in: Case C-540/03 *EP v Council* E.C.R. I-5769; Case C-428/05 *Viking* judgment of December 11, 2007.

[75] The Constitutional Treaty would have abolished of the Union's three pillar structure with the consequent extension of the jurisdiction of those Courts to cover third pillar matters.

The Lisbon Treaty will rename the Community Courts and makes further minor amendments to the Treaty articles governing the judicial system. One noteworthy point is that whereas art.222 EC states that the Court is to be assisted by eight Advocates General, *art.19 TEU* makes no reference to a maximum number of Advocates General. This would appear to leave the door open for the appointment of further Advocates General, which could help to address the issue of the Court's workload.[76]

Under the Treaty of Lisbon the name of the Court of Justice remains unchanged but the Court of First Instance would be renamed the "General Court" (*art.19 (1) TEU*) and judicial panels would be renamed "specialised courts" (*art.19 (1) TEU*). These specialised courts would be attached to the General Court, just as the Treaty of Nice envisaged that judicial panels would be attached to the CFI. In this respect, a particularly significant procedural change proposed is that new specialised courts should be established under the co-decision procedure and by qualified majority voting, rather than the current requirement of unanimous voting and consultation of the European Parliament.[77]

The Treaty of Lisbon maintains the amendments, first proposed in the Constitutional Treaty, to the provisions of art.230 EC. Two proposed changes to art.230 EC are particularly noteworthy (*art.263 TFEU*). Firstly, it is proposed that the Court should have jurisdiction to review the legality of acts of all EU bodies and agencies which are intended to produce legal effects vis-à-vis third parties. Under the current art.230 EC jurisdiction is limited to acts of the Council, Parliament, Commission and ECB. This is an important extension as many new agencies and bodies of the EU have been created in recent years with powers over sensitive matters of justice and home affairs in particular. Secondly, art.230(4) EC concerning locus standi in direct actions is replaced by a new paragraph which states that a natural or legal person may institute proceedings "against an act addressed to that person or which is of direct and individual concern to him or her, and against a regulatory act which is of direct concern to him or her and does not entail implementing measures" (*art.263 TFEU*). This formulation is intended to address some of the concerns expressed in case-law of the Court of First Instance and Court of Justice concerning the

---

[76] Poland argued at the Intergovernmental Conference that as a Member State similar in size to Spain it too should be awarded a permanent Advocate General.
[77] Art.III-359 (1) of the Treaty establishing a Constitution for Europe.

protection afforded to individuals by the current rules on locus standi in direct actions.[78]

## The Language Regime

One of the most difficult and controversial issues facing the Community Courts in the context of EU enlargement is the question of the Courts' language regime. Post-enlargement, all 20 official languages of the EU are employed at the Community Courts.[79] Much of the delay involved in processing cases results directly from the need to translate documents between these languages. The addition of 10 new official languages poses enormous organisational problems for the Court. As a result, it is often argued that a limit should be placed on the number of languages in use at the Courts. However, parties who are not able to use their native language in proceedings before the Courts would certainly be placed at a disadvantage and the legitimacy of proceedings before the Community Courts could therefore be called into question. In any event, it seems that a resolution of the language issue will not be found in the near future and a great deal of building work is currently taking place at the Kirchberg Plateau in Luxembourg in order to provide new office-space for all the translators and inter-preters from the candidate countries who have started taking up employment there over the past two years. Any change to the current language regime will require the unanimous approval of the Council[80] and politically it will be very difficult to achieve a consensus on limiting the number of languages in use at the Courts. Under the Treaty of Lisbon, it would be possible to change the language regime by a qualified majority vote (*art.342 TFEU* and *art.64 of the Protocol on the Statute of the Court of Justice of the European Union*).

## Procedural Reforms

A number of procedural reforms were discussed before the Treaty of Nice (Arnull, 1999: 522; Rasmussen, 2000, 1085) and have been

---

[78] A discussion brought to the fore by the Opinion of A.G. Jacobs in Case C-50/00 P *Union de Pequeños Agricultores* [2002] E.C.R. I-6677 and the judgment of the Court of First Instance in Case T-177/01 *Jego-Quere et Cie SA v Commission* [2002] E.C.R. II-2365.

[79] A 21st language, Irish, may also be used in proceedings before the Courts, although in practice it has never been used. From January 1, 2007, Irish was granted the status of a full official language of the EU.

[80] Art.64 of the Statute of the Court of Justice.

adopted subsequently with a view to making the work of the Community Courts more efficient. While the Court of Justice has, for some years, been able to settle preliminary ruling cases by means of a Reasoned Order under art.104(3) of its Rules of Procedure, the new art.104a EC now allows for the employment of an "expedited procedure" in appropriate cases. Also, it is now possible after Treaty of Nice for the Court to proceed to judgment without an Advocate General's opinion where a case raises no new point of law. As regards hearings, the Practice Directions issued by the Court of Justice in October 2004[81] emphasised that a party requesting a hearing must set out good reasons why it is necessary. Moreover, it was recently decided that Advocates General should, when issuing opinions in their own language, simultaneously issue their Opinion in one of five 'pivot' languages, namely French, English, German, Spanish or Italian, if their own language is not one of these languages. In view of the translation resources currently available to the Court, these are the five languages from which the text may be translated directly into all other languages. It also seems that in future only the text of preliminary questions, and not the whole file submitted to the Court, will be translated for circulation among the Member State governments. The Court is also introducing a system of selective publication, whereby the less important judgments will not be published in the European Court Reports, though they will still be available in the language of the case and in French on the Court's website. Moreover, it is hoped that a more efficient internal 'timetabling' of cases will speed up the efficiency of the Court's work (Jacobs: 2004).

## The Future Role of National Courts

An issue which has been widely debated among academic commentators over the past decade (Rasmusssen, 2000:1080), but which was completely ignored by the drafters of the Treaty of Nice, the Constitutional Treaty and Treaty of Lisbon is the issue of the relationship between the Community Courts and national courts. In order to relieve the workload crisis, it has often been suggested that greater powers of interpretation of Community law should be delegated to national courts. In particular, several quite radical suggestions for reform of the preliminary reference procedure have been debated over the years. Ideas put forward included restricting

---

[81] Available on the website of the Court of Justice.

the rights of national courts to send references to Luxembourg and allowing the Court of Justice to select only those questions which it finds most interesting while rejecting the others. From a structural point of view, the idea of setting up regional European Courts of Appeal has been contemplated. Another suggestion would have involved appointing a roving Community law judge to assist national supreme courts when dealing with matters of Community law. In the end, the drafters of the Treaty of Nice, conscious of the imminent enlargement of the Union, concluded that there is still a need for a strong central judicial authority to ensure the uniform and coherent development of Community law. This view was maintained in the process of elaborating both the Constitutional Treaty and the Treaty of Lisbon. In the future, however, as the principles and doctrines of Community law become more settled and widely understood the possibility of delegating greater interpretative powers to national judges is likely to arise again, possibly through developments in the case-law of the Court of Justice.

## Conclusion

As the judicial branch of a greatly enlarged EU of 27 Member States, the Courts at Luxembourg face unprecedented challenges in the years ahead. The reforms introduced by the Treaty of Nice were intended to prepare the Community Courts to deal with these challenges but the approach adopted at Nice was conservative (Arnull, 2006). The Treaty introduced enabling clauses which facilitate a gradual evolution of the courts system in the future, rather than bringing about any immediate or radical structural reform. These reforms are now in the process of being implemented, with the establishment of the EU Civil Service Tribunal constituting the most tangible result yet.

Implementation of the Treaty of Nice amendments has led to the emergence of a new three-tier Community courts structure which the Lisbon Treaty will maintain. The status of the Court of First Instance has been greatly enhanced by Nice and this court can be considered the 'workhorse' at the centre of the Community's judicial architecture. At a level above the Court of First Instance, a smaller Court of Justice will be left free to concentrate on fundamental constitutional issues and appeals raising questions of the unity and coherence of Community law. At a level below the Court of First Instance, new judicial panels will be given jurisdiction at first instance in certain highly specialised areas of Community law. The Nice reforms therefore maintain the tradition begun by the Single

European Act 1986 of providing for the establishment of new judicial bodies attached to existing institutions, while expanding the competences of established tribunals which have demonstrated an ability to handle specific competences of lesser importance.

The gradualist approach to reform adopted at Nice has the great merit of maintaining a continuity of development that is critical to the coherence and legitimacy of the Community's unique judicial system. It is this judicial system which has since the early days guaranteed integration through ensuring the principle of supremacy and protecting individual rights contained within the Treaty. The next chapter will examine how, and with what effect, the Court has upheld the rule of law in the EU.

# 3: The Rule of Law in the European Union

## 3.1 Introduction

The EU is based upon laws which it has the power to create and implement. Integration, based upon clear legal principles, would be impossible if it were not for the binding and uniform nature of EU law within all Member States. The Court of Justice has been charged with this task by art.220 EC and in Chapter 2 we considered the various Treaty provisions at its disposal. In this Chapter we shall consider *how* the Court has guaranteed Community rights, and promoted integration. The major beneficiary of the Court's strategy has been the individual who has used European law to challenge discriminatory or restrictive national law which has prevented the exercise of Treaty rights. The Court has, where necessary, declared invalid national rules which infringe Community law rights. Furthermore, Laenarts considers the ability of individuals to challenge both directly and indirectly Community acts as central to provision of coherent and effective judicial protection and is fundamental to the protection of the rule of law (Laenarts, 2007: 1632).

In the recent Opinion of A.G. Maduro in *Kadi*[1] (discussed in Chapter 10), the Advocate General was of the Opinion that even in the context of the EU's international law obligations these can only take effect in EU law under the conditions prescribed by the constitutional principles of the EU. Foremost of these principles is the principle that the Community is based on respect for fundamental rights and the rule of law.

In the protection of individual rights the Court has "constitutionalised" the Treaty and considered Treaty rights, such as those of free movement or citizenship as fundamental rights. The principles of direct effect, indirect effect and State liability (discussed below) have been developed by the Court as techniques through which Treaty rights are guaranteed, but in doing this the Court has been accused of judicial activism and has, at various times, clashed with national courts as to which institution is the final arbiter on the validity of Community law.

National courts have, since the early days, been concerned with the reach of Community law and in particular with the principle of supremacy which the Court established as early as the 1960s in *Van gend en Loos*[2] and *Costa v ENEL*.[3] In particular, national courts have been concerned in circumstances where EU law would appear to undermine or challenge domestic constitutional guarantees, such as the protection of fundamental rights. National courts, whose task it is to protect constitutional freedoms, have questioned how far those freedoms can be challenged by European law. Consequently a significant body of case law has developed in which the Court has sought to reconcile Community law and national law and allay fears that European law may undermine constitutionally guaranteed freedoms. Before considering how these disputes have been resolved it is necessary to examine the principle of supremacy and why it is central to EU integration.

## 3.2 The Principle of Supremacy

There is no provision in either the EC or EU Treaty stating that Community law is supreme. The principle of supremacy is a judicial

---

[1] C-402/05 *Yassin Abdullah Kadi v Council of the European Union and Commission of the European Communities*, Opinion of A.G. Maduro January 16, 2008.
[2] Case 26/62 *Van Gend en Loos* [1963] E.C.R. 1.
[3] Case 6/64 *Costa v ENEL* [1964] E.C.R. 585.

development and the commitment of the Court to upholding this is the single most identifiable reason why, despite the absence of a written Constitution, Community law has secured sophisticated and deep integration between the Member States.

The Constitutional Treaty included a provision which acknowledged the primacy of EU law. Article I-6 of this Treaty stated that "The Constitution and law adopted by the institutions of the Union in exercising competences conferred on it shall have primacy over the law of the Member States". For some Member States, notably the UK, this provision was unacceptable, despite accurately reflecting the legal status of EU law. Removing this reference to the primacy of EU law was one of the compromises which smoothed the way for final agreement of the Treaty of Lisbon 2007. The Treaty of Lisbon replaces art.I-6 of the Constitutional Treaty with a declaration[4] "recalling the existing case law of the European Court of Justice". The primacy declaration was clarified further in the final draft mandate and now reads:

"The Conference recalls that, in accordance with well settled case-law of the EU Court of Justice, the Treaties and the law adopted by the Union on the basis of the Treaties have primacy over the law of Member States, under the conditions laid down by the said case-law."

To reinforce this principle, the opinion of the Council Legal Service on the "Primacy of EC Law" will be annexed to the Final Act of the Conference. This states:

"It results from the case-law of the Court of Justice that primacy of EC law is a cornerstone principle of Community law. According to the Court, this principle is inherent to the specific nature of the European Community. At the time of the first judgement of this established case-law (Costa/ENEL, 15 July 1964, Case 6/64) there was no mention of primacy in the treaty. It is still the case today. The fact that the principle of primacy will not be included in the future treaty shall not in any way change the existence of the principle and the existing case-law of the Court of Justice.[5]"

---

[4] Declaration 17 concerning the primacy of EU law.
[5] Doc 11197/07 June 22, 2007 at *http://register.consilium.europa.eu/pdf/en/07/st11/st11197.en07.pdf* [Accessed April 10, 2008].

The principle of supremacy can be explained in the following terms. In situations of conflict between EU law and national law, EU law must prevail. The simplicity of defining the concept hides a rather more complex relationship that exists in the interaction between national law and procedure and the ECJ. Supremacy is now largely taken for granted, though some challenges still occur. In the *Metric Martyrs Case*[6] the applicant challenged a directive requiring produce that was not pre-packed to be sold in metric and not imperial measurements. The High Court dismissed the applicant's defence, which was based on the argument that as the Weights and Measures Act 1985 entered in to force after UK accession, this later statute impliedly repealed the European Communities Act (ECA) 1972. In such circumstances the defendant argued that UK law takes precedence over EU law. The English court dismissed these arguments and held that the ECA 1972, the primary legislation which provides for UK accession to the EU, has a "constitutional quality" which prevents implied repeal and thereby suggesting a degree of entrenchment.

The ECJ has established a clear body of case law which provides guidance to national courts, regarding their obligations to protect individual rights under Community law. The origins of the Court's commitment to the supremacy principle can be traced to the decision of *Van Gend en Loos* in which the Court stated that the EEC Treaty had "created a new legal order" which, in international law terms, was different both in substance and effect to other treaties, for example the ECHR. The Court stated that the EEC Treaty was intended to:

". . . confer rights upon individuals which became part of their legal heritage."

Though not stated expressly by the Court, this declaration would only make sense if EU law were supreme. The Court expanded this logic in *Costa v ENEL*. This case is important because it demonstrates how persons who are often referred to as "opportunistic litigants" have utilised Community law rights. This group can be defined as individuals who enforce Community rights before the ECJ to an extent which may not have been anticipated by the Treaty makers.

---

[6] See for example *Thorburn v Sunderland County Council* (*The Metric Martyrs Case*) [2002] 3 W.L.R. 247.

In *Costa v ENEL*, Costa was an Italian lawyer and small share-holder in Edison Volta (an Italian electricity company) sought to challenge a 1962 law which nationalised the electricity production and distribution industries. He refused to pay a bill of less than €2 and was brought before the lowest court in Italy which referred the case to the ECJ for a preliminary ruling under art.234 EC. The Italian government was adamant that no reference was necessary in such circumstances and that the obligation of the Italian court was to apply national law. The ECJ rejected this view and stated that *any* national court is entitled to seek an interpretation on the application of Community law from the ECJ:

"The integration into the laws of each Member State of provisions which derive from the Community, and more gener-ally the terms and spirit of the Treaty, make it impossible for the States, as a corollary, to accord precedence to a unilateral and subsequent measure over a legal system accepted by them on a basis of reciprocity. Such a measure cannot therefore be incon-sistent with that legal system. The executive force of Community law cannot vary from one State to another in deference to subsequent domestic laws, without jeopardising the attainment of the objectives of the Treaty. . ."

The statement has its roots firmly in the obligation arising out of art.10 EC (discussed below). By the reference to the "terms and spirit of the Treaty" the Court goes beyond merely stating that Community law takes precedence over national law. The intention of the Court is, through the use of teleological interpretation, to demonstrate that art.10 EC provides scope for a dynamic interpreta-tion of the Treaty. European law is to be considered as a new legal order which has a broader objective of integration. The Court places itself at the centre of this integration process and confirms that it will strike down measures which undermine the principle of supremacy.

Accepting the supremacy principle has proved problematic for all Member States. The cases of *Solange I* and *Simmenthal* demonstrate the conflict that national supreme courts have encountered when reconciling obligations of protecting fundamental rights under Community law and guaranteeing domestic constitutional provi-sions. In the UK the *Factortame* litigation demonstrates how the constitutional principle of parliamentary sovereignty has not always sat comfortably with supremacy (Gravells 1990:180; Craig, 1991:222). In this case the UK incorrectly transposed legislation under the

Common Fisheries Policy and required that boats fishing in UK territorial waters were 75 per cent British owned. These requirements prima facie infringed arts 12 and 43 EC. The applicants' sought an interlocutory injunction against the Crown to suspend the Merchant Shipping Act 1988 which implemented these requirements. This temporary injunction was to operate until such time as the question of whether the Act was compatible with Community law had been resolved. At first instance the English High Court rejected the applicants' claim and stated that interlocutory injunctions were not permitted against the Crown by virtue of s.21 of the Crown Proceedings Act 1947.

On appeal, the House of Lords sought a preliminary ruling from the ECJ asking whether it could dis-apply a domestic statute, namely the Crown Proceedings Act, and award an interim injunction. The Court responded:[7]

"It must be added that the full effectiveness of Community law would be just as much impaired if a rule of national law could prevent a court seised of a dispute governed by Community law from granting interim relief in order to ensure the full effectiveness of the judgment to be given on the existence of the rights claimed under Community law. It follows that a court which in those circumstances would grant interim relief. if it were not for a rule of national law, is obliged to set aside that rule."

Lord Bridge in the House of Lords stated in his judgment:

"Parliament has always loyally accepted the obligation to make appropriate and prompt amendments. Thus there is nothing in any way novel in according supremacy to rules of Community law in those areas to which they apply and to insist that. In the protection of rights under Community law, national courts must not be inhibited by rules of national law from granting interim relief in appropriate cases is no more than a logical recognition of that supremacy."

In circumstances where national law inhibited the individual from enjoying the rights granted under Community law, then it is the obligation of the national court to set that law aside. In this case the duty

---

[7] Para.21.

required the House of Lords to dis-apply the relevant provision of the Crown Proceedings Act. Though this challenges the principle of parliamentary sovereignty their Lordships viewed this course of action as being a necessity arising out of UK membership of the Community and based upon the provisions of s.2 (2) and (4) ECA 1972. The ECA while not using the word 'supremacy' states at s.2 (4) that:

"The provision that may be made under subsection (2) above includes, subject to Schedule 2 to this Act, any such provision (of any such extent) as might be made by Act of Parliament, and any enactment passed or to be passed, other than one contained in this Part of this Act, shall be construed and have effect subject to the foregoing provisions of this section; but, except as may be provided by any Act passed after this Act, Schedule 2 shall have effect in connection with the powers conferred by this and the following sections of this Act to make Orders in Council and regulations."

The House of Lords in *Factortame* interpreted this section purposively:

"The words 'is to be construed and take effect subject to directly enforceable Community rights' are to be understood *as having the same effect as if a section were incorporated in to the Merchant Shipping Act 1988 which enacted that the provisions with regard to the registration of British Fishing Vessels* (emphasis added) were to be 'without prejudice to the directly enforceable Community rights of nationals of any member state of the EC.'"

The effect of their Lordships' judgment is to impliedly include in to the Merchant Shipping Act 1988, and *all* UK legislation, a proviso that national law does not restrict the fundamental individual rights which are granted by Community law. The statement of the High Court in the *Metric Martyrs* case, that the ECA 1972 has a "constitutional quality" has the effect of entrenching the ECA in to UK law and consequently provides an enduring guarantee of supremacy of EU law within the UK (Wade, 1996).

## 3.3 The Protection of Fundamental Rights in EU Law

*Defining fundamental rights*

The Court has consistently acknowledged the role of the individual in European integration and that protection of individual rights can be identified as one factor contributing to economic integration. Judgments, such as *Konstantinidis* and *Johnson* have referred to Community law as providing individuals with fundamental rights and through the use of this rights based language the judgments have endowed the Treaties with a constitutional quality. The Treaties contain principles which are conventionally considered as fundamental rights, such as non-discrimination under art.12 EC. Other rights, for example equal pay under art.141 EC and the economic rights of the Internal Market, are not traditionally within fundamental rights discourse and provide a broader interpretation of rights within Community law by comparison to that of the ECHR.

The description of Community law rights as fundamental rights by the ECJ has elevated Community law rights to a status normally reserved for a domestic Bill of Rights. This has occasionally led to conflict with national constitutional courts that have not perceived Community law rights as having the same constitutional status, or offering an equivalent level of protection by comparison to human rights provisions within domestic constitutions.[8] In *Internationale Handelsgesellschaft* and *Simmenthal* the German and Italian Supreme Courts respectively were concerned that the fundamental rights protection which the constitutions guaranteed could be undermined by Community law. The two Supreme Courts contended that in such circumstances the principle of supremacy should not apply. The ECJ rejected these concerns and held that *every* national court without exception is under an obligation to apply Community law. Furthermore, any national court which sought to reserve for itself this right to resolve such conflicts was itself acting in a manner that incompatible with Community law. The Court of Justice stated in *Internationale Handelsgesellschaft*:

"the validity of a Community measure or its effect within a Member State cannot be affected by allegations that it runs counter to either fundamental rights as formulated by the

---

[8] See for example Case 11/70 *Internationale Handelsgesellschaft* [1970] E.C.R. 1125 and Case 92/78 *Simmenthal SpA v Ministero dello Finance* [1979] E.C.R. 777.

constitution of the State or the principles of a national constitutional structure."[9]

Similarly in *Simmenthal* the Court held:

"Every national court must, in a case within its jurisdiction, apply Community law in its entirety and protect rights which the latter confers on individuals and must accordingly set aside any provision of national law which may conflict with it, whether prior or subsequent to the Community rule."[10]

The judgment of the Court in *Internationale Handelsgeselschaft* is noteworthy because it defines judicial attitudes towards fundamental rights in Community law. The case is more commonly referred to as *Solange I*, which translates as "so long as" from German to English. This is because in its judgment the *Budesverfassungsgericht*, the German Federal Constitutional Court (FCC), stated it would only accept European integration 'so long as' it was based upon a respect for fundamental rights. The concerns of the FCC were based upon the principle that fundamental rights are entrenched in the German Constitution. Furthermore, the protection afforded to such rights in the Community legal order contained several regulatory gaps. Firstly, Community law included no definitive list of fundamental rights. Secondly, the EEC was not a signatory to the ECHR, and in *Opinion 2/94*[11] A.G. Jacobs confirmed that despite several Treaty developments, the EU still lacked the institutional capacity to sign the ECHR. Thirdly, the FCC was concerned that Community law might be adopted which is in breach of fundamental rights and that there is no remedy within Community law by which to challenge this. Finally, Community law in violation of fundamental rights cannot be challenged within the domestic legal systems because of its supremacy.

The ECJ addressed the concerns of the FCC by adopting a rights based language in its judgment, a practice which has become an increasingly common feature of ECJ judgments. The Court stated:

"Respect for fundamental rights forms an integral part of the general principles of Community law protected by the Court of

[9] *Internationale Handelsgeselschaft* at para.1134.
[10] *Simmenthal* at para.21.
[11] Opinion 2/94 *Accession by the Community to the European Convention for the Protection of Human Rights and Fundamental Freedoms* [1996] E.C.R. I-1759.

Justice. The protection of such rights, whilst *inspired by the constitutional traditions common to the Member States* (emphasis added), must be ensured within the framework of the structure and objectives of the Community."

The Court applied the ECHR as a benchmark for fundamental rights, which *all* Member States had subscribed to, and which provides a uniform minimum standard of fundamental rights protection across the Community. The Court of Justice stressed that European integration has its roots in the constitutional traditions of the Member States. This suggests that protection of fundamental rights in the domestic legal order constitutes not only a source of inspiration for the Court but also provides a binding standard (Lenaerts, 2003:877). Lenaerts argues that to form its judgments, the ECJ has regularly adopted teleological techniques, arising from comparative law, to draw upon the legal traditions of the Member States for guidance in the absence of an EU fundamental rights jurisprudence. The reference to legal traditions of the Member States is a mechanism through which the Court seeks to reassure and secure acceptance of its judgments by the Member States. The judgment of the Court in *Solange I* is an early example of this. For Lenaerts such comparative analyses and teleological reasoning in the application of Community law has been a key ingredient to the process of integration. Rather than being classified as judicial activism it is more appropriate to consider this as effective enforcement of Community law rights. (Lenaerts, 2003:879).

This approach demonstrates a monist interpretation by the Court of the relationship between EC law and international law. In *Mangold v Helm*,[12] (discussed in more detail below) the Court at para.74 refers to the general principle of non-discrimination being found in, inter alia international instruments cited in the preamble to dir.2000/78 for the establishment of a general framework for equal treatment in employment and occupation. The reliance upon and reference to international conventions and other instruments is one method through which to ensure that Community law norms are upheld and that rights are available to all citizens (Laenarts:2006). References to such international instruments may be considered as having an integrative effect and helps to guarantee the right.

Although the ECHR remains outside the Community legal order, it continues to be utilised as a point of reference for the ECJ. In *Nold*,

---

[12] Case C-144/04 *Mangold v Helm* [2005] E.C.R. I-9981.

the Court stated[13] that an additional source of inspiration for fundamental rights protection in Community law are:

"international treaties for the protection of human rights on which Member States have collaborated or of which they are signatories."

The reference to external human rights documents and comparative law techniques in *Solange I* and *Nold* is not necessarily an example of judicial activism per se. The judgments can be considered as the development of a human rights jurisprudence, in which a maturing judicial body draws upon established legal principles to ensure not only that human rights are protected, but that the scope of fundamental rights is extended.

The FCC in *Solange I* accepted the assurances of the ECJ and the obligations which supremacy demand but reserved the right to monitor how Community law was applied by the ECJ. In *Solange II*[14] the FCC referred to various developments in the Community since the judgment of *Solange I*, and particularly the Single European Act 1986 and case law concerning the protection of fundamental rights. It concluded that the protection of fundamental rights in the Community had reached a degree essentially comparable to the standard set by the German Constitution. On this basis the FCC stated that it would no longer exercise its jurisdiction to review secondary EC legislation by the standards of fundamental rights guaranteed by the German Constitution. It did, however, caution against a transfer of sovereign rights which may impinge upon the basic constitutional structure of Germany which encompassed the 'federal order' created by the Constitution.

The judgment of the FCC in *Brunner v Maastricht Treaty*[15] signalled a shift in focus with fundamental rights no longer being the primary cause of concern. In this judgment the FCC cautioned against the doctrine of supremacy being used as a justification for the development of the EU in an undemocratic manner. In particular, the FCC was concerned that further integration may alter the separation of powers and federal and institutional structure of Germany. The FCC concluded that the transfer of powers to the EU, and particularly those concerning Economic and Monetary Union, fell within the democratic principle guaranteed by art.38 of the

---

[13] Para.14.
[14] Case 345/82 *Wünsche Handelsgeselschaft v Germany* [1984] E.C.R. 1995.
[15] 89 BVerfGE 155 *Brunner v Maastricht Treaty* 155 [1994] 1 C.M.L.R. 57.

German Constitution. This provision precludes the transfer of powers to the EU if it leaves the *Bundestag* devoid of sovereign powers and is the decisive factor in the FCC's judgment.

The FCC adopted a cautious stance towards deeper integration and transfer of competence to the Community. It stated that if Germany were to participate in deeper integration then this must have parliamentary approval. Furthermore, any such extension must not offend the principle of subsidiarity in art.5 EC, which it considered to be a fundamental principle of EU law. The FCC rejected a dynamic interpretation of integration by stating that it will not accept extensions to the Treaty which occur through judgments of the ECJ. In particular the FCC stressed the need for democracy in EU decision-making and adherence to the principle of subsidiarity.

This line of cases in which the FCC engaged in a judicial dialogue with the ECJ over questions of supremacy and integration are noteworthy for several reasons. Firstly, they reinforce the position that the Community operates within a principle of the rule of law and should act where it has express competence. Secondly, Community action does not occur in isolation. It must be acceptable to the Member States and not offend long established principles of fundamental rights protection and democracy. Thirdly, the judicial dialogue in these cases demonstrates a mature legal order where the ECJ fulfils its role to guarantee the supremacy of Community law in partnership with the national courts.

## The Charter of Fundamental Rights

The Maastricht Treaty 1991 recognised the importance of the ECHR to EU integration. Article 6 (2) TEU provides that the EU will protect fundamental rights as contained within the ECHR and views them as being part of the general principles of EU law. Article 6 (2) TEU reflects the view which the Court of Justice first stated in the *Internationale Handelsgesellschaft* judgment. The characteristic of art.6 TEU is that the rights contained within are not dependent upon the pursuit neither of an economic activity nor on the existence of a professional or contractual relationship. The significance of art.6 TEU is that human rights standards of the Member States, based in large part upon the ECHR, are recognised as underpinning the process of EU integration and the Charter of Fundamental Rights is intended to reinforce this.

The Charter currently lacks a formal legal status having only been proclaimed at the Nice Council in 2000. Since then its value and application have been in some doubt. Until recently the ECJ was reluctant to make reference to the Charter in its judgments. The Constitutional Treaty would have incorporated the Charter, but under the Treaty of Lisbon the Charter will have "legally binding value" but it will not be reproduced in the Treaties (*art.6 (1) TEU*). *Article 6 (1) TEU* states:

> The Union recognises the rights, freedoms and principles set out in the Charter of Fundamental Rights of the European Union of 7 December 2000, as adapted at Strasbourg, on 12 December 2007, which shall have the same legal value as the Treaties.
>
> The provisions of the Charter shall not extend in any way the competences of the Union as defined in the Treaties.

The Charter will be re-enacted by the three main EU Institutions as part of their rules of procedure. *Protocol 7 of the Treaty of Lisbon* specifies the scope of application of the Charter and its relationship with the European Convention on Human Rights. A separate Protocol contains a declaration that neither in the UK nor in Poland may a national court or the Court of Justice declare domestic law as incompatible with the Charter. The effect of this exemption is questionable as it would appear to undermine fundamental principle of supremacy of EU law. Despite this Protocol the Charter could still have an indirect impact on UK and Polish law, particularly in cases where the Court ruled on Charter-related issues in other EU Member States. The exemption may also present problems for Germany, if it breaches a principle of reciprocity seen in *Internationale Handelsgeselschaft* and *Brunner v Maastricht Treaty* and under which the German Constitutional Court has in the past been prepared to accept the constitutionality of EU Treaties.

The Commission has provided no clear guidance on how the UK and Polish exemptions will operate. In its Opinion on the Draft Mandate for the 2007 Inter-Governmental Conference the Commission did not shed any light on its view of the legally binding nature of the Charter when combined with the obligation to apply EU law uniformly in all Member States. The Commission stated that:

> The Charter of Fundamental Rights will offer Europeans guarantees with the same legal status as the treaties themselves, bringing together civil, political, economic and social rights which the Union's action must respect. Its provisions will also

apply in full to acts of implementation of Union law, even if not in all Member States.[16]

The provisions of the Charter are designed to guarantee that citizens' basic rights and liberties are fully transparent at EU level, without disturbing the primary responsibilities of the Member States to protect human rights. The Charter does not replace domestic human rights provisions, including the ECHR. In this context, the Charter creates no new powers for the EU, nor does it alter any of the EU's existing powers. Furthermore, it will apply to Member States only when they are implementing EU law.

The interesting question is how the Court will react to the legally binding value of the Charter. The Court has refrained from making reference to the Charter as a means of protecting individual rights granted by the Treaty. In *BECTU*[17] while the Advocate General was prepared to make reference to the Charter the Court instead chose to rely solely on the content of the directive which was intended to confer specific rights on citizens. The case concerned the right to paid holiday leave (conferred by the Working Time Directive) by individuals who work on a series of short-term contracts. Under the UK regulations implementing the directive, the paid leave entitlement only accrued following 13 weeks employment by the same employer. BECTU, a trade union whose members were adversely affected by this precondition, argued that this was in breach of the terms of the directive.

Advocate General Tizzano stated that it was necessary to place the directive in the "wider context of fundamental social rights". In this regard, he examined a variety of international sources dealing with the right to a period of paid leave, before stating

"even more significant, it seems to me, is the fact that right is now solemnly upheld in the Charter of Fundamental Rights . . . in proceedings concerned with the nature and scope of a fundamental right the relevant statements of the Charter cannot be ignored".

While the Court acknowledged the importance of the right it did so without reference to the Charter. The Court did refer to an earlier

---

[16] COM (2007) 412.

[17] Case C-173/99 *Broadcasting, Entertainment, Cinematographic and Theatre Union (BECTU) v Secretary of State for Trade and Industry* [2001] E.C.R. I-4881.

document agreed by the Member States called the 1989 Social Charter in which rights to paid holiday were acknowledged.

Perhaps because of the non-binding nature of an Opinion, the Advocate General has referred to the Charter on several occasions. In Chapter 2 the views of A.G. Jacobs in relation to the Charter and its contribution to providing an effective remedy for citizens in the context of the application of art.230 EC was discussed. The Advocate General was firmly of the view that the Court should be mindful of art.47 of the Charter in cases of judicial review to ensure that individuals can challenge measures which affect their legal position. The CFI in the *Max Mobil*[18] judgment made reference to the Charter. In this case a mobile telephone company in Austria complained to the Commission about unfair regulation by Austria of access to mobile phone market. The Commission failed to act on some parts of its complaint and Max Mobil sought review of this decision not to act.

Finding in favour of Max Mobil, the CFI stated that art.41 of the Charter creates a duty of good administration which in this case required the Commission to make a diligent and impartial assessment of complaints. Furthermore, art.47 provides individuals with the right to an effective remedy and this implies a right for the applicants to seek judicial review of the Commission's actions. The Court of Justice has been reluctant to refer to the Charter primarily because of a floodgates argument in which it did want to see opportunistic litigants challenging EU law. That said the Court did refer to the Charter in the *Family Reunion Directive*[19] case in circumstances where the directive, in the Preamble, made specific reference to art.7 of the Charter which is intended to protect the right to family life. The Court stated:

". . . while the Charter is not a legally binding instrument, the Community legislature did acknowledge its importance by stating, in the second recital in the preamble to the Directive, that the Directive observes the principles recognised not only by Article 8 of the ECHR but also in the Charter."[20]

The discussion in relation to the Charter raises an important question of the relationship between the Charter and the ECHR. As

---

[18] Case T-54/99 *max.mobil* [2002] E.C.R. II-313.
[19] Case C-540/03 *Parliament v Council (Family Reunion Directive)* [2006] E.C.R. I-5769.
[20] Case C-540/03 *Parliament v Council (Family Reunion Directive)* [2006] E.C.R. I-5769 para.38. See also Case C-428/05 *Viking* judgment of December 18, 2007.

already stated A.G. Jacobs noted in *Opinion 2/94* that the EU lacked the legal and institutional capacity to become a signatory to the ECHR. The Constitutional Treaty provided for the EU to sign the ECHR in addition to, and not in place of, the Member States and the Treaty of Lisbon maintains this commitment (*art.6 (2) TEU*). Despite the EU not being a signatory to the ECHR this has not prevented the Court having to consider and protect the standards of human rights protection within the ECHR.

In the *Bosphorous Airways*[21] dispute the Court was faced with a dispute which raised questions both of the EU's Common Commercial Policy and the protection of human rights. The case is rare as it involved separate proceedings before the ECJ and the European Court of Human Rights.

Yugoslavian airways leased two airplanes to Bosphorous, a Turkish airline which sent one of the planes to Dublin for repairs. This occurred during the Balkan war and there were specific UN sanctions in place against the former Yugoslavia and therefore the plane was impounded in Dublin. The EU had implemented the sanctions through reg.990/93/EC.

Bosphorous Airlines sought a judicial review of the impoundment. The Court held that while there was an interference with the right to the peaceful enjoyment of possessions this was justified by the general interest in bringing an end to the war in Bosnia. Following the Court of Justice decision to uphold the Irish actions as compatible with the international obligations, Bosphorous Airways commenced an action before the European Court of Human Rights[22] in which it challenged the compatibility of the Court of Justice decision with art.1 of Protocol 1 of the ECHR concerning reviewable acts. In practice the substance of the dispute was a challenge to the compatibility of reg.990/93 with the ECHR, with the potential outcome that the European Court of Human Rights could be in conflict with the Court of Justice.

In respect of art.1 of Protocol No.1, the European Court of Human Rights stated that once adopted, reg.990/93 was "generally applicable" and "binding in its entirety" under art.249 EC. The Court of Human Rights further explained that reg.990/93 applied to all EU Member States, none of which could lawfully depart from any of its provisions. In addition, the direct applicability could not

---

[21] Case C-84/95 *Bosphorus Hava Yollari Turizm ve Ticaret AS v Minister for Transport, Energy and Communications* [1996] E.C.R. I-3953.
[22] *Bosphorus Hava Yollari Turizm v Ireland*, App. No. 45036/98 (Eur. Ct. H. R. June 30, 2005).

be, disputed as reg.990/93 had become part of Irish domestic law. The Court considered it entirely foreseeable that the Irish Minister for Transport would implement the impoundment powers contained in art.8 EC of reg.990/93 in such circumstances as arose in this case.

The Court of Human Rights justified the decision on the basis that Ireland had no choice but to take the steps necessary to comply with EC law. Furthermore, because EC law has an "equivalent protection" of human rights to that provided under the ECHR, the Court of Human Rights presumed that measures required by EC law comply with the ECHR. While the Court of Human Rights avoided a direct conflict with the Court of Justice it is debateable whether the protection of human rights is the same in both Courts. The other issue that is raised by the *Bosphorous* case is whether EU accession to the ECHR would improve the protection of fundamental rights?

Though accession by the EU to the ECHR may have political and symbolic reasons it is questionable whether there will be any improvement in the protection of fundamental rights such as those at issue in the *Bosphorous* case. The effects will be limited primarily because the ECHR is already accepted as the fundamental standard of human rights protection in all 27 Member States and this is also recognised within art.6 TEU. *Bosphorous Airways* is interesting because it is recognition by a judicial body, external to the EU, that the Court of Justice takes the protection of fundamental rights seriously. The substance of the dispute in *Bosphorous* was the absence of a judicial remedy before the Court of Justice. Should the Member States ratify the Treaty of Lisbon then the EU will eventually accede to the ECHR. Individuals may find increased scope, particularly in the light of the legally enforceable right contained in art.47 of the Charter to an effective remedy, to seek judicial review before the Court.

## *The scope of fundamental rights protection in Community law*

For Community law rights to be accessible to individuals they require an elevated status over domestic law which the judgments of the Court have guaranteed by the principle of supremacy. Community law has contributed to the bundle of fundamental rights which individuals enjoy through a process of judicial interpretation. One such example is the Court's judgment in the case of *Defrenne (No.2)*.[23]

---

[23] Case 43/75 *Defrenne v Sabena (No.2)* [1976] E.C.R. 455.

This case concerned the question of whether art.141 EC, which provides that "men and women should receive equal pay for equal work", had direct effect. Ms Defrenne was an air stewardess who during her period of employment had been paid less than her male counterparts. The Belgian government had failed to ensure the application of art.141 EC and Ms Defrenne claimed that as a result she had suffered direct and indirect discrimination. The ECJ concluded that while art.141 EC did not immediately appear to satisfy the criteria of direct effect, on a teleological interpretation, the objective was clear. The aim of art.141 EC was to prevent discrimination between men and women in employment. The ECJ's reasoning stressed a distinction between direct and indirect discrimination and concluded that only the former was caught by art.141 EC.

In addition to responding to the formal question of whether art.141 EC has direct effect the Court of Justice, used the judgment to provide much needed momentum to European integration. Specifically the Court highlighted that the EEC Treaty was not restricted to merely economic considerations. The Court held that:

"Article 141 EC also forms part of the social objectives of the Community, which is not merely a economic union, but is at the same time intended, by common action to ensure social progress and seek the constant improvement in the living and working conditions of their peoples. This double aim, which is at the same time economic and social, shows that equal pay forms part of the foundations of the Community."

This statement is important as it recognises that European integration is not a self-serving process intended to be for the benefit of a political or economic elite. Community law has at its core the objective of increasing citizens' rights and creating a scheme of protection and enforcement of those rights.

In *Defrenne (No.3)*[24] the Court went further and stressed the importance of guaranteeing individual social rights and in doing so referred to other external documents, namely the European Social Charter (1969) and Conventions of the International Labour Organisation (ILO). This adds weight to the argument of Laenarts that when the ECJ applies teleological reasoning draws upon external legal traditions and norms when doing so. Ms Defrenne challenged the different retirement ages for men and women imposed

---

[24] Case 149/79 *Defrenne v Sabena (No.3)* [1978] E.C.R. 1365.

by her employers, as being contrary to art.141 EC. The Court stated that this was a working condition and fell beyond the scope of the direct effect of art.141 EC remaining an issue for national law. The Court did take this opportunity to reinforce and, arguably develop, the statement made in *Defrenne (No.2)*. The Court stated that:

> "[t]he respect for fundamental personal rights is one of the general principles of Community law, the observance of which it has a duty to ensure. There can be no doubt that the elimination of discrimination based on sex forms part of those fundamental human rights."

The Court's description of the principle of non-discrimination as a "fundamental right" is noteworthy for two reasons. Firstly, the broad and arguably less traditional interpretation of what constitutes a fundamental right demonstrates a difference between the objectives of fundamental rights protection through the case law of the ECJ and that of the ECHR. The reference to other international documents such as the European Social Charter has a definitive integrative effect (Szyszczak, 2000:47). Rights within the European Social Charter, such as rights to collective bargaining, are not directly part of EC law, but they do form part of a wider source of international law protection of employment rights and as such should be recognised by EC law.[25]

Secondly, fundamental rights protection in Community law has a different centre of gravity to that of the ECHR. The ECJ has attached the label of a fundamental right to economic and non-economic rights alike and this interpretation is evident in the broader coverage of the EU's Charter of Fundamental Rights. The ECJ's judgments have consistently recognised the need to ensure that Community law does not restrict the fundamental rights protection afforded to individuals through existing domestic and international provisions. By so doing the Court is susceptible to criticisms of judicial activism, but this criticism ignores the argument of Szyszczak and of Laenarts that through teleological reasoning the Court has *broadened* the range of individual rights in substance relating to procedural values and remedies.

Supremacy is not mentioned explicitly in the Treaty but is the central principle of integration. In the *Solange I* judgment the ECJ held that adherence to the principle of supremacy overrides even

---

[25] See Case 4/73 *Nold v Commission* [1974] E.C.R. 491.

domestic constitutional provisions. The next part of this chapter considers supremacy and the techniques that the ECJ has employed to guarantee supremacy in the absence of an EU constitution. The discussion begins by examining art.10 EC, often described as the principle of solidarity which acts as a binding force on the Member States in the integration process.

## 3.4 Article 10 EC: The Principle of Solidarity

Article 10 EC is the key article of the EC Treaty and the closest to which the Treaty comes to refer to the principle of supremacy. This provision requires Member States not to act contrary to the objectives of the Treaty. Article 10 EC states:

> "Member States shall take all appropriate measures, whether general or particular, to ensure fulfilment of the obligations arising out of this Treaty or resulting from action taken by the institutions of the Community. They shall facilitate the achievement of the Community's tasks.
>
> They shall abstain from any measure which could jeopardise the attainment of the objectives of this Treaty."

This provision appears to be a rudimentary requirement for Member States, who have voluntarily signed the Treaty not only to refrain from acting contrary to Community law, but also to take positive steps to ensure that Treaty obligations are fulfilled. Consequently art.10 EC is referred to as the principle of solidarity. This solidarity is required to achieve the objectives set out in arts 2, 3 and 14 EC.

Article 10 EC guarantees communitarian action and supremacy at the domestic level and compliments the Community decision-making process. According to Temple Lang (1997:6) art.10 EC requires both administrative *and* judicial institutions to work actively to secure the observance of Community law and to prevent action which is inconsistent with the attainment of the Treaty's objectives. The ECJ has recognised this is essential for the uniform application of EC law. In *Factortame (No.2)*[26] the ECJ stated that:

---

[26] Case C-221/89 *R v Secretary of State for Transport Ex p. Factortame* [1991] E.C.R. I-3905.

"In accordance with the case-law of the Court, it is for the national courts, in application of the principle of cooperation laid down in Article 10 of the EEC Treaty, to ensure the legal protection which persons derive from the direct effect of provisions of Community law." (paragraph 19)

The Court's interpretation of art.10 EC has given the provision a constitutional quality. The ECJ has recognised that art.10 EC provides scope for teleological interpretation to secure the supremacy of Community law and there are four key mechanisms which have been developed. The first three principles are direct effect, indirect effect and state liability. These are mechanisms that have arisen out of the judicial dialogue under art.234 EC and their primary purpose is to ensure the unfettered availability of EC law rights in the Member States.

A final mechanism, namely the principle of effective remedies, requires Member States to compensate individuals in circumstances when their Community law rights have been infringed. The principle of effective remedies, firmly within the ambit of art.10 EC, operates as a deterrent to discourage Member States from acting contrary to Community law. In circumstances where individual rights have been infringed, for example the failure to transpose a directive within the specified time period, national courts will award damages to the individual against the Member State responsible if a loss has been suffered.[27] The purpose of such an award is to act as a deterrent for future breaches and to compensate the individual for the infringement of their rights. In *Marshall (No.2)*,[28] the ECJ held that any remedy awarded to an individual must be effective thereby prohibiting national legislation from placing an upper ceiling on the damages which can be awarded.

## 3.5 The Direct Effect of Community Law

Direct effect concerns the content of a legislative provision and refers to its capacity to give rise to rights for individuals which can be enforced before national courts. Direct effect is an important constitutional provision and the means through which individual

[27] Joined Cases C-6 and 9/90 *Francovich v Italian State* [1991] E.C.R. I-5357.
[28] Case C-271/91 *Marshall v Southampton Health Authority No.2* [1993] E.C.R. I-4367.

rights are guaranteed in the domestic law (Pescatore, 1983:158). It is important to distinguish direct effect from direct applicability which refers to the status of a Community provision in the domestic legal order (Winter, 1972:425). Treaty Articles and Regulations are directly applicable because they do not require any transposition to be implemented in the domestic legal order. Directives do not have automatic direct applicability as Member States implement these through existing domestic procedures but do so one the transitional period has expired.[29]

Direct effect is not a universal feature of all Community provisions including Treaty Articles. Individuals can plead a rule of Community law before their national courts but this will only occur if the criteria discussed in Chapter 1 have been fulfilled. Direct effect is arguably the most important mechanism through which the supremacy of Community law is maintained and national courts are under an obligation to ensure rights contained within the legislation are available and should use art.234 EC when they have doubt. The ECJ has consistently held that both Treaty Articles and Regulations have the potential of direct effect. Through cases such as *Van Gend en Loos*, *Van Duyn* and *Defrenne v Sabena* the Court has established prerequisite criteria for a provision to have direct effect. These are:

- the provision is clear and unconditional;

- the rights contained within the measure are expressed with sufficient precision; and

- in the case of directives only, the date for implementation of the directive has passed.

Application of these principles to Treaty provisions and Regulations raises little difficulty and they will commonly have direct effect. The area of controversy where the Court has been most active is with regard to directives. One issue that has arisen is whether an individual can rely upon a directive when the time period for implementation has not elapsed. *Inter-Environnement Wallonie v Région Wallonne*[30] the case concerned a challenge by an environmental pressure group to regulations on waste disposal from the Wallonne region of Belgium. The relevant directive had not come into force yet, as the implemen-

---

[29] Case 80/86 *Kolpinghuis Nijmegen BV (Criminal Proceedings)* [1986] E.C.R. 3969.
[30] Case C-129/96 *Inter-Environnement Wallonie v Région Wallonne* [1997] E.C.R. I-7411.

tation period had not expired. The Court held that Member States are required to "refrain from taking any measures liable seriously to compromise the result prescribed" by the directive during the implementation period. In such circumstances the national court must consider whether the measures are intended to be the definitive transposition.

If implemented correctly, individuals can rely upon the rights contained in a directive before their national court. In circumstances where the directive is incorrectly implemented, or not implemented at all, then providing that the transitional period has expired, an individual can rely on the directive itself. This is despite the fact that art.249 EC addresses a directive to Member States, not individuals. In situations of incorrect implementation national courts are required, through art.10 EC to interpret national law so far as possible in a manner which ensures compatibility with the directive. This teleological technique is referred to as indirect effect and is considered below.

In circumstances of incorrect implementation it may be possible to rely on the directive itself, provided that it has fulfilled the three criteria outlined above. The one restriction is that an individual can rely upon the directive in vertical relationships only. That is where the other party is the State, or according to the ECJ in *Foster v British Gas*,[31] an "emanation" of it. The Court has held in *Marshall (No.1)*[32] that directives cannot have horizontal direct effect and enforceable by one individual against another. The Court's reasoning is based upon a principle of consistent interpretation that it is the State's obligation to transpose the directive. Consequently it is the State, and not any private party, which is responsible for the absence of those rights from domestic law.[33] This reasoning has been criticised as restricting the scope of directives (Tridimas, 1994:621; Lenz et al, 2000:512) and has spawned a line of case law generically referred to as incidental horizontal direct effect which is considered below.

In the context of directives, the requirement that the other party be the State or an emanation of it is based on the principle that directives are only binding on the State and do not create enforceable rights inter partes. Yet since the 1980s the structure and competence of the State has changed profoundly, particularly with many State functions being

---

[31] Case C-188/89 [1990] E.C.R. I-3313.

[32] Case 152/84, *Marshall v Southampton Area Health Authority (No.1)* [1986] E.C.R. 723.

[33] Opinion of A.G. Lenz in Case C-91/92 *Facini Dori* [1994] E.C.R. I-1325 and A.G. Jacobs in Case C-316/93 *Vannetveld* [1994] E.C.R. I-763.

transferred to the private sector. The modern understanding of the State is therefore one based upon wholesale privatisation of certain sectors, for example utility services. Other structural changes include the development of public/private partnership financing arrangements, quasi-autonomous regulators who ensure competition and protect consumer interests, and contracting out of services which the State traditionally provided to ensure value for money for the taxpayer. The State has reduced in size and with it the opportunity for individuals to rely upon vertical direct effect.

*Foster v British Gas* concerned the question of whether a measure could have direct effect against a recently privatised utility company. While no longer part of the State, the Court held that the company remained an emanation of the State. Broadly this suggests that the company retains the exercise of some public function and has organs which are closely linked to the State. The Court highlighted several criteria which may lead to the conclusion that the body in question is an emanation of the State. The body should be:

- subject to the authority and control of the State;
- have special powers for that purpose; and
- provide a public service.

It is not clear from the judgment whether the 'test' is cumulative or that it is sufficient to satisfy only one of the requirements. Furthermore while some organs may fit within the definition within one Member State, there may be a difference in understanding and application of the criteria in another.

Despite the divergent interpretation of the State both public sector and privatised entities would appear to fulfil the *Foster* requirements. This raises a number of questions, not least whether it is appropriate for public concerns to be regulated under the same conditions as those within the private sector. The growth of competition within the Internal Market and decline in the role of the State inevitably call in to question the interpretation of the Court in *Foster*. Can the *Foster* criteria remain relevant propositions in an EU where the emphasis has shifted towards deregulation and competition? Szyszczak (1996:352) argues that the Court in *Foster* was primarily concerned with the effectiveness of Community law and ensuring that Community law rights were available as widely as possible through the principle of direct effect. She suggests that this judgment is part of a wider objective of making Europe more relevant to its citizens by enabling them to actively pursue their Treaty rights.

In *Foster* the Court was not concerned with wider economic and philosophical questions of what the role of the modern State should be. The Court was merely expressing a view on the relationship between the State and a privatised entity a short time after its privatisation. Furthermore, this judgment was delivered at a time when privatisation had not become widespread within the Community. Its sole purpose was to maximise the availability of Community law rights to citizens. It is only in the light of developments within the Member States since *Foster* that the continued relevance of the 'test' can be called in to question. National courts have been left to interpret the Foster criteria with mixed results. Judgments such as *Doughty v Rolls Royce* in the English Court of Appeal have cast doubt on the application of the *Foster* test[34] where it was held that Rolls Royce did not provide a public service when it was a nationalised industry. Despite its vagueness the Court of Justice has not abandoned *Foster* and views it as important part of its armoury in guaranteeing the effectiveness of Community law. Recently the Court has held that an Austrian body established to manage the country's motorway network fell within the *Foster* criteria.[35] In *Rieser* the Court affirmed that when a directive is not implemented in to national law within the required time then, providing it satisfies the direct effect criteria, it can be relied upon by an individual. In *Rieser* the Austrian State was the sole shareholder in Asfinag, the motorway management company. The Court highlighting the overall control, both financial and managerial, which this gave to the Austrian State[36]:

"It is entitled to impose objectives with regard to the organisation of traffic, safety and construction. Every year Asfinag is required to draw up a plan for the maintenance of the motorways and expressways and to submit to the State the calculation of the costs involved. Furthermore, every year within the periods necessary for the drawing-up of the State's budget, it must present to the State calculations with the estimated costs of planning, constructing, maintaining and managing motorways and national expressways."

---

[34] [1992] I.C.R. 538.
[35] Case C-157/02 *Rieser Internationale Transporte GmbH v Autobahnen- und Schnellstraßen-Finanzierungs-AG (Asfinag)* [2004] E.C.R. I-1477.
[36] Case C-157/02 *Rieser Internationale Transporte GmbH v Autobahnen- und Schnellstraßen-Finanzierungs-AG (Asfinag)* [2004] E.C.R. I-1477 at para.25.

What *Rieser* and other recent judgments such as *Vassalo*[37] and *Marrosou*[38] demonstrate is that the Court is wrestling with the need to guarantee effectiveness of Community law in an enlarged EU while simultaneously not undermining a long held principle that directives do not have horizontal effect. *Foster*, and the concept of an emanation of the State, has provided the Court with some latitude to balance these two competing principles. However, there is an increasing body of case law in which questions of direct effect arise in the context of disputes between two private parties in which the (non)implementation of a directive is a relevant factor. In such cases the Court faces a more complex challenge of guaranteeing effectiveness while not imposing burdens upon third parties.

## 3.6 Incidental Horizontal Direct Effect

Despite the Court's reluctance to permit horizontal direct effect there is a body of case law which has developed where the decision appears to be a de facto application of horizontal direct effect, but the Court denies that it is doing this. These are typically triangular situations which will involve the State and two private parties. In *Unilever Italia v Central Foods*[39] the case concerned Italian law on the labelling of extra virgin olive oil. Under Italian law olive oil could not be labelled as 'produced' or 'manufactured' in Italy unless the entire cycle of harvesting, production, processing and packaging took place in Italy. Any oil not meeting these criteria would be disposed of. Italy had failed to notify these technical standards as required by dir.89/183/EEC.[40]

The Court ruled that national technical regulations adopted in breach of dir.83/189/EEC were inapplicable and, accordingly, cannot be enforceable against individuals. The outcome in *Unilever* was that

---

[37] Case C-180/04 *Andrea Vassallo v Azienda Ospedaliera Ospedale San Martino di Genova e Cliniche Universitarie Convenzionate* [2006] E.C.R. I-7251.

[38] Case C-53/04 *Marrosu v Azienda Ospedaliera Ospedale San Martino di Genova e Cliniche Universitarie Convenzionate* [2006] E.C.R. I-7213.

[39] Case C-443/98 *Unilever Italia v Central Food* [2000] E.C.R. I-75352. See M. Dougan, (2001).

[40] Dir.83/189/EEC, which was aimed at preventing the appearance of barriers to the operation of the Internal Market, proved to be a basic instrument for the realisation of the Internal Market through the promotion of co-operation between the Member States and through the detection of fields in which joint action was revealed to be necessary.

the parties to the proceedings in national courts (the defendant in *Unilever*) could invoke dir.83/189/EEC against individuals in order to render the national legislation at issue inapplicable. The Court adopted similar reasoning to the application of dir.83/189/EEC in the *CIA Security* judgment.[41] It would be incorrect to interpret these judgments as the Court recognising that directives may have horizontal direct effect. Firstly, in *Unilever* the Court upheld the rule that a directive could not be relied upon when the defendant was an individual. However, the Court pointed out that the same reasoning could not be applied to the proceedings of the case. According to the Court, dir.83/189/EEC creates neither rights nor obligations for individuals and, furthermore, does not define the substantive scope of the legal rule on the basis of which a national court must decide the case before it. Consequently, a breach of this directive constitutes a substantial procedural defect and renders a technical regulation inapplicable.

Another explanation of the specific application of dir.83/189/EEC comes from the Opinion of A.G. Jacobs in the case of *Unilever*.[42] His reasoning is based on a comparison of the procedure provided for in the Directive with the procedures contained in reg.No.17 which until 2004 implemented the Treaty provision concerning Competition law[43] and in reg.No.659/1999 on State Aid. The purpose of all these measures is not the approximation of laws, but the establishment of a preventive control mechanism (Dashwood, 2007:98). Advocate General Jacobs correctly observes that dir.3/189/EEC might have been adopted in the form of a regulation rather than a directive and, consequently, he formulates the question whether the case law on the consequences of non-implementation of directives is of any relevance in proceedings involving a breach of notification procedure under the directive. Even though the Court did not make any reference to that argument, in any event the wording of the judgment implies that dir.83/189/EEC must be distinguished from other (traditional) directives.

The Court considered this issue in *Mangold v Helm*.[44] Again this case concerned a dispute between private parties. Mr Mangold, 56,

---

[41] Case C-194/94 *CIA Security v Signalson and Securitel* [1996] E.C.R. I-2201. See also Slot (1996).

[42] Opinion of A.G. Jacobs at para.79.

[43] Now replaced by Reg.1/2004.

[44] See 11 above. On the impact of *Mangold* see Editorial Comments, 'Horizontal direct effect—A law of diminishing coherence?' (2006) 43 *Common Market Law Review* 1.

brought proceedings against his employer, challenging the fixed-term nature of his contract. The Munich Employment Court asked the Court whether national rules on fixed-term employment contracts for older workers are in line with dir.1999/70 on fixed-term work and dir.2000/78 establishing a general framework for equal treatment in employment and occupation. Under German law, fixed-term employment contracts are only permissible where they are justified by an objective reason.

Article 14, para.3 of the national labour law on part-time and fixed-term employment contracts (TzBfG) included an exception for persons over 52 years old in relation to whom no objective reason is required. Prior to the transposition of dir.1999/70, that age had been 60. During transposition it was lowered to 58, and following the results of a governmental commission, it was further lowered temporarily to 52.

The Court found there had been no infringement in respect of dir.1999/70. A reduction of the protection which workers are guaranteed in connection with fixed-term contracts is not necessarily prohibited by the Directive where it is done independently of the directive's transposition. In this case, the cut-off age was lowered in order to encourage the employment of older workers in Germany, not to undermine a general level of protection for workers.

The Court considered that a national provision permitting fixed-term employment contracts to be offered to anyone over the age of 52, without restriction, constituted age discrimination, which breaches both the general Community law principle of equality and, more specifically, art.6 of dir.2000/78. Whilst the Court conceded that the TzBfG's public-interest purpose was a legitimate objective, it held that the means used to achieve that objective go further than is appropriate and necessary. It noted, in particular, that legislation such as the TzBfG could lead to a situation in which all workers aged 52 or over may lawfully be offered fixed-term contracts until they retire.

The referring court also asked questions concerning the applicability of dir.2000/78 to Mr Mangold's employment contract. In respect of its provisions on age, the directive did not have to be transposed into German law until December 2, 2006. The Court concluded however that, "it is the responsibility of the national court to guarantee the full effectiveness of the general principle of non-discrimination in respect of age, setting aside any provision of national law which may conflict with Community law". This is the case irrespective of whether the deadline for a directive's transposition has expired. The Court places a burden upon the national court to interpret the domestic provisions to ensure compatibility with Community and guarantee Treaty rights for *all* individuals.

In *Lindorfer*[45] A.G. Sharpston considered the operation of dir.2000/78 and how this fitted in with the general principle under Community law of non-discrimination. In particular the Advocate General examined whether the content of the directive justified the Court's reasoning in *Mangold*. The Advocate General took the view that a better reading of *Mangold* is not that there was in Community law a specific pre-existing principle of non-discrimination on grounds of age, but rather that discrimination on such grounds had always been precluded by the general principle of equality. Accordingly dir.2000/78 introduced a specific, detailed framework for dealing with that (and certain other specific kinds of) discrimination. The Advocate General argued that such an interpretation arises from para.76 of the *Mangold* judgment where the Court stated that "observance of the general principle of equal treatment, in particular in respect of age, cannot as such be conditional upon the expiry of the period allowed the Member States for the transposition of a directive intended to lay down a general framework for combating discrimination on the grounds of age". The Court in *Lindorfer* did not address this issue in its final judgment. However, the point made by A.G. Sharpston is an important one because it questions the reasoning used by the Court in *Mangold* and its application of a directive for which the time period for implementation had not yet passed.

In *Mangold* the Court refers to the *Simmenthal* judgment in support of its decision. This is problematic because *Simmenthal* was concerned with the direct effect of a Treaty Article rather than the provision of a directive the capacity of which to have direct effect is less certain.[46] In *Mangold* the Court makes no mention of the principle of consistent interpretation and, although it is clear in the facts that the case was brought against a private party, the Court made no specific reference in its reasoning to the implications this had for the effect of the directive or the general principle that it recognised. The Court appears to rule that the national court must give effect to its ruling, irrespective of the fact that the case is brought against a private party. This aspect of the *Mangold* judgment leaves open the possibility that the Court is prepared to move away from its earlier case law regarding the limitations on the direct effect of directives, which was

---

[45] Case C-227/04 *Lindorfer v Council* judgment of September 11, 2007.
[46] The Court has consistently held that Treaty provisions do have horizontal direct effect. See for example *Defrenne (No.2)* and *Bosman*.

followed by the introduction of the principle of consistent interpretation, and toward an insistence on the disapplication of national law
wherever it is inconsistent with Community law irrespective of the
question of direct effect.

Ross (2006) explains these judgments by arguing that while the
directives do not confer individual rights they do impose obligations
on the Member States, which have secondary consequences for
private parties. Consequently, the Court seeks to promote and
maximise the *effectiveness* of Community law wherever possible and,
while not explicitly applying a principle of horizontal direct effect,
the judgments do allow for private parties to apply Community law
against each other. Dashwood (2007: 106) argues that the judgment
in *Mangold* may be a turning point following which the horizontal
direct effect of directives will be permitted. But as Dashwoood
correctly concludes only time will tell on this point.

Effectiveness of Community law is a convincing justification of
the judgments and addresses a long standing criticism of the non-
horizontal application of EC law. Namely that individuals in purely
private legal relationships are at a disadvantage by comparison to
those who have a legal relationship with the State. By contrast to
Ross, Weatherill criticises this line of cases as eroding the rule that
directives do not have horizontal direct effect. According to
Weatherill (2001), the Court's justification of effectiveness is a
smokescreen for extending the scope of Community law and the
jurisdiction of the Court in to private legal relationships. Such
individuals are not without a remedy and can seek to enforce the
principle of State liability which is considered below.

## 3.7 The Principle of Indirect Effect

The provisions of directives which contain specific rights for individuals and are clear and unambiguous may, after the expiry of the
transitional period be pleaded against the State. Such rights cannot
be pleaded against a private party as directives have vertical and *not*
horizontal direct effect.

The result of this is that there is a clear discrepancy in the enjoyment of rights depending upon the relationship the individual enjoys
with the State. For example, a woman who is compulsorily retired at
the age of 60 by a private sector employer, which is in breach of the
principle of equal treatment in dir.76/207/EEC, cannot rely upon
the provisions of the directive. If the woman were employed by the

State she would be able to utilise the rights within the directive to challenge the decision. Clearly such a distinction is unsatisfactory, particularly as the role of the State in its capacity as an employer has altered. Thus the Court has addressed these problems through teleological means, using the principle of effet utile or effectiveness of Community law.

## *Interpretation of Community law: The Von Colson principle*

In *Von Colson v Land Nordhein Westfalen*[47] the issue centred on the implementation of the Equal Treatment dir.76/207/EEC. Two women who had applied for posts in a German prison had been rejected on grounds of sex, despite German transposition of the directive in to German law. The remedies which were open to the German Labour Court appeared to be limited to the re-imbursement of their travelling expenses to attend the interview at which they were ultimately discriminated against. The German court, using the art.234 EC procedure, referred questions to the ECJ concerning the adequacy of the national remedies within the context of the directive.

The Court stated that it is the *duty* of national courts to interpret provisions of national law "in the light of the wording and purpose of the directive".[48] Accordingly, if the national court had the discretion to do so, it should exercise its powers in a manner that remedies for sex discrimination should operate as a deterrent to such conduct. The Court considered this teleological approach as another method through which the objectives of art.0 EC could be guaranteed.

*Von Colson* was a case which concerned transposing legislation. But what would be the position in circumstances where existing national legislation conflicted with Community law? In such circumstances do national courts have the same duty to interpret national legislation to ensure compatibility with Community law? Furthermore would the teleological rule apply in circumstances where there was a horizontal relationship? In *Von Colson* the relationship was a vertical one, the defendant was the State and the directive did not fulfil the requirements of direct effect. The Court addressed the issue of horizontal indirect effect in the *Marleasing*.[49]

---

[47] Case 14/83 *Arcaro* [1984] E.C.R. 1891.
[48] Para.26.
[49] Case C-106/89 *Marleasing SA v La Comercial Internacional de Alimentacion SA* C-106/88 [1990] E.C.R. I-4135.

*Marleasing* concerned litigation in Spain between two private parties. The ECJ held that with regard to the question of pre-existing legislation this made no difference to the fact that the litigation concerned two private parties. All national law had to be interpreted to give effect to Community law without exception, even though the State was not a direct party to the proceedings. The Court's argument was that Member States are under an obligation to create the conditions for private parties to exercise their Community law rights. The Court suggested that art.10 EC requires national courts to interpret national law to ensure compatibility with Community law. This duty arose irrespective of the source of Community law. The duty of harmonious interpretation was not just a rule to mitigate against the limited scope of direct effect of directives. Interpretation, alongside the principle of direct effect, was a tool of securing supremacy (Hartley, 1998:212).

One question raised by *Marleasing*, which the ECJ did not answer, was what, if any, limits were there to the power of national courts to interpret legislation to ensure conformity? Would there be circumstances where the national legislation and Community law were so far apart that interpretation would not be possible? The Court has refined and narrowed the *Marleasing* principle and addressed this issue through subsequent judgments (Craig, 1997:525).

In *Kolpinghuis* the Court stated that no criminal liability could flow, by reason of interpretation, from the provisions of a directive which a Member State had failed to implement. Similarly a non-implemented directive could not give rise to obligations for an individual. In *Arcaro*,[50] the Court accepted that there would be limits to interpretation as a correctional tool. According to the ECJ national law should not be interpreted to attribute to it a meaning which it clearly was not intended to have. In such circumstances the national court should make a declaration of incompatibility with Community law.

The *Von Colson* judgment has created difficulties which the House of Lords identified in *Duke v GEC Reliance*.[51] This case concerned compatibility of the Sex Discrimination Act 1975 with dir.76/207/EEC. Their Lordships stated that as the UK Act was passed before the directive it would "be most unfair to the respondent to distort the construction of the 1975 Sex Discrimination Act in order to accommodate the meaning of the Equal Treatment Directive". Their Lordships were concerned that through interpreta-

---

[50] Case C-168/95 [1996] E.C.R. I-4705.
[51] [1988] A.C. 618.

tive techniques they would adopt the mantle of legislature and provide the Act with a meaning which Parliament had not intended.

The House of Lords has subsequently shown greater willingness to apply a more purposive interpretation to Equal Treatment legislation.[52] In *Webb v EMO Cargo*,[53] the House of Lords interpreted the Sex Discrimination Act to conform with dir.76/207/EEC on equal treatment in a manner which the Court of Appeal had previously rejected as a distortion of the statute. Their Lordships held that this could not be done if the impact of such purposive interpretation was to alter the meaning of domestic legislation.

Following the Court's judgment in the case of *Wagner Miret*[54] it would appear that the broad interpretative approach of *Marleasing* has been curtailed and in this case the ECJ stated that national courts should only interpret domestic law as far as possible to meet the requirements of the directive. Otherwise the national court should declare the national law incompatible leaving the individual to bring an action for damages against the offending state.

In Joined Cases *Pfeiffers v Deutsches Rotes Kreuz*,[55] the Court examined the principle of consistent interpretation and to what extent national courts may interpret domestic legislation to ensure consistency with Community law. The case concerned a dispute between two private parties. The German Red Cross, which operates a land-based rescue service using ambulances and emergency medical vehicles, agreed with employees in their various contracts of employment that a collective agreement was to apply, by virtue of which the employees' average weekly working time was extended from 38.5 hours to 49 hours. During *"duty time"* the emergency workers concerned had to make themselves available to their employer at the place of employment and remain continuously attentive in order to be able to act immediately should the need arise. Mr Pfeiffer and his fellow workers brought an action before the German Labour Court for a declaration that their average weekly working time should not exceed the 48-hour limit laid down by dir.93/104 on Working Time.

The Court held that periods of "duty time" must be taken into account in its totality in the calculation of maximum daily and weekly working time. It held that national legislation, such as that in

---

[52] For example, *Pickstone v Freemens plc* [1988] A.C. 66 and *Litster v Forth Dry Dock Ltd* [1990] 1 A.C. 546.

[53] [1992] All E.R. 43.

[54] C-334/92 *Wagner Miret v Fondo de Garantia Salarial* [1993] E.C.R. I-6911.

[55] Joined Cases C-397/01 to C-403/01 *Pfeiffer v Deutsches Rotes Kreuz* [2004] E.C.R. I-8835.

issue in these proceedings, that authorised periods of weekly working time in excess of 48 hours, including periods of duty time, was not compatible with art.6(2) of the directive.

The Court referred to its previous judgments in *Von Colson* and *Marleasing* and highlighted the obligation on Member States to achieve the result envisaged by the directive and their duty under art.10 EC. At para.111 of the judgment the Court stated that:

> "it is the responsibility of the national courts in particular to provide the legal protection which individuals derive from the rules of Community law and to ensure that those rules are fully effective".[56]

This interpretation was consistent with that expressed in *Von Colson*. But the Court went further and at para.113, the ECJ showed recognition of the discretion available to the national court, when it said that:

> "When it applies a domestic law, and in particular legislative provisions specifically adopted for the purpose of implementing the requirements of a directive, the national court is bound to interpret national law, so far as possible, in the light of the wording and purpose of the directive concerned in order to achieve the result sought by the directive and consequently comply with Article 249 EC."[57]

The Court further stated that the requirement for national law to be interpreted in conformity with Community law is inherent in the system of the Treaty, since it permits the national court, for the matters within its jurisdiction, to ensure the full effectiveness of Community law when it determines the dispute before it.[58] The judgment is important for its interpretation of what the full effectiveness of Community law means. In the judgment the Court recognised that there is a discretion available to the national court, but would appear to subsequently suggest that the discretion is extremely limited if the national court is to ensure the "full effectiveness of

---

[56] Joined Cases C-397/01 to C-403/01 *Pfeiffer v Deutsches Rotes Kreuz* [2004] E.C.R. I-8835, para.111.
[57] Joined Cases C-397/01 to C-403/01 *Pfeiffer v Deutsches Rotes Kreuz* [2004] E.C.R. I-8835, para.113.
[58] Joined Cases C-397/01 to C-403/01 *Pfeiffer v Deutsches Rotes Kreuz* [2004] E.C.R. I-8835, para.114.

Community law". The extent of this discretion is apparent when the Court states:

> Although the principle that national law must be interpreted in conformity with Community law concerns chiefly domestic provisions enacted in order to implement the directive in question, it does not entail an interpretation merely of those provisions but requires the national court to consider national law as a whole in order to assess to what extent it may be applied so as not to produce a result contrary to that sought by the directive.[59]

The principle of consistent interpretation imposes a wide-ranging obligation on the national court requiring it to examine not only implementing legislation but also any other legislation or other national law that could permit the national court to achieve the result sought by the directive. The Court recognises that it is a matter of national law how far the national court can go in order to achieve an interpretation of the national provision that is consistent with the relevant Community law. However, if it is possible for a consistent interpretation to be achieved by whatever methods permitted under national law, the national court is "bound to use those methods". Thus Community law requires the national court to apply the consistent interpretation if it is at all possible as a matter of national law to do so. It would appear that following the judgment in *Pfeiffer* the interpretive obligation of national courts is broader than that stated in *Wagner Miret*. Full effectiveness of Community law is the obligation for national courts and the boundaries for national courts to do this would appear to be pushed back

Indirect effect can only be of assistance to a litigant where national legislation exists and it is irrelevant as to whether it pre or post-dates the Community measure. This still leaves one situation outstanding, namely where there is an absence of national implementing legislation and where an individual has suffered a loss resulting from a failure by the State to implement the directive. In these circumstances it appeared as if an individual, notwithstanding art.10 EC, had no means of recourse. A failure to implement a measure which did not have direct effect also meant that there was no scope for indirect effect. The Court of Justice filled this legal vacuum, by developing the principle of indirect effect and creating an all-encompassing principle of State liability.

---

[59] *Pfeiffer* at para.115.

## 3.8 The Principle of State Liability

### *The Francovich judgment*

In *Francovich* the ECJ acknowledged a Community law remedy which requires Member States to pay compensation for loss or damage arising out a breach of Community law by the State (Ross, 1993:525). The State liability principle is based upon deterrence, but also, through the requirement to pay compensation, provides tangible proof that Community rights have a real value to EU citizens (Szyszczak, 1996:353).

In *Francovich* the Italian government had failed to implement Council dir.80/987/EEC which required the establishment of a system for guaranteeing to employees the payment of unpaid wages in the event of their employer's insolvency. The Commission had already brought a successful infringement action under art.226 EC against Italy for its failure to transpose the directive. Francovich and Bonifaci (the second applicant) had lost wages when their employer went in to liquidation. They commenced proceedings against the Italian State claiming it had a duty to pay their wages either through accepting the guarantees contained within the directive, or, as compensation for the State's failure to transpose the legislation. The ECJ stated that that directive did not meet the criteria of direct effect because the provision lacked sufficiently clarity and precision by leaving discretion to the State as to *how* the guarantee scheme would operate in practice. Yet the Court stated that the directive had a clear objective of protecting employees in circumstances similar to those of the applicants. In developing the principle of State liability the Court revisited its previous "constitutional" judgments to support its reasoning.

The Court, recalling the judgments of *Van Gend en Loos* and *Costa v ENEL*, reiterated that Community law is a distinct legal order which has created rights for individuals and corresponding obligations for Member States. It is the duty of Member States to ensure that these rights are fully available to all citizens and in these circumstances it would be inconsistent with the principle of full effectiveness of Community law if the applicants were denied compensation for the failure by the Italian State to implement the directive. The Court held[60]:

[60] Case C-69/90 [1991] E.C.R. I-5357, para.28.

"It follows that the principle of State liability for harm caused to individuals by breaches of Community law for which the State can be held responsible is inherent in the system of the Treaty."

The Treaty basis for State liability can be attributed to art.10 EC which places upon Member States an "obligation to nullify the unlawful consequences of a breach of Community law".[61] It remains a moot point whether the Court in *Francovich* actually created a new remedy or merely refined an existing one. Either way, the significance of the judgment cannot be understated primarily because of the requirement that each Member State should recognise a Community law remedy for breaches of Community law and not simply the application of a national remedy. In *Unibet*[62] the Court held that the principle of effective judicial protection of an individual's rights under Community law must be interpreted as requiring it to be possible in the legal order of a Member State for interim relief to be granted until the competent court has given a ruling on whether national provisions are compatible with Community law. This will occur in circumstances where the grant of interim relief is necessary to ensure the full effectiveness of the judgment to be given on the existence of the Community law rights. In *Unibet* the Court held that the principle of effective judicial protection of an individual's rights under Community law must be interpreted as meaning that, where the compatibility of national provisions with Community law is being challenged, the grant of any interim relief to suspend the application of national provisions until the final ruling is governed by the criteria laid down by the national law. This is subject to the proviso that those criteria are no less favourable than those applying to similar domestic actions and do not render practically impossible or excessively difficult the interim judicial protection of those rights.

*Unibet* illustrates that Community principles of an effective judicial remedy have created a scheme for enforcement of individual rights which is enforced domestically and based on Community law principles and judicial dialogue between the Court of Justice and national courts (Harlow, 1996:203). At the Community level the Commission will enforce a failure to implement a measure through art.226 EC and thus *Francovich* is a follow on action. At the national level an individual will seek compensation for the loss suffered through the infringement of Community law rights arising from the

---

[61] Para.27.
[62] C-432/05 *Unibet v Justitiekanslern* judgment of March 13, 2007.

breach and this is based on the principle of State liability. Crucially there is no need for a provision to be directly effective for an individual to bring a successful action.

In circumstances where there is a complete failure to implement a directive the Court in *Francovich* stated that three conditions are necessary to give rise to liability. These are:

- the directive grants rights to individuals;

- the content of those rights is identifiable form the directive itself; and

- there is a causal link between the breach of Community law by the Member State and the actual loss suffered by the individual.

Though State liability is a Community principle it is for national courts to apply it in the appropriate circumstances. This is commonly referred to as the national autonomy procedure and is part of the dialogue that exists between national courts and the ECJ. Though application of the principle is reserved for national courts, the ECJ has made it clear that State liability is central to ensuring the objectives of art.10 EC and that national courts have a duty to give effect to Community law. In *Francovich* the Court stated[63]:

"It is in accordance with the rules of national law that the State must make reparation for the consequences of the harm caused. In the absence of any Community legislation, it is a matter for the internal legal order of each Member State to determine the competent courts and lay down the detailed procedural rules for legal proceedings intended fully to safeguard the rights which individuals derive from Community law. . ."

In establishing the principle of State liability *Francovich* left several questions unanswered regarding the scope and application of the principle. The principle of direct effect was a clear method through which Community rights could be enforced in domestic courts in all cases, including incorrect implementation and non-implementation. In contrast, the *Francovich* judgment only referred to situations of non-implementation of Community law. Could State liability also apply to situations of incorrect implementation of Community law, or where a Member State had failed to adapt existing legislation? If

---

[63] Para.42.

the answer was "yes" then State liability would be more than just a remedy of last resort. Furthermore in situations of failure to adapt existing legislation, for example as occurred in *Marleasing*, State liability is a *more* effective remedy and deterrence than indirect effect as it dispenses with the need to consider horizontal indirect effect.

The *Francovich* judgment provided limited guidance as to whether the principle applied only in situations where fault could be established. Would *Francovich* also apply to non-fault situations? Craig argued, and this has been the general approach of the Court that when assessing the concept of fault the Court should seek assistance from the standard of non-contractual liability in art.288 EC (Craig, 1993:597). In the Joined Cases of *Brasserie du Pêcheur* and *Factortame III*[64] the Court addressed these questions refining and extending the principle of State liability.

## Refining the State liability principle

The *Brasserie du Pêcheur* litigation involved a claim by a French brewer against Germany for loss of profits incurred when it was prevented from selling its product because the beer did not meet the German Beer Purity laws. The Court had already held that the purity laws amounted to a breach of art.28 EC on the free movement of goods.[65] In *Factortame III* the claim was made by Spanish fishermen who were not able to secure access to British fishing quotas, action which the Court had ruled breached arts 12 and 43 EC.

The art.234 EC reference raised several questions. Firstly did the principle of State liability apply to breaches which arose from legislative measures? Secondly, was direct effect available in situations where the Community legislation in question satisfied the criteria for direct effect? Finally what were the criteria for State liability in these circumstances?

The Court stated categorically that State liability is available in *all* circumstances in which the State causes harm. The presence of the direct effect principle is irrelevant and will include situations, as in these two cases, where there are breaches of the Treaty itself. The Court's judgment expanded upon the basic State liability principle established in *Francovich* where the Court referred to art.10 EC as a justification for State liability. In these two judgments the Court followed this reasoning and expressly referred to art.220 EC which

---

[64] Joined Cases C-46/93 and C-48/93 [1996] E.C.R. I-1029.
[65] Case 178/84 *Commission v Germany* (*Beer Purity*) [1987] E.C.R. 1227.

requires the Court to ensure that the Community law is observed and art.288 EC on the non-contractual liability of the EU Institutions.

Article 288 EC provides the inspiration for the elaboration of the conditions for liability in *Brasserie du Pêcheur* and *Factortame III.* The Court stated that the three part 'test' in *Francovich* is relevant in the cases of non-implementation but reformulated the conditions under which liability will be established[66]:

- the rule of Community law must confer rights on individuals;
- the breach must be "sufficiently serious"; and
- there is a direct causal link between the breach and the damage suffered by the injured party.

The Court held at para.55 that a breach of Community law by a Member State will be sufficiently serious if it "manifestly and gravely disregards the limits of its discretion". The concept of 'manifest and grave' is borrowed from the *Schöppenstedt* judgment concerning the application of art.288 EC. The Court provided some limited guidance as to what amounts to manifest and grave:

". . . a breach of Community law will be sufficiently serious if it has persisted despite a judgment finding the infringement in question be established, or a preliminary ruling or settled case law of the Court on the matter from which it is clear that the conduct in question constituted an infringement."

The Court also examined the basis of liability and the judgment provides that the existence of a 'sufficiently serious breach' requires the presence of fault. What actually amounts to a sufficiently serious breach is a matter for national courts to decide. The House of Lords in *Factorame V*[67] provided greater clarity, and their Lordships suggested that a deliberate and prolonged breach, which is not remedied despite being brought to the attention of the Member State, would be manifest and grave and therefore sufficiently serious (Cygan:2000). In *Factortame V* the House of Lords applied significant weight to the fact that the Commission had notified the UK government on numerous occasions that the Merchant Shipping Act 1988 was contrary to Community law. It is therefore necessary to distinguish between a breach of Community law which is inadvertent,

---

[66] Para.51.
[67] *Factortame (V)* [1999] 3 W.L.R. 1062.

or remedied immediately upon being notified to the Member State by the Commission and one where the breach is persistent.

What has been the effect of *Brasserie du Pêcheur*? Does a breach of Community law actually gives rise to State liability? In *Denkavit*[68] and *British Telecommunications*[69] a failure to implement a directive where the directive was vague and unclear as to its content did not amount to a sufficiently serious breach. By comparison a complete failure to implement a directive will be very likely to amount to a sufficiently serious breach,[70] as was a restriction of rights under art.28 EC.[71] In *Robins*[72] the Court of Justice explored the issue of what action by the State would amount to a sufficiently serious breach. Approving the criteria laid down in para.55 *Brasserie du Pêcheur* and *Factortame III* the Court stated that if the Member State was not called upon to make any legislative choices and had only considerably reduced, or even no, discretion, the mere infringement of Community law may be sufficient to establish the existence of a sufficiently serious breach.[73] The Court highlighted that the discretion enjoyed by the Member State thus constitutes an important criterion in determining whether a sufficiently serious breach of Community law has occurred and that the discretion is broadly dependent on the degree of clarity and precision of the rule infringed. In *Robins* the UK argued that art.8 of dir.80/987/EEC, concerning the protection of employees in the event of the insolvency of their employer, was imprecise as to what constituted the minimum degree of protection required by the directive. The Court confirmed that in the light of the observations made by other Member States and the Commission there was no consensus as to what constituted minimum protection. Consequently the UK had a degree of discretion when implementing the directive and had not exceeded its discretion.

As with the concept of an emanation of the State under *Foster* the Court has adopted a broad interpretation of the State for the purposes of *Francovich* liability. In *Köbler* the Court confirmed, that the principle of State liability extends to national courts including supreme courts. The Court also held that in line with national

---

[68] Case C-283/93 [1996] E.C.R. I-5063.
[69] Case C-392/93 [1996] E.C.R. I-1631.
[70] Joined Cases C-178-/94 *Dillenkofer v Germany* [1996] E.C.R. I-4845.
[71] Case C-5/94 *Hedley Lomas* [1996] E.C.R. I-2553.
[72] Case C-278/05 *Robins v Secretary of State for Work and Pensions* judgment of January 25, 2007.
[73] Case C-278/05 *Robins v Secretary of State for Work and Pensions* judgment of January 25, 2007, para.71.

autonomy it is for the national law of Member States to determine the form of action for claiming damages for a breach of Community law by such a Court.

Though the Court in *Köbler* acknowledged that supreme courts were subject to the State liability principle it remained unclear when and under what conditions decisions of national courts of last resort could in fact lead to liability being imposed on Member States if such courts misinterpreted Community law. In some Member States, most notably Italy constitutional law severely restricted the circumstances in which such liability could be imposed and was limited only to circumstances where intentional fault or serious misconduct could be demonstrated. Furthermore, Italian law provided that interpretation of legal provisions or the application of such provisions to the facts of a case could not impose any liability. In *Tragehetti del Mediterraneo*[74] the constitutional restriction imposed by Italian law on the liability of the Supreme Court and the compatibility of these provisions with Community law was considered by the Court of Justice (Albors-Llorens, 2007: 271).

The Court held that the restriction imposed by Italian constitutional law on the availability of damages for the actions of Italian courts breached Community law. The Court stated that it was not permissible to limit damages to cases of intentional fault or serious misconduct by courts of last resort, and nor could interpretation of legal provisions, or the application of such provisions to the facts of a case, be entirely excluded by national law (Laenarts, 2007: 1641). One interpretation of the judgment in *Traghetti* is that State liability for judicial decisions in relation to failure to make an art.234 EC reference is an indirect form of appeal against the classification of a particular question as acte clair. The Court is directly challenging the decision of a national court and arguably the Court's judgment therefore decides the substantive issue of the dispute.

The only three conditions that must be fulfilled for Member State liability to arise are that a court of last resort commits a manifest infringement of Community law, that the rule of law infringed is intended to confer rights on individuals, and that there is a direct causal link between the breach and the loss or damage sustained. In relation to the condition requiring a manifest infringement of Community law, a number of factors, first mentioned by the Court in *Brasserie du Pêcheur*, will be taken into account (Ruffert, 2007, 481). This includes the degree of clarity and precision of the rule

[74] Case C-173/03 *Traghetti del Mediterraneo SpA v Italy* [2006] E.C.R. I-5177.

infringed, whether the error was intentional or excusable, whether the decision by the national court was incompatible with the position taken by a Community institution and whether the court of last resort breached its referral obligation under the third paragraph of art.234 EC. This merely restates existing factors first stated by the Court in *Brasserie du Pêcheur*. The Court failed to address the uncertainty arising from *Köbler* of when State liability would be permitted against a national court. This silence of what circumstances would *actually* lead to a successful claim have lead to suggestions by some commentators that the factual criteria to establish State liability of a national court will be set very high (Nassimpian, 2007: 826).

The principle of State liability has arguably contributed more than any other principle developed by the Court to constitutionalise the Treaties. It requires Member States to pay compensation for a breach of Community law and, as suggested by Szyszczak (1996), provides a direct connection between Community law and the citizen who receives compensation for the loss suffered arising from the breach.

The principle of State liability has also ensured the effectiveness of Community law. In *Courage Ltd v Crehan*[75] the Court ruled that an individual could not be prohibited from relying on art.81 EC because he had been a party to an anti-competitive agreement. The significance of this judgment is that the principle of State liability was applied in circumstances involving two private individuals, a question which had been debated since *Francovich* (Van Gerven, 1996:597). The Court held that a right of action in damages under the State liability principle must be available to an individual before national courts. In this case the Court focussed not on the issue of national procedural autonomy but rather on the nature and importance of the substantive Community law right at issue. The Court declared the hierarchical superiority of free competition as a constitutional norm protected by the EC Treaty and by the Court[76]:

"It should be borne in mind, first of all, that the Treaty has created its own legal order, which is integrated into the legal systems of the Member States and which their courts are bound to apply. The subjects of that legal order are not only the Member States but also their nationals. Just as it imposes burdens on individuals, Community law is also intended to give rise to rights which become part of their legal assets. Those rights arise not only where they are expressly granted by the

[75] Case C-453/99 [2001] E.C.R. I-6297.
[76] Para.19.

Treaty but also by virtue of obligations which the Treaty imposes in a clearly defined manner both on individuals and on the Member States and the Community institutions (see the judgments in Case 26/62 *Van Gend en Loos* [1963] ECR 1, Case 6/64 *Costa* [1964] ECR 585 and Joined Cases C-6/90 and C-9/90 *Francovich and Others* [1991] ECR I-5357, paragraph 31)."

The language of the Court is interesting because it has a constitutional quality through reference to the judgments in *Van Gend en Loos* and *Francovich*. These judgments have made a significant contribution to the protection of Community law rights. The Court also refers to art.81 EC as being a 'fundamental right' which reinforces the idea of constitutionality.

The judgment has a broader impact because it also supports the existence of an economic constitution. Economic rights such as art.81 EC are so fundamental that they must be accessible to individuals in horizontal situations and can be protected through the principle of State liability. In *Courage Ltd v Crehan* the Court has extended the scope of Treaty rights by coming back to first principles for the enforcement of these rights. The judgment reinforces the settled view that Community law is "a new legal order" that provides individuals with a bundle of rights and Member States together with the ECJ are under a positive obligation to ensure individual rights are effectively protected.

## 3.9 A Strategy for Enforcing Community Rights?

The techniques of the Court considered above provide an integrated scheme of principles through which an individual may enforce Treaty rights. In the words of art.10 EC they provide individuals with the tools to ensure that Member States "take all appropriate measures, whether general or particular to ensure the fulfilment of the obligations". Through this the Court has created a strategy by which the Treaty provisions have become constitutionalised. Consequently, the supremacy of Community law, and access to Community law rights has been achieved through these principles.

The judgments of the Court have reflected the objectives of the Treaty which can be defined as the written will of the Member States. The judgments have also perpetuated closer integration through the Court's us of teleological techniques. Whether the Court has been a judicially activist institution remains a matter of debate. On one level, the judgments of *Von Colson, Francovich, Traghetti del Mediterraneo* and *Courage v Crehan* are intended to give effect to Treaty provisions and permit individuals to enforce their Community law rights. On another level, judgments such as *Courage* have defined the extent of these Treaty rights by stating the basic principles of economic integration in the absence of such statements from the Treaty makers. For example, the principle of mutual recognition established by the Court in *Cassis* formed the philosophical basis of the 1985 White Paper on the Completion of the Internal Market.

The judgments in *Courage* and *Tragghetti* demonstrate the interconnectedness between the free movement rules and competition law which forms the basis of the modern governance techniques of the Internal Market. Consequently, the techniques used by the Court to enforce Internal Market rights have created an economic constitution forming the cornerstone of EU integration. The creation of the Internal Market is inconceivable without the contribution of the ECJ to ensure universal application of the common rules of Community law. The Court has played a central part in upholding the legal order established in the Community and this is a legal order founded upon the pursuit of economic integration.

# 4: Governance and Harmonisation

The EC Treaty confers no general competence to harmonise national laws (Weatherill, 2002). Article 5(1) EC states that the EC is competent only where so provided by the EC Treaty. "Non-economic" activities of the Member States remain outside of the legislative scope of Community law, for example, the provision of State education, health care services, although as we shall see in Chapter 5 this does not protect these areas where the non-discrimination principle contained in art.12 EC, or the Citizenship provisions of arts 17 and 18 EC apply. Similarly where there is an economic activity, the EC Treaty provisions may apply, for example, the application of the free movement and competition rules to sport or healthcare, even though the EU does not have *legislative* competence in the field.

Where the laws of the Member States differ, the creation of an Internal Market will be impeded. The differences between the Member States which may impede or hinder the development of an Internal Market may be addressed by a process of *negative integration*. This is where the Member States' laws are challenged either by using the direct effect of Community law in the national courts or through the enforcement processes of the Commission, using art.226 EC or more rarely, other Member States using art.227 EC.

From the *Cassis de Dijon*[1] ruling, and the various derogations allowed in the fundamental freedoms, as well as services of general economic interest in art.86(2) EC, the Member States may continue with laws and policies which prima facie infringe Community law. But these are seen as a justified *derogation* from the aims of creating an Internal Market. Any derogations are to be interpreted narrowly and are subject to the principle of proportionality. Member States may not plead a derogation from the EC Treaty rules where the Community has occupied the field and adopted harmonising measures.

Where the Member States laws and policies are divergent, and this divergence poses a threat to the Internal Market, the EC Treaty allows for *positive integration* to take place. This takes place through the creation of Community policies which harmonise the Member States' divergent practices and leads to the re-regulation of markets. The spill-over effect from what is a functionally broad programme of harmonisation is to extend Community law competence into a number of areas which are now seen as distinctive Community law disciplines: private law, consumer law, environmental law, social policy law, labour law, health care law, family law. In some instances these disciplines have been raised to the status of values within the Community and are to be mainstreamed through all Community policies. Article 3(2) EC mainstreams equality between men and women; art.6 mainstreams environment concerns and art.127 EC states that a "high level of employment" shall be taken into consideration in the formulation and implementation of Community policies and activities. Thus the integration programme, which is presented as an exercise in securing market freedoms through the creation of an Internal Market, has not only explicitly recognised the need for horizontal or flanking policies to support the four freedoms but has inevitably spilled-over into a number of broad policy areas and has committed the Community to a sustained commitment to rule-making at the Community level (Egan, 2001).

As a result of this expansion of objectives and competences there can be conflicts between the central Internal Market objectives of integration and the other recognised objectives of the Community. Article 95(3) EC recognises that non-market objectives should be given recognition in the legislative process. In recent cases the Court

---

[1] Case 120/78 *Rewe–Zentrale AG v Bundesmonopolverwaltung für Branntwein* [1979] E.C.R. 649.

has recognised the objectives of social legislation over internal market legal base objectives on which the legislation was justified.[2]

The breadth and expansion of Community objectives may also result in conflicting aims being present in one piece of legislation and the Court has ruled that where there are market and non-market objectives present which are not necessarily consistent with each other there needs to be a balanced interpretation of such legislation. In *Bodil Lindqvist*[3] the directive on the free movement of personal data has the aim of ensuring the free flow of personal data *and* the aim of safeguarding the fundamental rights of individuals. The Court recognised that these objectives may be inconsistent with each other but also that the directive itself provided mechanisms allowing for the different rights and interests to be balanced.

## 4.1 Exhaustive Harmonisation

The original approach of the EU of sectoral harmonisation, with a top-down centralised approach, proved to be unworkable especially after the Member States retained the power to block Commission proposals in the Council through the threat of the veto where a national interest was at stake. The idea of exhaustive harmonisation also spawned ridicule in the media and the popular imagination. Stories emerged of the "Euro-sausage" and images of the Commission: "If it moves—harmonise it!". But there are still some examples where exhaustive harmonisation is used where the Member States are able to agree that there is a need for common uniform rules.[4] However, the technique is used sparingly, firstly because it will take many years to reach agreement across 27 Member States on a measure involving exhaustive harmonisation but also because it is recognised that standardisation can stifle innovation and experimentation (Stuyck et al., 2006). The comitology process is one way in which the EU may introduce procedures to update exhaustive

---

[2] Joined Cases C-19/01, C-50/01 and C-94/01 *INPS v Alberto Barsotti* [2004] E.C.R. I-2005, paras 34 and 25.

[3] Case C-101/01 [2003] E.C.R. I-12971.

[4] See, for example, dir.76/56/EEC, OJ [1976] E.C.R. I-L262/1 which led to the Commission taking an infringement action against the UK (Case 60/86 *Commission v UK (Dim-Dip Headlights)* [1988] E.C.R. 3921). The directive contained an exhaustive list of lighting devices which did not include the dim-dip device required by UK law.

harmonisation measures in order to keep up to date with technical progress.[5]

Once the Community has entered the field the Member States are pre-empted from imposing their own standards and rules.[6] In a harmonised area the Member States may not use the justifications for derogations to the fundamental economic freedoms.

## 4.2 Optional Harmonisation

Some harmonisation directives provide for the option for producers to follow the provisions of the directive (Currall, 1984). This approach is not used often and it creates problems for intra-Community trade. The idea of optional harmonisation is that producers need only follow the provisions of a directive where they intend to trade the goods across an EU Member State frontier. If they do not intend to export the goods they have the option of complying with the directive.

## 4.3 Minimum Harmonisation

Minimum harmonisation is the most popular form of harmonisation, and represents a compromise, or half-way house for the Member States (Dougan, 2000; Rott, 2003). The Member States agree to minimum intervention through Community harmonisation techniques and are free to adopt or retain higher levels, especially in the fields of environmental protection, consumer protection and, especially, social policy. Minimum harmonisation became the routine approach after the ruling in *Cassis de Dijon* paved the way for a less intrusive form of regulation of the Internal Market: mutual recognition.

---

[5] Recognised by the Court in Case C-154/04 and C-155/04 *Alliance for Natural Health* [2005] E.C.R. I-6451.

[6] Case 60/86 *Commission v UK (Dim Dip Headlights)* [1988] E.C.R. 3921; Case C-2/90 *Commission v Belgium* [1992] E.C.R. I-4431.

## 4.4 Mutual Recognition: the New Approach

Ortino (2007:309) points out that mutual recognition is one of the most important legal instruments in international and transnational regulation: "Its basic function is to grant effect to foreign legal rules or acts occurring in the territory of another State." Mutual recognition plays an important role in European integration, for example, art.47 EC provides for directives to be adopted for the mutual recognition of diplomas, certificates and other formal qualifications and art.293 EC states that the Member States shall ensure the mutual recognition of companies and firms. The principle is found also in external relations Treaties of the EU and mutual recognition has extended into the area of criminal law (Peers, 2004; Bantekas, 2007).

Mutual recognition has a legislative base as well as a judicial base in case law. The necessity to reach consensus for unanimous voting in the Council meant that even where consensus was reached technological change had often over-taken Community harmonisation processes. A breakthrough in the integration process came as a result of a ruling of the Court's using a principle called "mutual recognition" (Armstrong, 2002). In *Cassis de Dijon*[7] the German authorities refused to allow a French liquor, Cassis de Dijon, to be sold as a liquor in Germany because it was weaker than the minimum alcohol content of liquors marketed as such in Germany. German liqueur had to have at least 25 per cent alcohol content whereas Cassis had between 15–20 per cent alcohol content. The German authorities claimed the rule was to protect consumers.

The Court introduced the idea of "home State control" stating that

". . . in the absence of common rules it is for the member States to regulate all matters relating to the production and marketing of alcohol and alcoholic beverages in their own territory".

Thus where a product was lawfully marketed in one Member State there was a presumption that it could be sold in other Member States without any further impediments to free trade. This was the idea of mutual recognition, although as we see below, what the Court is really interested in is whether the host State is imposing barriers to free trade. In fact the idea of mutual recognition owes as much to competition principles as it does to free trade. The Court looks at

[7] Above fn.1.

indistinctly applicable measures and finds them unlawful where they create an additional regulatory burden to foreign providers of a good or service, putting them at a competitive disadvantage with domestic providers. A Member State was allowed to rebut this presumption if it could show that there were certain interests (called "mandatory requirements") to be protected by the receiving State which had not been protected in the State where the goods were produced: public health, fairness in commercial transactions, fiscal supervision, consumer protection. Over time the Court has indicated that this is not an exhaustive list. The principle of proportionality applies.

The final limb of the *Cassis* principle was that home state control and mutual recognition reduced the need for exhaustive harmonisation at the Community level and the Community could move towards greater use of minimum harmonisation to harmonise Member State rules which resulted in continuing trade barriers.

The Court extended the mutual recognition principle to the field of services in *Saeger*.[8] Weiler (1999:367) argued that the name "mutual recognition" as a way of describing what the Court was doing in these cases is misleading and a better term would be "functional parallelism". He argues that what the Court was doing was applying ". . . a very conservative and fully justified application of the principle of proportionality". Thus, as Ortino (2007:314) explains the concept of functional equivalence is a derogation from the mutual recognition requirement: if there is no functional equivalence between the rules of the home state and the host state then a Member State may raise the derogation/justification found in the mandatory requirements doctrine (Bernard, 2002; Snell, 2002).

The Commission reacted quickly to the *Cassis* ruling and pushed for the greater use of mutual recognition, which was already recognised in the EC Treaty in art.49 EC (the mutual recognition of diplomas) and art.220 EC (the mutual recognition of companies). Mutual harmonisation became the backbone of the Commission's White Paper on Completing the Internal Market in 1985.

The legislative approach of mutual recognition is essentially a horizontal approach setting general principles across a range of sectors. A good example is seen in the directives which provide for the mutual recognition of educational and vocational qualifications which are discussed in Chapter 5. Differences between the Member States constitute a real barrier to the free movement of persons, and

---

[8] Case 76/90 *Saeger v Dennemeyer* [1991] E.C.R. I-4221.

yet, the Member States are reluctant to allow the Community to interfere in so sensitive an area as education and vocational training in order to harmonise such qualifications. Where intervention has been allowed it has been slow and piecemeal. Therefore the idea that comparable qualifications acquired in one Member State should also be recognised as an equivalent qualification in another Member State is a solution to a pervasive barrier to market integration.

Another aspect of mutual recognition is that it relies upon on private bodies to establish voluntary standards. This has raised concerns that the Commission is delegating its law-making powers. But the Commission argues that the standards are voluntary codes, not binding legislation. A number of organisations, CEN, CENELAC, ETSI, acting on a qualified majority vote on a mandate from the Commission establish essential technical specifications which are necessary for each mutual recognition directive. A manufacturer has a choice whether or not to conform with the specifications, but where the goods conform they will be tested and certified. Not surprisingly some of these decisions take time. There has also been criticism of the new approach to harmonisation from the perspective of quality in EU governance. The lack of accountability and transparency in the decision-making process, as well as the fear that the bodies may be influenced by powerful lobbying by interested groups while denying the opportunity for consumers to have a say, or participate in the decision-making processes, ("regulatory capture") are all criticisms.

The most well known technical specification mark is the "CE" found on many goods, for example, toys, and is therefore a kite mark signifying the product satisfies EU standards. But many consumers also see the technical specification mark as a guarantee of the *quality* of the goods. (Weatherill, 1995). Products manufactured in accordance with the technical standards are presumed to comply with the requirements of the harmonisation directive.[9] Under the minimum harmonisation approach the Community is concerned only with harmonising essential safety requirements. Once goods conform to these standards they are free to move freely throughout the Community. There are incentives for goods produced outside of the EU to conform also with the technical requirements as this will also allow for free movement throughout the EU, and this is why toys made in China, for example, will often bear the "CE" mark.

---

[9] Case 815/79 *Criminal Proceedings Against Gaetano Cremonini and Maria Luisa Vrankovich* [1980] E.C.R. 3583, para.13.

The new approach to harmonisation has also been questioned as to whether it will lead to a "race to the bottom". This is the idea that there will be a tendency for producers to move to the Member State which has the lowest standards. But in fact what has happened is a form of competitive regulation whereby Member States with higher standards provide a quality "kitemark" for goods and services produced under the higher national standards being recognised for the higher quality.

A final aspect of the mutual recognition and minimum harmonisation approaches is that the Member States are under an obligation to provide information concerning national measures which derogate from the principle of free movement of goods.[10] In order to provide greater transparency and an early warning system for any measures which impose technical requirements on goods.[11] This allows the Commission and other Member States to raise objections to such national measures before they can cause harm to the functioning of the Internal Market.

## Reflexive Harmonisation

Reflexive harmonisation is a newer form of harmonisation processes which have been identified as part of the move away from the top-down, exhaustive harmonisation approach. Reflexive harmonisation is explained as a process which is procedural in approach, allowing various new political actors in the integration process to use procedures established by the EU to promote a variety of local ("bottom-up", as opposed to "top-down") prescriptions for regulatory problems in the EU (Deakin, 1999).

Reflexive harmonisation also allows scope for experimentation at the local level, allowing a wider range of political actors to be involved in decision-making and implementation processes. It therefore resembles some of the ideas behind other forms of new economic governance, such as the open method of co-ordination. Examples of reflexive harmonisation are seen especially in the area of employment law and industrial relations where it has proved difficult to secure Community competence, for example, in the information and consultation provisions for workers and their representatives of The European Works Council Directive,[12] and also the

---

[10] Decision 3052/95/EC, OJ 1995 L321/1.

[11] Dir.98/34/EC, OJ 1998 L204/37.

[12] Council dir.94/45/EC, OJ 1994 L 254/64.

European Company.[13] Similarly the role of the social partners and the resulting Framework Directives adopted under the provisions relating to social law in arts 138 and 139 EC are examples of a newer form of harmonisation, linked with ideas of subsidiarity.

## New Governance

De Búrca and Scott (2006) describe the modern shift to new governance methods in the EU as a wide range of processes and practices that have a normative dimension but do not operate primarily, or at all, through the formal Community law-making mechanisms involving traditional command-and-control legal institutions. Two main forms of new governance techniques have made an important impact upon the EU governance processes in recent years: the open method of co-ordination and the Lamfalussy Process.

### (i) The open method of co-ordination

The phrase the "open method of coordination" (omc) was coined at the Lisbon Summit of March 2000. A legal base, for what is now generically identified as the omc, is seen in the use of new methods of co-ordinating policy in the arena of economic and monetary union, (BEPG) introduced in the Maastricht Treaty 1991 (now art.98 EC) (Hodson and Maher, 2001; Pisani-Frerry, 2006) and later, in the arena of employment policy (EES), introduced in the Amsterdam Treaty 1997 (arts 125–130 EC) (Ashiagbor, 2005.) Over time a number of omcs have developed with different structures and different forms of participation in the field of the environment, pensions and social protection, tax (Szyszczak, 2005; Zeitlin et al., 2005)

It is arguable that the advent of the omc in EU policy making and governance models is not so novel, or so recent, but merely builds upon the long tradition of soft law processes used in policy making (Senden, 2004; Armstrong and Kilpatrick, 2007; Trubek and Trubek, 2007)), the experimentation with new forms of governance (for example the commitment to proportionality, subsidiarity, the use of comitology, framework legislation networked administrative agencies), drawing upon the success of Commission monitoring of

---

[13] Council Reg.No. 2157/2001; Council dir.2001/86, OJ 2002 L294/22; EP and Council dir.2002/14 OJ 2002 L80/29.

traditional hard law directives and the peer review, "name and shame" mechanisms utilised in the implementation and monitoring of the Internal Market programme as well as the OECD (Schäfaer, 2006). The omc may also be seen as yet another aspect of experimental governance without entailing a systemic change to the underlying constitutional settlement of 1957 (Szyszczak, 2002). In this respect firm boundaries are drawn between "old" governance, or the Community method, and "new" governance which, to some extent exists outside the legal constitutional structures of the EU. The omc may also be characterised as part of an inherent logic within the EU of political actors switching from traditional to "better" or more "efficient" regulation in areas where some level of EU regulation is necessary but where it has been difficult to reach consensus on *what* level and *how* this should be achieved.

A uniting characteristic of new governance[14] is that it is seen as an experimental form of governance and decision-making; a response to the various regulatory shortcomings of the EU which manifested themselves in the last century. Such shortcomings include the limited decision-making capacity of the EU, buttressed by political concerns of the Member States to retain a residual sovereign capacity to direct and implement economic and social policies which are not seen as central to the integration project, the Court's continued role to set legal limits to the competence attributed to the integration project,[15] and the various criticisms of the powers of the EU, questioning the legitimacy of the decision-making processes and the powers attributed to the EU (Schmitter, 2000).

One normative analysis of the problem is provided by Scharpf (1999) who argues that the EU is bedevilled by systematic limits, or black holes, of non-decision. Regulatory competition forces Member States into a downward spiral and European decision-taking tends to end up lower than that of any single Member State. In his analysis a solution to the problem emerges by estimating the degree to which decision-making should be decentralised. But within the EU deadlock in decision-making is also reached because of institutional factors. The EU is a multi-level decision-making polity, with very few institutional mechanisms to achieve hierarchical co-operation and this contributes to the decision-making

---

[14] See Special Issue on Law and New Approaches to Governance in Europe (2002) 8.1. *European Law Journal.*

[15] Case C-376/98 *Germany v Parliament and Council (Tobacco Advertising)* [2000] E.C.R. I-8419.

deadlock. The situation is exacerbated by the creation of new Institutional models of decision making, giving bodies such as the European Parliament greater powers of co-decision and attaching importance to the views of other Institutions such as the Economic and Social Committee, the Committee of the Regions, the Economic and Policy Committee, the Employment Committee and the Social Protection Committee. For Scharpf a way out of this deadlock is to emphasise the horizontal and vertical *differentiation* of decision-making and to put in place mechanisms to determine the proper *choice* of decision-making arenas or patterns of linkages between the arenas to prevent decision-making breakdown.

A different approach to analysing the normative dimension of new governance in the EU is seen in the work of Joerges (1999). He argues that the Member States, and the political interests of the elites, as well as stakeholders in the EU decision-making processes of the EU, can break the decision making deadlock by *transforming* interests. This thesis argues that the Member States' preferences are influenced by continual discussion and exchange of arguments. An example of this is seen in the academic analysis of the use of comitology in the EU (Joerges and Vos, 1999). The outcome, it is claimed, is that expert deliberation in committees leads to Community-compatible interests.

These developments have shifted the focus of academic study of the EU away from the substantive issues of European integration towards a greater emphasis upon inquiry as to *how* the EU is emerging as a system of governance.

Soft law processes have played an important role in the governance of the Internal Market. Following quickly on the Court's ruling the Commission issued a Communication on *Cassis*, followed by the White Paper of 1985.[16] This which was an important policy document setting the agenda for next stage of economic integration. The Commission continued with a number of strategy papers, action plans which continued to outline the objectives of the Internal Market, setting targets and commenting on progress made, and the future direction of the Internal Market.

The implementation of the SEA 1986 and the 1992 project also led to greater monitoring of the Member States' implementation of the measures introduced to complete the Internal Market through the use of the Internal Market Score Board. This is a form of peer

---

[16] EC Commission, *Communication from the Commission Regarding the Cassis de Dijon judgment*, OJ 1980 L 256/2; White Paper, *Completing the Single Market*, COM(85) 310.

group review whereby Member States are "named and shamed" by the Commission. It has subsequently been used in other areas such as State Aid, the modernisation of social protection and immigration policy where a lighter touch is needed to persuade the Member States to align their national policies towards the aims of European integration.

The Lisbon process has used a variety of new governance tools to encourage the coordination of Member States' policies in an attempt to achieve a softer persuasive approach from the more heavy-handed harmonisation approach (Szyszczak, 2005). Each year targets are set for certain goals and Member States' progress is judged by benchmarking processes, peer review and a process of iteration: learning from each other.

The omc is not confined to a limited set of economic and employment, social protection policies, but has been extended into the flanking policies of the EU. The Commission is exploring its use in developing immigration policies, an area fraught with political sensitivity for the Member States,[17] environmental policy[18] and taxation.[19] It is ironic that the Member States have guarded their national competence in these sensitive areas while allowing incursions into that competence through the use of the new forms of economic governance (Szyszczak, 2002).

The use of the new approach to harmonisation, reflexive harmonisation and the new approaches to economic governance such as the omc reflect the fact that the Community uses multiple tools and a variety of political actors at various levels in the Community to implement its goals: multi-level governance. The goal of the Community today is first, to co-ordinate the new tools of economic governance, namely the Internal Market Strategy, the Broad Economic Policy Guidelines of the Member States and the Community and the European Employment Strategy. These are now streamlined and adopted on the same day. The second goal is to address the continuing pervasive barriers to market integration (taxation and procurement being two of the most problematic areas) as well as continued emphasis on the monitoring and enforcement of Community law, and the improvement in quality and the simplification of the Community rules: the regulatory environment in which the Internal Market operates (Weatherill, 2000).

---

[17] Commission, *Communication on an Open Method of Co-ordination for the Community Immigration Policy*, COM (2001) 387 final; Bogusz, 2004.

[18] Lenschow, 2002.

[19] Radaelli, 2003.

## *The Lamfalussy Process*

A committee of three "wise men" was established under the chair of Baron Lamfalussy to investigate why the Community approach to harmonisation in the commercial sphere, especially financial services, was so slow and difficult to maintain (Ortino, 2007). The Commission had introduced a Financial Services Action Plan (FSAP)[20] in 1999 proposing far-reaching change to the regulation, supervision and governance of financial markets. These markers needed to be liberalised, but also supervised, if the Internal Market project was to be successful. The resulting Lamfalussy Report identified that at each level of the Community decision-making processes (Commission initiative, the Council, the European Parliament and domestic implementation) there were problems resulting in obstructions and delay.[21] It was difficult to harmonise the national laws in this area and essentially many of the barriers to free movement resulted from non-State actors operating in the financial services' markets. Thus even the application of the mutual recognition/functional equivalence principle could not iron out the differences between financial services in the Member States and provide satisfactory protection for interested stakeholders (Avgerinos, 2003; Moloney, 2003; Wymeersh, 2005)). The Report also identified the incapacity of the Community system to prioritise issues, alongside a lack of flexibility. Thus a new faster-track procedure was proposed. Under the Lamfalussy process the Commission adopts detailed "Level 2" rules for financial markets based upon mandates in the related "Level 1" Directive or Regulation which has been adopted under the usual procedures. The Level I measures use the comitology process and have resulted in in a set of detailed measures, moving beyond minimum harmonisation and establishing the EU as "the primary regulator for the EC's financial markets" (Moloney, 2007:627) The Commission is advised by the Committee of European Securities regulators (CESR) which is composed of Member State Regulators. The Commission is supervised by the European Securities Committee (ESC) which is composed of Member State representatives. Level 3 of the Lamfalussy Process involves enhanced co-operation and networking between EU securities regulators, co-ordinated by the ESRC. The aim here is to ensure the practical consistent and equivalent transposition of Level 1 and

---

[20] *Implementing the Framework for Financial Markets: Action Plan*, COM (1999) 232.
[21] *Final Report of the Committee of Wise Men on the Regulation of European Securities Market* (Brussels, 2001).

2 legislation through the adoption of Guidelines and common standards. Level 4 addresses strengthened enforcement, especially in the hands of the Commission. As Moloney (2007:628) describes: "This explosive combination of process and regulatory reform led to massive reforms to financial market regulation delivered under the FSAP." The Commission has drawn upon the strengths of this new regulatory process to adopt a *White Paper on Financial Services Policy 2005–2010*[22] which attempts to consolidate the existing policies with a move towards broader policy orientations and assessing the effectiveness of EU intervention in financial markets.

The Lamfalussy Process has been extended to the regulation of banking, insurance and pensions.

## 4.5 Harmonisation and the Choice of Legal Base

Article 95 EC, introduced by the SEA 1986, provided a new legal base for harmonisation measures for the Internal Market using qualified majority voting. The Maastricht Treaty 1991 changed the procedure to the co-decision procedure, making greater use of the involvement of the European Parliament. Article 95 EC allowed measures to be adopted which have as their object the establishment and functioning of the internal market, as defined in art.14 EC. The growth in areas of EU competence has led to a number of disputes over the correct legal base for Internal Market measures. Paradoxically, the incremental growth of specific sectoral bases for Community-based measures had the effect of reducing the scope for general Internal Market legislation. But the situation was complicated by the fact that prior to the SEA the Internal Market legal base had been used to adopt a number of measures not strictly addressing the market-building focus of art.94 and 308 EC.

At the heart of the initial disputes was the issue of democratic participation in decision-making. Article 95 (1) EC is in a residual legal base, to be used only where there is no other suitable EC Treaty base.[23] But where the procedures under different legal bases are the same, the ECJ has allowed a dual legal base for measures.[24] The Court gave a broad interpretation to the scope of art.95(1) EC in

---

[22] COM (2005) 629.

[23] Case C-533/03 *Commission v Council (VAT)* [2006] E.C.R. I-1025.

[24] Case C-491/01 *Ex p. BAT* [2002] E.C.R. I-11453; *cf.* Case 211/01 *Commission v Council* [2003] E.C.R. I-8913).

*Titanium Dioxide*[25] where the use of art.95(1) EC was contested against the use of art.175 EC in a measure relating to the disposal of waste in the titanium dioxide industry. The Court argued that since environmental and health measures were a burden on undertakings, competition within the Internal Market could be distorted if the Member States' laws were not harmonised. The ruling was criticised for giving too broad an interpretation to art.95 EC: nearly all measures have a cost implication leaving the legal bases for other policies in a residual role. It was also felt that the Court was paying attention to procedural factors (art.95 EC involved the European Parliament in the co-operation procedure) over the actual *form* and *content* of the contested measure.

In contrast where a measure relating to the disposal of waste was adopted under art.175 EC the Court looked to the main objective of the directive and concluded that its purpose was the protection of the environment and that art.175 EC was a suitable legal base for such a measure. Article 95(1) was not suitable as the directive had only an incidental effect on harmonising market conditions within the Internal Market.[26] In the later case concerning *Beef Labelling*[27] the Court puts aside considerations of inter-institutional balance and greater democratic participation in decision-making for a more functional approach. The dispute was between the legal bases of art.95(1) EC and art.37 EC concerning an agricultural Regulation. The Court ruled that the aim of the Regulation was to re-establish stability in the beef and beef product market after the BSE crisis and that art.37 EC was the appropriate legal base. It was not relevant that the European Parliament wished to participate in the decision-making process.

In addition to the choice of a legal base, the Institutions must also take account of the principles of subsidiarity and proportionality. Initial academic discussion of whether subsidiarity was justiciable was not reinforced by rulings from the Court which has continued to show a reluctance to investigate whether the subsidiarity principle has been followed, preferring instead to focus upon formal procedural issues[28] or the necessity for Community-action.[29] Only in *Ex p. BAT*[30] did the Court investigate *why* there was a need for a

---

[25] Case 300/89 *Commission v Council* [1991] E.C.R. I-2867.
[26] Case C-155/91 *Commission v Council* [1993] E.C.R. I-939.
[27] Case C-269/97 *Commission and Parliament v Council* [2000] E.C.R. I-2257.
[28] Case C-233/94 *Germany v Parliament and the Council* [1997] E.C.R. I-2405.
[29] Case 84/94 *UK v Council* [1996] E.C.R. I-5755; Case C-377/98 *Netherlands v Parliament and Council* [1997] E.C.R. I-2405.
[30] Case C-491/01 [2002] E.C.R. I-11453.

Community-wide directive on tobacco products designed to remove the disparities which existed between the Member States.[31]

## 4.6 Limits to Community Competence

The classic understanding of art.95 EC is that it does not vest the Community legislator with "a general power to regulate the internal market".[32] Any measures based upon art.95 EC must actually and genuinely contribute to eliminating obstacles to trade and removing distortions of competition thus putting a limit upon unlimited exercise of Community competence and jurisdiction.[33] The recognition of the need for horizontal or flanking policies to support the Internal Market project, as well as the desire by some Member States to harmonise rules relating to social policy, migration, the environment, agriculture, health and safety, consumer protection has created tensions within the EU as to how far non-economic objectives can also be the subject of harmonisation within the EU using art.95 EC rather than a specific sectoral legal base for such measures. Some areas specifically reject the use of harmonisation, for example, health (art.152(4)(c) EC)[34] and employment (art.129 EC).

---

[31] The omc and after the Treaty of Lisbon 2007 is ratified, the use of incentive measures may be alternative, and more acceptable ways to handle such issues. See the attempt to develop an EU strategy to support Member States in reducing alcohol-related harm (COM (2006) 625) and the Green Paper, *Towards a Europe Free From Tobaccco Smoke: Policy Options at EU Level*, COM (2007) 27.

[32] Case C-376/98 *Germany v European Parliament and Council (Tobacco Advertising)* [2000] E.C.R. I- para.83.

[33] Case C-436/03P *European Parliament and Commission v Council* [2006] E.C.R. I-1025.

[34] Health issues are particularly problematic for the EU (see art.152(4) EC) As a result of the Treaty of Lisbon 2007 *art.168 (4) TFEU* provides that measures should be adopted in the area of public health *"in order to meet common safety concerns"* but it will be possible for the Union to harmonise standards of quality and safety in relation to medicinal products and devices *(art.168(4) TFEU)* where the Internal Market legal base of art.95 EC is currently used. The Union will also be able to adopt incentive measures in relation to cross-border threats to health, tobacco and alcohol abuse *(art.168(5) TFEU)*. But incentive measures should not be harmonisation measures. In contrast *art.168(7) TFEU* expands art.152(5) EC. Member States will be responsible for the definition of health policy and the delivery of health services. Member States shall include the management of health services and medical care in the allocation of resources assigned to them.

In *Tobacco Advertising*[35] the Court held that where there were two competing legal bases for a measure the principal rule is that the Internal Market base should be used where the aim is to improve the functioning of the Internal Market. Where the aim is to achieve another policy goal (for example, the protection of the environment, social policy) then the appropriate specific legal base should be used. Where there is no competence for the latter then the Internal Market legal base can be used irrespective of whether the Internal Market is ancillary to the objective being sought. Thus Internal Market issues cannot be disregarded when pursuing other ancillary goals of market integration. The Court indicates, conversely, that a measure which is aimed at enhancing the functioning of the Internal Market may be adopted, using art.95 EC as the legal base, even if its purpose is to promote another aim, for example, the protection of public health, which in principle is expressly excluded from Community law competence. In this respect the Court appears to enhance Community competence. This idea is seen in the later *Swedish Match* case. Tobacco for oral use was banned in a number of tobacco labelling directives and this ban was included in art.8 of dir.2001/37/EC which repealed and replaced earlier directives. This ban was challenged, and part of the case turned on the adequacy of using art.95 EC as a legal base for the directive. The Court departs from its earlier reasoning in the *Tobacco Advertising* judgment:

". . . where there are obstacles to trade or it is likely that such obstacles will emerge in future because the member States have taken or are about to take divergent measures with respect to a product or a class of products such as to ensure different levels of protection and thereby prevent the product or products concerned from moving freely within the Community, Article 95 EC authorises the Community legislature to intervene by adopting appropriate measures, in compliance with Article 95(3) EC and with the legal principles mentioned in the Treaty or identified in the case-law, in particular the principle of proportionality.

Depending on the circumstances, those appropriate measures may consist in requiring all the member States to authorise the marketing of the product or the products concerned, subjecting such an obligation of authorisation to certain conditions, or even provisionally or definitely prohibiting the marketing of a product or products (see, in the context of Council Directive

[35] Ibid, fn. 32.

92/59/EEC . . . on product safety . . ., Case C-359/92 Germany
v Council [1994] ECR I-3681, paras 4 and 33."[36]

Applying this reasoning to the prohibition of oral tobacco products, the Court recognises that the Member States acknowledged
that there were differences between the laws of the Member States
and that the "heterogeneous development" in the market for tobacco
products constituted an obstacle to trade and the free movement of
goods. But rather than facilitating trade the directive banned a
product. Arguably this is a public health choice to be made by individual Member states, not the Community legislator. This would
seem to be contrary to the reason put forward for the annulment of
the Tobacco Advertising Directive: the failure of the directive to
make any contribution to cross-border trade in advertising services.

The Court applied the reasoning from Swedish Match in *Tobacco
Advertising (No.2)*.[37] Following the annulment of the Tobacco
Advertising Directive a second directive was adopted by the
European Parliament and the Council, dir.2003/33/EC using art.95
EC as the legal base. Germany challenged the use of art.95 EC for
this measure. The Court ruled that art.95 EC allows the use of the
Internal Market legal base to respond to obstacles to trade and the
appropriate measure may require all the Member States to authorise
the marketing of the product or products concerned, subjecting the
obligation or authorisation to conditions, or even provisionally, or
definitively, *prohibiting* the marketing of a product.

There are arguments that the spill-over of competence from
Internal Market integration has led to the incidental expansion of
Community competence into new areas of regulatory activity
(Weatherill, 2004; 2005). This has been labelled "competence creep".

## 4.7 The Role of "Non-Economic" Values in the Integration Process

An important question today is how far the Community is, or should
be, only concerned with economic issues relating to the functioning

---

[36] Case C-210/03 *The Queen on the application of Swedish Match AB and Swedish Match UK Ltd v Secretary of State for Health* [2004] E.C.R. I-11893, paras 33 and 34. See also: Case C-434/02 *Arnold André GmbH & Co kg v Landrat des Kreises Herford* [2004] E.C.R. I-11825.

[37] Case C-380/03 *Germany v European Parliament and Council of the European Union* [2006] E.C.R. I-11573.

of the Internal Market, and how far other values should be a concern for the Community. A number of non-economic values were recognised in the original EEC Treaty, for example, in the derogations to the four freedoms, (expanded in the mandatory requirements of *Cassis de Dijon* and subsequent case law), as well as in art.86(2) EC (which recognises public services ("services of general economic interest")). We see that the Member States are allowed to plead a number of non-economic interests which may be balanced against the imperatives of market integration.

In the formation of legislative proposals the Commission is instructed to aim for a high level of protection for health, safety, environmental protection and consumer protection in its proposals based upon art.95(3) EC. A number of Community objectives must also be mainstreamed through Community policies: the environment, employment and gender equality. Other policies are not mainstreamed but have acquired a legitimacy in Community policies, for example, consumer policy, education and vocational training. Cultural policy is less openly articulated or developed; it is not a mainstreaming activity but art.151(4) EC states that:

"The Community shall take cultural aspects into account in its action under other provisions of this Treaty, in particular in order to respect and promote the diversity of its cultures."

Yet culture is a wide concept and has made an impression in many aspects of Community policy and litigation (Craufurd-Smith, 2004).

More recently it has been accepted that the Community can include (and indeed must include) other values in the integration process. Ideas of citizenship and fundamental, or human rights are present in the Court's case law. Community law, for example, can be held invalid if it fails to give sufficient protection to a fundamental right or infringes a human right.[38]

The Treaty of Lisbon 2007 amends the TEU by providing, for the first time, the values and objectives of the Union (*arts 2 and 3 TEU*).

## 4.8 Derogations from the Harmonisation Measures

The move towards qualified majority voting in Internal Market matters was softened for the Member States in art.95(4) and (5) EC

---

[38] Case C-5/02 *Rinke* [2003] E.C.R. I-12575.

by allowing a Member State to derogate from a harmonisation measure adopted under art.95 EC. But such derogations are carefully controlled and monitored by the Community governance process. Initially art.95(4) EC confined this derogation to measures existing at the time the harmonisation directive was adopted. Where a Member State deemed it necessary to maintain national provisions on grounds of "major needs" referred to in the justifications set out in art.30 EC or relating to the protection of the environment it could notify this request to the Commission. Under the original provisions of art.95(4) EC the Commission had to authorise this derogation before the Member State could continue with the national measure. For example, Sweden applied for a derogation from a harmonisation directive, dir.94/36,[39] under art.95(4) EC to continue with a prohibition against the use of an "E-additive", E124 cochineal red, in foodstuffs. Unfortunately the Commission failed to respond to the request. When litigation occurred in the national courts, the Court ruled that Sweden could not rely upon a national law which was inconsistent with dir.94/36/EC unless it had been specifically authorised to do so by the Commission.[40]

In fact the Member States have made little use of this derogation. Derogations sought related mainly to the use of certain chemicals and additives in foodstuffs. But in one case France was successful in annulling a Commission Decision granting a derogation to Germany from dir.91/173/EC.[41] The case was focused upon procedural issues, with the Court finding that the Commission had not investigated the impact of the derogation properly under art.95(4) EC.

The Treaty of Amsterdam 1997 extended the derogation to national measures adopted *after* the adoption of Community harmonisation measures. Under art.95(5) EC Member States may introduce new provisions based upon new scientific evidence relating only to the protection of the environment or the working environment on grounds of a problem specific to that Member State arising after the adoption of a Community harmonisation measure. The reason for the limited scope of the derogation in art.95(5) EC is given in *Commission v Denmark*.[42] When a measure is adopted under art.95(4) EC the Institutions are aware of the national provisions and choose to override them, or not take them into account, whereas

---

[39] OJ 1994 L237/4.
[40] Case C-319/97 *Criminal Proceeedings Against Kortas* [1999] E.C.R. I-3143.
[41] OJ 1991 L85/34.
[42] Case C-3/00 *Commission v Denmark* [2003] E.C.R. I-2643, para.65.

the adoption of *new* national measures under art.95(5) EC is more likely to jeopardise the attainment of the Internal Market.[43]

The Treaty of Amsterdam 1997 changed the procedural rules relating to the use of arts 95(4) and (5) EC. Under art.95(6) EC the Commission has six months to approve or reject national provisions after verifying whether or not the national measures are a means of arbitrary discrimination or a disguised restriction on trade between the Member States and whether they will jeopardise the attainment of an Internal Market. The six month period can be extended to twelve months in complex cases. But the Commission must respond to the notification within six months of the notification. If it does not, then art.95(6) EC states that the national measures are deemed to be approved. This overturns the ruling in *Kortas*.[44] Where the Commission approves of a Member State's derogation art.95(7) EC states that the Commission may also examine whether there should be a modification of the original harmonising directive, especially where the Member State's derogation provides a higher level of protection than the Community harmonisation measure.[45] Article 95(8) EC provides for special provisions in relation to any problems a Member State may encounter in the public health field which has already been the subject of harmonisation.

Article 95(9) EC introduced an expedited procedure, by way of derogation from arts 226 and 227 EC, to bring a Member State directly before the Court if the Commission, or another Member State, considers that a Member State is using the derogations in an improper manner. Finally, art.95(10) EC states that the harmonising measures shall, in appropriate cases, include a safeguard clause authorising the Member States to take for one (or more) of the non-economic reasons referred to in art.30 EC provisional measures, but these must be subject to a Community control procedure.

## 4.9 Governance and the Treaty of Lisbon 2007

Weatherill (2005) categories the governance approach to the use of Community powers as one based upon ex ante restraint by the political Institutions and ex post review by the Court. This has not

---

[43] Joined Cases T-366/03 and T-235/04 *Land Oberösterreich v Commission* [2005] E.C.R. II-4005.

[44] Case C-319/97 [1999] E.C.R. I-3143.

[45] Case C-3/00 *Commission v Denmark* [2003] E.C.R. I-2643, para.65.

proved to be an effective or acceptable constitutional mechanism to delimit the powers of the EU against the Member States and the constitutional principles governing the EU. As we shall see in the subsequent Chapters the impact of the fundamental free movement and competition provisions is now being felt in a number of areas where the EU does not have legislative competence. Equally the process started in the 1970s, of introducing a wider range of values into EU law alongside the economic aims of integration, was recognised in the Court's case law but not articulated fully in the basic EC Treaty.

The Treaty of Amsterdam 1997 did not address the competence issues of the EU squarely and the issues were not resolved in the Treaty of Nice 2000. The Declaration attached to the Treaty of Nice 2000 instigated a process that continued with the Laeken Declaration in December 2001 and the Convention on the Future of Europe, culminating in the failed Constitutional Treaty of July 18, 2004. The new IGC was set the task to clarify and re-organise the EC Treaty rules governing competence and also to institutionalise new political actors, particularly the national parliaments, and to monitor the exercise of Community powers. The Treaty of Lisbon 2007 sets out in greater detail the competences of the Union *(arts 4 and 5 TEU; arts 2–6 TFEU)*. Now competences fall into three distinct groups: exclusive competence, shared competence and a third group where the Union shall carry out actions to support and co-ordinate the actions of the Member States.

# 5: Four Fundamental Economic Freedoms*

Alongside a number of tasks, art.2 EC gives special prominence to the task of the Community of creating a Common Market and an economic and monetary union by implementing common policies or activities, which are referred to in arts 3 and 4 EC.[1] Article 14 EC *(art.26 TFEU)* provides the constitutional basis for the establishment of an Internal Market through the liberalisation of four basic factors of production: the free movement of goods, workers, services and establishment and capital.

After the Treaty of Lisbon 2007 the Union's objectives are altered in prominence. *Article 3 TEU* elevates the aim of promoting peace, the values and well-being of the Union's people *(art.3(1) TFEU)*, as well as offering its citizens an area of freedom, security and justice without internal frontiers. The latter involves ensuring the freedom of movement in conjunction with appropriate measures with respect

* With thanks to Dr Alina Tryfonidou for insightful and constructive comments on this Chapter.

[1] The Community is charged with promoting a harmonious balanced and sustainable development of economic activities, a high level of employment and of social protection, equality between men and women, sustainable and non inflationary growth, a high degree of competitiveness and convergence of economic performance, a high level of protection and improvement of the quality of the environment, the raising of the standard of living and quality of life, and economic and social cohesion and solidarity among Member States.

to external border controls, asylum, immigration and combating of crime (*art.3(2 TFEU*). *Article 3(3) TFEU* refers to the establishment of an Internal Market. Here we see a different balance between economic objectives and social objectives. The Internal Market shall work for the sustainable development of Europe based upon balanced economic growth and price stability, a highly competitive social market economy, aiming at full employment and social progress, and a high level of protection and improvement of the quality of the environment. The Internal Market shall also promote scientific and technological advance. There is a more explicit reference to the social aims and values of integration: combating social exclusion, discrimination, promoting social justice and protection, equality between men and women, solidarity between generations and protection of the rights of the child. The Union shall promote economic, social and territorial cohesion, and solidarity between Member States, respecting its rich cultural and linguistic diversity, ensuring Europe's cultural heritage is safeguarded and enhanced. In the *Protocol No. 6 On the Internal Market and Competition* it is stated that the Internal Market as set out in *art.3 TFEU* "includes a system ensuring that competition is not distorted." There is academic and political discussion as to how far the amendments down-grade the role of competition in the new Union, and this is discussed in Chapter 6.

The Internal Market is a field where the Union and the Member States shall have shared competence (*art.4 (2)(a) TFEU*. A number of provisions of the TFEU will have general application in the formulation of all policies: a high level of employment, the guarantee of adequate social protection, the fight against social exclusion, a high level of education, training and protection of human health *(art.9 TFEU)*. A new *art.10 TFEU* mainstreams the current art.13 EC non-discrimination areas of sex, racial or ethnic origin, religion, belief, disability, age and sexual orientation. Environmental protection (currently art.6 EC) continues to be mainstreamed in *art.11 TFEU,* alongside consumer protection in *art.11 TFEU* (currently art.153(2) EC). A new clause, *art.13 TFEU* implements the Protocol on the protection and welfare of animals, introduced by the Treaty of Amsterdam 1997.

The four freedoms were the central economic constitutional foundation stone of the Common Market with other policies seen as supplementary to the economic priorities of market building. The Single European Act 1986 created greater possibilities for the development of horizontal or flanking policies to the Internal Market, for example, an environmental policy, a consumer policy, a social policy and a vocational training policy. The creation of an economic and monetary union in the Maastricht Treaty 1991 led to the spill-over of Internal Market policies into a wider range of areas, many intruding into traditional areas of State sovereignty which had not been transferred to the Community. Since the Treaty of Maastricht 1993 the EU has faced opposition, at the grass roots level as well as at the Member State level, to expanding the competence of the Community.

Economic and monetary union created new challenges for the governance of the Internal Market. There was a greater need for common horizontal policies and the Commission was obliged to re-organise its policy-making strategies away from a vertical division of organisation to allow for the horizontal co-ordination of EU policies. This explains why new techniques of economic governance, such as the open method of coordination, have emerged during the 1990s to fulfil the ambitious aims set out in art.2 EC. From the SEA 1986 onwards, Community competence has increased into a number of these areas. The Court's case law has also extended the reach of Community law where national measures constitute a hindrance to the attainment of an Internal Market. The change of pace and governance techniques in the post-Lisbon era has allowed for greater co-ordination of a number of national policies without head-on legal clashes between the Member States and the Community Institutions over competence issues.

The four freedoms are distinct provisions in the EC Treaty and have evolved in different ways and at a different pace. There is now a tendency to use similar techniques in identifying barriers to market integration across the four freedoms as well as some convergence in the interpretation of the permissible derogations which can be raised by the Member States to justify the continuance of barriers to market integration. The convergence of the four freedoms is not without criticism (Snell, 2002; 2004). Are people really like goods? Can doctors be treated like bananas? The free movement of persons in the EU presents a special and complicated task for the Community, especially in the new culture of human rights and Citizenship protection and the aims in the post-9/11 world of creating an area of freedom, security and justice.

Securing an Internal Market has two dimensions: an *external* dimension which sets the economic boundaries, as well as the geo-political boundaries, to the area regulated by the EU and an *internal* dimension which is the aim of the Internal Market to dismantle internal frontiers and create a level playing field in relation to trade and competition within the geo-political area of the EU. It has not been easy to secure either the external or internal dimension to the

EU across the four freedoms, with free movement of persons presenting special difficulties.

## 5.1 The Four Freedoms as Fundamental Rights

The Court refers to the four freedoms as "fundamental" principles and "foundations" of the EC Treaty. The free movement of workers has been referred to as a fundamental right,[2] as has the free movement of goods.[3] New ideas of fundamental rights have emerged as substantive rights in EU legislation and the Court's case law. Such rights may complement and enhance the enforcement of the four fundamental economic freedoms but they may also act as a restraint upon the operation of the freedoms, especially in cases relating to the free movement of persons.[4]

The creation of an Internal Market and the liberalisation of trade are not ends in themselves (Szyszczak, 2000). The tasks and aims of economic integration must be balanced against other rights and values recognised in Community law *and* in the Member States' laws (De Witte, 2006).[5] This balancing act is seen in the scope for derogations from the four economic freedoms, contained in the EC Treaty: art.30, 39(3) and (4) EC, art.45 EC and in art.86(2) EC, which protects public services (known as "services of general economic interest" (SGEIs)) from the full rigour of market competition.

The Court has increased the range of derogations which are available describing such national measures as "mandatory" or "imperative" requirements designed to protect new values which have emerged since the EEC Treaty was adopted in 1957. Such mandatory requirements have involved consumer protection[6]; the protection of the environment[7], the protection of culture[8] improve-

---

[2] Case 152/82 *Forcheri v Belgium* [1983] E.C.R. 2323, para.11.

[3] Case C-228/98 *Dounias v Minister for Economic Affairs* [2000] E.C.R. I-577, para. 64.

[4] Case C-60/00 *Mary Carpenter* [2002] E.C.R. I-6279.

[5] Cf. Case C-341/05 *Laval*, judgment of December 18, 2007 and Case C-438/05 *International Transport Workers' Federation, Finnish Seamen's Union v Viking Line ABP, OÜ Viking Line Eesti*, judgment of December 11, 2007.

[6] Case 120/78 *Rewe Zentrale v Bundesmonopolverwaltung für Branntwein* [1979] E.C.R. 3961("Cassis de Dijon"); Case 178/84 *Commission v Germany* [1987] E.C.R. 1227 (Beer Purity); Case 252/83 *Commission v Germany* [1986] E.C.R. 3755 (Insurance Services).

[7] Case 302/86 *Commission v Denmark* [1988] E.C.R. 4607; Case 2/90 *Commission v Belgium (Walloon Waste)* [1992] E.C.R. I-4431; Case C-379/98 *PreussenElektra AG v Schleswag AG* [2001] E.C.R. I-2099.

[8] Case C-154/89 *Commission v France* [1991] E.C.R. I-659 (Tourist Guides). See Craufurd-Smith, 2004.

ment of working conditions[9] and the protection of pluralism in the media.[10]

The recognition of derogations to the fundamental freedoms has forced the EU to acknowledge that the right to trade is not absolute. This is illustrated in *Schmidberger v Austria*.[11] The Austrian authorities had authorised an environmental demonstration which had closed a motorway for nearly two days forming part of the Bremmer pass linking Germany and Italy, passing through Austria. A road haulage company attempted to claim damages for loss of business, claiming the Austrian authorisation contravened the free movement of goods provision, art.28 EC. The Court found the Austrian measure fell within art.28 EC but the Court and the Advocate General accepted the justification that the Austrian authorities were protecting the fundamental rights of expression and assembly, as guaranteed under arts 10 and 11 ECHR:

"It follows that measures which are in compatible with observance of the human rights thus recognised are not acceptable in the Community . . .

Thus, since both the Community and its member states are required to respect fundamental rights, the protection of those rights is a legitimate interest which, in principle, justifies a restriction of the obligations imposed by Community law, even under a fundamental freedom guaranteed by the Treaty such as the free movement of goods." (paras 73 and 74)

More recently the Court appears to have tipped the balance in favour of upholding the fundamental economic freedoms over fundamental rights. In *Viking*[12] the Court emphasises the primacy of freedom of establishment, imposing stringent criteria upon measures which are taken to protect workers' interests when such measures may interfere with the exercise of the freedom of establishment. In para.43 the Court recognises the right to strike in Community law:

---

[9] Case 155/80 *Oebel* [1981] E.C.R. I 1993; Case C-448/98 *Criminal Proceedings Against Guiot and Climatec SA* [2000] E.C.R. I-10663; Joined Cases C-369 and 376/96 *Criminal Proceedings Against Arblade and Arblade and Fils SARL and Leloup and Sofrage SARL* [1999] E.C.R. I-8453.

[10] Case C-368/95 *Vereinigte Familiapress* [1997] E.C.R. I-3689.

[11] Case C-112/00 [2003] E.C.R. I-5659.

[12] Case C-438/05 *International Transport Workers' Federation, Finnish Seamen's Union v Viking Line ABP, OÜ Viking Line Eesti*, judgment of December 11, 2007.

"In that regard, it must be recalled that the right to take collective action, including the right to strike, is recognised both by various international instruments which the Member States have signed or cooperated in, such as the European Social Charter, signed at Turin on 18 October 1961—to which, moreover, express reference is made in Article 136 EC—and Convention No 87 concerning Freedom of Association and Protection of the Right to Organise, adopted on 9 July 1948 by the International Labour Organisation—and by instruments developed by those Member States at Community level or in the context of the European Union, such as the Community Charter of the Fundamental Social Rights of Workers adopted at the meeting of the European Council held in Strasbourg on 9 December 1989, which is also referred to in Article 136 EC, and the Charter of Fundamental Rights of the European Union proclaimed in Nice on 7 December 2000 (OJ 2000 C 364, p. 1)."

But immediately, in para.44, this right may be subject to restrictions:

"Although the right to take collective action, including the right to strike, must therefore be recognised as a fundamental right which forms an integral part of the general principles of Community law the observance of which the Court ensures, the exercise of that right may none the less be subject to certain restrictions. As is reaffirmed by Article 28 of the Charter of Fundamental Rights of the European Union, those rights are to be protected in accordance with Community law and national law and practices. In addition, as is apparent from paragraph 5 of this judgment, under Finnish law the right to strike may not be relied on, in particular, where the strike is *contra bonos mores* or is prohibited under national law or Community law."

Thus the fundamental freedoms play a central role in European integration: they are seen as political rights and as constitutional rights. The four freedoms are an example of *negative integration* in that Member States are obliged to remove, and not put in place, any measures which will hinder the four freedoms. This is a concrete application of the fidelity or solidarity clause in art.10 EC. But the process of negative integration is also de-regulatory, dismantling Member

States' laws and regulations which are obstacles to the creation of an Internal Market. There is a need for some re-regulation at the Community level to protect legitimate interests such as consumer protection or the protection of the environment.

It is possible for the Member States to use a variety of *positive integration* techniques to secure the Internal Market through the use of the general Internal Market legal bases of art.94 EC and 95 EC, the residual legal base of art.308 EC, as well as specific legal bases pertinent to each individual freedom. Over the years the Community competence has expanded to create flanking policies in areas such as the environment, social policy, a consumer policy. Combined with litigation, using the direct effect of the EC Treaty provisions, as well as the secondary legislation fleshing out the bare bones of the EC Treaty, these processes of market building have deepened the *quality* of market integration.

We have seen that the role of individuals, and civil society generally, was downplayed in the early years of decision-making in the EU. But when we start to analyse *how* the four economic freedoms work, and the way in which they have been *made* to work, in favour of individual rights against the Member States we see the importance of the role of litigation using the concept of direct effect. This has led to ideas that the four fundamental freedoms confer basic rights of *economic citizenship* on natural and legal persons who are able to use these rights in the EU. But litigation has also exposed weaknesses in relying upon the four freedoms as the sole source of citizenship rights in an Internal Market. The major limitation of creating citizenship rights from the Internal Market provisions is that there must be some element of economic cross-border activity in order to trigger the rights. The Court has refused to entertain the idea of what is known as "reverse discrimination". This is where an individual seeks to rely on Community law against his or her own Member State without exercising any of the free movement rights. Thus while the practical, and sometimes inadvertent, spill-over of Community law into other areas outside of the core freedoms created the need for horizontal or flanking policies these policies have also contributed to the development of basic layers of citizenship rights which can be used against the home Member State. As we shall see in later Chapters the litigation has contributed to the development of general principles of Community law, alongside procedural rights and remedies.

## 5.2 Horizontal Direct Effect of the Four Freedoms

The EC Treaty rules relating to the four freedoms are addressed to the Member States. The competition rules of art.81 EC and 82 EC were designed to address the barriers to market integration which could be raised by private actors operating in the market. Today it is recognised that barriers to market integration may be raised by regulatory power and *private power* as much as by the public power held by Member States. Competition law has addressed the abuse of market power by private firms and in the liberalisation process has placed positive duties upon the actors in the liberalised sectors (Szyszczak: 2007). The effects of liberalisation and privatisation, the so-called "rolling back the frontiers of the State", which have been felt in Europe from the 1980s, has placed a number of duties upon private actors to provide goods and services previously provided by the State. A growing interest in placing public duties on private power has led the ECJ to explore, albeit tentatively, the horizontal direct effect of the fundamental freedoms[13] since the rules of the Internal Market are far-reaching in terms of negative and positive duties to promote market integration.

In a series of cases[14] the Court ruled that arts 28 and 29 EC were addressed to the Member States and not private persons. But in *Dansk Supermarked*[15] the Court gave an indication that private persons should be bound directly by art.28 EC. This is seen as an obiter dictum, and in a later case the Court has expressly denied the horizontal direct effect of art.28 EC.[16] The Court has applied art.28 EC to the delegation of State powers to private bodies. To hold otherwise would make it easy for a Member State to evade the application of art.28 EC.[17] Similarly a Member State is responsible in ensuring and maintaining the free movement principles where the actions of non-State actors (for example angry farmers[18] and environmental protestors)[19] may impede the free movement provisions (Lohse, 2007).

---

[13] Baquero Cruz, 2002; Van den Bogaert, 2002.
[14] Cases 177 and 178 *van de Haar Vlaamse* [1984] E.C.R. 1787; Case 311/85 *Vlaamse Reisbureaus* [1987] E.C.R. 3801; Case 65/86 *Bayer v Süllhofer* [1988] E.C.R. 5249.
[15] Case 58/80 *Dansk Supermarked* [1981] E.C.R. 181, para.17.
[16] Case C-159/00 *Sapod Audic* [2002] E.C.R. I-5031, para.74.
[17] Joined Cases C-266 and 267/87 *Royal Pharmaceutical Society* [1989] E.C.R. 1295; Case C-325/00 *Commission v Germany* [2002] E.C.R. I-9977.
[18] Case C-265/95 *Commission v France* [1997] E.C.R. I-6959.
[19] Case C-112/00 *Schmidberger v Austria* [2003] E.C.R. I-5659.

In contrast to the case law under art.28 EC, the Court has explored the use of the horizontal direct effect in the area of free movement of workers and applied art.39 EC to a horizontal situation in *Bosman*[20] and *Angonese*.[21] The situation in *Bosman* could be characterised as "semi-horizontal" in that the football regulatory body was, indeed, not part of the State, however, it regulated collectively an economic activity and thus it had sufficient power to impede the free movement of goods. *Angonese* took the case-law on horizontal direct effect one step further by establishing that art.39 EC is horizontally directly effective, at least when there is (direct or indirect) discrimination on the grounds of nationality. Here this was a situation where a private bank required of job applicants a certificate of bilingualism. The Court drew an analogy with the horizontal direct effect of the equal pay principle in art.141 EC. The Court ruled that art.39 EC should apply to private parties as well as public authorities, otherwise there would be inequality in the application of the free movement principle. The distinction between *Angonese* and *Bosman* is important, because in the context of the other free movement of persons provisions, the Court has adopted the *Bosman* principle but has not (at least not yet) followed *Angonese*.

In two cases concerning the right of trade unions to take collective action *Laval*[22] and *Viking*[23] the Court recognised that such action could amount to a restriction on the right to provide services and the freedom of establishment. On the question of horizontal direct effect the Court refers to established case law:

". . . according to settled case-law, Articles 39 EC, 43 EC and 49 EC do not apply only to the actions of public authorities but extend also to rules of any other nature aimed at regulating in a collective manner gainful employment, self-employment and the provision of services (see Case 36/74 *Walrave and Koch* [1974] ECR 1405, paragraph 17; Case 13/76 *Donà* [1976] ECR 1333, paragraph 17; *Bosman*, paragraph 82; Joined Cases C-51/96 and C-191/97 *Deliège* [2000] ECR I-2549, paragraph 47; Case C-281/98 *Angonese* [2000] ECR I-4139,

---

[20] Case C-415/93 *Union Royale Belge de Societé de Football Association v Bosman* [1995] E.C.R. I-4921.

[21] Case C-281/98 *Roman Angonese v Cassa di Risparmio di Bolzano* [2000] E.C.R. I-4139.

[22] Case C-341/05 *Laval*, judgment of December 18, 2007.

[23] Case C-438/05 *International Transport Workers' Federation, Finnish Seamen's Union v Viking Line ABP, OÜ Viking Line Eesti*, judgment of December 11, 2007.

paragraph 31; and Case C-309/99 *Wouters and Others* [2002] ECR I-1577, paragraph 120)."[24]

## 5.3 The Four Fundamental Economic Freedoms

*The Free Movement of Goods*

*(i) The Customs Union*

The customs union forms the economic basis of the integration project in relation to goods. The legal nature of the customs union is set out in art.23 EC *(art.28 TFEU)*. A customs union is differenti- ated from other forms of economic integration in that it creates an external frontier for goods entering the EU based upon a Common Customs Tariff (CTT) allowing foreign goods to enjoy rights to free movement within the EU once they have entered the EU legally. This is called the right of free circulation and also allows for the free movement of goods originating *within* the Member States of the EU.

The existence of a CTT entails the development of a common commercial policy for the EU. Otherwise trade policy between the EU and the rest of the world may not be beneficial for certain Member States and an uneven trade policy conducted on a unilateral basis between a Member State and third countries may not be of benefit to the EU as a whole.

The evolution of a Common Commercial Policy for the EU is seen as another layer of the economic constitution of the EU, but it has been slower in developing (Cremona, 1990). Article 133(1) EC gives the Community power for

"the conclusion of tariff and trade agreements, the achieve- ment of uniformity in measures of liberalisation, export policy and measures to protect trade such as those to be taken in the event of dumping or subsidies."

Proposals are made by the Commission and can be adopted by the Council by qualified majority vote (art.133 (2) and (4) EC). Under these powers measures have been taken to adopt a

---

[24] Case C-438/05 *International Transport Workers' Federation, Finnish Seamen's Union v Viking Line ABP, OÜ Viking Line Eesti*, judgment of December 11, 2007, para.33.

Common Customs Code[25] as well as protective measures to protect the EU against what are seen as unfair trade practices by third country importers such as dumping[26] and subsidies by third country governments.[27]

The Court defined the concept of "goods" for the purposes of Community law as products which can be valued in money and which are capable, as such, of forming the subject of commercial transactions.[28]

## *The Common Commercial Policy*

Article 25 EC (*art.30 TFEU*) prohibits customs duties (tariffs) and charges having an equivalent effect on goods crossing an internal frontier of the EU; customs duties are allowed at the EU's external frontier but once goods have passed through this external frontier they are deemed to be in free circulation. Article 25 EC applies to all fiscal measures, however small, which make imported products more expensive, and therefore less competitive, than home produced products. Statistical levies, charges for health inspections, taxes on the export of art works have all been found to be covered by art.25 EC. In *Van Gend en Loos*[29] the ECJ ruled that art.25 EC was directly effective against a Member State (vertical direct effect).

Article 25 EC does not provide for any justifications, exemptions or derogations from its provisions but in *Commission v Germany*[30] the Court outlined three situations where a fiscal charge would fall *outside* of the scope of art.25 EC. First, where the charge relates to an internal system of dues applied systematically and in accordance with the same criteria to domestic products and imported products; second, where the charge constitutes payment for a service in fact rendered to an economic operator of a sum in proportion to the service; finally where the charge attaches to inspections carried out to fulfil obligations imposed by Community law.

The first situation refers to another tool within the EC Treaty which addresses common internal policies of the EU aimed at combating measures which may act as trade barriers and result in unfair competition between domestic products and imported

---

[25] Council reg.2913/92, OJ 1992 L302/1.
[26] Council reg.384/96, OJ 1996 L56/1.
[27] Council reg.2026/97, OJ 1997 L288/1.
[28] Case 7/68 *Commission v Italy (Art Treasures)* [1968] E.C.R. 423.
[29] Case 26/62 [1963] E.C.R. 1.
[30] Case 18/87 [1988] E.C.R. 5427.

products, art.90 EC (*art.110 TFEU*).[31] Article 90 EC is directly effective and addresses taxation. Although various inroads into the area of domestic taxation have been made through litigation using the free movement provisions, taxation continues to be an area where Member States have the autonomy to determine their own taxation schemes. Article 93 EC provides the means to harmonise legislation concerning turn-over taxes, excise duties and other forms of indirect taxation to the extent that such harmonisation is necessary to ensure the establishment and functioning of the Internal Market. Article 90 EC allows the Member States to adopt taxation systems which are based upon objective criteria, unrelated to the origin of goods. But art.90 EC captures both direct discrimination[32] and indirect discrimination.[33]

The application of art.90 EC is not always easy. Article 25 EC and art.90 EC are mutually exclusive.[34] Goods which are subject to different taxation levels must be shown to be *similar* to fall within art.90(1) EC; or to be *in competition* with each other to fall within art.90(2) EC. The Court abandoned its initial formal approach, asking if the goods fell within the same fiscal, customs or statistical classification[35] and now uses an approach which looks at the factual comparison of the goods combined with an economic analysis.[36]

Many of the cases concern the different taxation of alcoholic beverages. Is beer similar to wine or whisky? Is beer in competition with other alcoholic beverages? These are crucial questions, not only to trigger the use of art.90 EC, but also in relation to remedies. If goods are *similar*, then any discrimination must be eliminated by the equalisation of taxes imposed on domestic and imported products. Where goods are *in competition* the State must remove the protective aspects of the taxation system, that is, the tax may continue to be different for both products provided that it reflects objective differences between the two goods.[37]Additionally, to ensure the effectiveness of Community law, Member States must allow for the repayment of any charges which are contrary to art.90 EC, subject to a limitation where there would be unjust enrichment.[38] A damages

---

[31] Case 193/85 *Co-frutta* [1987] E.C.R. 2085.
[32] Case 57/65 *Lütticke v Hauptzollamt Saarlouis* [1966] E.C.R. 205; Case C-313/05 *Brzeciński v Dyrekto Izby Celnej w Warszawie* [2007] E.C.R. I-513.
[33] Case 112/84 *Humblot* [1985] E.C.R. 1367.
[34] Case C-313/05 *Brzeciński v Dyrekto Izby Celnej w Warszawie* [2007] E.C.R. I-513.
[35] Case 45/75 *REWE v HZA Landau* [1976] E.C.R. 181.
[36] Case 106/84 *Commission v Denmark* [1986] E.C.R. 833.
[37] Case 170/78 *Commission v United Kingdom* [1983] E.C.R. 2265.
[38] Case 68/79 *Hans Just I/S* [1980] E.C.R. 501.

claim is available using national procedural rules, subject to the proviso that the claims based upon Community law rights must be not less favourable than those governing similar national law actions and do not make the exercise of Community law rights virtually impossible or excessively difficult.

## Measures Having an Equivalent Effect to a Quantitative Restriction

The free movement of goods also addresses non-fiscal barriers to trade. These are measures which concern both imports and exports such as quotas, export/import bans or may cover measures which concern the marketing, presentation or content of goods. These are called measures having an equivalent effect to a quantitative restriction. A Member State may have good justifications for controlling the import and export of goods through non-fiscal measures based upon public policy, consumer, or environmental concerns. Articles 28 EC (*art.34 TFEU*) (imports), art.29 (*art.35 TFEU*) (exports) and art.30 EC *(art.36 TFEU)* (justifications) address the permissible scope of this balance between a Member State's legitimate interests to control the movement of goods in and out of its territory and the liberalisation of the flow of goods in the EU.

In 1983 the Community attempted to trouble shoot any disruption to trade between the Member States by adopting a directive[39] which required the Member States to notify in advance to the Commission any new technical standards.[40] The Commission would then consult with other Member States as to whether the proposed new standards would produce obstacles to trade. The Court gave this clearance system added weight in *CIA*[41] when it ruled that a Member State could not apply technical standards to individuals in the home state where such standards had not been notified under the directive. Non-notification was a substantial procedural defect rendering such technical regulations inapplicable.[42]

The Court moved away from looking only at measures which may be *discriminatory* against foreign imports, to adopting a broader test, set out in *Dassonville*[43]:

---

[39] Dir.83/189/EEC, now repealed by dir.98/34/EC, OJ 1998 L204/37.
[40] Case C-65/05 *Commission v Greece (Computer Games)* [2006] E.C.R. I-10341.
[41] Case C-194/94 [1996] E.C.R. I-2201.
[42] Case C-443/98 *Unilever* [2000] E.C.R. I-7535, para.45.
[43] Case 8/74 *Procureur du Roi v Dassonville* [1974] E.C.R. 837, para.5.

"All trading rules enacted by Member States which are capable of hindering, directly or indirectly, actually or potentially, intra-Community trade are to be considered as measures having effect equivalent to quantitative restrictions."

This cast the net of art.28 EC wide (Gormley, 2006; Maduro, 1997) leading to extensive litigation with traders using Community law to challenge national regulatory rules.[44] In *Cassis de Dijon*[45] the Court took the *Dassonville* test a step further by identifying *indistinctly applicable* rules which may also be caught by art.28 EC.[46] An indistinctly applicable rule is a measure which applies to domestic and imported goods but in fact imposes a greater burden on imported goods. This is because an importer must comply with the home state rules on production and marketing as well as the rules of the importing State. Where these rules are different this creates a double burden, often imposing extra costs upon the importer to adapt the products to the requirements of the importing State. The fact that an exporter may now have to conform to 27 Member States' requirements underlines the need for harmonisation of essential laws and standards, but also reinforces the reason why the Court in *Cassis* introduced the idea of home state control and mutual recognition. In *Cassis de Dijon* the Court ruled that:

". . . in the absence of common rules it is for the Member States to regulate all matters relating to the production and marketing of alcohol and alcoholic beverages in their own territory."

But in relation to *indistinctly applicable* rules the Court saw the need to allow the Member States a wider margin of discretion in the justifications they might raise in order to take the potential restriction of trade outside of the application of art.28 EC: a rule of reason. The Court in *Cassis* accepted that:

"Obstacles to movement in the Community resulting from disparities between the national laws relating to the marketing

---

[44] Gormley, 2008, describes the Commission's division specialising in art.28–30 EC infringements ". . . was in the late 1980s becoming ever more like a free legal aid centre for traders within the Community."

[45] Case 120/78 *Rewe Zentrale v Bundesmonopolverwaltung für Branntwein* [1979] E.C.R. 649.

[46] Joined Cases C-158/04 and C-159/04 *Alfa Vita Vassilopoulos AE* [2006] E.C.R. I-8135.

of the products in question must be accepted in so far as those provisions may be recognised as being necessary in order to satisfy mandatory requirements relating to the effectiveness of fiscal supervision, the protection of public health, the fairness of commercial transactions and the defence of the consumer."

Unlike the derogations contained in art.30 EC, discussed below, the list of mandatory requirements is not exhaustive and has been added to by the Court in relation to, inter alia, protection of the environment, working conditions, protection of national and regional socio-cultural objectives, financial equilibrium of a social security system, the protection of fundamental rights and freedom of the press. The Court has also applied the proportionality principle. As we saw in the previous chapter, the Commission used *Cassis*, and the principle of mutual recognition, to form the basis of a new regulatory approach to kick start the integration project in the 1980s.[47]

In many cases the source of the barriers to trade within the Internal Market will be "product requirements". In *Rau*[48] a Belgian requirement that margarine was to be sold in cubes (in order to avoid confusion with butter) was found to be an indistinctly applicable measure having an equivalent effect to a customs duty because imported margarine would need to be repackaged, adding to costs, in order to be sold in Belgium.[49] But the Court was also asked to rule on the compatibility of Member States' rules regulating the "marketing" of products. For example, restrictions on advertising, the way goods are produced and sold. In the "*Buy Irish*" case[50] the ECJ held that the national measures need not be legally binding.

The wide scope of this test allowed for a period of opportunistic litigation testing how far art.28 EC could become an economic due process clause, allowing for challenges on *all* domestic measures which impinged upon commercial freedom (Maduro, 1997). There was, for example, no de minimis test built into the application of art.28 EC and therefore virtually any form of State regulatory activity, or even policy, could be caught by art.28 EC. For some

---

[47] EC Commission, *Communication from the Commission Regarding the Cassis de Dijon judgment*, OJ 1980 C 256/2; White Paper, *Completing the Single Market*, COM (85) 310.

[48] Case 261/81 *Rau* [1982] E.C.R. 3961. See generally, Ellis, 1999.

[49] Other examples include: Case 407/85 *Drei Glocken GmbH v USL Cenro-Sud and Provincia Autonoma di Bolzano* [1988] E.C.R. 4233; Case 286/86 *Ministère Public v Deserbais* [1988] E.C.R. 4907; Case 182/84 *Criminal Proceedings against Miro BV* [1985] E.C.R. 3731.

[50] Case 249/81 *Commission v Ireland* [1982] E.C.R. 4005.

commentators this was seen as an abuse of the free movement provisions (Steiner, 1992). It allowed for Community law to be used to challenge policies made by democratic elected governments governing their own territory (Szyszczak, 2000). For example, in the UK challenges made by traders (usually large DIY stores) challenging the legislation which prevented shops from trading on a Sunday (Rawlings, 1993). Not all commentators are critical of this litigation strategy. Weatherill (2002) argues that it is a useful modernising device and allows for challenges to protectionist national rules.

The extension of art.28 EC to the marketing rules of a Member State appeared to take the scope of art.28 EC too far into the autonomy of the Member States, especially in matters which would not be legitimately harmonised under art.95 EC (Davies, 2005) but also undermined the principles of home state control established in *Cassis de Dijon*. The Court of Justice was deluged with preliminary references from the national courts using art.234 EC to question and challenge regulatory aspects of national law. This in turn created an environment where the search was on to create limits to the scope of art.28 EC (White, 1989).

The Court re-appraised its post-*Cassis* case law in *Keck and Mithouard*.[51] Two traders sold goods at a loss, contrary to French law. In their defence they pleaded art.28 EC making the tenuous claim that the French law restricted the volume of sales of imported goods. The Court continued with the *Cassis* test in relation to "product requirements", but in relation to "selling arrangements" the Court stated that such arrangements would be caught by art.28 EC only where there was discrimination, *in law and in fact*, against the foreign products. Thus Member State regulations which apply to the conditions under which a good is produced, for example, employment and social law, town planning, criminal law, environmental legislation are considered to be too incidental to the effect on inter-state trade and are not caught by art.28 EC unless discrimination can be shown. Wilsher (2008) argues that the Court deliberately avoided a discrimination approach in the *Cassis/Dassonville* formula, pointing to the complexity, but also the limitations of using the concept under the GATT regime. Wilsher finds that in practice the use of a discrimination model has proved to be incoherent in analysing non-product rules and this has led to uncertainty when national courts have been asked to apply *Keck*.

---

[51] Joined Cases C-267 and 268/91 [1993] E.C.R. I-6097.

Commentators criticised the lack of reasoning in *Keck*, and saw the formal differentiation between product requirements and selling arrangements as artificial.[52] Advocate General Jacobs pointed out in his Opinion in *Leclerc*[53] that a total ban on advertising a certain kind of product would be a marketing rule and therefore using only a discrimination test would be inappropriate. More recently, A.G. Fennelly[54] and Oliver and Roth (2004) have argued that *Keck* does offer an appropriate mechanism for the operation of the four freedoms in an Internal Market. It is argued that *Keck* reflects the different effects of product-related and selling rules. The former affect *access* to a market, whereas marketing rules do not impede access to the market but Member States may still discriminate against foreign produced goods. Oliver and Roth acknowledge that there is still little clarity as to when, and how, market access is impeded, and the Court seems to continue addressing the application of art.28 EC on a case by case basis. In two cases decided in 2004 the Court looked at the German system of coping with environmental problems created by drinks packaging. Producers and distributors of drinks in non-re-usuable packaging are subject to charge a deposit and take packaging, but these provisions can be complied with by participating in a global collection scheme. But this option is withdrawn if for two consecutive years the percentage of drinks marketed in reusable packing in Germany falls below a certain threshold. An infringement action was brought against Germany and two Austrian exporters of soft drinks to Germany challenged the rules in the German courts, as being contrary to art.28 EC. In a preliminary ruling, *Radlberger Getranke and S. Spitz*,[55] the Court found this was an indistinctly applicable rule and that it incurred costs for all producers. But producers established outside of Germany use considerably more non-reusuable packaging than German producers. Therefore the German rules hinder the marketing of drinks from other Member States. The Court accepted the German justification for the rules: the protection of the environment. But found that this must satisfy the principle of proportionality. This would be satisfied only if there is a reasonable transitional period which ensures that every producer and distributor can actually participate in the system. This was a matter for the national

---

[52] Reich, 1994; Enchelmaier, 2003, Tryfonidou (2007a).
[53] Case C-412/93 [1995] E.C.R. I-182.
[54] Case C-190/98 *Volker Graf* [2000] E.C.R. I-495, paras 18–19.
[55] Case C-309/02 [2004] E.C.R. I-11763.

court to assess. In the infringement action, *Commission v Germany*[56] in assessing the rule that mineral water must be bottled at source the Court held that the German legislation did not satisfy the principle of proportionality because the transitional period was only six months which was not long enough to allow foreign producers to adapt their procedures.[57]

The Court is willing to apply art.28 EC when a distortive effect on competition can be shown, and will also look at statistical evidence.[58]

The Court has not applied the *Dassonville* test to the *export* of goods, a situation which is covered by art.29 EC. Instead the Court applies a discrimination test.[59]

In *Jersey Potatoes*[60] the Court found a law prohibiting producers in Jersey from exporting their potatoes to the UK unless a number of regulatory conditions were met was likely to interfere with the pattern of trade between Jersey and the UK and gave an advantage to production for the domestic market. In *Jersey Potatoes,* the movement of goods between Jersey and the UK was considered to be movement within one and the same Member State and thus, if there was no other cross-border element, the situation would qualify as purely internal to the UK (see paras 42–54). However, the Court found that the situation was not purely internal to a Member State, because the fact that all Jersey Potatoes were sent to the UK meant that it was "certainly conceivable" that *some* of those potatoes would be further exported to other Member States and, thus, there would be a *potential* effect on the exportation of goods from Jersey to *other Member States* via the UK (see paras 65–66 of the Judgment for arts 23–25 EC and paras 78–81 for art.29 EC).

[56] Case C-463/01 [2004] E.C.R. I-11705.

[57] The debate on the scope of the regulatory autonomy of the Member States after *Keck* continues within the Court. See, for example: Joined Cases C-158/04 and C-159/04 *Alfa Vita Vassilopoulos AE* [2006] E.C.R. I-8135; C-142/05 *Mikkelsson v Roos* nyr, (Opinion of A.G. Kokot of December 14, 2006); C-110/05 *Commission v Italy* [2006] nyr,(Opinion of A.G. Lèger of October 5, 2006).

[58] Cases C-34-36/95 *De Agostini* [1997] E.C.R. I-3843; Case C-405/98 *Konsumentombudsmannen (KO) and Gourmet International Products AB (GIP)* [2001] E.C.R. I-1795; Case C-416/00 *Morellato* [2003] E.C.R. I-9343. Cf. Case C-20/03 *Burmanjer et al* [2005] E.C.R. I-4133 where the Court held that it did not have sufficient information to reach a decision; Case C-444/04 *A-Punkt Schmuckhandels GmbH v Schmidt* [2006] E.C.R. I-3617 where the Court was unable to decide whether the prohibition on marketing in private homes would affect the sale of imported products more than domestic products. See Kurzer, 2001; Craufurd-Smith, 2004.

[59] Case 15/79 *Groenveld* [1979] E.C.R. 3409; Case 155/80 *Oebel* [1981] E.C.R. 1993.

[60] Case C-293/02 *Jersey Produce Marketing Association Ltd v States of Jersey* [2005] E.C.R. I-9543.

## Reverse Discrimination

One limitation of the rules on the Internal Market is that they do not cover examples of what is known as "reverse discrimination" (Shuibhne, 2002). In the previous Chapter we saw that art.95 EC may only be used as a legal base for Internal Market measures where there is a sufficient inter-state element.[61] Reverse discrimination is the situation where the national measures discriminate against domestic goods. The immunity of reverse discrimination from the reach of the Internal Market rules reflects a level of national autonomy reinforced by the *Cassis* doctrine of home state control. In *Mathot*[62] a Belgian law requiring butter produced in Belgium to conform to certain packaging requirements, without similar requirements imposed upon imported butter, was held not to infringe art.28 EC. The Court explained in paras 7–8 of *Mathot*, that reverse discrimination falls outside of the scope of art.28 EC because it does not impede the importation of goods from other Member States. The *Cassis* principle and the principle of reverse discrimination allows for competition between products to continue and allows the Member States to give a competitive edge to domestic products by insisting on different, and higher standards, for domestically produced products.

In a discrete group of cases the Court has applied the free movement of goods provisions to situations which are wholly internal to a Member State where goods move from geographically distinct territory to another part of a Member State's territory[63] and in *Pistre* the Court applied art.28 EC to a situation which was wholly internal to France.[64] In subsequent cases the Court has applied art.28 EC in cases where there was no inter-state element to the free movement of goods.[65] This corresponds with tentative developments

---

[61] Case C-376/98 *Germany v Commission (Tobacco Advertising)* [2001] E.C.R. I-8419. But cf. C-465/00 *Österreichischer Rundfunk* [2003] E.C.R. I-4989, paras 41–42; C-101/01 *Lindqvist* [2003] E.C.R. I-12971 and C-380/03 *Germany v Parliament and Council (Tobacco Advertising II)* [2006] E.C.R. I-11573. There the Court seems to have accepted that legislation drafted under art.95 EC can, also, be applied to purely internal situations: there is no need for an inter-state element in all instances.

[62] Case 98/86 *Criminal Proceedings against Mathot* [1987] E.C.R. 809.

[63] Case C-363/93 *Lancry* [1994] E.C.R. I-3957; Cases C-485-6/93 *Simitzi v Kos* [1995] E.C.R. I-2665; Case C-72/03 *Carbonati Apuani Srl v Comune di Carara* [2004] E.C.R. I-8027.

[64] Case C-321/94 *Pistre* [1997] E.C.R. I-2343.

[65] Case C-448/98 *Guimont* [2000] E.C.R. I-10663, para.23; Case C-293/02 *Jersey Produce Marketing Organisation Ltd v States of Jersey and Jersey Potato Export Marketing Board* [2005] E.C.R. I-9543.

in other areas of free movement, for example, persons,[66] services,[67] capital.[68]

## Justifications and Derogations from the Free Movement Rules

Article 30 EC provides a set of justifications for the Member States to derogate from the principle of free movement of goods. This is an exhaustive list, drawn up, and un-amended since 1957. The list is based upon classic public policy concerns: public morality, public policy, public security, protection of health and life of humans, animals, plants, the protection of national treasures possessing artistic, historic or archaeological value or the protection of industrial and commercial property.

The Member States' scope to use the derogations is circumscribed by the fact that the derogations can only be invoked in the absence of Community measures in the field.[69] Member States' discretion is also curtailed by the application of the principle of proportionality and by the fact that derogations from a fundamental Treaty principle should be interpreted strictly. The Court has ruled also that the derogations cannot be used to serve economic objectives,[70] although in some of the more recent cases relating to the organisation of health care schemes in relation to the free movement of services the Court appears to re-work economic justifications into acceptable heads of justification.[71]

In recent years the Court has not always adhered to the strict distinction between distinctly applicable measures which can be justified by reference to art.30 EC and indistinctly applicable measures which may be justified by reference to the *Cassis* mandatory requirements principle.[72] But in other cases the Court adheres to the

---

[66] Case C-281/98 *Roman Angonese v Cassa di Risparmio di Bolzano* [2000] E.C.R. I-4139. See the Opinion of A.G. Sharpston in Case C-212/06 *Government of the French Community and Walloon Government v Flemish Government* June 28, 2007.

[67] Case C-6/01 *Anomar v Portugal* [2003] E.C.R. I-8621; Case C-458/03 *Parking Brixen* [2005] E.C.R. I-8585.

[68] Joined Cases C-515 and 527-540/99 *Reisch v Salzburg* [2002] E.C.R. I-2157; Case C-300/01 *Salzmann* [2003] E.C.R. I-4899.

[69] Case C-1/96 *R v MAFF Ex p. Compassion in World Farming* [1988] E.C.R. I-1251.

[70] Case 7/61 *Commission v Italy* [1961] E.C.R. 317.

[71] Case C-385/99 *Müller-Fauré VG v Onderlinge and van Riet v Onderlinge* [2003] E.C.R. I-4509.

[72] Cases C-34-36/95 *Konsumentombudsmannen v De Agostini* [1997] E.C.R. I-3843; Case C-120/95 *Decker v Caisse de maladie des employés privés* [1998] E.C.R. I-1831; Case C-379/98 *Preussen Elektra AG v Schleswag AG* [2001] E.C.R. 2099; Case

formal distinctions.[73] In the case law of the other fundamental freedoms the Court has started to blur the distinction between distinctly applicable and indistinctly applicable rules, speaking of hindrances to trade or market integration. The time may come whereby the distinctions in terms of the justifications are abandoned and we see the emergence of a generic "public interest" justification across the case law of all four freedoms (Szyszczak, 2002).

Derogations are often seen as "special pleading", protecting national interests of the Member States. There are arguments to suggest that the Community has an interest in recognising a range of public interest, non-market values both in the adoption of harmonising measures and in the justifications in art.30 EC and the Court's case law under *Cassis*. To recognise a wider range of Community values other than purely economic concerns precludes the use of the special pleading derogations by the individual Member States and creates a consensus on Community values (Gerstenberg, 2002).

A procedure for the exchange of national measures derogating from the principle of free movement of goods has also been established in Decision 3052/95.[74] In response to a number of protests against foreign goods where farmers blocked roads and ports in France the Member States introduced reg.2679/98 and a resolution on the free movement of goods.[75] Where there is an obstacle or a potential obstacle to the free movement of goods the Member State concerned must inform the Commission of the obstacle and explain what it is going to do to remove the obstacle to free trade. The Commission may request the Member State to take measures to remove obstacles to the free movement of goods.

## 5.4 The Free Movement of Persons

*Citizenship of the Union*

The nature of free movement of persons law has changed and expanded since 1957, largely due to the wide interpretation of EC Treaty provisions by the Court and, after the Treaty of Maastricht 1991, the introduction of the Citizenship provisions, in arts 17–22

---

C-472/99 *Clean Car Autoservice v Stadt Wien and Republik Österreich* [2001] E.C.R. I-9687. Barnard, 2001.

[73] Case C-224/97 *Ciola Vorarlberg* [1999] E.C.R. I-2517.

[74] OJ 1995 L 321/1.

[75] OJ 1998 L 337/8. See Case C-265/95 *Commission v France* [1997] E.C.R. I-6959.

EC (*arts 20 and 25 TFEU*). Cases involving the interpretation of these provisions confer rights on non-economically active citizens.[76]

The focus of the free movement of persons revolves around the dual imperatives of the economic character of this right and the requirement of nationality of a Member State.[77] Free movement centred essentially on the fundamental principle of non-discrimination based on nationality (art.12 EC, *art.18 TFEU*). The Court has moved the concept of free movement along the lines of the free movement of goods by looking at non-discriminatory measures which may be a barrier or disincentive to free movement.[78] Like the free movement of goods, the free movement of persons is subject to exceptions, which tend to be vigorously defended by Member States. Similar issues of reverse discrimination arise, alongside the issue of whether the free movement provisions may have horizontal effect against private parties.

The free movement of persons is thus a complex and an extensive economic right, a social right, a fundamental human right and a citizenship right in Community law. This multidimensional range of rights has grown from a fragmented legal base in the EC Treaty and secondary legislation as well as the case law of the European Court. The Court has stated that common principles should apply across the rights to free movement of persons[79] but the various rights have evolved at a different pace. Attempts were made to de-couple rights to free movement from the necessity to exercise a cross-border *economic* activity in a set of Residence directives adopted in the early 1990s.[80] A right of residence in another Member State could be claimed provided that the person was financially self-sufficient. Today the EU is focusing upon consolidating these rights, with the Court building the right of Citizenship as the fundamental legal basis for free movement rights:

---

[76] Case C-60/00 *Carpenter* [2002] E.C.R. I-6279; Case C-200/02 *Chen* [2004] E.C.R. I-9925, and Case C-209/03 *Bidar* [2005] E.C.R. I-2119.

[77] See Case C-369/90 *Michelletti* [1992] E.C.R. I-4239 and Case C-192/99 *R v Secretary of State for the Home Department Ex p. Manjit Kaur* [2001] E.C.R. I-1237).

[78] Case C-415/93 *URBSFA v Bosman* [1995] E.C.R. 4921; Case 384/93 *Alpine Investments* [1995] E.C.R. I-1141; Case C-55/94 *Gebhard* [1995] E.C.R. I-4165.

[79] Case C-363/89 *Roux v Belgium* [1991] E.C.R. I-273.

[80] Council dir.90/364 (General Right of Residence), OJ 1990 L 180/26; Council dir.90/365 (Residence for ex-employees and the self-employed) OJ 1990 L 180/28; Council dir.93/96 (Right of Residence for Students), OJ 1993 L 317/59.

"Union citizenship is destined to be the fundamental status of nationals of the Member States, enabling those who find themselves in the same situation to enjoy the same treatment in law irrespective of their nationality, subject to the exeptions as are expressly provided for."[81]

The original EC Treaty had ideas of "citizenship" scattered across it, based upon the non-discrimination on grounds of nationality principle in art.12 EC and developed by the Advocates General and ECJ.[82] The Treaty of Maastricht 1991 introduced a limited set of ad hoc Citizenship rights. The initial reaction to the paucity of the rights attached to Union citizenship led many commentators to see the concept as an embarrassment. After a tentative start, the right to free movement, found in art.18 EC (*art.21 TFEU*) combined with the non-discrimination principle in art.12 EC has provided the basis for the new approach to Citizenship.[83] The Citizenship concept, linked with fundamental human rights concepts, is extending the right to free movement to areas previously thought to be outside of the scope of Community law.[84]

Article 18 EC is a weak legal basis for Citizenship to become the "fundamental status" of nationals of one of the Member States of the EU. Citizenship is only granted to nationals of one of the Member States. Yet, with the development of a range of flanking policies, it is now possible for third country nationals, legally resident[85] in the EU, to rely upon a set of citizenship based rights, such as the right to equality of treatment, consumer rights, employment rights. Article 18 EC does not outline what other migration and non-discrimination rights might be available for family members who are

---

[81] Case C-184/99 *Gryzelczyk* [2001] E.C.R. I-6193; Case C-224/98 *D'Hoop* [2002] E.C.R. I-6191; Joined Cases C413/99 *Baumbast and R v Secretary of State for the Home Department* [2002] E.C.R. I-7091; Case C-200/02 *Chen* [2004] E.C.R. I-; Case C-224/02 *Pusa* [2004] E.C.R. I-5763. Case C-1/05 *Jia* [2007] E.C.R. I-1.

[82] See for example, A.G. Jacobs' Opinion in Case C-168/91 *Konstantinidis* [1993] E.C.R. I-1191.

[83] Joined Cases C413/99 *Baumbast and R v Secretary of State for the Home Department* [2002] E.C.R. I-7091; Case C-200/02 *Chen* [2004] E.C.R. I-9925. Cf. Case C-86/96 *Martínez Sala* [1998] E.C.R. I-2691 where the Court uses art.17 EC combined with art.12 EC and avoids the issue of looking at the status of the economic activity of the migrant.

[84] Case C-200/02 *Chen* [ 2004] E.C.R. I-9925; Case C-456/02 *Trojani* [2004] E.C.R. I-7573; Case C-209/03 *Bidar* [2005] E.C.R. I-2119; Case C-258/04 *Ioannis Ioannidis* [2005] E.C.R. I-8275 27; Case C-11/06 *Rhiannon Morgan v Bezirksregierung Köln* judgment of October 23, 2007 (not yet reported). See Dougan (2005, 2006); Golykner, 2004, 2006; White, 2005.

[85] See: Case C-109/01 *Secretary of State for the Home Department v Akrich* [2003] E.C.R. I-9607 and Case C-1/05 *Jia* [2007] E.C.R. I-1 (Tryfonidou, 2007).

not EU Citizens. The Court has created these rights through its case law in *Baumbast* and *Chen*. In *Baumbast* the Court constructs an argument which carefully avoids ruling upon the exact scope of family rights derived from art.18 EC (Szyszczak, 2004). Article 18 EC does not detail what limits there are to the right to free movement. Under the economic rights to free movement the Member States are allowed some discretion to refuse admission and deport EU migrants. The Court relies upon art.12 EC and equality of treatment in order to create substantive rights for EU migrants deriving rights from art.18 EC, but as Maduro (2000) points out, in order to achieve true equality of treatment, and integration of persons into the host State, positive measures may also be necessary.

The new ideas embracing Citizenship as the fundamental status for nationals of the Member States may be capable of making inroads into the concept of reverse discrimination. The language of *Grzelczyk* is sufficiently wide to cover reverse discrimination. But in a later case the Court goes further:

". . . a citizen of the Union must be granted in all Member States the same treatment in law as that accorded to nationals of those member States who find themselves in the same situation. It would be incompatible with the right to free movement were a citizen, in the Member State of which he is a national, to receive treatment less favourable than he would enjoy if he had not availed himself of the opportunities offered by the Treaty."[86]

A new Citizenship directive, dir.2004/38/EC,[87] came into force on April 30, 2004, with a transitional implementation period until April 30, 2006. This directive confers benefits on *all* EU Citizens, whether economically active, or not. These rights amend reg.1612/68/EEC which formed the core of the rights attached to free movement of workers and repeals, inter alia, dirs 64/221/EEC and 68/360/EEC, which facilitated free movement of persons in the EU. The new directive enhances the rights of family members, irrespective of their nationality and registered partners and non-married partners can be recognised as members of the family. Family members will be able to retain their residence rights in the EU in the

---

[86] Case C-224/98 *D'Hoop* [2002] E.C.R. I-6191, para.30.
[87] OJ 2004 L 158/77.

event of divorce, death or departure from the Member State of the European Citizen. After five years of residence citizens will have the right to permanent residence in the host State.

The new approach to Citizenship rights in the EU creates an inherent tension between the historical development of rights associated with an "economically active" migrant and the new basis of rights which are de-coupled from economic activity. Arguably the sophisticated set of rights which have developed from the free movement provisions will continue to reward the economic migrant and provide incentives for people to move in the EU to create an active labour market. The Citizenship Directive continues to differentiate between economically active Citizens and other persons who move between the Member States. For example, art.7(1) grants workers and their families a right of residence in the host State beyond the three month guarantee given to Citizens. This residence is protected if the worker becomes incapacitated, suffers involuntary unemployment or takes up vocational training. Rights of family members are also secured even if the worker goes to work in another Member State (art.17). Under art.7(3) workers cannot be expelled from the host State even if they become a burden on social security system, although the Member State may legally expel the worker and his/her family on public policy/security grounds.

The Treaty of Lisbon 2007 introduces references to EU Citizenship in the provisions on Democratic Principles (*Title II, TEU*) and makes some amendments to the EC Treaty provisions on Citizenship. The most important amendment is the "Citizens' Initiative" which allows a proposal for Union action to be initiated by a petition of at least one million signatures (*art.11 TFEU*). A cause of concern for the UK was the increased power of the Council to adopt by unanimity vote measures in the field of social security and social protection for migrants (*art.21 TFEU*). In relation to the change from unanimity voting to QMV in relation to social security measures for migrant workers in *art.48 TFEU* the UK government negotiated an "emergency brake" whereby the matter can be referred to the European Council if the Member State believes that the proposed measure would affect important aspects of the domestic social security system.

## *Securing the External Frontier of the EU*

One of the European Union's objectives is to create an area of freedom, security and justice. The aim of this objective is to secure internal free movement for Citizens of the Union and third country nationals (TCNs) who have entered the EU legally.[88] Recent case law has extended the rights of TCN family members sometimes using human rights concepts (Hedemann-Robinson, 2001; Szyszczak, 2004). Some TCNs have limited economic rights to enter the EU to exercise an economic activity under international agreements made between the EU and third States, for example the EEA agreement, the Europa Agreements leading up to the 2004 enlargement of the EU in May 2004, Agreements with Turkey,[89] Morocco, Algeria, or Russia.

Admission of TCN migrants has always been a sensitive economic and political issue for the EU. Some Member States encourage such migration as it is an essential part of the economy and allows for flexibility within labour markets. Indeed, managed migration at the Community level is seen as an important aspect of managing the European Employment Strategy and attaining the Lisbon Strategy goals.[90] Other Member States, particularly States with economic problems, or forming part of the external frontier of the EU, are concerned to retain control migration flows, especially from irregular migrants (Bogusz et al., 2004). Historically this issue has been a major site for a battle of competence between the Member States, who wish to retain sovereignty in the area of immigration control and the treatment of TCNs in their own territory, and the Community, which claims to have a collective economic and political interest in managing migration and the treatment of TCNs.[91]

Community competence over matters relating to the external borders of the EU and for the control of the free movement of persons has developed in a slow, incremental fashion, but in recent years political events and the threats posed by the migration of legal and illegal migrants have compelled the Member States to co-operate more closely on securing the external frontiers of the EU.

Some of the Member States were willing to co-operate on removing the internal frontiers to free movement and attempting to secure an external border through closer co-operation on visa policy

---

[88] Case C-459/99 *MRAX v Belgium* [2002] E.C.R. I-6591, Joined Cases C-413/99 *Baumbast and R v Secretary of State for the Home Department* [2002] E.C.R. I-7091; Case C-60/00 *Mary Carpenter* [2002] E.C.R. I-6279 (Tryfonidou, 2007b).

[89] The EC–Turkey Association Agreement 1963 gives the most extensive rights to TCNs legally resident in the EU. The Agreement continues to generate litigation which contributes to the general principles of Community law and the free movement provisions: Case C-502/04 *Torun v Stadt Augsburg* [2006] E.C.R. I-1563.

[90] Commission, *Communication on Immigration, Integration and Employment* COM (2003) 336 final.

[91] Joined Cases 281, 283–285/85 *Germany, France, Netherlands, Denmark, United Kingdom v Commission* [1987] E.C.R. 3203.

for TCNs as well as co-operate on law enforcement. In 1985 the Schengen Agreement was signed by a sub-group of EU States and was implemented through a Convention in 1990. This was essentially an inter-governmental agreement, operating outside of the Community-law framework. Although the crossing of the internal "frontiers" between the Member States of Schengenland has become easier the price for the abolition of such formalities has been tougher checking of TCNs at the external frontier of Schengenland and closer police co-operation which has had a number of implications for civil liberties (Curtin and Meijer, 1995).

The Treaty of Maastricht 1991 introduced a third inter-governmental pillar (Title VI TEU) which included co-operation in relation to Justice and Home Affairs matters. For example, the crossing of external borders, immigration, asylum, drug addiction, fraud, judicial co-operation in civil and customs matters, police co-operation. The discussion of such sensitive matters outside of the judicial and democratic control of the main body of Community law raises concerns over secrecy, lack of transparency and accountability.

A new art.100c EC was introduced which allowed the Council to determine which TCNs should have a visa in order to enter the EU. Labour market issues relating to conditions of employment for TCNs were addressed in art.137(1)(g) EC. The Treaty of Amsterdam built upon this method of co-operation by transferring a number of areas relating to the free movement of persons (asylum, immigration and the crossing of external borders) into the EC Treaty in what is currently Title IV of the EC Treaty. This area has been brought within the normal channels of EU decision-making and also the jurisdiction of the ECJ. But only courts or tribunals against whose decision there is no judicial remedy can make references to the ECJ (art.68(1) EC).[92] The Court does not have jurisdiction on measures relating to the crossing of internal borders, the maintenance of law and order and safeguarding internal security (arts 62(1) and 68(2) EC). The UK, Ireland and Denmark opted-out of some of these provisions.

A new concept of an "area of freedom, security and justice" was introduced by the Treaty of Amsterdam 1997 (Walker, 2004, Hatzopoulos, 2008). At the European Council Meeting at Tampere in 1999 the Member States developed these principles, giving them structure by including roles for Europol and Eurojust as well as establishing a European Police College. The Tampere principles

---

[92] In Case C-51/03 *Georgescu* order of March 31, 2004 (a reference from a first instance criminal court was rejected).

also recognised the need to treat TCNs fairly and to respect human rights principles, especially when dealing with asylum and refugee claims. The Treaty of Amsterdam 1997 incorporated the Schengen Agreement and Convention into the main body of EC law. The UK and Ireland continue to remain outside of the Schengen arrangements although they have been allowed to cherry pick participation in some of the Schengen measures such as police and judicial co-operation on criminal matters.[93] This has led to a fragmentation of the legal base for handling the external dimension of free movement of persons as well as different priorities in relation to the aims of securing a common external frontier and the aims of securing internal free movement under the Internal Market aims.

The rise in terrorist acts, international crime in the form of drug and people trafficking and money laundering altered the mood of the Member States and the attempts to obtain a balance in securing the external frontier and treating TCNs fairly was altered towards a security-focused agenda. The Hague Programme spelt out the increased security needs of Europe:

"A key element in the near future will be the prevention and repression of terrorism . . . Preserving national security is only possible in the framework of the Union as a whole. The EU is no longer just concerned with external security but also security within the EU: 'Freedom, justice, control at the external borders, internal security and the prevention of terrorism should henceforth be considered indivisible within the Union as a whole'."[94]

The Hague Programme was implemented through an Action Plan.[95]

---

[93] There is also a "lock-out" rule in the Schengen Protocol which allows the participating Member states to refuse the UK permission to participate in measures which built upon earlier measures when the UK had not opted in. See Case C-77/05 *United Kingdom v Council* and Case C-137/05 *United Kingdom v Council,* judgment of December 18, 2007 where the UK was refused participation in new measures establishing a Borders Agency (FRONTEX) and setting biometric standards for passports.

[94] EU Council, *The Hague Programme: Strengthening Freedom, Security and Justice in the European Union*, Council Doc 16054/04, 4.

[95] COM (2005) 184; Commission, *Implementing the Hague Programme: The Way Forward* COM (2006) 331.

The aim of the Constitutional Treaty was to bring all areas relating to the external dimension (police-co-operation and judicial co-operation) into the main body of EU competence. As a result of the Treaty of Lisbon 2007 the policy of the "Area of Freedom, Security and Justice" is found in *arts 67 TFEU and Protocol No.11*. The whole policy has been removed from the TEU and re-drafted to create a single co-ordinated policy. The policy falls under the legislative competence of the Union and is justiciable by the Court.[96] However, there is a five-year transitional period from the date of entry into force of the Treaty of Lisbon 2007 where the Court will not have jurisdiction to review measures that have entered into law before the Treaty of Lisbon entered into force, unless the measures have been amended subsequently (*Protocol No.11 on Transitional provisions art.9 and 10*). The Commission has the right of initiative but in matters relating to judicial co-operation in criminal matters, and police co-operation the right of initiative is shared between the Commission and a quarter of the Member States (*art.76 TFEU*). National Parliaments will be involved in the judicial co-operation in criminal matters and police co-operation (arts 82–89 TFEU) and are also able to review proposed legislation under the protocol on Subsidiarity (*arts 69 and 81 TFEU* and *Protocol No.2*).

The Schengen Protocol has been amended to take into account the effects of the UK and Ireland opting out of a measure where this produces problems on operability or has financial consequences. The Council can urge the UK and Ireland to opt-in to a provision or ask them to bear the financial cost (*Protocol on the Position of the UK and Ireland, art.4a*).[97]

There is an "emergency brake" built into the provisions on judicial cooperation in civil and criminal matters, concerning mutual recognition of judgments and criminal offences (*arts 81, 82(3) and 83(3) TFEU*). If a Member State opposes a draft framework law the matter will be sent to the Council for discussion.

The EU has already moved towards a better managed external frontier in relation to visas, asylum and refugee policy, the control of irregular migration, trafficking and a policy of returning migrants to

---

[96] There is an exception in *art.276 TFEU* in that the Court has no jurisdiction to review the validity or proportionality of operations carried out by police or other law enforcement agencies of a Member State or the safeguarding of internal security.

[97] *Protocol No. 11 on Transitional Provisions, art.10* applies a similar procedure to the transitional provisions.

the home State.[98] There is a directive on Family Reunification[99] and a directive on Long Term Residents.[100] Other immigration matters in relation to TCNs currently remain within the competence of the Member States.[101] However, in recent years the EU has stepped up the co-ordination of the Member States' policies on irregular and illegal migration (Bogusz et al., 2004). The Commission has issued a Communication on illegal migration[102] followed by an Action Plan[103] as well as the adoption of dir.2001/40[104] on the mutual recognition of decisions on the expulsion of TCNs, and dir.2001/51 on harmonising financial penalties imposed on carriers transporting undocumented TCNs.[105] A Framework Decision has also been adopted to strengthen the penal framework of illegal migration[106] and a Framework Decision, 2002/629/JHA relating to penalties for trafficking humans.[107]

## Free Movement of Workers

Article 39 EC (*art.45 TFEU*) was intended as a dynamic right, to allow workers to move freely to take up jobs where there were labour and skills shortages. The right is broad in scope, allowing for a number of positive social rights, as well as family migration[108] and social rights, in addition to the principle of non-discrimination on grounds of nationality (Davies, 2003). Such rights are seen as embry-

---

[98] See: Commission, *A Common Agenda for Integration: Framework for the Integration of Third Country Nationals in the European Union* COM (2005) 389; Presidency Conclusions, Brussels European Council December 14–15, 2006.

[99] Council dir.2003/86/EC, OJ 2003 L251/12. Cf. art.8 allows the Member States to require that a sponsor of a TCN family member to have stayed lawfully within the territory for two years prior to the family reunification. This was unsuccessfully challenged in Case C-540/03 *European Parliament v Council (Family Reunification Directive)* [2006] E.C.R. I-5769. art.4 (1) contains a derogation for children who arrive in a member state independently of the rest of the family. Here a Member State may require that the child meets the criteria for integration in its own domestic legislation. Again, despite references to art.8 ECHR, and arts 7 and 24(2) (3) of the Charter of Fundamental Rights for the EU the Court dismissed the challenged to the legality of the directive.

[100] Council dir.2003/109/EC, OJ 2004 L16/44.

[101] Case C-109/01 [2003] E.C.R. I-9607.

[102] COM (2001) 548.

[103] COM (2006) 733.

[104] OJ 2001 L149/34. This used art.63(3) as the legal base but because it is part of the Schengen *acquis* the UK and Denmark do not participate.

[105] OJ 2001 L187/45 The UK participates in this directive but Ireland and Denmark do not.

[106] Framework Decision 2002/946/JHA OJ 2002 L328/1.

[107] OJ 2002 L203/1.

[108] Case C-291/05 *Eind*, judgment of December 11, 2007.

onic fundamental social rights and have been built upon in the Court's jurisprudence, extending the basic right to have both *vertical*[109] and *horizontal*[110] direct effect in the national courts. In *Angonese* the Court applied art.39 EC to a situation where a private bank required of job applicants a certificate of bilingualism from a local authority. The Court drew an analogy with the horizontal direct effect of the equal pay principle in art.141 EC. The Court ruled that art.39 EC should apply to private parties as well as public authorities, otherwise there would be inequality in the application of the free movement principle.

The right to free movement for workers is one of the core economic rights of the Internal Market contained in art.14 EC. It is also accepted as a fundamental right in the 1989 Charter of Fundamental Rights of Workers. As a substantive economic right the right to free movement of workers is subject to detailed Community law regulation. To fall within the concept of a "worker" for the purposes of art.39 EC brings with it the right to non-discrimination on grounds of nationality (art.12 EC) and triggers access to a number of economic, social and political rights within the host State,[111] as well as rights to family migration which were originally found in reg.1612/68/EEC and are now consolidated in dir.2004/38/EC (Barret, 2003). Regulation 1408/71 co-ordinated social security arrangements between the Member States. (Golynker, 2006; Cousins, 2007). Some of these social rights are now recognised as Citizenship rights and the entitlement to social security benefits and social services is recognised in art.34 of the Charter of Fundamental Rights (CFR). Article 35 CFR states that everyone has the right of access to preventative healthcare and medical treatment.

In order to take advantage of the right to free movement a person must possess the nationality of one of the Member States. The Member States retain the right to determine their own nationality laws and this, therefore, is a limitation on the right to free movement. But the ECJ has ruled that since free movement is such a fundamental economic right the Member States must *apply* their nationality laws so

---

[109] Case 167/73 *Commission v France* 1974] E.C.R. 359; Case 41/74, *Van Duyn v Home Office* [1974] E.C.R. 1337.

[110] Case C-415/93 *Union Royale Belge de Societe de Football Association v Bosman* [1995] E.C.R. I-4921; Case C-281/98 *Roman Angonese v Cassa di Risparmio di Bolzano* [2000] E.C.R. I-4139; Case 36/74 *Walrave and Koch v AUCI* [1974] E.C.R. 1405; Case C-472/99 *Clean Car Autoservice v Stadt Wien and Republik Österreich* [2001] E.C.R. I-9687.

[111] Case C-147/03 *Commission v Austria* [2005] E.C.R. I-5969. Cf. Case C-386/02 *Baldinger* [2004] E.C.R. I-8411 with Case C-400/02 *Merida* [2004] E.C.R. I-8471.

as to give effect to the right to free movement.[112] A Member State may continue to check that people invoking the right to free movement have the most fundamental qualifying condition: possessing the nationality of a Member State[113] Members of the worker's family who are TCNs may be asked for additional visas; the list of TCNs who need a visa when crossing an external border is set out in Council reg.539/2001.[114]

In *MRAX* [115] the Court stated that where a TCN spouse did not have a visa a refusal of entry would be disproportionate if TCN spouse could prove his/her identity and marriage and there was no evidence of risks covered by derogation on grounds of public policy public health or public security. *MRAX* may be confined to the situation where the TCN spouse joins the migrant *directly* from a non-EU State. In *Akrich*[116] the Court limited the right to free movement of spouses where a TCN spouse had not entered the Community external frontier in a lawful manner.

A second condition is that the person must be a "worker". There is no definition of a worker in the EC Treaty but the definition has implications for the scope of a wide range of Community employment and social law. The Court has ruled that the concept of a worker is a Community law concept. To rule otherwise would mean that the trigger for such a fundamental economic right will vary from Member State to Member State and would undermine the principle of free movement of workers.[117]

The Community law test is a functional test, summarised in *Lawrie-Blum*,[118] that:

> "for a certain period of time a person performs services for and under the direction of another person in return for which he receives remuneration."

It is for the national court, as a matter of fact, to decide if the test is satisfied. But the concept of a worker, drawn from the economic right to free movement is also relevant for applying rights to free

---

[112] Case C-369/90 *Micheleti v Delagación del Gobierno en Cantabria* [1992] E.C.R. I-4239.

[113] Case C-378/97 *Wijsenbeek* [1999] E.C.R. I-6207.

[114] Council reg.539/2001, OJ 2001 L81/1.

[115] Case C-459/99 *MRAX v Belgium* [2002] E.C.R. I-6591.

[116] Case C-109/01 [2003] E.C.R. I-9607.

[117] Case 75/63 *Unger v Bestuur der Bedrijfsvereniging voor Detail handel en Ambachten* [1964] E.C.R. 1977; Case 53/81 *Levin v Staatssecretaris van Justitie* [1982] E.C.R. 1035; paras 11–12.

[118] Case 66/85 [1986] E.C.R. 2121, paras 16–17.

movement under agreements with third countries as well as Community-based employment rights.[119] As a result a wide range of economic activity falls within the scope of art.39 EC. Various sporting activities such as football[120] have been held to fall within the scope of an economic activity, as well as an apprenticeship, prostitution, community-based work, part-time work, a retired worker[121] and work-seekers.[122] In *Collins*[123] an Irish-American national, had moved between the UK and America, working intermittently. When he entered the UK to look for work he was refused a social benefit, a job seekers' allowance which was available to UK nationals looking for work. The Court acknowledged that Collins was not a "worker" within the meaning of art.39 EC and had no right of residence in the UK. But the Court argued that in the light of his status as an EU Citizen he could rely upon the prohibition on the grounds of nationality contained in art.12 EC and art.39(2) EC to claim a social benefit intended to facilitate access to employment.

The final trigger for art.39 EC is that the worker, or work-seeker, must have crossed a Member State frontier. Thus art.39 EC cannot be used to trigger more favourable rights to a situation which is wholly internal to a Member State.[124] Community law may provide more favourable immigration rights, especially for members of a migrant workers' family, when the free movement principle has been triggered legally.[125]

If these three conditions are met a worker has the right to move to another Member State to accept offers of employment or to look for work.[126] He/she is protected by the principle of

---

[119] Case C-265/03 *Simutenkov* [2005] E.C.R. I-2579.
[120] Case C-415/93 *Union Royale Belge de Société de Football Association v Bosman* [1995] E.C.R. I-4921; *Simutenkov ibid.*
[121] Case C-224/02 [2004] E.C.R. I-5763.
[122] Case C-292/89 *R v IAT Ex p. Antonissen* [1991] E.C.R. I-745.
[123] Case C-138/02 [2004] E.C.R. I-2703.
[124] Case C 175/78 *R v Saunders* [1979] E.C.R. 1129.
[125] Case C-370/90 *R v IAT and Surinder Singh Ex p. Secretary of State for the Home Department* [1992] E.C.R. I-4265. *cf.* the Court's reliance upon the *exercise* of free movement rights in C-109/01 *Akrich* [2003] E.C.R. I-9607 and Case C-200/02 *Chen* [2004] E.C.R. I-9925.
[126] Art.39 (4) EC contains an exemption for access to posts in the public service. This is narrowly construed (Case 149/79 *Commission v Belgium* [1980] E.C.R. 381) and does not apply if a worker is admitted to work in the public service (Case 152/73 *Sotgui v Deutsche Bundespost* [1979] E.C.R. 153. It is question of fact as to how many of the duties carried out in the post are seen as an exercise of public authority in the general interests of the State: Case C-47 *Anker et al. v Bundesrepublik Deutschland* [2003] E.C.R. I-10447; Case C-4-05/01 *Colegio de Oficiales de la Marina Española v Administracion del Esatado* [2003] E.C.R. I-10391.

non-discrimination[127] on grounds of nationality, and as we have seen, the Court has moved beyond a pure discrimination approach to also include measures imposed by a Member State which impede access to the labour market.[128] The economic right to free movement is based upon a fundamental right to *leave* a Member State, thus, any provisions which *preclude or deter* a national of a Member State from a Member State are incompatible with the EC Treaty.[129] The free movement of workers differs from the free movement of goods because, since the ruling in *Groenveld*, the Court has applied a *discrimination* test to the *export* of goods from a Member State.

In addition, the migrant worker acquires a number of positive rights. For example, the migrant worker is entitled to move freely within the territory of a Member State, to stay in the Member State for the purposes of employment, to bring his/her family to the host state and for the family to be admitted to education and vocational training schemes, the right for the family members to stay in the home state to continue the education, alongside a primary carer who may be a third country national, the right to take up employment without encountering discrimination on the grounds of nationality and the right of the worker and his family to remain in the Member State after the work has ended as a result of retirement or illness/invalidity. The fact that a migrant worker derives positive rights from Community law leads to the possibility of reverse discrimination taking place where migrant workers receive more rights than the nationals of a host state.

## Derogations from the Right to Free Movement

The right to free movement is not absolute. It is subject to a number of derogations which Member States may invoke on a case by case basis. Article 39(4) EC (*art.45(4) TFEU*) allows the Member States to exclude *access* to posts in the public service from the free movement and non-discrimination principle: art.39 (3) EC (*art.45(3)*

---

[127] This may include direct discrimination: (Case 13/76 *Donà* [1976] E.C.R. 1333; Case C-415/93 *Union Royale Belge de Societé de Football Association v Bosman* [1995] E.C.R. I-4921) and indirect discrimination (Case 222/86 *Heylens* [1987] E.C.R. 4097.

[128] Case C-415/93 *Bosman* [1995] E.C.R. I-4921; Case C-109/04 *Kranemann v Land Nordrhein-Westfalen* [2005] E.C.R. I-2421. See: Toner, 2004; Spaventa, 2007.

[129] Case C-10/90 *Masgio v Bundesknappschaft* [1991] E.C.R. I-1119 paras 18–19; Case C-415/93 *Bosman* [1995] E.C.R. I-4921, para.104); Case 232/01 *Van Lent* [2003] E.C.R. I-11525.

*TFEU*). Article 45 EC (*art.51 TFEU*) has a similar restriction where the post involves the exercise of official authority. This is intended to have the same function as art.39 (4) EC in relation to establishment. Article 39 (4) EC (*art.53 TFEU*) allows the Member States to use public policy,[130] public security and public health grounds to prevent foreigners from entering their territory. The public security and public policy grounds may be used to deport foreigners. These derogations were developed in Council dir.64/221/EEC, which was repealed and replaced when dir.2004/38 came into operation on April 30, 2004.

These are classic derogations drawn up in 1957 and which the Court has ruled are exhaustive, unlike the derogations to the free movement of goods which were expanded upon in *Cassis*.[131] This reflects the protection of the sovereignty of the Member States in sensitive areas. But EU law has made inroads into that sovereignty. The derogations relate to a fundamental economic right of the EC Treaty and must be interpreted restrictively[132] and are subject to the principle of proportionality and the principle of respect for fundamental human rights.[133] For example, the derogations cannot be used to serve economic ends and there are procedural rights contained within Community law and the general principles of Community law.[134] The objective justification exception also applies to free movement of workers cases, when there is indirect discrimination on the grounds of nationality or non-discriminatory obstacles to the free movement of workers. The Member States' traditional executive powers are also subject to judicial review.[135]

---

[130] Case 41/74 *Van Duyn v Home Office* [1974] E.C.R. 1337; Case C-268 *Jany* [2001] E.C.R. I-8615.

[131] Case C-17/92 *FDC* [1993] E.C.R. I-2239; Case C-388/01 *Commission v Italy* [2003] E.C.R. I-721.

[132] Case C-441/02 *Commission v Germany (Italian Migrants)* [2006] E.C.R. I-3449; (Nic Shuibhne, 2005–2006).

[133] Joined Cases C-482/01 and C-493/01 *Orfanopoulos v Land Baden-Würtemberg* [2004] E.C.R. I-5257; Case C-60/00 *Carpenter v Secretary of State for the Home Department* [2002] E.C.R. I-6279.

[134] Case 36/75 *Rutili* [1975] E.C.R. 1219; Joined Cases 115 and 116 *Adoui and Cornuaille* [1982] E.C.R. 1665; Joined Cases C-65/95 and C-111/95 *R v Secrertary of State for the Home Department Ex p. Singh Shingara and Abbas Radiom* [1997] E.C.R. I-3343.

[135] Case 41/74 *Van Duyn v Home Office* [1974] E.C.R. 1337; Case C-348/96 *Criminal Proceeedings against Calfa* [1999] E.C.R. I-11; Case C-114/97 *Commission v Spain* [1998] E.C.R. I-671.

*Free Movement of Services*

The free movement of services, found in art.49 EC (*art.56 TFEU*), is a residual category of free movement (art.50 EC, *art.57 TFEU*). As a result of changes in technology, the industrial base and the liberalisation of global services the provision of services is now a dominant form of economic activity, contributing some 70 per cent of GDP in the EU as the industrial base of Europe has changed with greater reliance upon the service sector for the creation of jobs and economic activity. The rise in the importance of services to the European economy is matched by an increasing interest in regulating services at the Community level and a body of case law exploring the scope of this freedom. Distinct areas are emerging where the basic free movement of services' provision is creating distinct sectoral approaches to questions relating to the free movement of companies, healthcare,[136] gambling[137] and broadcasting.[138]

The free movement of services is a complicated concept as it may be triggered by a variety of economic activities: a person may move to another Member State to *provide* services; a consumer may move to another State to *receive* services; both the service provider and the consumer may move; the service itself might move (for example a fax, telephone, internet, electronic commerce services, satellite TV); or neither the service provider nor the consumer may move. Another feature of the provision of services is the *range* of activity caught by the provision. It can include the self-employed, for example a taxi driver or hairdresser, as well as organised business in the banking, financial commercial sectors. Some sectors have received closer attention from the Community, for example, the creation of a Financial Services Action Plan,[139] and a general directive on

---

[136] Case C-159/90 *SPUC v Grogan* [1991] E.C.R. I-4685; Cases C-368/98 *Vanbraekel e.a.* [2001] E.C.R. I-5363; Case C-157/99 *Smits* [2001] E.C.R. I-5473; Case C-385/99 *Müller-Fauré* [2003] E.C.R. I-4509; Case 56/01 *Inizan* [2003] E.C.R. I-12403; Case C-193/03 *Bosch* [2004] E.C.R. I-9911; Case C-8/02 *Leichtle* [2004] E.C.R. I-2641; Case C-145/03 *Keller* [2005] E.C.R. I-2529; Case C-372/04 *Watts* [2006] E.C.R. I-4325; Case C-466/04 *Acereda Herrera* [2006] E.C.R. I-5341; Case C-444/05 *Stamatelaki* [2007] E.C.R. I-3185.

[137] Case C-275/92 *Schindler* [1994] 1039; Case C-67/98 *Zenati* [1999] E.C.R. I-7289; Case C-243/01 *Gambelli* [2003] E.C.R. I-13031; Case C-124/97 *Läärä* [1999] E.C.R. I-6067; Joined Cases C-338/04 &360/04 *Placanica* [2007] E.C.R. I-1891.

[138] Case 352/85 *Bond* [1988] E.C.R. 2085; Case C-288/89 *Gouda* [1991] E.C.R. I-4007; Case 11/95 *Commission v Belgium* [1996] E.C.R. I-4115; Case C-245/01 *RTL Television* [2003] E.C.R. I-12489.

[139] Commission Communication of May 11, 1999, "Implementing the Framework for Financial Markets: Action Plan" COM (1999) 232 final.

Services[140] has been adopted in an attempt to liberalise this sector even further. This is because the Community secondary legislation and the case law on services, while creating general principles, does not address in detail the remaining barriers to free markets.

The free movement of services has made inroads into narrowing down the scope of the reverse discrimination principle by finding that certain economic activity has a potential cross-frontier element, and is not wholly internal to a Member State.[141] The most far-reaching, and controversial ruling is that of *Carpenter*[142] where the free movement of services protected the right to family life of a service provider. A Philipine wife of a British man who provided services in other Member States was able to resist a deportation order. It was argued that she stayed at home to look after her husband's children from a previous marriage. If she was deported this would impair the husband's ability to provide services in another Member State. The case has been criticised, in the broad interpretation given to a *hindrance* to provide services in another Member State but is rationalised and viewed more of a "Citizenship" case than a case explaining the scope of the free movement of services provisions. There was no discrimination present, and the effect upon the provision of services was incidental. However, the outcome of the *Carpenter* case is analogous to the pre-*Keck* case law in the area of free movement of goods.

Services are not defined in detail in the EC Treaty. Article 50(1) EC states that services are "normally provided for remuneration".[143] Changes in the State provision of many public services, through contracting out, public-private finance partnerships and the use of economic, market-based principles has brought a lot of traditional State provision of services within the potential scope of the free movement rules of the EU. The Court has not produced a workable "bright line" to distinguish when State activity is caught by the Internal Market and competition rules of the EC Treaty and when State activity is "non-economic" and remains outside of the reach of Community law (Szyszczak: 2004). A number of cases have arisen where restrictive rules on the availability of social and public services provided on an economic, market footing have been tested

---

[140] Dir.2006/123, OJ L 376/36.

[141] Case C-76/90 *Säger* [1991] E.C.R. I-4221; Joined Cases C-369 and 376/96 *Arblade* [1999] E.C.R. I-8453; Case C-58/98 *Corsten* [2000] E.C.R. I-7919; Case C-51/96 *Deliège* [2000] E.C.R. I-2549; Case C-458/03 *Parking Brixen* [2005] E.C.R. I-8585.

[142] Case C-60/00 [2002] E.C.R. I-6279.

[143] Case 263/86 *Belgium v Humbel* [1988] E.C.R. 5365; Case C-159/90 *SPUC v Grogan* [1991] E.C.R. I-4685.

against the free market principles.[144] This may have de-stabilising effects upon national welfare systems (Hatzopoloulos, 2002; Newdick, 2006)

*Gebhard*[145] provided some clarification of the definition of services, distinguishing them from the right of establishment. Services are provided on a temporary basis and should be distinguished from establishment by reference to the duration of the service, its regularity, periodicity or continuity. Although the Court was realistic to recognise that in order to provide services in a Member State the establishment of an infrastructure, for example, offices, staff, consulting rooms, chambers, is not incompatible with the nature of a service where such an infrastructure is necessary to perform the service.

Recipients of services are free to travel to another Member State in order to receive services by virtue of art.6 of dir.2004/38 which replaced dir.73/148.[146] It is this right which has been used in the "health care tourists" cases where individuals travel to another Member State to receive immediate and/or superior medical services (van der Mei, 2002; Davies, 2004).

The Court has treated the export of services in the same way as it has approached the issue in relation to workers in *Bosman*. In *Alpine Investments*[147] Dutch restrictions on cold calling for financial services which were framed in a neutral manner and were non-discriminatory, were scrutinised as impeding the free movement of services since they restricted access of the service provider to the markets of other Member States where cold calling was permitted.[148] Exporters of the service would be subject to a double burden, of having to obey two or more sets of national regulatory rules, making the service less competitive. This approach, however, makes a significant inroad into the principle of "home state control" and highlights the need for Community harmonisation of such regulatory measures.

Directive 73/148/EEC extended the rights of immigration and residence in relation to services by requiring the Member States to abolish restrictions not only in the provision of services but also for

---

[144] C-157/99 *Geraets-Smits and Peerbooms* [2001] E.C.R. I-5473; Case C-385/99 *Müller-Fauré* [2003] E.C.R. I-4509.

[145] Case C-55/94 [1995] E.C.R. I-4165.

[146] OJ 1973 L172/14. However most case law uses art.49 EC as a directly effective right: Joined Cases 286/82 and 26/83 *Luisi and Carbone v Ministero del Tesoro* [1984] E.C.R. 377; Case C-355/98 *Commission v Belgium (private security firms)* [2004] E.C.R. I-9289.

[147] Case C-384/93 [1995] E.C.R. I-1141.

[148] Case C-243/01 *Piergiorgio Gambelli* [2003] E.C.R. I-13031.

providers of services. A number of cases have concerned workers employed by service providers who are then sent to another Member State to work. The lack of harmonisation of social and labour laws in the Community allows for competition between regulatory systems of the Member States with incentives for employers to establish themselves in a Member State with lower labour and payroll costs. In *Commission v Belgium*[149] the Court held that a Belgium law requiring service providers to carry an identity card issued by the Belgian Ministry of the Interior was in breach of art.49 EC. The right of residence is only available for the corresponding time that a service is being provided, or received. More far-reaching cases are *Rush Portuguesa*[150] and *Van der Elst*[151] where the Court ruled that a service provider may take a workforce composed of workers not entitled to the right of free movement under art.39 EC to another Member State provided that they have been admitted to the home state by legal means. At that time, the harmonisation of the Member States' labour and social laws was very under-developed and in order to avoid a "race to the bottom" in terms of lowering labour standards the Court ruled that the host State may apply its own labour standards to the migrant posted workforce.[152] However, the Court will assess the proportionality of the measures in a strict way.[153] These cases reveal the necessity for Internal Market law to "spillover" into the areas of harmonising Member States' employment and social laws. The cases led to the adoption of a directive on posted workers dir.96/71/EC[154] However, with enlargement, new problems have emerged where employers are shifting their labour sources to Member States from central and eastern Europe where wages are lower.[155]

Many of the issues relating to free movement of services involve the elimination of *discriminatory* measures which act as barriers to free movement.[156] In the same way as the Court approached "distinctly applicable" and "indistinctly applicable" obstacles to free

---

[149] Case C-355/98 [2000] E.C.R. I-1221.
[150] Case C-113/89 [1990] E.C.R. I-1417.
[151] Case C-43/93 [1994] E.C.R. I-3803.
[152] But see Joined Cases C-165/98 *Criminal Proceedings against Andre Mazzoleni and Inter Surveillance Assistance SARL* [2001] E.C.R. I-2189; Case 493/99 *Commission v Germany* [2001] E.C.R. I-8163.
[153] Case C-493/99 *Commission v Germany* [2001] E.C.R. I-8163. Cf. Case C-255/04 *Commission v France* [2006] E.C.R. I-5251.
[154] OJ 1998 L18/1.
[155] Bercusson, 2007.
[156] Case 33/74 *van Binsbergen* [1974] E.C.R. 1299; Case C-288/89 *Gouda* [1991] E.C.R. I-4007; Case C-17/92 *FDC* [1993] E.C.R. I-2239.

trade in relation to goods, the Court has also recognised such a distinction in relation to freedom to provide services. The leading judgment on indistinctly applicable measures is an infringement action, *Commission v Germany* known as "the insurance cases".[157] Here the Court found that German rules requiring insurance companies to be both established and authorised in Germany was a double burden, increasing the costs of insurance services provided by non-German service providers and therefore in breach of arts 49 and 50 EC. The Court accepted that insurance services were a sensitive sector and that there were good mandatory requirements of consumer protection justifying a continued interest in the German regulation of insurance services where such interests were not adequately protected in the home State. While the authorisation requirement was a proportionate response to such needs, the residence/establishment requirement was not.

The free movement of services follows the other freedoms in relation to handling issues of equality of treatment in the *exercise* of the right to free movement. Issues of direct discrimination on grounds of nationality, which is contrary to art.12 EC, have arisen in relation to social advantages[158] and also indirect taxation.[159]

As with the other freedoms the Court has increasingly looked to *market access* as a criterion for determining whether or not a breach of the free movement provisions has occurred.[160] In *Mazzoleni*[161] the Court refers to a

"restriction . . . which is liable to prohibit, impede or render less advantageous the activities of a provider of services."

In other cases the Court has also used ideas of tackling measures which hinder or impede access to a market[162] or deter recipients from using a service.[163]

The Court has accepted that Member States may justify such measures by imperative reasons in the public interest where the home

---

[157] Case 205/84 *Commission v Germany* [1986] E.C.R. 3755.
[158] Case 186/87 *Cowan* [1989] E.C.R. 195; Case 63/86 *Commission v Italy* [1988] E.C.R. 29; Case C-484/93 *Svensson* [1995] E.C.R. I-3955; Case C-45/93 *Commission v Spain* [1994] E.C.R. I-911.
[159] Case C-17/00 *De Coster* [2001] E.C.R. I-9445.
[160] Case C-76/90 *Säger* [1991] E.C.R. I-4221; Case C-384/93 *Alpine Investments v Minister van Financiën* [1995] E.C.R. I-1141; Case C-275/92 *Schindler* [1994] E.C.R. I-1039.
[161] Case C-165/98 *Mazzoleni* [2001] E.C.R. I-2189, para.22
[162] Joined Cases C-430 and 431/99 *Sea-Land Service Inc* [2002] E.C.R. I-5235.
[163] Case C-55/98 *Skatteministeriet* [1999] E.C.R. I-7641.

State does not provide adequate protection.[164] The Court will scrutinise these reasons for proportionality[165] and also for legitimacy.[166] This wider justification, based upon the *Cassis* approach, has modernised the rather limited EC Treaty justification contained in art.45 EC (*art.51 TFEU*) which reflects the 1957 public policy/public interests justifications of that era. In *Omega*[167] the police authorities in Bonn, Germany, issued a prohibition order against Omega, a company which had introduced a laser sport which targeted humans by using sensory tags. A British company supplied the equipment and the technology for the laser sport. The police took the view that games for entertainment which simulated killing were contrary to human dignity and constituted a danger to public order. The Court took the view that the prohibition order affected the freedom to provide services under art.49 EC. But the Court acknowledged that the Community and the Member States are required to respect fundamental rights. The protection of fundamental rights was a legitimate interest which could be used to justify a derogation from Community law obligations, even if the Community law obligations guaranteed a fundamental freedom under the EC Treaty. Provided that the German measures necessary and proportionate they could be used to restrict a service even though another Member State had chosen a different way of protecting human rights. In this case the protection of human dignity which was being protected by the prohibition order corresponded to the level of protection the German constitution aimed to guarantee within Germany and the order banned only human targets in laser games. It was, therefore, proportionate.

The Court will allow a Member State to justify rules which are restrictive where they are designed to prevent an abuse of rights.[168] But the Court is careful to balance the freedom to provide services against a Member State's claims that the freedom has been exercised merely to abuse local regulatory laws when in fact a legitimate service is being provided in another Member State.[169]

---

[164] Case C-272/94 *Guiot* [1996] E.C.R. I-1905.

[165] Joined Cases C-369 and 376/96 *Arblade* [1999] E.C.R. I-8453; Case C-180/89 *Commission v Italy* [1991] E.C.R. I-709 ("Tourist Guide" cases).

[166] Case C-67/98 *Zenatti* [1999] E.C.R. I-7289, but *cf.* C-124/97 *Läärä* [1999] E.C.R. I-6067; Case C-6/01 *Anomar* [2003] E.C.R. I-8621; Case C-243/01 *Gambelli* [2003] E.C.R. I-3031; Case C-42/02 *Diana Elisabeth Lindman* [2003] E.C.R. I-13519.

[167] Case C-36/02 [2004] E.C.R. I-9609.

[168] Case C-148/91 *Vereniging Veronica Omroep Organisatie v Commissariaat voor de media* [1993] E.C.R. I-487.

[169] Case C-56/96 *VT4 Ltd v Vlaamse Gemeenschap* [1997] E.C.R. I-3143.

Of significant political importance is the litigation often known as "health care tourism" where nationals of a Member State have taken advantage of the right to move to *receive* services as a way of avoiding non-existent or inadequate medical care, or waiting lists, in the home state.[170] The Court has applied art.49 EC to hospital treatment and to medical benefits in kind.[171] The Court ruled that patients could rely upon art.49 EC to challenge rules which prevented or made it more difficult to seek appropriate health care in another Member State, for example, the need for prior authorisation before travelling to receive health care services. The Court accepted that a Member State could justify such rules where considerations of planning and the financial equilibrium of healthcare schemes are taken into consideration. These justifications are perilously close to economic considerations which the Court has ruled are not valid justifications for impeding the four fundamental freedoms (Snell, 2005). It may be that the time has come for the Court to reassess this justification in the light of the expanding scope of Community law and the changes in State and private provision for various services. The Court seems to take a softer line on such sensitive public services, and the provision of social facilities for a Member State's population as a whole. The rise of such litigation begs the question as to whether there should be more specific Community law rules handling such sensitive issues. The omc is being used to co-ordinate a dialogue between the Member States to reduce the disparities in the way health care services are provided. This would minimise the ad hoc litigation which is gradually chipping away at the Member States' sovereignty in sensitive areas.

## The Services Directive, 2006/123/EC[172]

The Lisbon Process saw the liberalisation of services as playing a pivotal role in reaching the goal of making the EU the most dynamic, knowledge-based society by the year 2010. From the late 1980s onwards Europe had seen a wave of privatisation and liberalisation taking place as more and more services were exposed to competitive markets (Szyszczak, 2007). However, national restrictions continued to make the provision of services across frontiers difficult and the Commission was set the task of devising a directive

---

[170] Case C-158/96 *Kohll* [1998] *E.C.R.* I-1931; Case C-120/95 *Decker* [1998] E.C.R. I-1831; Case C-368/98 *Vanbraekel* [2001] E.C.R. I-5363.
[171] Case C-157/99 *Geraets-Smits and Peerbooms* [2001] E.C.R. I-5473; Case C-385/99 *Müller-Fauré* 2003] E.C.R. I-4509. See Davies, 2002; Hatzopoulos, 2002.
[172] OJ 2006 L 376/28.

to liberalise services. The original draft, presented by Commissioner Bolkestein, proposed a model of liberalisation for services based upon deregulation by using the "country of origin principle", that is, a service provider should be subject to only one law in the country in which he/she was established. This was seen as a step too far. There would be few means for the home State to control the provision of services in another Member State and there were fears that it could lead to social dumping leaving consumers with few rights and protections. The Commission redrafted the proposal following amendments from the European Parliament. The new proposal, presented by Commissioner McCreevy, dropped the country of origin principle (De Witte, 2006; Davies, 2007; Flower, 2006–2007) as well as reference to social provisions.[173]

Article 2(1) of the directive states that the directive applies to services supplied by providers established in a Member State. Services are outlined in the Preamble, Recital 33, in a broad way and also by reference to art.50 EC and the GATS. However a number of services are excluded: financial services, electronic communication services and networks, private security services and social services (art.2(2)) as well as healthcare services, gambling. However such services remain subject to the underlying EC Treaty base on services, art.49 EC.

The country of origin principle is changed to the idea of freedom to provide services in art.16(1). A Member State must ensure free access to, and free exercise of, a service activity in its territory and Member States must not make access to, or exercise of, service activity subject to compliance with any requirements which do not respect the free movement principle.[174] There is a set of derogations: public policy, public security, public health and the protection of the environment. In the Preamble, Recital 41, the concept of "public

---

[173] The Commission also issued a Communication on the Posted Workers' Directive: COM (2006) 159.

[174] Restrictions which are prohibited are set out in art.16(2): an obligation on the provider to set up an establishment in the host state; an obligation on the service provider to obtain authorisation from competent authorities of the host state (for example entry onto a register, registration with a professional body) except where provided for in Community legislation; a ban on the provider creating an infrastructure (for example offices, consulting rooms) which are necessary for the provision of a service; the application of specific contractual arrangements between the provider and recipient of services which restrict the provision of the service; an obligation to possess an identity document specific to the exercise of a service activity, any other requirements (with the exception of health and safety matters) which affect the use of equipment and material which are an integral part of the service provided; any restrictions on the freedom to provide services in respect of the recipients of services.

policy" is referred to "as interpreted by the Court" and covers the protection against a genuine and sufficiently serious threat affecting one of the fundamental interests of society and may include issues relating to human dignity, the protection of minors, vulnerable adults, animal welfare. Public security may embrace issues of public safety. While this list includes aspects of the Court's case law it does not specifically address the generic public interest justifications suggested by the Court in recent years (Szyszczak, 2007) other than through the obligation contained in art.3(3) that the Member States must apply the provisions of the directive in compliance with the rules of the EC Treaty on free movement of establishment and services. Article 18 sets out a safety net for the Member States to apply case-by-case derogations in exceptional circumstances.

## 5.5 Procurement

The State continues to be a huge buyer of a number of goods and services, and also must supply certain services and create tangible objects to supply services, for example, the building of a transport infra-structure (roads, bridges, railways), hospitals, schools. The procurement of these goods and services still occupies a large part of Community GDP. States tender to favour their own nationals, either openly or covertly by creating procurement conditions which make it easier for national firms to comply with. Thus tackling discrimination on the grounds of nationality was one of the first tasks of a Community procurement policy. Surprisingly the original EEC Treaty did not address procurement as a separate issue. It was only after the completion of the Internal Market, that greater attention was placed on the regulation of State procurement activity.

The lack of a Treaty base entailed the use of the general Internal Market base of art.95 EC to provide a detailed set of tools to regulate procurement. (Trepte, 2007). Directives were adopted regulating procurement in works, supply and services contracts as well as public utilities in water, transport, telecommunications. In addition a directive on review procedures (remedies) was adopted. More recently the Community has had to adopt policies on defence procurement, e-commerce and address the special forms of public-private financing initiatives. In 2004 the procurement directives were modernised to take account of developments in markets, especially the effects of liberalisation and two new directives were adopted on the public sector and for utilities.[175]

## 5.6 Freedom of Establishment

The right of establishment is available to natural persons who are nationals of a Member State and also to legal persons. Thus, the right applies to companies and to the self-employed. Since the 2004 enlargement process it has provided the legal base whereby migrants have been able to migrate to work in Western Europe, circumventing the transitional provisions on the free movement of workers.[176] Article 43 EC (*art.49 TFEU*) bases the right of establishment on the right to take up and pursue activities in another Member State without discrimination. In the *Factortame* litigation the Court described the right of establishment as:

"the actual pursuit of an economic activity through a fixed establishment in another Member State for an indefinite period."[177]

As with other fundamental economic freedoms the concept of establishment is not defined in the EC Treaty and it has been left to the Court of Justice to provide working definitions of the concept. In *Gebhard*[178] the Court stated:

". . . the concept of establishment within the meaning of the Treaty is therefore a very broad one, allowing a Community national to participate, on a stable and continuous basis, in the economic life of a Member State other than his State of origin and to profit therefrom, so contributing to social and economic penetration within the Community in the sphere of activities as self-employed persons."

---

[175] Dir.2004/18, OJ 2004 L134/1, and dir.2004/17, OJ 2004 L134/114.
[176] Case C-268/99 *Jany* [2001] E.C.R. I-8615; Joined Cases C-151/04 and 152/04 *Nadin* [2005] E.C.R. I-11203.
[177] Case C-221/89 *R v Secretary of State for Transport Ex p. Factortame* [1991] E.C.R. I-3905, para.20.
[178] Case C-55/94 *Gebhard v Consiglio dell'Ordine degli Avvocati e Procuratori di Milano* [1995] E.C.R. I-4165 para.25. The permanent presence in the Member State must be established for the free movement of establishment provisions to apply: Case C-386/04 *Centro di Musicologia Walter Stauffer* [2006] E.C.R. I- 8203, para.19.

The right of establishment can be exercised by being a shareholder[179] or a director of a company.[180] More recent cases brought under the Europe Agreements have enhanced the concept of "self-employment". These cases arose because, under the Europe Agreements and under the terms of Accession Treaty 2004, some Member States were concerned that there would be a flood of migrant workers from the Central and Eastern European accession States and therefore restricted the right of free movement of workers. But there were no restrictions on the right to provide services and the right of establishment. In *Jany*,[181] a case concerning Czech and Polish prostitutes, offering services in the Netherlands, the Court distinguished the "self-employed" from "workers" in that the self-employed work outside of the relationship of subordination and take economic risks not taken by workers and they are paid directly, and in full, for their services. In *Ex p. Barkoci and Malik*[182] the Court stated that a self-employed person could conduct "activities of an industrial or commercial character, activities of craftsmen, or activities of the professions of a Member State."

## Freedom of Establishment and Individuals

The right of establishment is a complicated right as it may give rise to claims by individuals as well as companies. Rights under art.43 EC embrace the right to take up activities as a self-employed person on the same terms as nationals of the host State and also the right to exercise an activity, as well as family residence rights and the right for the self-employed and their families to remain in the host State.[183] Many of the issues mirror the problems faced by migrant workers under art.39 EC. Immigration and residence rights were granted under Dir.73/148/EEC[184] and such rights are extended to a self-employed person's family. In *Roux*[185] a requirement to register with the relevant authorities in the host State and the penalty for failure

---

[179] Case 182/83 *Fearon v Irish Land Commission* [1985] E.C.R. 3677; Case 251/98 *Baars v Inspecteur der Belastingdienst Particulieren/Ondernemingen Gorinchem* [2000] E.C.R. I-2728; Case C-212/97 *Centros v Erhvervs-og Selskabsstyylrelsen* [1999] E.C.R. I-1459; Case C-470/04 *Keller Holding* [2006] E.C.R. I-2107.
[180] Case C-221/89 *Factortame II* [1991] E.C.R. I-3905.
[181] Case C-268/99 *Jany v Staatssecretaris van Justitie* [2001] E.C.R. I-8615.
[182] Case C-257/99 *R v S/S for the Home Department Ex p. Barkoci and Malik* [2001] E.C.R. I-6557, para.50.
[183] Council Dir.75/34/EEC OJ 1975 L14/10.
[184] OJ 1973 L172/14. Repealed by dir.2004/38/EC.
[185] Case C-363/89 *Roux v Belgium* [1991] E.C.R. I-273.

to register, deportation, were held to be inconsistent with the rights conferred by art.43 EC. Problems have arisen in exercising the right to freedom of establishment. Often a person in business may wish to set up a second office, a secondary establishment, in order to exercise economic activities in more than one Member State. Some Member States forbid secondary establishment, arguing that they wish to maintain local regulation over business and professional activities. In *Klopp*[186] the Court ruled that a ban on secondary establishment used by the Paris Bar was contrary to art.43 EC. This was a forward-looking judgment in that the Court held that while it was legitimate for the Paris Bar to want to exercise control over lawyers practising locally a *ban* on secondary establishment, forcing lawyers to give up their primary establishment, was out of proportion given that lawyers were able to maintain contact with their clients and the French courts through modern methods of transport and telecommunications.[187] Where there is indirect discrimination the State may be able to justify rules which are objective.[188] Other cases have involved more overt forms of discrimination based upon nationality which is contrary to Community law and cannot be justified under one of the Treaty derogations.[189]

The Court has moved on from considering rules based only on nationality discrimination to consider rules which are non-discriminatory but nevertheless prevent access to the local market. This is very similar to the indistinctly applicable rules considered in relation to goods in *Cassis de Dijon*. In *Gebhard*[190] the Court ruled:

"national measures liable to hinder or make less attractive the exercise of fundamental freedoms guaranteed by the Treaty must fulfil four conditions: they must be applied in a non-discriminatory manner; they must be justified by imperative requirements in the general interest; they must be suitable for securing the objective which they pursue; and they must not go beyond what is necessary in order to obtain it . . ."

---

[186] Case 107/83 [1984] E.C.R. 2971.
[187] See also Case C-140/03 *Commission v Greece (opticians)* [2005] E.C.R. I-3177 where a Greek law forbidding opticians from dispensing their services from more than one outlet was held to effectively amount to restriction on the free movement of establishment despite the absence of discrimination in the measure.
[188] Case 292/86 *Güllung* [1988] E.C.R. 111.
[189] Case 2/74 *Reyners v Belgian State* [1974] E.C.R. 631.
[190] Case C-55/94 [1995] E.C.R. I-4165.

The Court has imposed some limits on this test where the alleged impediment and the allegation of restricting access to a market is too remote.[191] But other cases, for example, prior authorisation for a trade fair [192] a language requirement imposed upon dentists[193] and a restriction on multi-disciplinary partnerships between lawyers and accountants[194] have been held to be restrictions on the freedom of establishment. As with the other fundamental economic freedoms, such restrictions may be justified by the Member State, subject to the principle of proportionality.

One of the major obstacles for individuals wishing to provide services or establish themselves within another Member State is the requirement of professional qualifications. The development of an education policy for the EU has been a contested area since the Member States still seek to maintain control over such a fundamental area of national identity. Vocational training has also been part of the open method of co-ordination processes relating to the European Employment Strategy.

The principle of mutual recognition of qualifications has underpinned the Community legislative approach and has been used by the Court to liberalise free movement in the professions. Article 47 EC allows the Council to adopt directives on the mutual recognition of diplomas using the art.251 EC procedure. Directives have been adopted over the years, for example dentists, vets, doctors, nurses, lawyers services, architects. The sectoral approach to mutual recognition proved to be too slow and so the Community adopted two horizontal mutual recognition directives. Council dir.89/48/EEC[195] covers the mutual recognition of qualifications gained through tertiary education of at least three years duration and not covered in a specific sectoral directive. Council dir.92/51/EEC[196] extended the principle to diplomas and qualifications obtained through work or a course of study post-secondary education of less than three years duration. As part of the ongoing modernisation process the Commission introduced a new directive to streamline the sectoral directives. Directive 2005/36/EC[197] replaced and repealed the earlier directives to create a more flexible and streamlined mutual recogni-

---

[191] Case C-1909/98 *Graf v Filzmozer GmbH* [2000] E.C.R. I-493, para.25.
[192] Case C-439/99 *Commission v Italy* [2002] E.C.R. I-305.
[193] Case C-424/97 *Haim II* [2000] E.C.R. I-5123.
[194] Case C-309/99 *Wouters* [2002] E.C.R. I-1577.
[195] OJ 1989 L 19/16.
[196] OJ 1992 L209/25.
[197] OJ 2005 L255/22.

tion process. The transitional period for the directive expired on October 20, 2007.

The mutual recognition process was slow in developing, partly because the original art.47 EC required unanimity voting. As a result case law has produced far-reaching principles which may be used to remedy the barriers to integration which different education and training systems create. In *Thieffry*,[198] an early case recognising the principle of mutual recognition, the ECJ ruled that Member States were bound by the principle of solidarity, as set out in art.10 EC and the principle of non-discrimination, as set out in art.12 EC. In the later case of *Vlassopoulou*[199] a Greek lawyer with Greek and German qualifications did not satisfy the exact qualifications for the mutual recognition approach to be applied but nevertheless the ECJ accepted that national rules on qualifications may have ". . . the effect of hindering nationals of the other Member States in the exercise of their right of establishment" guaranteed under art.43 EC. The Court invoked art.10 EC, ruling that Member States were under a duty to co-operate in the exchange of information to allow comparisons to be made to determine the equivalence of qualifications. The Court affirmed the duty to give reasons for decisions, allowing such decisions to be reviewable by the courts to ensure that any national rules and regulations were compatible with Community law.[200]

An example of the extensive protection provided by Community law to facilitate the free movement of persons is seen in *Bobadilla*. Here a Spanish national was refused a permanent post at a Spanish museum on the ground that her English postgraduate qualification was not equivalent to a Spanish qualification. The English qualification fell outside of the scope of the two horizontal mutual recognition directives and was not covered by a sectoral directive. Nevertheless the Court ruled that the museum was obliged to assess whether Bobadilla's knowledge and qualifications were of an equivalent standard required under the Spanish regulations for the post.[201]

The kinds of issues which have arisen in exercising the freedom of establishment go beyond pure market access issues and embrace the need to extend the principle of equal treatment to the *exercise* of professional activities, for example the ability to rent property to

---

[198] Case 71/76 [1977] E.C.R. I 765.
[199] Case C-340/89 [1991] E.C.R. I-2357, para.15.
[200] Case C-104/91 *Borrell* [1992] E.C.R. I-3003; Case 222/86 *UNECTEF v Heylens* [1987] E.C.R. 4097.
[201] Case C-234/97 *Bobadilla* [1999] E.C.R. I-4773. See also Case C-108/96 *MacQuen* [2001] E.C.R. I-837; Case C-313/01 *Morgenkesser* [2003] E.C.R. I-13467.

exhibit artistic works,[202] access to social housing[203] equal treatment in relation to taxation, especially taxation based upon residence requirements[204] as well as rules which may lead to the double payment of social security contributions in the home state and the host State.[205]

## Freedom of Establishment and Companies

The harmonisation of company law in the EU has been slow and faced difficulties because of differences in corporate structure across Europe and political differences on the form such regulation should take (Armour, 2005; Schön, 2005). The free movement of services and establishment provisions have been used as a means of circumventing barriers to free movement faced by corporate entities. Turning attention to issues relating to the freedom of establishment and legal persons (companies) the issues are exacerbated by the fact that companies may want to retain their registered head office (the "seat") in the home State but establish branches, agencies or subsidiaries in other Member States in order to conduct business at the local level. Company law in the Member States of the EU is not fully harmonised (Edwards, 1999; Wouters, 2000).

One fundamental difference between the Member States is the approach taken to deciding *where* a company is actually located: the place of incorporation or the place where the economic activity really takes place. Some States take an approach which identifies where the predominant economic activity is exercised. Other States use a more formal "place of incorporation" approach. The harmonisation of company law in the EU has been slow and the Member States are anxious to impose restrictions upon the movement of companies where they suspect that migrating companies may try to evade local laws and regulations.

One example is the case of the *Daily Mail*.[206] This company, which produces a national newspaper in the UK, wanted to move its central management and control to the Netherlands but also to maintain its legal personality and status as a company in the UK. There were a number of tax advantages to this plan. It needed the prior approval of the UK Treasury to do this but relocated to the

---

[202] Case 197/84 *Steinhauser v City of Biarritz* [1985] E.C.R. 1819.
[203] Case 305/87 *Commission v Italy* [1988] E.C.R. 29.
[204] Case C-80/94 *Wielockx* [1995] E.C.R. I-2493; Case C-107/94 *Asscher* [1996] E.C.R. I-3089.
[205] Case C-53/95 *Inasti v Kemmler* [1996] E.C.R. I-703.
[206] Case 81/87 [1988] E.C.R. 5483.

Netherlands before receiving such approval. The ECJ dismissed the argument that the requirement of prior approval for such a relocation was contrary to arts 43 and 48 EC. The Court recognised that a company must be anchored in at least one Member State for regulatory rules to apply and that in the absence of harmonising measures Member States were able to regulate the movement of companies. Thus, if the *Daily Mail* had wanted to establish a subsidiary in the Netherlands the UK would have had to justify rules which prevented the partial emigration of the economic activities of the *Daily Mail*. It would still be open for the UK to raise a justification based upon public policy considerations of combating tax evasion.[207]

The case can be viewed as the Court prompting the Member States to move forward on the harmonisation of company law; a hint which was ignored by the Member States. Later developments suggest that the ruling in the *Daily Mail* case may be at odds with the developments in relation to the free movement of services and capital, and the more general shift towards looking at rules which are a "hindrance" to free movement. This has led to the Court chipping away at the Member States' national laws governing company law.

The change in approach is seen in *Centros*[208] which concerned two Danish nationals who were shareholders in a private company incorporated in the UK. The shareholders applied to have a branch of the company registered in Denmark where the economic activities of the company took place. The company had never traded in the UK but had taken advantage of the more lenient incorporation rules of the UK which, inter alia, did not require minimum capital requirements. The Danish authorities refused to register a branch of the company arguing that the device was being used to evade the tougher Danish regulation of companies. The Court found the refusal to register the branch, the secondary establishment, an obstacle to free movement of establishment, since it was not an attempt to evade the Danish rules. This was a legitimate *exercise* of the right to free movement within the EU. Although the Danish regulators could take steps to counteract fraudulent use of the free movement provisions; the outright refusal to register the secondary establishment was a disproportionate response.

*Inspire Art*[209] concerned Dutch rules on minimum capital requirements and Directors' liability which prevented foreign companies from exercising economic activity in the Netherlands except through

---

[207] Case C-200/98 *X AB and Y AB v Riksskatteverket* [1999] E.C.R. I-8261.
[208] Case 212/97 [1999] E.C.R. I-1459.
[209] Case C-167/01 [2003] E.C.R. I-10155.

a branch. The Court accepted that any justifications for the rules to prevent abuse of Dutch laws and regulations could only be carried out on an individual basis. A general rule, impeding the right of establishment, was disproportionate.

In *Überseering*[210] the Court was faced with a more complicated issue. In a private dispute a Dutch company, Überseering, sued a German company for defective work carried out in Germany. All the shares of Überseering had been acquired by two German nationals before the litigation commenced. Under the German law Überseering had transferred its centre of administration to Germany but did not satisfy the German rules relating to incorporation and therefore did not have the legal capacity to bring proceedings. Überseering was still legally incorporated in the Netherlands. The ECJ ruled that the requirement to re-incorporate the company under German law in order to obtain access to the German legal system was a double burden, "an outright negation of freedom of establishment". These cases reveal that the Court is willing to allow regulatory competition to encourage free movement.

A host State cannot insist that a company's business be conducted through a primary establishment.[211] In *Factortame*[212] the Court ruled that a nationality condition on the owners of ships or the shareholders and directors was a breach of art.43 EC and was also contrary to art.294 EC. The residency and domicile rules were unjustified forms of indirect discrimination, but the requirement that a vessel had to be managed and its operations directed and controlled from within the UK was compatible with Community law since it essentially coincided with establishment which implies a fixed establishment. But this could not preclude the registration of a secondary establishment in the UK.

In addition to barriers to market access companies have also faced problems in access to economic activities,[213] and validation of qualifications provided by an education establishment[214] and relating to equality of treatment in relation to tax treatment.[215]

---

[210] Case C-208/00 [2002] E.C.R. I-9919.

[211] Case C-101/94 *Commission v Italy* [1996] E.C.R. I-2691.

[212] Case C-213/89 *R v Secretary of State for Transport Ex p. Factortame Ltd* (I) [1990] E.C.R. I-2433; *R v Secretary of State for Transport Ex p. Factortame Ltd* (II) [1991] E.C.R. I-3905.

[213] Case 3/88 *Commission v Italy* [1989] E.C.R. 4035.

[214] Case C-153/02 *Neri* [2003] E.C.R. I-3555.

[215] Case 270/83 *Commission v France* [1986] E.C.R. 273; Case C-250/95 *Futura Participations SA* [1997] E.C.R. I-2471; Case 311/97 *Royal Bank of Scotland plc v Elliniko Dimosio (RBS)* [1999] E.C.R. I-2651; Case C-330/91 *Ex p. Commerzbank* [1993] E.C.R. I-4017.

A variety of factors may be seen as a deterrent to migrating companies. In *Commission v Italy*[216] the Court held that an Italian law providing that only companies in which all, or a majority of shares were directly, or indirectly, in public or State ownership could conclude agreements for data processing systems for public authorities "essentially favoured Italian companies" and breached art.43 EC. The rules were not justifiable. In *Pfeiffer Großhandel*[217] Pfeiffer owned a large supermarket in Austria (Plus KAUF PARK). It obtained a court order restraining Löwa a rival German discount store operating in Austria from using the trade name "Plus" The Court held that an order against a company established in another Member State was liable to constitute an impediment to the realisation of a uniform advertising concept at Community level, contrary to art.43 EC, on the ground that it might force Löwa to adjust the presentation of its business according to the place of establishment. The Court recognised that the primary aim of the Austrian law was to safeguard trade names against the risk of confusion and could be justified by overriding requirements in the general interest thus the Court order was proportionate.

Contrast *Neri*[218] with the *Sevic*[219] case. In *Neri* a British company (ESE) created 12 branches in Italy where for a fee it provided courses which were validated by Nottingham Trent University leading to a BA degree. Neri enrolled on one such course and discovered the Italian authorities did not recognise her degree although it was recognised as a degree in the UK. The Court held that the Italian laws were there to protect educational standards but were likely to deter students from enrolling on the courses and seriously hinder the pursuit by SE of its economic activities in Italy. In *Sevic* the Court examined the compatibility of a German law allowing only for mergers between companies established in Germany. It was argued that the German law would deter the exercise of freedom of establishment and was contrary to art.43 EC. The Court recognised that national rules could be justified on the grounds of protecting the interests of creditors, minority shareholders and employees, as well as protecting the effectiveness of fiscal supervision and the fairness of commercial transactions. However the German law did not satisfy the principle of proportionality.

---

[216] Case 3/88 *Commission v Italy (Data Processing)* [1989] E.C.R. 4035.
[217] Case C-255/97 *Pfeiffer Großhandel GmbH* [1999] E.C.R. I-2835.
[218] Case C-153/02 *Neri v ESE* [2003] E.C.R. I-13555.
[219] Case C-411/03 *Sevic Systems* [2005] E.C.R. I-10805.

Direct taxation is an area jealously preserved by the Member States, but successive Court rulings are gradually chipping away at this autonomy. In *Marks and Spencer plc v David Halsey (HM Inspector of Taxes)*[220] a challenge was made to the UK's corporation tax scheme which allows for group relief under which a company may surrender its losses to another company in the same group carrying on trade in the UK. This allowed the company to deduct those losses from its taxable profits. Marks and Spencer plc argued that the rules were incompatible with the freedom of establishment. The Court ruled that a group relief scheme which did not allow a parent company to deduct the losses incurred by its subsidiaries established abroad from its taxable profits was in principle compatible with Community law but it was a restriction upon the freedom of establishment to preclude the possibility for the parent company to deduct losses incurred by non-resident subsidiaries if the parent could show that the losses were not (and could not) be taken into account in the member state of residence of the subsidiary companies. The approach in Marks and Spencer was based upon a restrictions analysis but in other cases a restrictions analysis was combined with a discrimination analysis.[221]

## 5.7 Free Movement of Capital

Capital should be one of the easiest commodities to move freely within the EU but in practice the Member States have been reluctant to liberalise this economic freedom, and the free movement of capital continues to be the least developed of the four economic freedoms (Peers, 2002; Usher, 1994, Flynn, 2002) but also is the only economic freedom where the original EEC Treaty provisions have been repealed and replaced now forming arts 56–59 EC, *arts 63–66 TFEU*).

The original free movement of capital provisions envisaged that the liberalisation of capital would take place in stages, using directives adopted under art.69 EEC and by the end of the transitional period. The EEC Treaty provisions were drafted in what the

---

[220] Case C-446/03 [2005] E.C.R. I-10837. See Kingston (2006–07).
[221] Case C-196/04 *Cadbury's Schweppes v CIR* [2006] E.C.R. I-7995; Case C-524/04 *Thin Cap* [2007] E.C.R. I-2107; Case C-231/05 *Oy AA* [2007] E.C.R. I-6373; Case C-347/04 *Rewe Zentralfinanz* [2007] E.C.R. I-2647.

Court in *Casati* called "less imperative terms".[222] In this case the Court ruled that complete free movement of capital could undermine the economic policy of the Member States or create an imbalance in the balance of payments. Therefore art.67(1) EC was not directly effective and free movement of capital should be available only to the extent necessary to ensure the proper functioning of the then Common Market. As a result the free movement of capital differs from the other three freedoms in that it has developed from detailed secondary legislation into a directly effective EC Treaty principle (Usher, 2005).

Some 20 years after the end of the transitional period Council dir.88/361/EEC[223] brought about the full liberalisation of capital movements and in its Annex set out a list (a nomenclature) of the capital movements which includes current payments covered by the directive which is still referred to in the case law.[224] Thus loans and mortgages, the taxation of dividends, guarantees linked to the provision of services, the use of golden shares by governments when publicly owned companies are privatised have all been held to fall within the scope of the directive. Shortly after this directive was adopted the Maastricht Treaty 1991 introduced new rules on capital movements and payments which were broad in nature, and legally complete, allowing for the direct effect of the relevant EC Treaty provisions.

Article 106(1) EC required the Member States to authorise means of payment as consideration for trade in goods, persons, services or capital. This therefore distinguishes the means of payment from the free movement of goods. In *R v Thompson*[225] the Court stated that art.106 EC was perhaps the most important provision in the EC Treaty for the attainment of a Common Market. Article 106(1) EC was declared directly effective in *Luisi and Carbonne*.[226]

The Court explained the distinction between art.106 and art.67 EC.[227] Current payments covered by art.106 EC involved such transactions as the transfers of foreign exchange as remuneration for a service whereas art.67 EC covered free movement of capital such as the investment of funds. This distinction became less important after the Treaty of Maastricht 1991.

---

[222] Case 203/80 *Criminal Proceedings Against Casati* [1981] E.C.R. 2595, para.19.

[223] OJ 1988 L178/5.

[224] Case C-222/97 *Manfred Trummer and Peter Mayer* [1999] E.C.R. I-1661.

[225] Case C-7/78 *R v Thompson* [19787] E.C.R. 2247, para.22.

[226] Cases 286/82 and 26/83 *Luisi and Carbone v Minisero del Tesoro* [1984] E.C.R. 377.

[227] Case 308/86 *Ministère Public v Lambert* [1988] E.C.R. 4369, para.10.

However, the Court has not been consistent in determining whether an activity should be categorised as a capital movement or as falling within the scope of the other Treaty freedoms.[228]

Articles 56–60 EC are the backbone of the second stage of Economic and Monetary Union (EMU), applying to all of the Member States, not just those States which have moved to the second stage of EMU. Article 56 EC is vertically directly effective[229] and applies to movements within the EU as well as movements to, and from, third countries. This raises the question as to whether the overlap between the capital movement rules open up the other freedoms to third country nationals who are operating in the Internal Market where the free movement of workers, services, goods and establishment overlap with the free movement of capital rules.[230]

Article 67 EC uses a discrimination model to establish the free movement of capital prohibiting discrimination on the grounds of nationality, the place of residence and the place where capital is invested. The issue of direct discrimination has dominated the case law.[231] In the *Golden Shares*[232] cases the Court has recognised the concept of indirect discrimination and followed the ideas seen in the services and goods case law of looking for a hindrance to free movement of capital. Such hindrances may be justified by public interest defences, subject to the principle of proportionality.[233]

Article 58 EC contains two derogations from the principle of free movement of capital. The first derogation applies to tax payers. Member States may distinguish between tax payers who are not in the same situation with regard to their place of residence or where

---

[228] Case C-410/96 *Criminal Proceedings Against Ambry* [1998] E.C.R. I-7875; Case C-35/98 *Verkooijen* [2006] E.C.R. I-4071; Joined Cases C-397/98 and C-410/98 *Metallgesellschaft and Hoechst v Inland Revenue* [2001] E.C.R. I-1727; Case C-524/04 *Test Claimants in the Thin Cap Litigation v Commissioners of Inland Revenue* [2007] E.C.R. I-2107; Case C-112/05 *Commission v Germany (Volkswagen Golden Shares)* judgment of October 23, 2007.

[229] Case Joined Cases C-163/94, C-165/94 and C-250/94 *Criminal Proceedings Against Sanz de Lera* [1995] E.C.R. I-4830 para.41.

[230] Cases C-163, 165 and 250/94 *Sanz de Lera* [1995] E.C.R. I-4821; Case C-452/04 *Fidum Finanz* [2006] E.C.R. I-9521; Case C-290/04 *FKP Scorpio Konzertprduktionen* [2006] E.C.R. I-9461; Case C-101/05 *Skatteverket v A*, judgment of December 18, 2007.

[231] Case C-302/97 *Klaus Konle v Republik Österreich* [1999] E.C.R. I-3099; Case C-423/98 *Albore* [2000] E.C.R. I-5965.

[232] Case C-463/00 *Commission v Spain* [2003] E.C.R. I-4581; Case C-367/98 *Commission v Portugal* [2002] E.C.R. I-4731; Case C-98/01 *Commission v UK* [2003] E.C.R. I-4641 (Szyszczak, 2002).

[233] Case C-463/00 *Commission v Spain* [2003] E.C.R. I-4581; Case C-367/98 *Commission v Portugal* [2002] E.C.R. I-4731; Case C-98/01 *Commission v UK* [2003] E.C.R. I-4641 (Szyszczak, 2002).

their capital is invested (Snell, 2007).[234] The second derogation is a broader derogation using the traditional grounds of public policy or public security.

In *Manninen*[235] a challenge was made to Finnish legislation which did not allow shareholders to benefit from a tax credit on dividends where the company is established in another Member State. The Court recognised that direct taxation remained within the competence of the Member States. But the Court found that the Finnish rules involved a restriction on the free movement of capital within the meaning of art.56 EC. Looking at the justifications for the rules the Court rejected the argument based upon art.58(1)(a) EC. This should be interpreted restrictively and was limited by art.58(3) EC which is directed at arbitrary discrimination and disguised restrictions. In order to fall within art.58(1) EC it must be shown that the difference in treatment must concern situations which are not objectively comparable, or be justified by overriding reasons in the general interest. And comply with the principle of proportionality.

One overriding reason which may be raised by the Member States is the need to safeguard the cohesion of the tax system.[236] But to date a Member State has not satisfied the principle of proportionality when applying the derogation to a fundamental Treaty freedom. In *Manninen* the Court shows how a less restrictive approach could be taken to preserve the cohesion of the national system. A direct link must be established between the tax advantage concerned and the offsetting of that advantage by a particular tax deduction The objective pursued by the tax legislation should also be examined. In the Finnish case the objective was to prevent double taxation. The Court saw the link between the tax advantage and the offsetting tax deduction and why the Finnish rules were necessary to achieve this. But granting to a shareholder in a company established in another Member State a tax credit calculated by reference to the corporation tax paid by the company in the Member State would be a less restrictive measure while at the same time not threatening the cohesion of the tax system.

---

[234] Case C-279/93 *Schumacker* [1995] E.C.R. I-225; Case C-204/90 *Bachmann v Belgium* [1992] E.C.R. I-249 (Vanistendael, 1996; Wattel, 1996).

[235] Case C-319/02 *Manninen* [2004] E.C.R. I-7477.

[236] Case C-204/90 *Bachmann* [1992] E.C.R. I-249; Case C-300/90 *Commission v Belgium* [1992] E.C.R. I-305. See Wathelet, 2001.

# 6: Competition Law and Policy

The competition rules are found in arts 81 and 82 EC addressing the regulation of agreements and dominant positions in the market exercised by non-State (private) economic entities (or as the EC Treaty calls them "undertakings"). Although addressed to private undertakings these provisions may also be used against the State, albeit in exceptional circumstances. The EC Treaty also has competition provisions addressing special rights granted to undertakings and state monopolies in art.86 EC and a regime of State Aid control in arts 87–88 EC. One of the most significant areas of distortion of trade and competition, public procurement does not have an EC Treaty base and is regulated through secondary legislation (Trepte, 2007). Traditionally from an academic perspective competition law and policy and the Internal Market "trade" rules have been viewed as separate areas. However early litigants saw how the competition rules complement the rules relating to the four freedoms which form the fundamental economic core of the Internal Market (Maduro, 1998; Szyszczak, 2007). Many of the early cases used art.28 EC *and* the competition law provisions against the Member States, particularly art.86 EC, but also the combination of arts 10, 81 and 82 EC. It has been argued that the Court was hesitant to use the competition law provisions against the Member States because, with the exception of art.86(2) EC, there was no scope to allow a State's economic activity to be justified or exempted from the application of the full force of the rules of the market. This explains why art.28 EC was the chosen route of the Court in the initial cases exploring the boundaries of the constitutional division of power in the market (Szyszczak, 2004).

Under the current EC Treaty competition is not an objective of the Community but a policy tool to achieve the aims and objectives of European integration. The four freedoms and the competition rules, together with directly enforceable individual economic rights, combined with the guarantee of competition as an economic value bestow a quality of a liberal economic constitution upon the EC Treaty. Under the current EC Treaty arrangements art.4 EC charges the Member States and the Community to conduct their economic policies:

"... in accordance with the principle of an open market economy with free competition."

In relation to economic and monetary policy art.98 EC states that

"The Member States and the Community shall act in accordance with the principle of an open market economy with free competition, favouring an efficient allocation of resources, and in compliance with the principles set out in Article 4."

The importance attached to art.4 EC is seen in *CIF* where it is used as a "fidelity clause".[1] In *Courage v Crehan*[2] the Court refers to the fundamental political and constitutional building blocks of Community law to stress the role of competition policy in European integration:

"It should be borne in mind, first of all, that the Treaty has created its own legal order, which is integrated into the legal systems of the Member States and which their courts are bound to apply. The subjects of that legal order are not only the Member States but also their nationals. Just as it imposes burdens on individuals, Community law is also intended to give rise to rights which become part of their legal assets. Those rights arise not only where they are expressly granted by the Treaty but also by virtue of obligations which the Treaty imposes in a clearly defined manner both on individuals and on the Member States and the Community institutions (see the judgments in Case 26/62 *Van Gend en Loos* [1963] ECR 1, Case 6/64 *Costa* [1964] ECR 585 and Joined Cases C-6/90 and C-9/90 *Francovich and Others* [1991] ECR I-5357, paragraph 31)."

---

[1] Case C-198/01 *CIF v Autorità Garante della Concorrenza e del Mercato* [2003] E.C.R. I-8055, para.47.
[2] Case C-453/99 *Courage v Crehan* [2001] E.C.R. I-6297, paras 19–20.

Since the Treaty of Maastricht 1991, the extent of the *balance* between free market ideas and legitimate public interests of the Member States has been part of an ongoing debate within the EU. The balance between economic concerns and social concerns has always been in the background in the political processes of the EU, as well as the case law of the European Court. The Lisbon Process, while recognising the need for a balance between what are see as *competing values* of the EU, emphasised the need for a competitive economy and this tipped the balance in favour of economic priorities.

The framers of the Constitutional Treaty wanted to make competition an objective of the EU and competition was classified as an exclusive competence of the Union (art.I-13(1)(b)). However, over the summer of 2007, in the discussions over the future Treaty of Lisbon 2007, France led a move to "downgrade" the significance of competition in the new Treaty. The final result is that competition is not mentioned amongst the Community objectives in the new Treaty on European Union (*art.3 TEU*). However the Internal Market is one of the Community objectives (*art.3(3) TEU*) and the Internal Market includes a system ensuring that competition is not distorted (*Protocol on the Internal Market and Competition*).[3]

Under the Treaty of Lisbon amendments competition is an exclusive competence of the Union (*art.3(1)(b) TFEU and art.3(6) TEU*): "The Union shall pursue its objectives by appropriate means commensurate with the competences which are conferred upon it by the treaties (*art.3(6) TEU)*. However, the reference to an economic policy based upon "the principle of an open market economy with free competition" is moved from the Principles Chapter to the Economic Policy Chapter (*art.119 TFEU*). What does this mean? Has competition been down-graded? One approach in answering this question is to compare the current EC Treaty with the Lisbon amendments. Currently competition is not an objective of the EC/Union. In the current EC Treaty competition is an *instrument* of policy. It can be argued that from the Treaty of Lisbon competition indirectly becomes an objective of the Union through its explicit link with Internal Market objective in the *Protocol on the Internal Market and Competition*. Arguably this Protocol challenges the widespread, US-inspired, moves to detach competition from market integration, limiting it to mere efficiency considerations.

In recent years the competition rules have also influenced the development of an industrial policy for the EU. Although the

---

[3] The Protocols have the same legal value as the Treaties (art.51 TEU).

Commission has developed an industrial policy through the use of soft law it was not until the Treaty of Maastricht 1991 that such a policy was included in the EC Treaty (Sauter, 1997; Szyszczak, 2007; Kroes, 2007).

The competition rules are found in arts 81–89 EC. Competition policy addresses the barriers to market integration which can be raised by the State and non-State actors, particularly private firms. The rules are interpreted in a teleological way by the European Courts since competition is one of the *tasks* of the Community set out in art.2 and is also mentioned as an *activity* in art.3(g) EC.[4] Also of importance in understanding EC competition law is the principle of subsidiarity in art.5 EC and the fidelity clause of art.10 EC. The principle of non-discrimination on the grounds of nationality contained in art.12 EC plays a role in many cases dealing with access to markets and distribution of goods and services. Overall the principle of proportionality underpins the approach of the Court in reviewing anticompetitive acts of the State and private parties and the Commission's response to such conduct.

The founders of the Common Market recognised that it was pointless to create a Common Market where State barriers to market integration were dismantled but private barriers continued. A multinational firm operating across a number of Member States can cause as much damage to free trade and market integration by dividing up its operations along national lines as can a State. Market power may also disrupt the competitive conditions of a market, denying customers choice and denying competitors entry to the market. Similarly collusion and agreements between smaller firms can also divide up the Internal Market creating anti-competitive effects. The State may actively encourage this form of collusion by regulating how certain goods and services are delivered. Ownership of intellectual property rights is an important tool in promoting innovation, research and development but the exercise of such rights may prevent market access and divide up the Internal Market along territorial lines. Although aimed primarily at private undertakings, the Court has argued that art.81 EC and art.82 EC may also be applied to State activity. This explains why, therefore, there is a need to create a complementary approach between the rules of trade, the Internal Market, and the rules of competition (Mortelmans, 2001; Baquero-Cruz, 2002; Szyszczak, 2004 and 2007).

---

[4] Case 6/72 *Europemballage Corp and Continental Can Co Inc v Commission* [1973] E.C.R. 215.

In 1957 few Member States had a developed system of competition law. The EC Treaty coincided with the new system of competition law established in post-war Germany at the behest of the US. Germany led the evolution of Community competition law in the 1960s and 1970s and the early development of a Community competition system was influenced by the US anti-trust system (Gerber, 1998). Over time the EU and the individual Member States have created a distinctive *European* system of competition law[5] which may sometimes clash with the operation of US anti-trust policy in the globalised economy (Fox, 2003; cf. Bloom, 2005).

EC competition law and policy is often seen as different from other competition and antitrust regimes in two particular dimensions. Firstly, it is aimed at promoting the public and private integration of European markets. Alongside the free movement provisions of the Internal Market the competition rules form a central plank of the economic constitution of Europe. A second dimension is that EU competition law and policy recognises that it pursues a variety of aims beyond the narrow view of promoting efficiency in markets. Other goals have been articulated: ensuring consumer welfare, protecting social interests and protecting the competitive structure of markets. Another concern of modern competition law in the EU has been the prevention of the abuse of excessive market power, either by the State or private parties. The focus upon the restraint of private power in the market has been seen by Amato (1997) as a part of the process of upholding the fundamental freedom of individuals: a foundation stone of liberal democracy.

From the late 1990s competition law has been undergoing a process of modernisation.[6] This has included procedural and institutional changes involved the de-centralisation of competition enforcement alongside what is termed a "more economic approach" to the interpretation of the substantive law of competition (Wurmnest, 2007). The year 2002 is often seen as a turning point in the modernisation of competition law. Philip Lowe was appointed as the Director General of Competition in the Commission and introduced a tougher economic dimension to competition policy and investigations, creating a role for a Chief Economist at the Commission. 2002 was also the year in which the CFI annulled three high profile merger

---

[5] Slot, 2004.

[6] The institutional beginnings of this process are usually traced back to the Commission's Green Paper on Vertical Restraints in EC Competition Policy of January 22, 1997.

decisions of the Commission,[7] of which one has resulted in substantial damages being awarded against the Commission.[8] This signalled to the Commission the need to ensure that its investigations were carried out with a degree of economic rigour to show how alleged anti-competitive behaviour harmed competition in Europe.

In 1957 the Commission was placed at the centre of the enforcement of the rules. Even today, the European Courts recognise that the Commission has a broad economic discretion to monitor and enforce competition law.[9] Regulation 17/62 provided the Commission with a central and monopolist role to regulate arts 81 and 82 EC. But because the competition rules also produce direct effect within the national legal order there may be conflict in the respective powers of national courts and the Commission, especially where a justification or exemption from the non-application of the competition rules is pleaded. By using the preliminary ruling procedure national courts have contributed to the growth of a body of case law which refines the principles upon which the EU competition policy is built. Thus the body of policy-making and decision-taking built up by the Commission has acquired a normative status and provided the legitimacy for the competition policy of the EU.

The enlargement of the EU, alongside the growing internationalisation of trade, made the Commission's monopolist role unworkable. The Commission attempted to lessen its workload in the monitoring and enforcement of competition law by adopting Block Exemptions and guidance on policy through soft law Notices and Communications. At the same time, increasing the workload, special rules developed to regulate mergers ex ante.

Regulation 1/2003/EC[10] introduced the de-centralisation of the enforcement of arts 81 and 82 EC to the national level, repealing reg.17/62/EEC. This has liberated the Commission from its excessive workload, allowing it to focus upon the real "trouble cases" for the

---

[7] Case T-5/02 *Tetra Laval BV v Commission* [2002] E.C.R. II-4381; Cases C-12/03 P and C-13/03 P *Commission of the European Communities v Tetra Laval BV* [2005] E.C.R. II-987; Case T-48/03 *Schneider Electric v Commission*, Order of January 31, 2006; on appeal Case C-188/06P *Schneider Electric v Commission* [2007] E.C.R. I-35; Case T-342/99 *Airtours v Commission* [2002] E.C.R. II-2585.

[8] Case C-188/06P *Schneider Electric v Commission* [2007] E.C.R. I-35. An action for damages has also been lodged by Airtours (now MyTravel): Case T-212/03 pending.

[9] Case C-141/02P *Commission v T-Mobile Austria GmbH formerly max.mobil Telekommunikation Service* [2005] E.C.R. I-1283.

[10] OJ 2004 L1/1.

EU as well as engaging in sector inquiries.[11] It has also led to the creation of new actors, committees of experts to advise on competition policy and a network to co-ordinate developments in the Member States to ensure that there is not too much divergence in the application of competition law at the national level (Szyszczak, 2005; Ehlermann and Atanasiu, 2003). However, there are also fears that the European networks may result in too much confidential information being exchanged between national authorities. (Reichelt, 2005).

At the same time as the enforcement of competition has been linked to regulatory as well as competition bodies at the national level private enforcement has been encouraged[12] albeit with doubts as to whether this is the correct course for competition policy to take since there is a school of thought that competition law enforcement should be left in the hands of a public regulator (Wils, 2003; Eilmansberger, 2007; Kominos, 2007, 2008; Eilmansberger, 2007).

## 6.1 Article 81 EC

Article 81 EC addresses agreements and other forms of co-operation between private parties which may affect competition within the EU and segment markets, in the same way that national boundaries may present obstacles to the free movement of goods, services, establishment and capital.

Article 81 (1) EC prohibits any kind of agreement or collusion between undertakings which has the object *or* the effect of preventing, restricting or distorting competition. Article 81(2) EC makes any agreement which infringes art.81(1) EC void. This was a clever self-policing device. Until reg.1/2003 came into force it was possible for undertakings to notify their agreements to the Commission and for the Commission to grant a negative clearance, or, if the agreement infringed art.81(1) EC but was beneficial to the integration project, to be granted an individual exemption. The work load of the Commission became so great that a number of Block Exemptions were introduced allowing firms to mould agreements into business practices which did not require prior approval from the

---

[11] The most recent being a sector inquiry into the pharmaceutical industry launched in February 2008.

[12] Case C-453/99 *Courage v Crehan* [2001] E.C.R. I-6297; Joined Cases C-295-298 *Manfredi* [2006] E.C.R. I-6619.

Commission. The option of notification is now lost. Under the decentralisation of competition law introduced in reg.1/2003/EC firms must self-assess whether the agreement is caught by art.81(1) EC and whether it would satisfy the conditions for an exemption under art.81(3) EC.

## Definition of an Undertaking

The use of the word "undertaking" in competition law is a deliberate attempt to include as many economic actors as possible within the ambit of competition law. The definition of an undertaking has also been one of the devices used in EU law to create a bright line between State activity which is economic and should be subject to the rules of the Internal Market and competition law, and activity which is purely public or social in nature and remains within the autonomy of the State. (Szyszczak, 2004). As with other definitions such as the concept of a "worker" under art.39 EC, the Court has ruled that the definition of an undertaking is a Community law concept and it is irrelevant as to the national definition of legal status and the way in which the undertaking is financed. In *Höfner and Elser v Macrotron*[13] a Federal Employment Placement Office in Germany was held to be engaged in economic activity. At para.21 the ECJ states that:

> "the concept of an undertaking encompasses every entity engaged in an economic activity, regardless of the legal status of the entity and the way in which it is financed."

Thus artists, inventors, a pension fund, the International Federation of Football Association, customs agents and even members of the Amsterdam Bar have all been held to constitute "undertakings" for the purposes of EU competition law (Townley, 2007). On the other side of the bright line examples of cases where an a body has been held not to be an "undertaking" include a French municipal authority with a concession to supply funeral services, *Bodson v Pompes Funèbres des Régions Libérés SA*,[14] and compulsory sickness funds created by statute in Germany *AOK Bundesverband v Ichthyol-Gesellschaft Cordes, Hermani and Co.*[15]

---

[13] Case C-41/90 [1991] E.C.R. I-1979.
[14] Case 30/87 [1988] E.C.R. I-2479.
[15] Cases C-264/01, C-354/01, C-355/01 [2004] E.C.R. I-1283. For an example of non-economic activity see: Cases C-284/04, C-369/04, *T-Mobile Austria e.a.* judgment of June 26, 2007.

In *SELEX*[16] the Commission used the earlier Court ruling in *SAT*[17] to find that Eurocontrol was not an undertaking and therefore not subject to the competition rules. The CFI found that powers exercised by SAT were different from the situation in the earlier ruling but found that most of the activities exercised by Eurocontrol in the field of air navigation were non-economic but one activity was economic: that of giving assistance to national administrations. However the CFI found that there was no breach of the competition rules.

Article 81 EC requires an agreement or collusion between undertakings. One issue is whether art.81 EC can apply where undertakings are sufficiently linked to form one economic entity, for example, a parent and its subsidiary. In *VihoEurope BV v Commission*[18] Parker Pen Ltd sold stationery products through local subsidiaries. Parker Pen Ltd refused to deal with Viho, a Dutch office equipment wholesaler. Viho complained that the distribution system was a set of agreements between undertakings which divided up the EU market. On appeal to the ECJ the Court noted that Parker Pen Ltd held 100 per cent of the shares in the subsidiaries and that sales and marketing were directed by the parent company. Thus Parker Pen Ltd and its subsidiaries formed a single economic unit within which the subsidiaries did not enjoy real autonomy. The Court makes the point, however, that the large undertaking may run the risk of infringing art.82 EC. Articles 81 EC and 82 EC are not mutually exclusive.[19]

As a result of privatisation and liberalisation more complex issues of liability for anti-competitive behaviour are emerging.[20]

## *Agreements and Concerted Practices*

Article 81 EC is framed broadly to outlaw "all agreements between undertakings, decisions by associations of undertakings and concerted practices which may affect trade between Member States and which have as their object or effect the prevention, restriction or

---

[16] Case T-155/04 2006] E.C.R. I-4797 on appeal Case C-113/07.

[17] Case C-364/92 [1994] E.C.R. I-43.

[18] Case C-73/95P [1996] E.C.R. I-5457.

[19] Case 85/76 *Hoffman La-Roche and Co AG v Commission* [1979] E.C.R. 461; Case T-51/89 *Tetra Pak Rausing SA v Commission (Tetra Pak I)* [1990] E.C.R. II-309.

[20] Recently the Court held that a successor undertaking may be liable for competition infringements of a previous undertaking, even where the previous undertaking continues to exist: Case C-280/06 *Autoritá Garanté della Concurenza e del Mercato v Ente tabacchi italiani*, judgment of December 11, 2007.

distortion of competition within the common market." The idea behind such a broad rule is to ensure an optimal degree of competition by making undertakings behave independently on the market. Article 81 EC is a curious paradox between attempting to capture far too much behaviour which may not be anti-competitive, but in fact may have pro-competitive benefits for European integration and on the other hand failing to recognise that anti-competitive behaviour may also take place without formal co-operation, for example, secret "gentleman's agreements", signalling, price leadership policies. It is important to distinguish between two forms of agreement: those where the *object* is the restriction of competition and those with a more benign object but the *effects* might be anti-competitive. When the parties enter into an agreement whose object is anticompetitive (for example, because they wish to cartelise to fix prices, or share markets) they will wish to keep this agreement hidden from the competition authorities. In these cases the Commission will often look for a "smoking gun", for example, an email, a fax documenting that parties had engaged in cartel-like behaviour. More recently whistle-blowing has brought to light these secret forms of agreement with the incentive of a waiver or reduction in the fine for the whistle-blower. The difficulty which the Commission may encounter is how to distinguish between cartel-like behaviour which is caused by the parties agreeing to restrict competition expressly, and cartel-like behaviour which is the result of the particular market conditions that create incentives for parties to behave as if there were a cartel. Economists would distinguish between *express* and *tacit* collusion, and while the economic effect is the same, competition law only catches express forms of collusion.

In the absence of a clear written agreement the CFI has held that there must be a "concurrence of wills" between at least two parties. In *Commission v Bayer*[21] the Commission argued that there was a tacit agreement between Bayer and its wholesalers to partition the Internal Market and maintain high prices. There was no Internal Market in pharmaceutical products and in one product, Adalat, the price was fixed by health authorities in France and Spain at a level around 40 per cent less than the price in the UK. Wholesalers began to import Adalat into the UK to exploit the price difference. Bayer's subsidiaries began to impose caps on the amount of Adalat supplied in France and Spain. Bayer argued that this was unilateral conduct and that the Commission has stretched the concept of an "agree-

---

[21] Case T-41/96 [2000] E.C.R. II-3383; on appeal Case C-2/01 and C-3/01P [2004] E.C.R. I-23.

ment" too far. The CFI annulled the Commission Decision. On appeal the ECJ accepted that the use of measures which prevented or hindered parallel imports is not per se evidence of an agreement. The policy did not require co-operation between wholesalers but in certain circumstances it may be necessary to look at the intention of the parties.

Article 81 (1) EC also prohibits decisions between associations of undertakings which produce anti-competitive effects. This may encompass the constitution of the association[22] or the code/ regulations under which the members of the association operate,[23] even if the code is non-binding,[24] and professional regulations.[25]

Concerted practices are also brought within the scope of art.81(1) EC. This has created controversy since firms operating in oligopolistic markets argue that they behave in parallel by reacting to the same market conditions. In *ICI v Commission* (Dyestuffs)[26] the Court explained that there was a difference between an agreement and a concerted practice, providing a definition of the latter as:

". . . the object is to bring within the prohibition of [Article 81(1) EC] a form of coordination between undertakings which, without having reached the stage where an agreement properly so-called has been concluded, knowingly substitutes practical cooperation between them for the risks of competition.

By its very nature, then, a concerted practice does not have all the elements of a contract but may inter alia arise out of co-ordination which becomes apparent from the behaviour of the participants."

In the later case of the *Sugar Cartel*[27] the Court added to this definition with the words that the participants

" . . . knowingly substituted for the risks of competition practical cooperation between them, which culminated in a situation which did not correspond to the normal conditions of the market."

[22] *National Sulphuric Acid Association,* OJ 1980 L 260/24.
[23] *Visa International-Multilateral Interchange Fee,* OJ 2002 L 318/17.
[24] Case 45/85 *VDS v Commission* [1987] E.C.R. 405.
[25] Case C-303/ 99 *Wouters v Algemene Raad van de Nederlandse Order van Advocaten* [2002] E.C.R. I-1577.
[26] Cases 6 and 7/73 *Istituto Chemioterapico Italiano SpA and Commercial Solvents Corp v Commission* [1974] E.C.R. 223, paras 64 and 65.
[27] Cases 40-48, 50, and 54-56/73 [1975] E.C.R. 1663.

Proving a concerted practice may be difficult. In *Sugar Cartel* the Court stated that the facts must be looked at as a whole, but in *Hüls AG v Commission* (Polypropylene Cartel)[28] the Court made the Commission's task easier by stating that the anticompetitive effects of the concerted practice on the market do not have to be shown.

## Preventing, restricting or distorting competition

To be caught by art.8(1) EC an agreement must have as its object *or* effect a restriction of competition (Odudo, 2001, 2006). Some illustrations of the kinds of agreements potentially caught by the competition rules are found in art.81(1) EC, for example, price fixing, market sharing. In *Consten and Grundig v Commission*[29] the Court held that the effect on competition does not necessarily have to be detrimental. This allowed for a broad interpretation of art.81 (1) EC, casting the net of Community competition law wide.

The agreement must analysed in the totality of the economic and legal context within which it operates.[30] The Commission has codified its own practice and the Courts' case law. In 2004 the Commission produced a set of Guidelines as part of the implementation of the modernisation programme related to reg.1/2003/EC.[31]

## May Affect Trade Between Member States

This part of art.81(1) EC has traditionally been interpreted as the dividing line between Community competence to regulate competition and national competence. The Commission and the European Courts look at the effects of an agreement or concerted practice. Even a local agreement within one Member State may affect competition in the Internal Market. The language used in one of the earliest rulings on this phrase echoes the language of free movement of goods used in *Dassonville*[32]:

"For the requirement to be fulfilled it must be possible to forsee with a sufficient degree of probability on the basis of a

---

[28] Case C-199/92P [1995] E.C.R. I-4287.

[29] Cases 56 and 58/64 [1966] E.C.R. 299.

[30] Case 23/67 *Brasserie de Haecht SA (No. 1) v Wilkin* [1967] E.C.R. 407.

[31] Communication from the Commission, *Guidelines on the application of Article 81(3) of the Treaty,* O J 2004 C 101/97. At paras 21–27, the Commission explains how the words "object or effect of restricting, preventing or distorting competition" operate.

[32] Case 8/74 *Procureur du Roi v Dassonville* [1974] E.C.R. 837.

set of objective factors of law or of fact that the agreement in question may have an influence, direct or indirect, actual or potential, on the pattern of trade between Member States."[33]

In the Guidelines associated with reg.1/2003 there is a document entitled *Guidelines on Effect of Trade Between Member States* which summarises the Court's case law.[34]

### (i) De minimis

The Court[35] and the Commission have accepted a de minimis principle in relation to the effects on competition and the effects on trade between Member States. The Commission Notice of 2001 restricts the principle to the *competition* aspects of the infringement of art.81(1) EC[36] and the 2004 Guidelines explain the application of a de minimis approach on the effects on trade between Member States.[37]

### (ii) Article 81(3) EC

The wide application of art.81 (1) EC caught many agreements and business practices of undertakings. The Commission was not willing to use a "rule of reason" and preferred to use the possibility of an individual exemption under art.81(3) EC as the process for deciding if certain kinds of agreement could be beneficial for the Internal Market (Monti, 2002).[38] There are four conditions to be met for art.81(3) EC to apply, with the applicant bearing the burden of showing all four conditions are met. The agreement must: (1) lead to an improvement in the production of goods or services; (2) lead to

---

[33] Cases 56 and 58/64 *Etablissements Consten SA and Grundig-Verkaufs-GmnH v Commission* [1966] E.C.R. 299, 341.

[34] Commission Notice, *Guidelines on the effect on trade concept contained in Articles 81 and 82 of the Treaty*, OJ 2004 C 101/ 81.

[35] Case 5/69 *Völk v Vervaecke* [1969] E.C.R. 295.

[36] *Commission Notice on Agreements of Minor Importance Which Do Not Appreciably Restrict Competition Under Article 81(1) of the Treaty establishing the European Community (de minimis)*, OJ 2001 C 368/11.

[37] *Commission Notice Guidelines on the effect on trade concept contained in Articles 81 and 82 of the Treaty*, OJ 2004 C101/ 86.

[38] See Case T-112/99 *Métropole Télévision (M6) v Commission* [2001] E.C.R. II-2459.

an improvement in the distribution of goods and services; (3) promote technical progress; (4) promote economic progress. Efficiency gains can be included in the consideration of art.81(3) EC and other benefits such as social benefits, for example, improving the stability of the labour market or environmental concerns have been used to justify an exemption under art.81(3) EC. The Commission provided guidance on the scope of art.81(1) EC through soft law. Under the new decentralised regime of enforcement of competition law undertakings must assess the balance between art.81 (1) and (3) EC on their behaviour. The Commission has issued Guidelines on the Application of art.81(3) EC.[39]

## Fines, Whistle-Blowing, Leniency and Settlements

Other aspects of the modernisation of competition law are a shift in focus to creating greater deterrence of anticompetitive conduct by a new fining policy emphasising that higher fines will be imposed where breach of the competition rules is intentional or negligent.[40] The Commission has also encouraged whistle blowing by issuing a Leniency Notice.[41] In 2005 the Commissioner for Competition, Neelie Kroes also indicated that the US-style plea bargaining system would be introduced whereby an undertaking could get a rebate from the fine it would otherwise have to pay if it elected not to contest the Statement of Objections issued by the Commission.

## The Application of art.81 EC to State Activity

The Court has used art.81 EC in conjunction with art.10 EC, the fidelity or solidarity clause to create a doctrine which imposed restraints upon the economic policy of the Member States. The Court established that the Member States were prevented from depriving the competition rules of their effet utile, that is their effectiveness. In Au Ble Vert[42] the Court suggested that State legislation which makes anti-competitive behaviour redundant, and thus restricting competition, would infringe art.81 EC. This was extended to cover, firstly, any State measures (even including a mere policy) which imposed, or facilitated or reinforced the effects of restrictive

---

[39] OJ 2004 C 101/1.
[40] Guidelines on the Method of Setting Fines Imposed Pursuant to Article 23(2)(a) of Regulation No 1/23, OJ 2006 C 21/02.
[41] Commission Notice on Immunity From Fines and Reduction of Fines in Cartel Cases, OJ 2006 C-298/17.
[42] Case 229/83 [1985] E.C.R. 1.

agreements[43] and, secondly, where the State delegated to undertakings the responsibility to take measures of economic policy which restricted, or had the potential to restrict, competition.[44] This approach coincided with the era pre-*Keck* where the Court gave an expansive interpretation to art.28 EC. In a series of rulings delivered at the same time as the ruling in *Keck* the Court reigned in this expansive approach to the application of art.81 EC to State activity.[45] This self-imposed judicial restraint towards State intervention where there was no Community interest at stake was called the "November Revolution" by Reich (1994). Reich argues that these cases were a significant turning point in the Court's constitution building of the EU, with an implicit rejection of a liberal economic Constitution. But the Court continues to accept that art.81 EC can apply to State activity but will normally find legislative and regulatory activity of the State acceptable, provided that the principles of proportionality and non-discrimination are observed (Szyszczak, 2007).

## 6.2 Abuse of a Dominant Position

Article 82 EC addresses the competition issues which arise where a firm has the capacity to behave unilaterally on the market because of the strength of its economic power. Holding a monopoly or a dominant position is not per se a problem for EU law; it is the way the dominance is used, the abuse of market power which attaches a special responsibility for dominant firms. Article 82 EC addresses the power held by corporate groups, multinational companies[46] as well as collective dominance of a market by more than one undertaking. The idea of collective dominance is controversial since where there are a few firms operating in an oligopolistic market such firms will argue that they react in a similar way to the same market conditions. The CFI[47] has defined collective dominance as where two or more independent economic entities are:

---

[43] Case 123/83 *BNIC v Clair* [1985] E.C.R. 402.
[44] Case 231/83 *Cullet v Leclerc* [1985] E.C.R. 305.
[45] Case C-185/91 *Reiff* [1993] E.C.R. I-5801; Case C-2/91 *Meng* [1993] E.C.R. I-5751; Case C-245/91 *OHRA* [1993] E.C.R. 5851.
[46] Case 6/72 *Europemballage Corp and Continental Can Co Inc v Commission* [1973] E.C.R. 215; Cases 6 and 7/73 *Istituto Chemioterapico Italiano Spa and Commercial Solvents Corp v Commission* [1974] E.C.R. 223.
[47] Cases T-68, 77 and 78/89 *Società Italiano Vetro SpA v Commission ("Flat Glass")* [1992] E.C.R. II-1403.

"... united by such economic links that, by virtue of that fact, together they hold a dominant position."

In later cases the ECJ ruled that contractual or other links in law are not essential for a finding that there is collective dominance but other connecting factors could be taken into account in an economic assessment and in particular in an assessment of the structure of the market in question.[48]

Even more far-reaching is the ruling in a case under the merger regulation,[49] where the CFI held that evidence of a collective dominant position may be found where the economic links between the undertakings are formed only by:

"... the relationship of interdependence existing between the parties to a tight oligopoly within which, in a market with appropriate characteristics, in particular in terms of market concentration, transparency and product homogeneity, those parties are in a position to anticipate one another's behaviour and are therefore strongly encouraged to align their conduct in the market."

Article 82 EC is skeletal in form. There must be a dominant position in the Common Market, or a substantial part of the Common Market; there must be an abuse of that position, with art.82 EC providing a set of illustrations as to how abuse might occur, and there must be an effect on trade between Member States. There has been less case law on art.82 EC and it has been used predominantly against non-EU multinational firms. The Commission has produced less soft law guidance on art.82 EC.

In contrast to art.81 (3) there is no possibility of an "exemption" from an abuse of a dominant position. Thus an institutional history was never developed between the Commission and dominant firms where a dialogue could develop on what kind of behaviour was acceptable by a dominant firm and less predictability for competitors or consumers as to what abusive conduct would be tackled by the Commission. The Court also appeared unsympathetic to justifications of defences raised by the dominant firms.[50]

---

[48] Cases C-395 and 396/96P *Compagnie Maritime Belge Transports SA v Commission* [2000] E.C.R. II-1365.
[49] Case T-102/96 *Gencor v Commission* [1999] E.C.R. II-753, para.276.
[50] See inter alia: *Tetra Pak* (conduct was an alleged response to the market); *Michelin, Hoffmann-La Roche* (aiding consumers and the market); *United Brands* (no market power).

Over the years the Court has accepted that an objective justification for an alleged abuse of a dominant position may be made, subject to the principle of proportionality. The difficulty with art.82 EC is that it has been applied ex post and undertakings may not realise that they are in a dominant position or that there behaviour is an abuse of a dominant position. In *Continental Can*[51] the Court applied art.82 EC to changes in the *structure* of the market. Over time it was realised that art.82 EC was not an adequate tool to deal with the competition problems emerging from the increase in take-overs and mergers in the EU and in 1989 a separate regulation was adopted to handle mergers.

## What is a Dominant Position?

It was left to the ECJ to define dominance. Dominance does not exist in the abstract; it is tied up with the relevant market in which the firm trades. In some instances the State will create a legal monopoly, especially where an undertaking is given exclusive rights to perform a service or produce goods. During the 1990s greater emphasis was placed upon tackling the abuse of such monopolies as ideas of liberalisation of State regulated markets swept across Europe.

A central idea in the Court's definition of dominance is the ability of a firm to act independently. At para.65 of the ruling in *United Brands*[52] the Court provides the classic definition of dominance built up through its case law. A dominant position:

"... relates to a position of economic strength enjoyed by an undertaking which enables it to prevent effective competition being maintained on the relevant market by giving it the power to behave to an appreciable extent independently of its competitors, customers and ultimately of its consumers."

In *Hoffman-La Roche*[53] the ECJ emphasised that a dominant position did not preclude some competition, but to attract art.82 EC the dominant firm must be able to influence the conditions of competition on the market.

---

[51] Case 6/72 *Europemballage Corp and Continental Can Co Inc v Commission* [1973] E.C.R. 215.

[52] Case 27/76 *United Brands Co and United Brands Continental BV v Commission* [1978] E.C.R. 207.

[53] Case 85/76 *Hoffmann-La Roche and Co AG v Commission* [1979] E.C.R. 461.

The test for the relevant market for these conditions to exist in has given rise to controversy and criticism. There are two relevant markets to consider. The first is the product market; the second is the geographical market. The Commission would like to define relevant markets narrowly in order to show that the firm is dominant. Whereas the accused dominant firm(s) would like to draw the markets as wide as possible to show that there are other competitors. The issue is how far are products interchangeable so that if a dominant firm exploits its economic position (for example by raising prices) consumers will have the opportunity to switch to alternative products. The Commission will look at the use of the product, price and characteristics. This kind of test is not always easy to apply. If the price of draught beer is raised what does the seasoned beer drinker do? Switch to lager? Or wine? Is he or she just thirsty and will drink mineral (or tap) water?

In relation to the product market a dominant firm is keen to show that products within a market are interchangeable and that it is competing alongside a number of different products. The facts of *United Brands* illustrate the point. United Brands was a vertically integrated firm. It owned banana plantations in Central and South America and also distributed the bananas under a trade mark protected name "Chiquita". It held between 40–45 per cent of the market share of branded bananas and held sufficient economic power to control the way its bananas were sold by wholesalers. United Brands argued that the "relevant market" was fresh fruit in general.

The Commission and the ECJ took a much narrower view arguing that the banana was a separate market because the banana had unique physical, functional and economic characteristics. Using studies by the Food and Agricultural Organisation it was argued that there was a low cross-elasticity between bananas and other fruit. Bananas were available all year; the only other fruits which were available all year were apples and oranges. Other fruits such as peaches or grapes were seasonal. Consumers did not substitute other fruits for bananas; other fruits were not interchangeable.

What caused most controversy and criticism of this decision, however, was that the Court recognised a distinct *separate consumer market* which would not substitute other fruits for the banana: the very young, the old, and the sick. This group of consumers, was not the whole of the market, and neither the Commission nor the Court showed *how* United Brands was able to exploit the banana market (for example, charging high prices to this group of consumers). The Commission, in the face of the criticism of the decision, refined its ideas that a distinct group of customers will be relevant for market definition to cover the situation where such customers constitute a separate market and the dominant firm is able to exploit this separate market.[54] But other cases show the tendency of the Court to uphold the narrow view taken by the Commission of the relevant market. For example, in *Michelin*[55] the CFI upheld the Commission Decision finding an abuse of a dominant position in the market for new replacement tyres for lorries, buses and similar heavy vehicles. These are perhaps extreme examples but they show the intuitive approach taken by the Court and the Commission towards controlling excessive power in the market.

The geographical market test determines the Community jurisdiction. In the *Sugar Cases* the Court stated that

"the pattern and volume of the production and consumption of the said product as well as the habits and economic opportunities of vendors and purchasers must be considered."[56]

It is the *volume* of trade which is a significant factor. This has meant that a number of ports and airports have been held to fulfil the "substantial part of the Common Market" criteria.[57] In some cases a single Member State has also been held to occupy a substantial part of the Common Market.

The Commission and the Court also use various indicators in order to show that a firm is dominant in a particular market.[58] The most obvious indicator to look for is the *amount* of the market share the dominant firms holds in the relevant market. The higher the market share, with "very large shares", are taken by the Court as indicative of dominance, or at least a presumption of dominance, unless the alleged dominant firm can show that there are "exceptional circumstances".[59] The market share should be held over a period of time. Looking at the case law, 50 per cent appears to be

---

[54] *Commission Notice on the Definition of the Relevant Market for the purposes of Community Competition Law*, OJ 1997 C372/5, para.43.

[55] Case T-203/01 [2003] E.C.R. II-1.

[56] Joined Cases 40-48/73, et al. [1975] E.C.R. 1663, para.371.

[57] Case C 179/90 *Merci convenzionali Porto di Genova SpA v Siderugica Gabrielii SpA* [1991] E.C.R. I-5889; Case 66/86 *Ahmed Saeed Flugreisen and Silver Line Reisburo GmbH v Zentrale zur Bekampfung unlauteren Wettbewerbs eV* [1989] E.C.R. 803.

[58] *Commission Notice on the Definition of the Relevant Market for the Purposes of Community Competition Law*, OJ 1977 C 372/5.

[59] Case 85/76 *Hoffmann-La Roche and Co AG v Commission* [1979] E.C.R. 461. See Case T-201 /04 *Microsoft*, judgment of September 17, 2007 where the market share of 90% of the had been built up.

threshold for determining that there are very large market shares when the rebuttal of the presumption of dominance comes into play.[60]

Where market shares are lower, then other factors, or indicators are used. These factors relate predominantly to *access* to the market. These will include the structure of the market: what are the shares of competitors? Vertical integration of the undertaking's activities bringing about economies of scale and control over the production and distribution process is an important indicator. This may also lock in customers and consumers to the particular brand or a secondary market such as spare parts, after sales services. Other examples from the case law include ownership of intellectual property rights; state regulation, for example the creation of a legal monopoly; superior technology and efficiency; access to financial resources; raw materials or "key inputs" (for example, airline slots); advertising; overall size; strength and range of products: the ability to cross-subsidise or engage in predatory pricing. In some cases it is the dominant firm which supplies the evidence, either from internal documents used by the Commission, or from claims made by the firm itself. For example, AKZO described itself as "the world leader in the peroxides market".

## *Abuse*

Article 82 EC lists *examples* of what constitutes an abuse of a dominant position. These examples show how a dominant undertaking may exploit its market power against other competitors and also to the disadvantage of consumers. Many cases involve the pricing policies (unfair purchase or selling prices) of dominant firms (Bishop, 1991). By and large, the attack has been upon the *supply* of goods/services on the market but it is recognised that a dominant firm may be monopsonist, one example might be where a supermarket in a dominant position exploits its buying power against suppliers. But neither the Court, nor the Commission, can act as a price regulator. There are arguments that in the absence of barriers to entry and legal restraints, competition law should not intervene to regulate prices. A successful firm should be allowed to reap the benefits of efficiency and success otherwise there are disincentives for innovation. Excessive prices may force customers to change brands and attract new competition to the market.

---

[60] Case C-62/86 *AKZO Chemie BV v Commission* [1991] E.C.R. I-3359.

One concern over pricing policy is the issue of predatory pricing. This is where an undertaking prices its product so low that competitors are forced out of the market. When this occurs with goods coming from outside of the EU this is called "dumping" and the Commission has the power to impose duties on such imported products to raise the price and protect home produced goods. A dominant firm may target certain customers with low prices to fend off a competitor. It can do this by squeezing profit margins or cross-subsidising products. In *France Télécom v Commission*[61] the CFI upheld the Commission's decision to fine Wanadoo (which later merged with France Telecom) confirming that it held a dominant position in the market for Internet access. Wanadoo had eight times more Internet subscribers than its nearest rival and in the later merger with France Telecom enjoyed new advantages as a result of its association with the French telecommunications incumbent. Wanadoo had engaged in predatory pricing first, because prices below average variable costs give grounds for assuming that a pricing practice is eliminatory and secondly, prices below average total costs, but above average variable costs, must be regarded as abusive if they are determined as part of a plan for eliminating a competitor. The CFI held that the Commission was correct in its choice and application of the method of calculating the rate of recovery of costs which led it to conclude that there was predatory pricing and that the Commission furnished solid and consistent evidence as to the existence of a plan of predation. The CFI held that it was not necessary to establish in addition proof that Wanadoo had a realistic chance of recouping its losses. Wanadoo could not rely on an absolute right to align its prices on those of its competitors in order to justify its conduct. Even if alignment of prices by a dominant undertaking on those of its competitors is not in itself abusive or objectionable, it might become so where it is aimed not only at protecting its interests but also at strengthening and abusing its dominant position.

A dominant firm may also use pricing strategies to divide up the Internal Market along geographical lines. By maintaining the geographical divisions with other measures (which are also addressed under art.81 EC) such as preventing parallel imports, limiting supplies, using intellectual property rights to prevent access to the market, or divide the Internal Market along territorial lines. The Court has allowed dominant firms to refute such allegations of

---

[61] Case T-340/03 [2007] E.C.R. II-107.

abuse by showing that there are objective market conditions which explain price differences between the geographical areas. These would include transport costs, costs of licensing or intellectual property rights.

Another form of differential pricing strategies which has come under scrutiny is the use of loyalty rebates and discounts which tie in customers.[62] Rebates are a common business practice. The dominant firm will argue that there are cost savings where discounts are given for quantity buying but there must be a correlation between the discount and the saving. In contrast loyalty discounts are seen as problematic since they prevent customers from obtaining supplies from competitors and will usually prevent competitors from offering their goods at a price which can induce the customer to switch supplier.[63]

## (i) Tying

A dominant firm may lock in customers of a primary market by limiting the choices of goods or services on a secondary market. It may be that the primary market is competitive but the dominant firm may not allow for competition in, say, after sales care, or servicing, or spare parts for its products which are not be interchangeable with spare parts from competitors. This ties the customers to buy these products from the dominant firm. The issue of finding abuse from tying or lock-ins is therefore bound up with the definition of the relevant market. In *Van den Bergh Foods Ltd v Commission*[64] a manufacturer of ice cream products included an exclusivity clause in its distribution agreements for the "impulse buying" market of ice cream. Freezer cabinets were made available at a nominal sum and maintained by the manufacturer on condition that they were used for the exclusive use of its products. In *Hilti*[65] a supplier of nail guns engaged in a number of practices to ensure its customers of the nail gun also bought nails from it. This included

---

[62] Case T-203/01 *Michelin v Commission* [2003] E.C.R. I-4071; Case T-219/99 *British Airways v Commission* [2003] E.C.R. II-5917; Case C-95/04 [2007] E.C.R. I-2331.

[63] Joined Cases 40-48/73, 50, 54-56/73, 111/73, 113/73 and 114/73 *Coöperatieve Vereniging 'Suiker Unie' UA v Commission (European Sugar Cartel)* [1975] E.C.R. 1663; Case 85/76 *Hoffmann-La Roche and Co AG v Commission* [1979] E.C.R. 461.

[64] Case T-65/98 [2003] E.C.R. II-4653; on appeal Case C-552 /03 P *Unilever BestFoods (Ireland) Ltd v Commission,* Order of September 28, 2006.

[65] Case T-30/89 [1991] E.C.R. II-1439.

inter alia, discounts where guns and nails were bought together but also refusing to supply customers who bought nails from other suppliers. In *Hugin*[66] the Court held that the relevant market for establishing dominance was the spare parts for Hugin cash registers. Hugin was the sole supplier of the spare parts and therefore abused a dominant position by refusing to supply the spare parts to a small firm which sold, leased, serviced, repaired Hugin cash registers. In *Digital*[67] the Commission found that there were two separate markets for the maintenance of Digital computers: maintenance of hardware and software. The services were not interchangeable. *Microsoft* concerned the tying in of software markets. The CFI held that the Commission was correct to conclude that Microsoft breached art.82 EC by bundling Windows Media Player into the Windows Personal Computer Operating System.[68]

### (ii) Refusals to supply

In *Commercial Solvents*[69] the Court found that Commercial Solvents was using its dominant position on the raw material market to affect competition, and to drive a competitor out of business by refusing to supply a derivative product. Commercial Solvents wanted to vertically integrate its operations and enter the derivatives market. The Commission ordered Commercial Solvents to resume supplies of the products in order to keep a competitor in the market. Interestingly most of the supplies of the product which was used to make drugs to fight tuberculosis were exported outside of the EU. The Commission and the Court were concerned to maintain the competitive structure of the market. In *United Brands*, a dominant firm refused to supply a long-standing customer who had advertised competing brands of bananas. While the Court accepted that a dominant firm can protect its commercial interests it found the cutting off of banana supplies to be a disproportionate response. In *Hugin* the dominant firm cut off supplies of spare parts to a customer.

---

[66] Case 22/78 [1979] E.C.R. 1869. The Commission did not show that trade between the Member States was affected.

[67] Commission Press Release IP/97/868.

[68] Commission Decision March 24, 2004 COMP/C-3/37.792. Case T-201/94, judgment of September 17, 2007, Kühn and Caffarra (2005).

[69] Cases 6/73, 7/73 *Istituto Chemioterapico Italiano SpA and Commercial Solvents Corp v Commission* [1974] E.C.R. 223.

In *Microsoft*[70] the CFI upheld the Commission's finding that Microsoft had abused a dominant position by refusing to supply its competitors with inter-operability information.

## (iii) Essential Facilities

From the refusal to supply cases the Commission began to entertain the idea of an "essential facilities" doctrine, an idea found, but not always upheld in US anti-trust principles. This doctrine concerns *access* to a facility supplied or controlled by a dominant undertaking in an upstream market rather than the supply of products (Doherty, 2001; Nagy, 2007). The early cases concerned access to transport facilities,[71] but the doctrine is of relevance to networked industries in the liberalisation process.

An essential facilities doctrine using competition law has been greeted with much comment and criticism. If we look carefully at the European Court's case law we see that there is a judicial reluctance to admit the doctrine into Community law, but, at the same time, the "refusal to deal" principle contained within art.82 EC has been used in such a way that the European approach is far more intrusive that the US case law. As we have seen, in relation to abuse of a dominant position courts cannot step in and act as a regulators. Too much intervention in markets will destroy incentives for efficiency, innovation and investment (Areeda, 1990). If there is a breakdown in the competitive structure of a market this is better handled through regulation rather than litigation. In the liberalisation process access to networked services and the infrastructure is regulated specifically.[72]

In *Oscar Bronner*[73] access to a newspaper distribution system created by a dominant firm was sought by a small distributor. The Court referred to its earlier case law on refusal to supply. It did not refer to the concept of "essential facilities". The Court took a narrow approach. Arguing that before an abuse of a dominant posi-

---

[70] Case T-201/04, judgment of September 17, 2007.

[71] *British Midland/AerLingus,* OJ 1993 L96/34; *Sealink/B&I Holyhead Interim Measures* [1992] 5 C.M.L.R. 255; *Sea Containers Ltd/Stena Sealink* [1994] OJ 1995 L15/8; Cases T-374-375, 384 and 388/94 *European Night Services v Commission* [1998] E.C.R. II-3141.

[72] For example, in the area of telecommunications, now called "electronic communications", European Parliament and Council dir.(EC) 2002/19 on access to, and interconnection of, electronic communications networks and associated facilities, OJ 2002 L108/7.

[73] Case C-7/97 [1998] E.C.R. I-7791.

tion could be found for failing to grant access to a facility owned or developed by the dominant undertaking three conditions should be met: firstly, the refusal should be likely to eliminate all competition in the downstream market; secondly, the refusal must be incapable of objective justification; thirdly, the access to the facility must be indispensable; there must be no actual or potential substitute for the facility requested.

In relation to intellectual property rights the Court has accepted that a refusal to grant licences *may* be an abuse of a dominant position.[74] In *Magill*[75] the Court applied its refusal to supply case law to a refusal by TV stations which owned the copyright in television listings to allow a new competitor Magill, to enter the market to supply a *new* comprehensive TV guide. The Court viewed the TV stations as holding a monopoly in a raw material.

The idea of an essential facilities doctrine has been limited in *IMS Health GmbH & Co OHG v NDC Health GmbH & Co KG*.[76] IMS had created a brick system for dividing Germany into segments for the analysis of data for regional sales of pharmaceutical products. This had become an industry standard. NDC had tried to create a competing system with no success and applied for a licence to use the IMS system. IMS refused the application which would have given a competitor access to its brick system. IMS sought to use its copyright protection against NDC in the German courts. An art.234 EC reference was made to the ECJ. NDC made a complaint to the Commission. The Commission ordered interim measures against IMS, using the *Magill* ruling, ordering IMS to grant NDC a licence. IMS appealed this decision but the CFI and ECJ suspended the interim measures until after the art.234 EC.

In the ruling the ECJ does not refer to a concept of essential facilities. The Court sets out three cumulative conditions to be fulfilled before a refusal to license a copyright protected product can be an abuse of a dominant position. There must be a *new* product involved (*Magill*); access to the copyright protected product must be indispensable so that the refusal to supply the information will exclude any, or all, competition on a secondary market; the refusal to supply must be unjustified. In neither *Oscar Bronner* nor *IMS* does the ECJ offer any indication of what amounts to a legitimate justification for refusing to supply. In *Microsoft* the Commission rejected Microsoft's

---

[74] Case 238/87 *AB Volvo v Erik Veng* [1988] E.C.R. 6211; Case 53/87 *CICCRA Maxicar v Renault* [1988] E.C.R. 6039.
[75] Cases C-241/91 P *RTE and ITP v Commission* [1995] E.C.R. I-743.
[76] Case C-418/01 [2004] E.C.R. I-5039.

justification that the refusal to supply interface information for its software was necessary to protect innovation.

## Abuse Affecting the Structure of a Market

The Court has expanded these examples by applying art.82 EC to conduct which affects the structure of the market.[77] Later cases have applied art.82 EC to behaviour which weakens competition on the market. In *Michelin*[78] the Court states:

"The concept of abuse is an objective concept relating to the behaviour of an undertaking in a dominant position which is such as to influence the structure of a market where, as a result of the very presence of the undertaking in question, the degree of competition is weakened and which, through recourse to methods different from those which condition normal competition in products or services on the basis of transactions of commercial operators, has the effect of hindering the maintenance of the degree of competition still existing in the market or the growth of that competition."

The Court signalled that private firms who acquire market power are regarded as having a "special responsibility" which forbids the firm from abusing a dominant position and behaving in ways which may be tolerated by competitors in the same market who do not enjoy such significant market power. This led Amato to comment:

"Market power, just because it is conceptually accepted, is thus loaded with the burdens and limits which, according to the general principles more of public than of private law, bear upon whoever holds power."[79]

Advocate Generally Fenelly used the term "super dominant" for the first time in *Compagnie Maritme Belge.*[80] Over time the Court has suggested that undertakings who are "super-dominant" also have special responsibilities in the way they behave.[81] Super dominance

---

[77] *Continental Can,* above fn.46.
[78] Case 322/81 [1983] E.C.R. 3461.
[79] Amato, 1997:66.
[80] Cases C-395 and 396/96P [2000] E.C.R. I-1365, para.137.
[81] Case C-333/94 P *Tetra Pak International SA v Commission* [1996] E.C.R. I-5951; Case T-228/97 *Irish Sugar plc v Commission* [1999] E.C.R. II-2969; *Football World Cup* 1998 OJ 2000 L 5/55.

brings with it a special responsibility towards the competitive process and conduct is more likely to be categorised as abuse under art.82 EC.

## Objective Justification of the Behaviour of a Dominant Firm

Article 82 EC forbids the abuse of a dominant position, therefore there is no scope within the wording of the Treaty provision to condone or grant an exemption for abusive behaviour. But the Court and the Commission have developed the concept of "objective justification" to allow for behaviour which is pursued for legitimate commercial reasons. Examples of this justification are seen in the Commission Decision in *Eurofix-Bauco/Hilti*[82] where a producer of nail guns tied the sale of nails to its guns for safety reasons. The Commission has allowed a dominant firm to cut off supplies to a bad debtor in *BBI/Boosey & Hawkes*.[83]

## Effect on Trade Between Member States

The requirement that there must be an effect upon trade between Member States for art.82 EC to bite is a jurisdictional device demarcating competence between Community law and national law. In *Hugin* the Court quashed the Commission's decision finding an abuse of art.82 EC because the activities of the firm which relied upon the spare parts was confined to the area of London and there was no inter-state trade. It was also argued that if the firm went out of business it would not upset the competitive structure of the market. But in other cases art.82 EC has been applied even if there is no alteration to the flow of goods or services between Member States but where the behaviour may alter the structure of competition.[84]

The Commission is now looking at whether art.82 EC should be modernised in the same way that art.81 EC has been scrutinised. It is arguable that art.82 EC has provided enough flexibility to handle the new problems which have emerged such as whether there should be an essential facilities doctrine, issues of collective dominance and super-dominance. Where art.82 EC is not a useful tool then special rules of regulation have been used in the liberalised sectors and also

[82] OJ 1988 L65/19.
[83] OJ 1988 L286/36.
[84] Cases 6 and 7/73 *Istituto Chemioterapico Italiano SpA and Commercial Solvents Corp v Commission* [1974] E.C.R. 223.

in the field of merger control. There is some criticism that the Commission has focused too much upon the supply side and neglected the possibilities of abuse in markets where there is a monopsony. Also there are arguments that because art.82 EC applies ex post more guidance could be given to undertakings to avoid abusing a dominant position.

## Article 82 EC and State Activity

The activities of the State, where it creates a public monopoly, or assigns special or exclusive rights to an undertaking to provide goods or services on the market, may also be caught by art.82 EC. However art.82 EC is not used on its own and is used in conjunction with art.86 EC and arts 10 and 12 EC (Szyszczak, 2007). This has resulted in many Member States adapting and even dismantling public monopolies in Europe in the wake of the creation of an Internal Market post-1992. The use of art.81 EC and 82 EC in this way is seen as a procedural approach (Harm, 2002). The Court is careful not to criticise a particular Member State's policy but finds certain behaviour contrary to the competition rules of the EU.

## Mergers

Mergers are an important tool of industrial policy and are more likely to occur when cross-border trade develops (Szyszczak, 2007: Kroes, 2007). Until the adoption of a Regulation in 1989 (Venit: 1990) there was no systematic approach to mergers in the EU although the Commission had expressed an interest in controlling what were termed "concentrations" since the 1960s (de Jong, 1966–1967). Articles 81 EC and 82 EC were stretched to cover situations where a merger had the potential to disrupt competition but it was recognised that a system of ex ante regulation of mergers was necessary where there was a Community dimension. At the national level merger control was very under-developed.

Community competence to regulate mergers is contentious since it is arguable that mergers do not constitute anti-competitive behaviour but alter the structure of competition on the market. There was an underlying industrial policy objective in the EU of increasing the scale of national and European firms to enable them to compete in globalised markets. This was seen by encouraging the use of joint ventures. Many of the early cases investigated by the Commission were alleged to have a political motive, rather than an economic analysis of the harm the merger might cause (Szyszczak, 2007:18).

To allow the Member States to retain some control over national industry policy merger control was divided between Community and national competence. However, in recent years this jurisdictional divide has led to problems of what is termed "economic patriotism" since the current regulation of mergers does not address situations where national mergers or take-overs either take place within one Member State in a significant industry, or where the Member State steps in to block mergers in a sensitive sector (Scott, 2006).[85]

The Merger Regulation applies to "concentrations". This occurs when two or more independent undertakings merge their activities or where there is a change in control of an undertaking. The approach for determining Community competence to regulate mergers is based upon the turnover of the undertakings. There are two alternative sets of thresholds in art.1 of reg.139/2004.[86] One threshold relates to the "worldwide turnover" and the other relates to the "Community-wide turnover". This is a different approach from the application of arts 81 and 82 EC which uses the "effect on trade between Member States" as the determinant of Community competence. A new Merger Task Force (which has now been disbanded) was created and prior notification of mergers was mandatory with the Commission obliged to take Phase I and Phase II investigations and reach decisions within strict time limits.

The parties to a merger are allowed to raise justifications (or defences), for example that there would be efficiencies in the merger; art.2(1)(b) of reg.139/2004 refers to "the interests of immediate consumers, and the development of technical and economic progress".[87]Another possible defence which has emerged is that of the "failing firm".[88] In the *Guidelines on the assessment of horizontal mergers*[89] the Commission sets out the policy in this area. The basic requirement is that the deterioration of the competitive structure that follows the merger cannot be said to be caused by the merger. Three criteria must be met. Firstly, the allegedly failing firm would be forced out of the market in the near future because of financial

---

[85] See Case C-196/07 *Commission v Spain* judgment of March 6, 2008.

[86] Council reg.(EC) No 139/2004 of January 20, 2004 on the control of concentrations between undertakings (the EC merger regulation), OJ 2004 L 24/1. On July 10, 2007 adopted a new Commission Consolidated Jurisdictional Notice under Council reg. (EC) No.139/2004 on the control of concentrations between undertakings (the "merger regulation").

[87] Korsnas/AD Cartonboard, COMP/M.4057; Inco/Falconbridge, COMP/M. 4000.

[88] Joined Cases C-68/94 and C-30/95 *French Republic and SCPA v Commission (Kali and Salz)* [1998] E.C.R. I-1375 (Monti, 2007).

[89] *Guidelines on the assessment of horizontal mergers under the Council Regulation on the control of concentrations between undertakings*, OJ 2004 C31/5, paras 89–91.

difficulties; secondly, there is no less anti-competitive alternative purchase than the notified merger and finally, in the absence of the merger the assets of the failing firm would inevitably exit the market.

Mergers may be cleared by the Commission subject to "commitments".[90] These are also known as remedies. The parties to a merger may also agree to restrictions directly related and necessary to the implementation of a merger (known as ancillary restraints) Recital 21, art.6(1)(b) and art.8(1) and (2) the Commission must consider these restrictions as part of its assessment of the merger.[91]

The Commission was overwhelmed with work and published a number of soft law Notices and Communications to provide guidance on policy. But the Commission was criticised for not taking into account sufficient economic factors in its decisions and a series of high profile defeats in the CFI[92] forced the Commission to re-appraise its practice in relation to mergers.

The Merger Regulation was amended in 2004 as part of the general modernisation package of reforms to competition law which took place with enlargement. The Regulation is supplemented with soft law to provide guidelines on how certain mergers should be handled.[93] Additionally a Chief Competition Economist was appointed and a new internal panel was created to scrutinise the initial investigations of a merger by the Commission staff.

---

[90] Art.6(2); 8(2) and Recital 30 reg.139/2004. The Commission also published a Notice on Remedies: See for example, Case T-177/04 *EasyJet v Commission* [2006] E.C.R. II-1931 where EasyJet unsuccessfully challenged the commitments undertaken by Air France and KLM but the CFI emphasised that in accepting commitments the Commission must act in accordance with proportionality. But compare Case T-282/02 *Cementbouw v Commission* [2006] E.C.R. II-319 where the CFI held that the Commission was permitted to accept all commitments offered [voluntarily] by the parties even if the commitments went beyond what was strictly necessary for the purpose of maintaining competition in the market.

[91] Case T-251/00 *Lagardère SCA and Canal+ SA v Commission* [2002] E.C.R. II-4825.

[92] Case T-342/99 *Airtours plc v Commission* [2002] E.C.R. II-2585; Case T-310/01 *Schneider Electric v Commission* [2002] E.C.R. II-4071; Case T-80/02 *Tetra Laval v Commission* [2002] E.C.R. II-4519. In October 2001 the Commission found the acquisition of Legrand by Scheider to be incompatible with the Common Market and in January 2002 ordered Schneider to divest. Schneider appealed to the CFI for annulment of the Decisions but prepared to divest itself of Legrand. The CFI annulled the Commission Decision blocking the merger and in Case T-351/03 *Schneider Electric v Commission,* judgment of July 11, 2007 the Commission was found to have been in breach of an essential procedural requirement in not allowing Schneider to make representations and awarded damages against the Commission. A similar damages action has been lodged by MyTravel (formerly Airtours) as a result of its merger with First Choice which was blocked by the Commission. This claim is different since it is based on the Commission's alleged errors of assessment and not the breach of a procedural requirement.

[93] For example, *Guidelines on the assessment of horizontal mergers under the Council Regulation on the control of concentrations between undertakings*, OJ 2004 C31/5.

The major change under the new Regulation is the test used to determine if a merger is likely to affect competition in the Internal Market. Under the original Merger Regulation the Commission was able to block a merger if it could show that the merger would create, or strengthen, a dominant position and that effective competition would be significantly impeded (Kokkoris, 2005; Soames and Maudhuit, 2005). As a result of the case law from art.82 EC the Commission found it easy to presume that if the merger created or strengthened a dominant position then competition would also be impeded. Under the new Regulation the wording is reversed and requires the Commission only to show that the merger would significantly impede competition; the creation of dominance is only one example of a situation where competition would be impeded.[94]

The change in approach resulted from some controversial decisions taken by the Commission. The Commission clashed with the US over the blocking of a merger between General Electric and GE Honeywell.[95] This was a proposed conglomerate merger which was deemed to be so strong that the massive economic strength which would be created would undermine rivals and dominate a range of markets.[96] In the same year the Commission blocked a conglomerate merger between *Tetra Laval and Sidel.* On appeal the CFI found that the Commission had committed manifest errors of assessment and quashed the Commission's Decision; the ECJ upheld the CFI ruling.[97]

A second reason given for the change was that the Commission argued that the old test failed to capture mergers in oligopolistic markets. The original test in the Merger Regulation could not address unilateral effects which emerge from oligolopoly behaviour. But the Commission had used the Merger Regulation to block mergers which led to the creation of a collective dominant position. Although the Commission lost its appeal of its decision in *Airtours*[98] the CFI confirmed that it was possible to use the old test of the Merger Regulation to regulate mergers ex ante in oligopoly markets

---

[94] Art.2(3).

[95] *General Electric/Honeywell* OJ 2004 L 48/01; on appeal Case T-209/01 and 210/01 (Gerber, 2003).

[96] Burnley, 2007. See also Case T-464/04 *Impala v Commission* [2006] E.C.R. II-2289; on appeal Case C-413/06 P, Opinion of A.G. Kokott, December 13, 2007, Wright (2007).

[97] Case T-5/02 *Tetra Laval BV v Commission* [2002] E.C.R. II-4519; Case C-12/03P, [2005] E.C.R. I-987; Case C-13/03P [2005] E.C.R. I-1113.

[98] Case T-342/99 *Airtours plc v Commission* [2002] E.C.R. II-2585.

that created a risk of co-ordinated anti-competitive behaviour but the Commission had wanted to go further than this and block mergers that led to tacit collusion through co-ordinated effects. As we have seen, it is more difficult to prove tacit collusion under art.81 EC ex ante.

# 7: The Application of the Competition Rules to Economic Activities of the State

States may create barriers to economic integration by using policies and tools which are related to competitive conditions of the market in their own territory. This may produce spill-over effects which affect trade between Member States by preventing access to domestic markets. But the effects may be wider where the State activity disrupts the competitive structure of markets by the use of the extraordinary political and economic power it enjoys in the Internal Market. In 1957 there was no clear policy towards regulating State intervention in the market. The Member States were divided as to how far State intervention could, and should, be tolerated in a Common Market. Many States were continuing to use, and to believe in, active State intervention in the market in order to re-build the worn-torn economies of Europe. Particularly in networked sectors (utilities, telecommunications, transport) there are economies of scale in placing the production and delivery of certain services in one co-ordinated owner. Many States continue to see State-owned undertakings, and even whole sectors, as national champions and find it difficult to accept that the goods and services produced can also be supplied by private actors. One feature of the role played by competition policy is how sharp divisions between the Member States on the *role* of State intervention have been ironed out by the use of the competition rules.

Acceptance of the role the State can play in the market is seen in the belief that States are free to choose between public and private ownership in art.295 EC:

"This Treaty shall in no way prejudice the rules in Member States governing the system of property ownership."

The Member States have attempted to use this clause to protect State intervention in sensitive areas. But the ECJ has refused to allow art.295 EC to be used to shield economic activity and direct intervention in the market, from the scrutiny of, and compliance with, Community law.[1] Nevertheless, cases continue to arise where the State argues that the activity in question is non-economic and therefore not subject to the rules of the EC Treaty at all.[2] The Commission has attempted to draw some bright lines between "non-economic" activity and "economic" activity caught by the EC Treaty.[3] These bright lines are not always consistent, or always followed by the European Courts, who continue to use a number of legal tests to decide if State activity is caught by the EC Treaty rules (Szyszczak, 2004, 2007). The European Courts appear to be using an approach analogous to the pre-*Keck* approach under art.28 EC: drawing the net of Community law as wide as possible but then allowing exemptions or justifications from the application of the free movement and competition rules where there is a public interest at stake.[4] The difficulty with this approach under competition law is that the competition rules were not drafted in a way which allows for the range of justifications, exemptions and derogations which are available under the four economic freedoms.

---

[1] Joined Cases T-228/99 and T-233/99 *WestLB v Commission* [2003] E.C.R. II-445; Case C-209/00 *Commission v Germany* [2002] E.C.R. I-11695.

[2] Cases C-264, 306, 354 and 355/01 *AOK* [2004] E.C.R. I-2493; Case T-319/99 *FENIN v Commission* [ 2003] E.C.R. II-357.

[3] European Commission, Communication on Services of General Interest in Europe, COM (2000) 580 final, p.3; Report to the Laeken European Council on Services of General Interest COM (2001) 598 final; Non-Paper Services of General Economic Interest and State Aid, November 12, 2002; Report From the Commission on the state of play in the work on the Guidelines For State Aid and Services of General Economic Interest, *http://europa.eu.int/comm/competition/state_aid/others/sieg_en.pdf*; Green Paper on Services of General Interest, COM (2003) 270 final; White Paper on Services of General Interest COM (2004) 374 final.

[4] These activities continue, despite the Court of Justice signalling that there are limits to economic integration: Case C-376/98 *Germany v Commission* [2000] E.C.R. I-8419.

*The economic rationale* for why the State intervenes in the economy is far more complex than the legal analysis. The most important economic rationale for State intervention in the market is commonly defined by a "market failure". The main examples of market failure are where there are external costs or benefits arising from an activity which do not accrue to the person bearing or enjoying it. Examples are pollution, a negative externality to those who are damaged by it; or research, a positive externality to those that benefit from it, and which may justify an intervention to internalise those costs or benefits. Public goods are another example of perceived market failure, when they would not be normally provided by the private sector. The inevitable result is the under-supply or non-supply of these necessary goods or services. Income distribution may be another reason why the State may intervene to redistribute income and wealth in a more equitable way.

In addition to the economic explanations, the political context is clearly an important motivator of public intervention in the economy. The clearest examples are the powers to impose taxes and to introduce legislation. These are natural prerogatives of the State. The decision to intervene in the presence of a market failure, and the choice of the appropriate tool, may be influenced by political reasons, such as the social impact or acceptability of a given measure, the lobbying of more organised interests which may lead to the "capture" of public institutions' decision-making. Historical and cultural/ideological trends influence the State's decision and there is a wide variety of conceptions on the role of the State in the economy depending upon different kinds of legal-economic constitutions (divided broadly: liberal v socio-democratic traditions). Thus the State may intervene in the economy in various ways, such as: direct ownership/operation of undertakings, for example, as a public monopoly; regulation (for example, labour, safety, environmental standards; rules on importing/exporting, selling, advertising, supplying, products and services); State Aid to undertakings and industries; public procurement. Under certain circumstances, State intervention in the market may be caught by EC competition rules.

## 7.1 Public Monopolies and Bodies Granted Special or Exclusive Rights

The Member States used State monopolies to rebuild their economies after the Second World war, actively encouraging national champions to supply public services such as postal services, utilities (gas, electricity, water), telecommunications and broadcasting. These monopolies could perform social functions as well as raise money for the State (Szyszczak: 2002; 2004; 2007) and were seen as natural monoplies. Public monopolies and undertakings which were given special or exclusive rights were tolerated but they were subject to the rules on free movement of goods, under what is now art.31 EC, and also the competition chapter of the EC Treaty, especially the State Aid rules and art.86 EC (Buendia Sierra, 1999).

Article 86(1) EC states that the rules of the internal market and of competition law shall apply to such undertakings. Public monopolies are bound by the free movement rules of the EC Treaty, including the rules on procurement and the rules in arts 81 and 82 EC (which are normally perceived to apply to private undertakings), as well as the State Aid provisions.

A central issue in the litigation involving the State is whether there is an "undertaking" pursuing an economic activity. The State will try to argue that such bodies are performing traditional State duties which are not competitive. So, for example, special rules have developed protecting State social security schemes from the competition rules.[5] Each situation is judged on a case-by case basis. For example, a public *body* was charged with the maintenance and improvement of air navigation safety, collecting route charges levied on users of airspace. The body was considered to be a public authority and was not considered to be an undertaking:

" . . . it is in the exercise of that sovereignty that the states ensure . . . the supervision of their airspace and the provision of air navigation control services."[6]

In another case the Court held that anti-pollution supervision

" . . . constitutes a mission of general interest which is part of the essential tasks of the state relating to the environment within the public se domain."[7]

---

[5] Joined Cases C-159/91 and C-160/91 *Poucet and Pistre* [1993] E.C.R. I-666; Case C-218/00 *Battistello* [2002] E.C.R. I-691.

[6] Case C-364/92 *SAT v Eurocontrol* [1994] E.C.R. I-43, para.20. *Cf.* the later analysis by the CFI in Case T-155/04 *SELEX* [2006] E.C.R. II-4797; on appeal case C-13/07.

[7] Case C-343/95 *Diego Cali v Servizi ecologici porto di Genova SpA* [1997] E.C.R. I-1580 para.23.

In many cases the issues relating to the infringement of the competition rules and public monopolies relate to the abuse of a dominant position addressing *how* public and private dominant firms should behave in competitive markets. The Commission in its *Twentieth Report on Competition Policy* in 1990 had focused upon the pervasive State barriers to market integration:

". . . it is felt that at the present stage of economic integration in the Community the barriers are greatest in markets currently subject to State regulation".[8]

The close scrutiny of public monopolies during the 1990s created an impetus for the Member States to liberalise various sectors as it became clear that Member States could not continue with public monopolies which were inefficient and protectionist. It was also recognised that ownership of a network sector could be separated from the operation of the network and competition introduced in the supply of goods and services within the network. Changes in technology, as well as consumer expectations, created the conditions for the State to shift some of its traditional duties on to private, non-State actors. During the 1990s new hybrid undertakings were conceived, supplying traditional State goods and services under competitive conditions. This led to a shift in the balance between the State and market, in harmony with the Internal Market programme, but also created tensions between the vertical (Member State-Community) and horizontal (the Community Institutions inter se) division of power in the EU.

Article 86(2) EC provides an exemption from the application of the Internal Market and the competition rules for undertakings which provide "services of general economic interest" if it can be shown that the application of the EC Treaty rules would obstruct the performance, in law or in fact, of the tasks assigned to them. Baquero Cruz (2005) has called this a "switch rule". However the Court sees it as a derogation from a fundamental EC Treaty provision and in principle should be interpreted restrictively and is subject the principle of proportionality. It must also be shown that the development of trade must not be affected to such an extent as would be contrary to the interests of the Community.

A central argument for retaining a monopoly to provide services of general economic interest (SGEIs) is the necessity for cross-subsidisation. For example, universal postal services are provided

---

[8] Case C-41/90 *Höfner v Macrotron* [1991] E.C.R. I-1979.

efficiently in urban areas but less efficiently in remote or rural areas. Thus a State-provided postal service is able to offset the extra costs of the rural or remote postal services against the profits from the urban service. A commercial competitor may challenge the monopoly by cream-skimming the efficient postal services and not offer the less efficient rural/remote services.

This was the situation in *Corbeau*.[9] A private operator offered a superior postal service and charged less to collect and deliver mail than the State postal service in the Belgian city of Liège. The State postal service viewed this as cream skimming and brought criminal proceedings against Corbeau. The ECJ held that the creation of the State monopoly was a restriction on competition which was incompatible with the Common Market but found that it could be justified because there was a service of general economic interest consisting of the obligation to ensure a basic postal service at similar tariffs and similar conditions throughout Belgium. The Court viewed the use of a monopoly as proportionate since the undertaking providing the service should have the benefit of economically acceptable conditions. This included the use of cross-subsidisation to offset the losses in the unprofitable sectors against profits in the more profitable sectors.

In later cases the Court has taken a generous view of the proportionality principle accepting that the State cannot take the same risks as a private competitor and has not asked the State to show that the service of general economic interest can be provided in a way which does not use a monopoly or is less restrictive of competition.[10] The latter approach would seem to necessary in order to satisfy the principle of proportionality. But the increasing liberalisation of markets in Europe has shown that there are other ways of funding and providing services of general economic interest beyond the use of State monopolies. The liberalisation process regulates the provision of such services, which are termed "universal services" (Szyszczak, 2001). This has led to greater challenges and litigation focusing upon the way in which these services are funded and provided in the sectors not liberalised. In the case law of the European Courts, and the practice of the Commission, there are a number of tensions with disagreements as to whether the provision of such services are special and should be subject to non-market principles or whether

---

[9] Case C-320/91 *Corbeau* [1993] E.C.R. I-2568.

[10] Case C-159/94 *French Gas and Electricity Monopolies* [1997] E.C.R. I-5815; Case C-158/94 *Italian Electricity Monopoly* [1997] E.C.R. I-5789; Case C-157/94 *Dutch Electricity Monopoly* [1997] E.C.R. I-5699. Soriano, 2003.

competition law and policy should be used to open up services of general economic interest to open market (competitive) principles.[11]

The use of opportunistic litigation to challenge State monopolies in the 1990s led to the creation of a new Constitutional provision in the EC Treaty at the Amsterdam IGC in 1997. Article 16 EC recognises a positive role for services of general economic interest in

" . . . the shared values of the Union as well as their role in promoting social and territorial cohesion. . .".

While the Member States and the Community are charged with ensuring that such services operate on the basis of principles and conditions which enable the services to fulfil their missions art.16 EC does not provide a legal base to develop the role of services in the future EU. Article 16 EC contains a proviso that it is without prejudice to arts 73, 86 and 87 EC. This means that the competition law provisions apply and restrict the operation of art.16 EC. Thus services of general economic interest remain a derogation to the general competition and free market rules, but with a paradoxical duty placed upon the Member States and the Community to promote such services in competitive markets (Ross, 2007).

As a result of the Treaty of Lisbon 2007 art.16 is amended and forms *art.14 TFEU.* This provides a legal base for new legislation on services of general economic interest, but somewhat paradoxically the Union is not given competence in this area. *Article 14 TFEU* is accompanied by *Protocol 9 on Services of General Interest.* Article 1 of the Protocol affirms that:

"The shared values of the Union in respect of services of general economic interest within the meaning of Article 14 of the Treaty on the Functioning of the European Union include in particular:

- the essential role and the wide discretion of national, regional and local authorities in providing, commissioning and organising services of general economic interest as closely as possible to the needs of the users;

---

[11] C-280/00 *Altmark Trans GmbH and Regierungspraesidium Magdeburg v Nahverkehrsgesellschaft Altmark GmbH* [2003] E.C.R. I-7747; Joined Cases C-83/01 P, C-93/01 P and C-94/01P *Chronopost SA, La Poste v Commission* [2003] E.C.R. I-6993.

- the diversity between various services of general economic interest and the differences in the needs and preferences of users that may result from different geographical, social or cultural situations;
- a high level of quality, safety and affordability, equal treatment and the promotion of universal access and of user rights."

Article 2 of the Protocol states that the provisions of the Treaties do not affect in any way the competence of Member States to provide, commission and organise non-economic services of general interest.

Article 36 of the Charter of Fundamental Rights recognises, as a fundamental right, "access to services of general economic interest as provided for in national laws and practices, in accordance with the Constitution, in order to promote the social and territorial cohesion of the Union." Only *access* to such services is covered by this provision but it could be interpreted broadly to cover the terms and conditions and the *way* such services are provided.

Since 1996 the Commission has attempted to consolidate the Courts' case law on SGEIs through the use of soft law. In the face of increased litigation, especially in the State Aid field, the Commission adopted a White Paper on Services of General Interest and has implemented a package of measures to regulate such services in the EU.[12] However plans to adopt a Framework Directive in this field have been abandoned in the light of the new art.14.[13]

Article 86(3) EC is an unusual provision. It gives the Commission a monopolist position in the monitoring and enforcing art.86 EC. It also provides a rare legal base for the Commission to use directives or Decisions addressed to the Member States to ensure that art.86 EC is observed without involving the Council and the European Parliament. As with art.232 EC, the Commission cannot be compelled to act.[14]

---

[12] White Paper on Services of General Interest, COM (2004) 374 final. Commission Communication on Services of General Interest COM (2007) 725 final; Commission Working Document on the Application of Article 86(2) EC to State Aid in the form of psc (SEC(2007) 1516 final); Working Document on the application of public procurement rules to social services of general interest (SEC(2007) 1514); Working Document on progress made since the 2004 White Paper on SGIs (SEC(2007) 1514).

[13] Commission Communication Accompanying the Communication on 'A Single Market for 21st Century Europe: Services of General Interest Including Social Services of General Interest: A New European Commitment, COM (2007) 755 final.

[14] Case C-141/02P *Commission v T-Mobile Austria GmbH formerly max.mobil Telekommunikation Service* [2005] E.C.R. I-1283.

The Commission has used this legal base to create normative measures. Initially the Commission used this legal base as a preventative legal tool, adopting directives on Transparency in financial arrangements between Member States and public undertakings.[15] The Commission also used art.86(3) EC to open up the telecommunications market to liberalisation and this caused controversy. In 1988 the Commission adopted the Telecommunications Terminals directive[16] on the basis of art.86(3) EC. It was argued that this legal device imposed new obligations upon the Member States and circumvented the participation of the Member States (and the then limited role of the European Parliament) in the Community legislative procedure. In a legal challenge to the directive the Court gave a wide interpretation to the preventative functions of directives and recognised that art.86(3) EC could be used to specify to *all* of the Member States the obligations that derived from the EC Treaty.[17] This wide-ranging ruling, together with the case law under art.86(1) EC, provided the incentive for the Member States to consider the liberalisation of public monopolies more closely and to use art.95 EC (the legal base for Internal Market measures) for further liberalisation measures. In this way they controlled the structured opening up of markets previously insulated from competition.

## 7.2 State Aid

States may create barriers to integration and free competition within the Internal Market by giving aid and subsidies to national firms. This kind of intervention in markets plays a major role in the industrial policy of the Member States and often is *expected* of the Member States in order to promote social, environmental and regional policies. State aid may be granted to help firms in financial distress; it is expected of the State to save jobs which might be vulnerable in a failing firm. During the oil crisis of the 1970s Member States were obliged to rescue struggling firms and direct intervention of the State in the economy rose dramatically. But this form of retrenchment failed, leading to pressure on public enterprise and public finances.

---

[15] Commission Dir.80/723, OJ 1980 L195/35; amended by Commission Dir.85/413, OJ 1985 L229/20; Commission Dir.93/84, OJ 1984 L54/16, Commission Dir.2000/52/EC, OJ L 2000 193/75.

[16] Commission Dir.(EEC) 88/301, OJ 1988 L131/73.

[17] Case C-202/88 *Telecommunications Terminal Equipment* [1991] E.C.R. I-1223.

State Aid creates distortions in the market. Until the 1990s, when the completion of the Internal Market turned greater political attention to the pervasive barriers created by State intervention in markets, the Commission used a diplomatic approach towards the control of State Aid in the Internal Market. By the end of the 1990s a tougher approach was taken towards controlling State Aid at the EU level, firstly by encouraging the reduction of the amounts of State Aid (expressed as a percentage of GDP) and secondly, by encouraging the use of horizontal State Aid. It is felt that the latter is less anti-competitive and promotes European integration.

In the Commission's Ninth Survey on State Aid in the European Union, (COM (2001) 403 final, para.2) the Commission explains why State Aid is a problem for European integration:

"A key element of Competition policy is Community State Aid control, the benefits of which are clear. State aid can frustrate free competition by preventing the most efficient allocation of resources and posing a threat to the unity of the Internal Market. In many cases, the granting of State aid reduces economic welfare and weakens the incentives for firms to improve efficiency. Aid also enables the less efficient to survive at the expense of the more efficient. In addition to creating distortions within the Internal Market, the grant of State aid can affect trade between the EU and third countries thereby encouraging them to adopt retaliatory measures that may be a source of further inefficiency. . ."

The Member States singled out the control of State Aid in the Lisbon Process:

"State aid distorts competition and, whether or not it has an impact on trade between member states, may damage the allocative efficiency of the European economy. In particular, it modifies economic incentives and so may cause the inefficient allocation of scarce private resources to industries receiving aid and away from others. State aid may also encourage rent-seeking behaviour and "capture" of government by industries, and moral hazard in the case of failing industries. Like other government expenditures, the financing of State aid also raises the issue of the marginal cost of public funds, i.e. the loss of efficiency due to taxation.

The consequences of State aid in terms of inefficient functioning of product markets imply that the European

Commission's control of State aid needs to be supplemented by an effort of self-discipline on the part of the member states themselves. In view of the cross-border spill-over effects of State aid, this self-discipline can be more rigorous and politically acceptable if the efforts of the Member States are co-ordinated. To this end, since 1999 recommendations on State aid are included in the framework of the Broad Economic Policy Guidelines (BEPG)."[18]

The Stockholm European Council Meeting in 2001 agreed, for the first time, an objective indicator to benchmark Member States' expenditure on State Aid by expressing such expenditure as a percentage of GDP. The enforcement and monitoring of State Aid was enhanced by the introduction of a State Aid Scoreboard and a State Aid Register. The most recent State Aid Score Board of Autumn 2007 reveals that not all of the Member States are reluctant to give up the use of State Aid and that State Aid continues to be directed at the manufacturing and service sectors.[19]

Articles 87–89 EC address States Aids. These provisions are skeletal in form and have been implemented and modernised by the use of soft law and Block Exemptions.[20] State Aids are, in principle, incompatible with the Internal Market and therefore prohibited unless they are granted an exemption by the Commission in accordance with the procedure under art.88 EC and the procedural Regulation which was introduced in 1999 and modernised by a Regulation in 2004 (Sinnaeve, 2007). The Member States are bound also by the fidelity clause of art.10 EC.

## Exemptions, Justifications and Derogations

Article 87(2) EC grants a number of automatic exemptions from the application of the State Aid rules covering aid for natural disasters, exceptional circumstances, or having a social character granted to individual consumers. The latter must not discriminate according to the origin of the products concerned. Article 87(2) (c) is unusual in that it allows for aid to be granted in certain areas of Germany. This provision is to be phased out in amendments made by the Treaty of Lisbon 2007 (*art.107(2)(c) TFEU*). The ECJ construed this provision

---

[18] Lisbon European Council, March 2000 SN 100/1/100 point 17.

[19] The Score Board can be found at: *http://europa.eu.int/comm/competition/state_aid/ scoreboard/*. [Accessed April 11, 2008]

[20] Vademecum Community Rules on State Aid (last updated February 15, 2007).

narrowly referring to the economic disadvantages created by the division of Germany in 1948, for example, the loss of markets. Thus art.87(2) (c) EC has little practical role to play after the reunification of Germany.[21]

Under art.87(3) EC the Commission may *exempt* certain aid schemes from the competition rules and has produced a range of soft law to provide guidance in this field.

A slightly more complicated exemption from the State Aid rules is the application of art.86(2) EC where State Aid is given to provide a service of general economic interest. The State Aid rules do not provide for this as an exception but the wording of art.86(2) EC speaks of the *non-application of the competition rules* to a service of general economic interest and this can justify the reading over of this exception from the rules on state monopolies to the State Aid arena. The Commission is prepared to grant exemptions using art.86(2) EC. The ECJ in *Altmark*[22] has provided guidelines to establish if funding of services of general economic interest is indeed caught by the State Aid rules. It is not clear if funding which falls outside of the *Altmark* criteria, but within art.86(2) EC, should be notified and approved by the Commission. Arguably *all* potential State Aid should be cleared, or approved, by the Commission but there are arguments that aid which satisfies art.86(2) EC is *not* caught by the State Aid rules.

Article 73 EC creates an exception for transport in the field of State aid where finance is used for transport coordination or for the provision of a service of general economic interest.

The production of, and trade in arms, munitions and war material set out in art.296(2) EC are also subject to special rules under the EC Treaty. Because this provision is part of the general and final provisions of the EC Treaty it affects all the EC Treaty rules, including the provisions relating to competition. Member States are given a wide discretion in matters relating national defence and security. Where State Aid is granted relating to a measure affecting internal security the competition rules do not apply. The Member State does not have to notify the aid to the Commission and the Commission may not use the procedure under art.88 EC to examine the aid. But the Commission is still under a duty to ensure the measure does not adversely affect the conditions of competition in relation to products which are not intended for specifically military purposes

---

[21] Case C-301/96 *Germany v Commission* [2003] E.C.R. I-9919; Case C-277/00 *Germany v Commission* [2004] E.C.R. I-3925.

[22] Case C-280/00 *Altmark* [2003] E.C.R. I-7747. Cf. Case 289/03 *BUPA v Commission* judgment of February 12, 2008.

(art.296(1)(b) EC). If there is a distortion of competition under art.298(1) EC the Member State and the Commission must examine how the measure can be adjusted to comply with the competition rules. But the Commission is not required to adopt a Decision or address a Decision or directive to the Member State. If the Commission believes that art.296 EC cannot be relied upon by the Member State it may used the ordinary State Aid procedures to investigate the aid set out in art.88(2) EC.

## Definition of a State Aid

There is no definition in the EC Treaty as to what is a State Aid. This is deliberate. It allows for flexibility in tackling the wide range of measures States can resort to in order to support domestic firms. Over the years Commission practice, and the rulings of the European Courts, have created a set of criteria which must be satisfied for a measure to be classed as a State Aid. There must be a measure which confers a benefit or an advantage which favours certain undertakings; the benefit or advantage must be granted by, or come from, the instruction of the State and involve State resources; the measure must distort or threaten to distort competition and affect trade between the Member States. In the case law little attention is paid to the last two criteria, but there are differences of opinion between the European Courts and the Commission on the application of a de minimis rule. The Commission has published a number of Communications on de minimis aid and in 2001 adopted a regulation.[23] In contrast the ECJ has rejected the use of a de minimis rule.[24]

Only aid granted by a Member State or through State resources falls within the concept of a State Aid in art.87(1) EC. In *Neptun*[25] the Court gave this concept a narrow meaning requiring that the measure must be *directly* at the expense of the State. In *Stardust Marine*[26] the question arose as to whether aid granted by public or private bodies created by the State constituted State Aid. The ECJ ruled that even if the State is in a position to control an undertaking, and to exercise a dominant influence over its operations, actual exercise of that control cannot be automatically presumed. The ECJ held

---

[23] Commission reg.(EC) 69/2001 of January 12, 2001 on the application of arts 87 and 88 of the EC Treaty to de minimis aid, OJ 2001 L10/30.
[24] Case C-280/00 *Altmark* [2003] E.C.R. I-I-7747.
[25] Joined Cases C-72 and C-73/91 *Sloman Neptun Schiffahrts AG v Seebetriebsrat Bodo Ziesemer der Sloman Neptun Schiffahrts AG* [1993] E.C.R. I-887.
[26] Case C-482/99 *France v Commission* [2002] E.C.R. I-4397.

that an inquiry should be made in each individual case and set out a series of indicators to be applied. There is no "aid" "granted" from the State or its resources when the State distorts competition among undertakings or goods and services by placing an extra burden on certain economic agents or activities (Schon, 2006).[27] In *Pearle*[28] a reference was made asking if charges imposed on its members by a trade association, governed by public law, which represented traders in optical equipment was an illegal State aid. The charge was a compulsory, earmarked levy to finance a collective advertising campaign for opticians. Despite being levied by a public body the charge was not a State aid. The monies used for the advertising campaign came directly from the members of the trade association, no the State.

There may be State Aid present where an agreement does not accord with normal commercial practice.[29]

## Private Economy Investor Test

A filter used by the Commission to determine if there is a State Aid is the use of the "private economy investor test".[30] This is used to test if a State measure is a legitimate market investment, or whether the State is subsidising a firm in a way which is likely to disrupt competition. Without such a test commercial activity by the State would be paralysed and the Commission would be inundated with notifications of potential State Aid. The test has been criticised since it is argued that it is a hypothetical test. A private investor would often not be willing to invest in failing firms in the same way that the State feels an obligation to invest for social and political reasons. It is also argued that, subject to the constraints on public expenditure under the Growth and Stability Pact and the Broad Economic Policy Guidelines of the Community and the Member States, the State has a deeper pocket than a normal private investor. As is discussed below, investments in firms are often made merely because the State is willing to a guarantee or underwrite a firm. In this respect the State has a better credit rating than other economic

[27] Case C-308/01 *GIL Insurance Ltd v CCE* [2004] E.C.R. I-4777; Case C-526/04 *Laboratoires Boiron SA* [2006] E.C.R. I-7529.

[28] Case C-345/02 *Pearle* [2004] E.C.R. I-7139.

[29] Joined Cases T-116/01 and T-118/01 *P&O European Ferries (Vizcaya) SA and Diputación Foral de Vicaya v Commission* [2003] E.C.R. II-2957; appeal Case C-442/03 [2006] E.C.R. I-4845.

[30] Case C-142/87 *Belgium v Commission* [1990] E.C.R. I-959.

actors. Despite the criticisms, the private investor test continues to be used by the Commission, for example in the Commission Decision in 2004 against State Aid given to Ryan Air in the concessions it obtained to land at Charleroi Airport in Belgium.

Another case which is illustrative of the way the test operates is the case of the German public bank WestLB. Here a complaint was made to the Commission by the federation of private banks in Germany concerning the contribution of certain assets by the Land Nordrhein-Westfalen to WestLB. It was argued that the loans made were a form of State Aid because the rate of return on the investment was only 0.6 per cent after tax whereas a private investor would have expected a rate of return of 9.3 per cent after tax.

Although the CFI found that the Commission had not given sufficient reasons for its Decision the CFI did hold that the profitability of the beneficiary is not conclusive but should be taken into account for the purpose of determining whether the public investor behaved in the same way as a market economy investor or whether the beneficiary obtained an economic advantage which it would not have obtained under normal conditions. The Commission ordered the German government to collect €3 billion in State Aid, plus interest, which had been given to the German public banks from the 1990s. WestLB was the largest recipient of such aid, totalling some €979 million.[31]

The application of the private economy investor test involves complex economic assessment and the European Courts are reluctant to interfere with the Commission's assessment, although in some recent cases the CFI has been prepared to limit the Commission's discretion.[32] A major issue is how to handle the problem of cross-subsidisation in public monopolies supplying a service of general economic interest in what is known as a "reserved sector", alongside their increasing involvement with commercial activity in liberalised markets.[33] Such cases have arisen in the postal sector which is undergoing a structured liberalisation. The former State monopolies have often retained the provision of a service of general economic interest in providing a basic postal service which is protected from competition. But aid or benefits which are allowed to provide the service of general economic interest may also be used to

---

[31] Joined Cases T-228/99 and T-233/99 *WestLB v Commission* [2003] E.C.R. II-445; Case C-209/00 *Commission v Germany* [2002] E.C.R. I-11695.

[32] Case T-11/95 *BP Chemicals v Commission* [1998] E.C.R. II-3235.

[33] Case C-39/94 *SFEI* [1996] E.C.R. I-3547; Case T-613/97 *UFEX v Commission* [2000] E.C.R. II-4055.

cross-subsidise activities in the commercial sector, making it difficult for competitors to break into these markets which have been opened up to competition.

The CFI in *UFEX* decided that more was required than merely showing that a public undertaking providing a service of general economic interest was paid the full costs for the provision of logistical and commercial assistance provided to its subsidiary which was acting in the commercial competitive sector. Instead the CFI stated that the Commission should have checked that the payment received by the parent company was comparable to that which would be demanded by a private holding company not operating in a reserved sector pursuing a structural policy and guided by long-term prospects.

The ECJ set the CFI judgment aside and referred the case back to the CFI.[34] The ECJ stressed the importance of the service of general economic interest provided by La Poste, pointing out that the huge, and often uneconomic network that La Poste had created to provide a universal postal service could not be assessed by a purely commercial approach and indeed such a network would never be created by a private operator. Since such comparisons would be hypothetical only the available and verifiable elements of the aid should be assessed. This ruling appears to be incompatible with the ruling of *Altmark* but also appears to be line with the reasoning in *Stardust Marine* of granting greater commercial freedom to public companies.

The Court has also recognised a new category of a "Private Ceditor" test relating to the way in which the state pursues debts.[35]

## Problems with Privatisations

With liberalisation came the selling-off of State assets: privatisations (Devroe, 1997; Szyszczak 2001). A question arises as to whether the Member States have under-sold assets and whether this can be a form of State Aid. Favourable terms can be offered to investors from the Member State to keep assets within national ownership and can be used to repay political favours. The Commission would prefer State assets to be sold by an open, transparent and unconditional bidding procedure to avoid any doubts that there may be State Aid involved in privatisations.[36] But the Commission has accepted

---

[34] Joined Cases C-83/01 P, C-93/01 P and C-94/01P *Chronopost SA, La Poste v Commission* [2003] E.C.R. I-6993.

[35] Case T-36/99 *Lenzing AG v Commission* [2004] E.C.R. II-3597; on appeal Case C-525/04P *Spain v Lenzing* judgment of November 22, 2007

[36] 1991 XXI Report on Competition Policy, para.248.

expert valuations of State assets.[37] A sale to the highest bidder will not always eliminate a suspicion of State Aid, particularly where a substantial amount of public finance is used to enable a sale to take place.[38]

## Different Kinds of State Aid

The Commission classifies State Aid into four kinds of categories. Group A aids are grants and tax exemptions; Group B is the type of aid favoured by France, equity participation in the firm; Group C are soft loans and tax deferrals and Group D are guarantees. The last kind of State Aid creates controversy because often no tangible form of aid or subsidy passes from the state to a firm.[39] In the new Member States 41 per cent of the total aid over the period 2000–2003 was in the form of guarantees, whereas guarantees make up only 3 per cent of the identifiable aid in the old Member States.

## New Aid

Surprisingly it was not until 1999 that the Commission's practice in relation to the procedures for handling State Aid were codified in a regulation. It is assumed that State Aid is illegal per se unless it can be justified. A new State Aid must be notified to the Commission and approved before it can be put into operation. The Commission has two months in which to act.[40] After two months, if there is no decision, a Member State may notify the Commission that it is proceeding with the aid and the Commission is barred from objecting to the aid.

In the two-month period the Commission may initiate a formal investigation. The Commission must, as far as possible, endeavour to take a Decision within 18 months from the opening of the procedure. If no Decision is forthcoming then the Member State may request that a Decision be taken within two months. But if a Member State has supplied insufficient information to the Commission to enable it to determine the compatibility of the State Aid with the Common Market there is a presumption of a negative decision. The Commission enjoys a broad discretion in its decision-making powers but the principle of proportionality plays an important role. The

[37] *Koninklijke Schelde Groep,* OJ 2003 L14/56, para.79.
[38] Opinion of A.G. Jacobs Joined Cases C-278/92, C-279/92 and C-280/92 *Spain v Commission* [1994] E.C.R. I-4103, para.30.
[39] Friend, 2004; Nicolaides, 2005.
[40] Case 120/73 *Lorenz v Germany* [1973] E.C.R. 1471; arts 4(5)–(6) of reg.659/1999.

State Aid Register allows for greater transparency in seeing how the Commission develops policy and allows the Member States an insight into what is acceptable aid.

If a Member State fails to notify new aid, or introduces new aid during the Commission's preliminary or formal examination of the proposed aid, the Member State is in breach of art.88(3) EC. The aid is unlawful, notwithstanding the fact that the Commission may ultimately have come to the conclusion that the aid was unlawful. Any recipients of such unlawful State Aid will be under an obligation to repay the aid with interest.[41]

The Commission has exclusive power to find the compatibility of an aid with the Common Market. Over the years the Commission has created a body of soft law processes to develop policy in this area. From 1999 onwards it has adopted legislation in the form of Block Exemptions creating procedural rules for the regulation of State Aid[42] and allowing certain kinds of aid to be exempt from notification, for example horizontal aid, de minimis aid, small and medium size enterprise, employment with re special sectoral rules applying to agriculture, fisheries, transport shipbuilding and steel. As part of the modernisation of State Aid[43] the Commission has issued a draft proposal for a general Block Exemption.[44]

### State Aids and Services of General Economic Interest

Commission dir.80/723, which was adopted by the Commission using art.86(3) EC, addressed the need for transparency in State Aid applied to public undertakings. This directive used a de minimis rule but did not usurp the normal Commission powers to control State Aids. This directive, as amended,[45] aims to enforce transparency by extending the rules on the separation of accounts to any undertaking that enjoys a special or exclusive right under art.86(1) EC or that is entrusted with a service of general economic interest and receives State Aid in any form whatsoever. Such State Aid is now included in the Commission's surveys of State Aid.

---

[41] Case C-39/94 *SFI v La Poste* [1996] E.C.R. I-3547.

[42] Council reg.(EC) 659/1999, OJ 1999 L 83/1, now modernised by Commission reg.(EC) No. 794/2004, OJ 2004 L140/1.

[43] *Commission, State Aid Action Plan. Less and Better Targeted State Aid: A Road Map for State Aid Reform 2005–2009*, COM (2005) 107 final.

[44] *http://ec.europa.eu/comm/competition/state_aid/reform/gber3_en.pdf*. [Accessed April 11, 2008)

[45] Commission dir.80/723, OJ 1980 L195/35; amended by Commission Dir.85/413, OJ 1985 L229/20; Commission dir.93/84, OJ 1984 L54/16, Commission dir.2000/52/EC, OJ 2000 L 193/75.

A contentious issue is whether payments or other benefits for services of general economic interest are State Aid or whether they are merely compensatory payments for services provided. The difficulty with a compensation approach is that often it is difficult to assess how much a service of general economic interest would cost because often such services are not provided in competitive markets. In *Ferring*[46] the ECJ held that a tax exemption provided to wholesale distributors of pharmaceutical products was *not* a State Aid since it compensated the pharmaceutical companies for providing a service of general economic interest. The Court demanded a necessary connection between the additional costs incurred by the distributors providing the service and the tax exemption. If the exemption was greater than the costs incurred there was the possibility of trying to justify the advantage or benefit under art.86(2) EC. This justification/exemption is not written into the rules on State Aid but can be read across from art.86 EC in that a Member State is asking for the non-application of the *competition* rules to its activities.

In principle it is hard to see how a Member State can justify payments/benefits in excess of the cost of a service of general economic interest and still satisfy the principle of proportionality contained in the application of art.86(2) EC. But the Court has accepted that when supplying such services the State is not acting as a normal commercial undertaking and may have to invest in risky undertakings to ensure the delivery of public services.[47]

A difficulty with applying art.86(2) EC, which has not be answered directly by the European Courts, is whether a Member State must notify new State Aid which is covered by art.86(2) EC. It is arguable that in order to maintain the integrity and transparency of the State Aid system, and to preserve the central regulatory role of the Commission, the State is still under an obligation to notified new aid which can benefit from an art.86(2) justification.

In the *Altmark*[48] ruling the ECJ took a prescriptive approach setting out firm criteria to be satisfied in order to find that any aid or benefit was compensation for the provision of a service of general economic interest. The Court adopted a *compensation approach* provided that four conditions were met. Firstly, the recipient undertaking must actually have a clearly defined service of general

---

[46] Case C-53/00 *Ferring v ACOSS* [2001] E.C.R. 6639.
[47] Joined Cases C-157/94 *Commission v Netherlands* [1997] E.C.R. I-5699; Case 158/94 *Commission v Italy* [1997] E.C.R. I-5789; Case 159/94 *Commission v France* [1997] E.C.R. I-5815; Case C-160/94 *Commission v Spain* [1997] E.C.R. I-5851.
[48] Case C-280/00 *Altmark* [2003] E.C.R. I-7747.

economic interest to discharge. Secondly, the parameters on the basis on which compensation is calculated must be established in advance and in an objective and transparent manner in order to avoid conferring an economic advantage which may favour the recipient undertaking over competing undertaking undertakings. Thirdly, the compensation must not exceed what is necessary to cover all, or part, of the costs incurred in the discharge of the service of general economic interest, taking into account relevant receipts and a reasonable profit for discharging those obligations. Finally, where there is no public tendering system to choose the provider of the service of general economic interest the level of compensation must be determined by an analysis of the costs which a typical under-taking, well run and adequately provided for to meet the require-ments of a service of general economic interest would have incurred in discharging those obligations taking into account the relevant receipts and a reasonable profit for discharging the obligations.

The last criterion is controversial since the Court seems to be steering the Member States towards a procurement process for providing services of general economic interest. Where there is no procurement process it may be difficult to find a comparator under-taking to benchmark the costs of providing a service of general interest. (Szyszczak: 2004). Using a procurement process does not necessarily rule out the possibility of illegal State Aid.[49] When a public contract does not correspond with a normal trade agreement illegal State Aid may be present.[50]

The Court applied its *Altmark* criteria in *Enirisorse*.[51] This was an indirect challenge to a claim that there was a service of general economic interest in providing port services in Cagliari, Italy. Enirisorse loaded and unloaded domestic and foreign goods at Cagliari using its own personnel and equipment and not the services of the port authority. It challenged the requests for payment for these services by the Ministry of Finance claiming that the Italian decree under which the port services were created was contrary to Community law. The Court found that none of the four criteria in *Altmark* were met and therefore the financing of the port authority system was a State Aid within the meaning of art.87(1) EC.

---

[49] Bartosch, 2002.

[50] Joined Cases T-116/01 and T-118/01 *P&O European Ferries (Vizcaya) SA and Diputación Foral de Vicaya v Commission* [2003] E.C.R. II-2957; on appeal Case C-442/03 and C-471/03 [2006] E.C.R. I-4845.

[51] Cases C-34-38/01 [2003]. But cf. Case T-289/03 *BUPA*, judgment of February 12, 2008.

In the follow-up to *Ferring* the national court pointed out that in applying the *Altmark* criteria use is made of data to which the economic operator who alleges that there is state aid does not have access. Attorney General Tizzano argued that the burden of proof should remain with the complainant who asserts that there is illegal State Aid. In contrast the ECJ stated that a national court is required to use all procedures available to it under national law, including ordering necessary measures of inquiry in particular production of documents in order to secure effectiveness.[52]

## *Existing State Aid*

Existing aid includes State Aid exempted under art.87(2) EC. Each year the Member States must submit an annual report on all State Aid schemes. These rules only apply to aid schemes, not individual aid. Existing individual aid cannot be challenged. If an existing aid becomes incompatible with the Common Market the Commission can order its immediate termination, or termination within a reasonable time.[53] If the Member State fails to follow the Commission's Recommendation the Commission must then initiate a formal investigation procedure.

The Court extended the definition of existing aid contrary to the express wording of reg.659/1999 by including a system of aid that existed in a certain market which had been closed to competition but had been liberalised.[54] The aid was to be regarded as "existing aid" from the date of liberalisation of the market.

There is an under-used procedure in art.88(2) EC whereby the Council, acting by unanimity vote, may overrule the Commission's decisions on new and existing aids if this justified by exceptional circumstances. This procedure was used in 2002 when the Portuguese government asked the Council to approve aid to pig farmers. The Commission had taken a Decision that earlier aid was incompatible with the common market. The Portuguese government wanted to grant new aid which corresponded in amount to the aid which had been declared invalid. The Council adopted a Decision under art.88(2) EC and this was challenged by the Commission using art.230 EC, arguing that the Council had exceeded its competence, or in the alternative, that the Council had committed a manifest

---

[52] Case C-526/04 *Laboratoires Boiron SA* [2006] E.C.R. I-7529.
[53] Joined Cases C-182/03 and C-217/03 *R Belgium and Forum 187 ASBL v Commission* [2003] E.C.R. I-5479, para.124.
[54] Joined Cases T-298/97, 312/97, 313/97, 315/97, 600–607/97, 1/98, 3–6/98, 23/98 *Alzetto Mauro v Commission* [2000] E.C.R. II-2319.

error of appreciation in concluding that there were "exceptional circumstances" and that the Council's Decision was not adequately and correctly reasoned.[55]

## The Special Problem of State Aid in the New Member States

The enlargement of the EU on May 1, 2004 created new problems for State Aid control. Eight out of the 10 accession States have only recently become market economies. There is still a political tendency to look to State intervention in the market as a political and social policy tool. The EU used a system of close monitoring of State Aid in the Accession Reports which took place in the run up to the enlargement in 2004. Under the Europe Agreements, which were the bilateral framework agreements between the EU and each candidate country establishing the legal framework for the adaptation of national legislation to the acquis communautaire, each accession State had to adopt and implement a national State Aid law and a national authority responsible for State Aid.

The Commission approved a series of transitional State Aids to address particular problems associated with accession. In particular aid was needed to support the financial sector, coal, steel, agriculture and the new accession States continue to direct aid towards particular sectors, rather than implementing the Lisbon and Stockholm objectives of directing aid towards horizontal projects. Additionally many accession States use incentive measures, such as tax breaks, to encourage investment.

Where State Aid was identified as incompatible with the Common Market the accession States had to adapt or abolish the aid. In order to prevent incompatible State Aid continuing after enlargement a new surveillance mechanism covering all sectors except for transport and agriculture was introduced, known as the "existing aid" mechanism. In transport and agriculture measures could be counted as existing aid provided that they were notified to the Commission by August 31, 2004. These measures enjoy the protection of a sunset clause which allows the new Member States a longer period of time, until April 2007, to ensure the compatibility of the measures with Community law.

During the first phase of this surveillance mechanism in 2002 some 222 measures were approved by the Commission and listed in the Treaty of Accession. During the second phase a new mechanism

---

[55] Case C-110/02 *Commission v Council* [2004] E.C.R. I-6333.

called the "interim procedure" approved some 278 measures as existing aid. New State Aid measures were notified to the Commission right up until April 30, 2004 and at the time of writing (May 2005) a number of State Aid measures from this period are still being assessed by the Commission.

There was a huge incentive for the new Member States to bring their State Aid into effect before May 1, 2004. Any State Aid granted after that date becomes new aid. The total State Aid granted by the accession states in the four years before May 1, 2004 was some €5.7 billion per year. Three accession states, Poland, Czech Republic and Hungary, accounted for 86 per cent of this aid.

The Treaty of Accession used the distinctions between "existing aid" and "new aid" which are found in the EC Treaty. The Commission will not necessarily approve aid which was approved by national authorities prior to accession. Existing aid is aid which existed prior to entry into force of the accession Treaty and has not changed materially in the interim. Such aid also embraces aid which has been authorised by the Commission or the Council (or is deemed so authorised) or is aid which has been paid prior to the 10-year limitation period set out in art.15 of reg.659/1999. This aid was listed in Annex IV, Chapter 3 to the Accession Treaty.

To be included in Annex 4, the measure had to reviewed, and approved, by the national authority and the Commission did not object to the measure in the framework of the information and consultation mechanisms established by the Europe Agreements. Annex 4 was closed on November 1, 2002. From November 2002 until May 1, 2004 a transitional period was in operation and it is expected that a second list of approved existing aid measures will be adopted. Aid granted prior to December 10, 1994 is deemed to be existing aid per se.

The Commission can modify a measure for the future which is deemed to be "existing aid" by using appropriate measures. It cannot order recovery. But there is a presumption that existing aid is legal until the Commission has taken an adverse decision.

## National Courts and Repayment of Illegal State Aid

The Commission adopted a *Notice on Co-operation Between the National Courts and the Commission in the State Aid Field* (Flynn, 2003).[56] The national court's role is to safeguard rights which individuals enjoy as a result of the direct effect of the prohibition

---

[56] OJ 1995 C312/8.

laid down in the last sentence of art.88 (3). The court should use all appropriate devices and remedies and apply all relevant provisions of national law to implement the direct effect of this obligation placed by the Treaty on Member States.

A national court must, in a case within its jurisdiction, apply Community law in its entirety and protect rights which that law confers on individuals. It must therefore set aside any provision of national law which may conflict with it, subsequent to the Community rule.[57] The judge may, as appropriate and in accordance with applicable rules of national law and the developing case-law of the Court of Justice grant interim relief, for example by ordering the freezing or return of monies illegally paid, and award damages to parties whose interests are harmed.

The Court of Justice has held that the full effectiveness of Community rules would be impaired and the protection of the rights which they grant would be weakened if individuals were unable to obtain redress when their rights are infringed by a breach of Community law for which a Member State can be held responsible; the principle whereby a State must be liable for loss and damage caused to individuals as a result of breaches of Community law for which the State can be held responsible is inherent in the system of the Treaty.[58] A national court which considers, in a case concerning Community law, that the sole obstacle precluding it from granting interim relief is a rule of national law, must set aside that rule.

In *CELF*[59] the Court addressed the difficult question of whether a national court should recover aid which had been granted by a Member State before the aid was officially notified but when notified was declared to be compatible with the Common Market under art.87 EC. Normally the non-notified aid would be declared illegal and should be repaid with interest. The Court took a pragmatic solution and held that a national court is not bound to order the recovery of the aid for the whole period of its use but should order recovery (with interest) for the period of unlawfulness. The national court may also uphold claims for damages as a result of the implementation of the non-notified aid.

The Commission must order the recovery of new State Aid which is put into operation before a Commission decision or state aid which exists without having been notified to the Commission. A recovery decision can only be avoided if it would infringe a general

---

[57] Case C-119/05 *Lucchini Sidurgeri* [2007] E.C.R. I-6199.
[58] Case C-6 and 9/90 *Francovich v Italian State* [1991] E.C.R. I-5357.
[59] Case C-199/06 *CELF*, judgment of February 12, 2008.

principle of Community law. It is difficult to apply this defence. The most obvious general principle of Community law which could be infringed is the principle of legitimate expectations. If the Commission makes a mistake, for example, wrongly classifying the aid, or does not follow time limits this situation could give rise to legitimate expectations.

Recovery of the illegal State Aid is through national law.[60] The State Aid must be repaid with interest. No time limit is set for recovery; the Regulation speaks of recovery "without undue delay". While a Member State is under a duty of good faith as a result of the solidarity/fidelity clause of art.10 EC the monitoring and enforcement of recovery of illegal State Aid does not have any clear cut rules. Usually the Commission asks a Member State in the recovery Decision to inform it within two months of the steps taken.[61]

A weakness of the State aid enforcement regime is that the Member State that has acted illegally but it is the *recipient* which is punished. A competitor who has been harmed by an illegal State Aid could bring a *Francovich* action for damages against the State.

## 7.3 Competition Policy and a Community Industrial Policy

The Commission has interpreted competition policy widely. By allowing competition policy to pursue a number of objectives, for example, the promotion of integration, efficiency, the competitiveness of European industry, and albeit limited in extent, wider social objectives competition policy has internalised an industrial policy for the EU. This goes beyond the EC Treaty base for an industrial policy which was first introduced by the TEU 1991. This coincided with a greater range of aims and objectives for European integration, including ideas of social rights and citizenship.

Article 3 (1) (m) EC states that the activities of the Community shall include "the strengthening of the competitiveness of Community industry". Title XVI allows the Commission to coordinate the Member States' actions in this field (art.157(2) EC). The Community and the Member States are to ensure that the

---

[60] Case C-404/00 *Commission v Spain* [2003] E.C.R. I-6695, para.22. Art.14(3).

[61] See the current problems where the recipient was unable to repay the State Aid: Case T-416/05 R *Olympiakes Aerogrammes AE v Commission*, Order of June 26, 2006; Case C-419/06 *Commission v Greece*, judgment of February 14, 2008.

conditions necessary for the competitiveness of the Community' industry exist. The Council may support action taken by the Member States to achieve the objectives of the industrial policy (art.157 (3) EC). But express Community competence in the field of industrial policy is simply not evident in the EC Treaty. Arguably through the competition policy pursued under arts 81 and 82 EC, the Community, through the policy of the Commission and the European Courts, has found a more interventionist role for an industrial policy of the EU. The close connection between industrial policy and competition policy is recognised explicitly by the Commission in policy documents.[62]

By 2004 the EU had a wide-ranging and sophisticated set of competition tools, and a fair degree of consensus on competition policy for the EU. Enlargement, combined with a dependency upon an almost monopolistic role for the Commission in the policy-making, monitoring and enforcement of competition law, created the necessity to refocus the central role and energy of the Commission on aspects of anticompetitive behaviour which attracted attention at the Community level, especially the pursuit of hard core cartels. As a result of de-centralisation, all the Member States have been obliged to introduce national competition rules which mirror arts 81 EC and 82 EC.

The control of private power in the market has led to ideas of an economic constitution. Competition policy has imposed a number of restraints not only on the sovereignty of the Member States but also on the behaviour of undertakings. Although the main focus has been upon the anti-competitive *behaviour* of undertakings, Community competition law has proved to be flexible enough to reach into regulating the *structure* of competition in the EU. Particularly in relation to dominant undertakings a special responsibility has been placed upon them not to jeopardise the aims of European integration. This in turn has led to structural adjustments at the national level, including the rationalisation of mergers at the Community level. The effects of the competition policy have had an impact upon direct State intervention in the market, changing quite fundamentally the Member States' attitudes towards their role in competitive markets. As a result competition law and policy has not only complemented the Internal Market but added a new dimension: an industrial policy which encompasses new concepts of social and economic goals for European integration.

---

[62] EC Commission, *Fostering Structural Change: An Industrial Policy for an Enlarged Europe,* COM (2004) 274 final.

The development of an EU industrial policy and the application of the competition rules to Member State economic activity gradually led to changes in the Member States attitude towards direct State intervention in the market. The European Courts' use of the procedures of EU law, rather than openly prescribing a particular form of economic policy has shifted the political balance away from Member State power towards the rule of economic law (Szyszczak, 2007). The Member States' retreat from economic sovereignty has led to the scope for competition to exist in markets previously protected from competition. This can be seen as a process of de-regulation in the same way that the four freedoms, especially the free movement of goods, created de-regulation of trade barriers inhibiting market integration. A major problem in the field of competition, however, is that the Community lacks the competence to re-regulate where intervention in the market is necessary. The EU realised that general competition principles were insufficient to handle the new problems of controlling market power where markets were liberalised. During the 1990s the EU witnessed a degree of experimentation, of using competition *and* regulatory principles to manage the liberalisation of sensitive sectors such as telecommunications, postal services and utilities. Thus new paradigms are emerging for the management of the new economy (Graham and Smith, 2004; Bavasso, 2004).

However, the Community lacks a fully developed industrial policy and also lacks competence for re-distributive policies. This explains why the Court has been cautious in areas affecting services of general economic interest. In areas where liberalisation of markets has taken place the legal base of the Internal Market has provided the justification for, and the means to re-regulate markets at the EU level.

# 8: Core Policies: the Common Agricultural Policy and Economic and Monetary Integration

## SUMMARY

8.1 The Common Agricultural Policy of the EU

8.2 Economic and Monetary Integration

## 8.1 The Common Agricultural Policy of the EU

A pressing concern in 1957 was to feed the people of Europe and reduce reliance on exports of agricultural products. The Common Agricultural Policy (CAP) is one of the oldest, most controversial and the most financially burdensome policies of the EU. It has been described by A.G. Geelhoed as "characterised by direct and radical intervention in economic practices concerning the production, processing and marketing of agricultural, products".[1] The objectives of the CAP have been sustained over time but the policies to achieve those objectives have been overhauled several times (MacMchon, 2007). The 1992 MacSharry Reforms were introduced as a response to the GATT Uruguay Round of 1986 which included discussion of international trade in agricultural products for the first time,[2] resulting in the Agreement on Agriculture. New rules were introduced for trade restrictions used to protect human, animal and plant health in the Sanitary and Phytosanitary Agreement. In 1997 reforms were made as part of the Agenda 2000 reforms of agriculture and the structural funds in preparation for enlargement of the EU.[3] As a result of continued public criticism of a wide range of alleged failures to address animal welfare issues, rural development,

---

[1] Case C-228/99 *Silos e Mangimi Martini SpA v Ministero delle Finanze dello Stato* [2001] E.C.R. I-8401, para.33.

[2] As discussed in Chapter 10 for the first time at the GATT/WTO the Commission negotiated on behalf of the Community/EU: See *Opinion 1/94* [1994] E.C.R. I-5267.

[3] COM (97) 2000.

the effects of the EU policy on agriculture and the developing countries and the EU's inability to handle major food crises and ensure the safety and quality of food, further reforms were made in 2003 (Kosior, 2005; Grant, 2006. Chalmers, 2005).

*Article 13 TFEU* introduces the Protocol on the protection and welfare of animals from the Treaty of Amsterdam 1997. This is a new wide-ranging mainstreaming clause:

"In formulating and implementing the Union's agriculture, fisheries and transport, internal market, research and technological development and space policies, the Union and the member States shall, since animals are sentient beings, pay full regard to the requirements of animal welfare, while respecting the legislative or administrative provisions and customs of Member States relating in particular to religious rites, cultural traditions and regional heritage."

After the Treaty of Lisbon 2007 agriculture will be an area of shared competence between the Union and the Member States (*art.4(2)(d) TFEU*). Article 32 EC (*art.38 TFEU*) will be amended to include fisheries in the CAP.

Article 33 EC (art.39 *TFEU*) states that the aim of the CAP as "to increase agricultural productivity". This policy is to be achieved around two pillars: the common organisations of the market and rural (structural) development (Usher, 2002; Cardwell, 2004). The first pillar, the common organisations of the market (COM), creates separate markets for different agricultural products regulated to protect the markets from normal market conditions. Article 34(1) EC (*art.40 TFEU*) states that the organisation of markets shall take either the form of common rules on competition, compulsory co-ordination of various national market organisations or a European market organisation, depending upon the product concerned. In *De Samvirkende Danske Landbofeninger* the Court describes a COM as:

"The essential aim of the machinery of the common organizations of the market is to achieve price levels at the production and wholesale stages which take into account both the interests of Community production as a whole in the relevant sector and those of consumers, which guarantee market supplies without encouraging over-production."[4]

---

[4] Case 297/82 *De Samvirkende Danske Landbofeninger* [1983] E.C.R. 3299, para.13.

Amongst the mechanisms used to achieve common organisations of markets are financial aid for the production, marketing and price support, which can include guaranteed purchases of agricultural goods where there is over-production or a slump in demand. This approach resulted in over-production of certain agricultural products, with a concentration of quantity over quality resulting the notorious beef and butter "mountains" and the magical wine and milk "lakes".

The EU policy has faced opposition at the international level because in effect it is a protectionist policy allowing EU producers access to subsidies. Together with EU-wide import quotas, or even bans,[5] European agricultural producers enjoy a huge degree of protection against external competition.

Attempts were made to restrain support for over-production during the 1980s, including placing an overall ceiling on agricultural expenditure which had registered at 87 per cent of the overall Community budget in 1970. The MacSharry Reforms (1992) focused upon a reduction in Community prices for certain sectors (mainly cereals and beef production) to align EU prices with global prices. This was to bring the EU into line with WTO obligations, as well as opening up the EU market to foreign competition. Producers were given payments *not* to produce certain goods in order to break the tendency towards over-production. The impending enlargement of the EU created new pressures, not only to reform the CAP but also to reform the structural policy of the EU, resulting in the *Agenda 2000* package of measures.[6] The policy of price reduction was continued and a new fund was established to give pre-accession aid through the Special Accession Programme for Agriculture and Rural Development (SAPARD).

More recent reforms have continued the MacSharry approach but stronger links have been made with the second pillar of addressing what is termed the multifunctional nature of agriculture, linking payments to animal welfare, environmental issues and rural development schemes. In 2005 the Commission issued a Communication,

---

[5] For example the high profile cases brought before the WTO Disputes Panel and Appellate Body on the EU ban on the marketing of hormone-treated beef on the grounds of consumer safety which excluded US and Canadian beef from the EU market; the marketing of GM crops which excluded products from the US, Canada and Argentina (Cardwell and Rodgers, 2006). The ability to use the WTO rules in the domestic courts was curtailed by the ECJ refusing to grant direct effect to the WTO or to allow judicial review of EU legislation in the context of WTO obligations: Case C-149/96 *Portugal v Council* [1999] E.C.R. I-8395; Case C-377/02 *Van Parys* [2005] E.C.R. I-1465.

[6] COM (97) 2000.

*Simplification and Better Regulation for the Common Agricultural Policy.*[7]

The second pillar has become more significant after the 2004 enlargement as this addresses rural development. It is essentially a structural policy for the CAP. During the 1970s the CAP had focused upon modernisation of farms, facilitating early retirement of agricultural workers and training. The impact of enlargement brought an increase in the number of farmers in the EU: an increase of 57 per cent, bringing less productive and less mechanised agricultural activity into the CAP through a set of transitional measures.[8] As part of the *Agenda 2000* reforms a new Regulation was adopted to simplify and reorganise rural development allowing for greater flexibility and decentralised policies to emerge.[9] Member States could choose from a range of measures in creating rural development plans some of which were funded under the EU Structural Funds.[10]

In 1991 a programme called *Links Between Actions for the Development of the Rural Economy* (LEADER) was adopted which promoted the use of local action plans which were eligible for support from the Structural Funds. There are criticisms of the programme in that support for rural development funding is contingent on matched funding from the Member State and thus the move towards greater de-centralisation results in an uneven use of the Structural Funds. The current rural development programme runs from 2007–2013. A new funding instrument, the European Agriculture Fund for Rural Development, is central to three core objectives. Firstly, increasing the competitiveness of the agriculture sector by providing support for re-structuring; secondly, supporting land management to enhance the countryside environment; thirdly, strengthening the quality of life in rural areas and promoting economic diversity.

The CAP relies heavily upon secondary legislation which is adopted using art.37(2) EC as the legal base. The legal base originally used unanimity voting in the Council and in the planned change to QMV in January 1966 the President of France, De Gaulle,

---

[7] COM (2005) 509 final proposing a simplification of the legal framework for the COMS; Revised COM (2006) 822.

[8] These measures were some of the most contentious aspects of the 2004 enlargement and continue to be challenged: Case T-257/04 *Poland v Commission* pending; T-04/06 *Poland v Commission* pending.

[9] Council reg.1257/99, OJ 1999 L160/80; amended by Council reg.1783/2003, OJ 2003 L270/70. The current Regulation is Council reg.1698/2005, OJ 2005 L277/1.

[10] For example: measures promoting good practice in animal welfare, improving food quality, promotion of organic food.

famously refused to give up sovereignty in this field, leading to the Luxembourg Accords 1966 which for several years stymied the development of the EEC by allowing the Member States to exercise (or threaten) the use of the veto in the Council.

A significant legal feature of the CAP is that the Commission has been delegated significant discretionary powers[11] to implement the overall policy of the CAP as well as overseeing its day to day administration.[12] But the CAP also relies upon the cooperation of the Member States to implement the CAP as well as administer and match funding. Thus it is not surprising that the CAP has generated a vast array of litigation, which in turn has contributed to the development of the fundamental principles of Community law outlined elsewhere in this book. Some examples include the famous mandatory requirements in *Cassis de Dijon*,[13] discussed in Chapters 3 and 4, the *"Schoppenstedt"*[14] formula, the test for non-contractual liability of the Institutions, the test for standing to bring a claim for judicial review in *Plaumann*,[15] development of the fundamental principles of Community law, for example the right to property (*Hauer*),[16] the principle of equality (*Rückdeschel*),[17] the principle of proportionality (*Internationale Handelsgesellschaft*).[18]

In recent years the EU has faced mounting pressure to handle various food crises which have been linked or regulated by the CAP, for example BSE,[19] or dioxins in chickens or genetically modified foods or foot and mouth disease. Inevitably the CAP is intertwined

---

[11] Case 5/67 *Beus* [1968] E.C.R. 83; Case 5/73 *Balkan Import-Export GmbH v Haupzollamt Berlin-Packhof* [1973] E.C.R. 1091; Case C-280/93 *Germany v Council (Bananas)* [1994] E.C.R. I-4973.

[12] The ECJ approved the delegation of power in Case 25/70 *Einfuhr-und-Vorrasstelle v Köster* [1970] E.C.R. 1161, para.9: ". . . without distorting the Community structure and the institutional balance, the management committee enables the Council to delegate to the Commission an implementing power of considerable scope."

[13] Case 120/78 *Rewe-Zentrale AG v Bundesmonopolverwaltung für Branntwein* [1979] E.C.R. 649.

[14] Case 5/71 *Aktien-Zuckerfabrik Schöppenstedt v Council* [1971] E.C.R. 975.

[15] Case 25/62 *Plaumann and Co v Commission* [1963] E.C.R. 95.

[16] Case 44/79 *Hauer v Land Rheinland-Pfalz* [1979] E.C.R. 3727.

[17] Case Joined Cases 117/76 and 16/77 *Rückdeschel v Hauptzollamt Hamburg-St Annen* [1977] E.C.R. 1753.

[18] Case 25/70 *Internationale Handelsgesellschaft mbH v Einfuhr-und Vorratsstelle für Getreide und Futtermittel* [1970 E.C.R. 1125.

[19] Commission Decision 96/239/EC, OJ 1996 L78/47 (which was unsuccessfully challenged by the UK: Case C-180/96 *United Kingdom v Commission (British Beef Ban)* [1998] E.C.R. I-2265 and Commission Decision 96/385, OJ 1996 L151/39; Commission Decision 98/692/EC (unsuccessfully challenged by France in Case C-1/00 *France v Commission* [2001] E.C.R. I-9989).

with other EU policies, most notably the free movement of goods provisions but also external relations, and flanking (or horizontal policies), for example, consumer protection, food safety and food quality, public health and environmental protection. As we shall see in the next Chapter the EU has only a limited competence in these areas and the flanking policies are mostly of recent origin and are partially developed. These factors have raised legal questions of competence and the use of the correct legal base. For example, in *United Kingdom v Council (Hormones in Beef)*[20] the UK unsuccessfully argued that where a measure harmonises national laws in the interests of consumers art.94 EC (which requires unanimity voting in the Council) should be used in preference to the QMV procedures required in art.37 (2) EC. But the expansion of EU competence in the sphere of public health as a result of art.152(4) EC has allowed the European Parliament to have greater involvement through the co-decision procedure and QMV where the measures relate to the veterinary and phyto-sanitary fields which have as their direct objective the protection of public health.

## 8.2 Economic and Monetary Integration

As we have seen in Chapter 4, the free movement of capital provisions of the Internal Market were the least developed of the four fundamental economic freedoms. It was not until 1988, as part of the Single Market Programme, that secondary legislation was introduced to liberalise capital movements within the EU. In the Treaty of Maastricht 1993 the original EEC Treaty provisions on free movement of capital were repealed and the new, modernised capital movement provisions were brought into line with the other economic freedoms and complemented a new set of measures designed to achieve economic and monetary union (EMU)[21] and a single European currency.

An economic union is often seen as the ultimate goal of the original EEC Treaty, brought about by the creation of a customs union and a common market (Swann 2000). The original EEC Treaty referred to the co-ordination of the economic policies of the

---

[20] Case 68/86 *United Kingdom v Council (Hormones in Beef)* [1988] E.C.R. 855.
[21] Cf. *Opinion 1 /91 on the European Economic Area (EEA) Agreement* [1991] E.C.R. I-6079 where the Court states that an objective of the EEC was achieving economic and monetary union.

Member States and art.104 EEC required each Member State to pursue the economic policy needed to ensure the equilibrium of its overall balance of payments and to maintain confidence in its currency and art.105 EC required co-ordination of economic policies to attain those objectives. There was no mention of *monetary* union. The question of whether or not the EU needs a monetary union, and indeed whether or not it is an optimal economic area for a monetary union is a political and economic question. However the introduction of EMU has had a major impact upon a range of EU policies, including the CAP, discussed above. What is sometimes called the "spill-over" effects of EMU has led to the need for greater horizontal co-ordination of EU policies and the creation of new spheres of competence, or partial competence, for the EU in a range of horizontal or flanking policies.

The Member States made the first political announcement to work towards economic and monetary union (EMU) in 1969 at The Hague Summit.[22] The Werner Committee proposed that EMU should be achieved by 1980.[23] The collapse of the Bretton Woods system (which had guaranteed the stability of international exchange rates since 1944) shook the international financial community resulting in the European currencies floating against each other. A flexible European scheme of managed exchange rates was established, called "the Snake" to keep the European currencies loosely aligned, but this was not effective and in 1979 the European Monetary System (EMS) was created along with an Exchange Rate Mechanism (ERM) and European Currency Unit (ECU). The currency crises of the early 1990s revealed the weakness of this system. The ECU was set using a basket of currencies and the ERM then pegged each national currency at a rate against the ECU. The rate could only be altered unanimously. The ERM allowed each currency a margin of fluctuation up to 2.25 per cent, but in the event of a crisis where a currency could not maintain its position, its membership of the ERM was suspended. However in September 1992 and July 1993 the UK was obliged to leave the ERM and the continuing crises in international monetary markets forced the ERM to expand the fluctuation margins to a meaningless 15 per cent band.

---

[22] Final Communiqué of the Conference of Heads of State or Government on December 1 and 2, 1969, para.8. See Snyder (1999).

[23] Ad Hoc Committee presided over by P. Werner, Report to the Council and the Commission on the Realisation by Stages of Economic and Monetary Union in the Community (Luxembourg, October 8, 1970), *Supp to EC Bulletin* 11–1970).

The weakness of the ERM system was the failure to co-ordinate the Member State economies (Swann, 2000).

The SEA 1986 did not address EMU directly. There is reference in the Preamble to the 1972 commitment of the Heads of State or Government towards progressing towards EMU. The SEA 1986 set the seeds for greater cooperation in economic and monetary policy by inserting a new art.102a EC into the EC Treaty. Jacques Delors headed a Committee which produced a Report in 1989[24] providing the blue print for the implementation of a three stage plan for EMU delivered through the TEU (Treaty of Maasticht 1991).[25] The Delors Report recommended the creation of an independent European System of Central Banks which would have price stability as the central goal, and that there should be centralised control over national fiscal policies.

The first stage of EMU was the completion of the Internal Market, closer economic convergence between the Member States and membership of all the Member States in the ERM. The second stage involved the creation of a European System of Central Banks (ESCB) which would co-ordinate national monetary policies and formulate a common monetary policy for the EU. The third stage involved the fixing of the exchange rates and the creation of a single currency[26] managed by the ESCB.

Of significance also from the Treaty of Maastricht is the wording of art.4(1) EC, creating an economic constitutional clause which sets out the constitutional principle of economic management:

". . . the activities of the Member States and the Community shall include . . . the adoption of an economic policy which is

---

[24] The Delors Report: Committee for the Study of Economic and Monetary Union, *Report on Economic and Monetary Union in the European Community* (Luxembourg, OOPEC,1989).

[25] Note the discussion of the difficulties in getting the Maastrict Treaty 1991 ratified left EMU in a precarious position. Not all of the Member States were fully committed to EMU. The UK reserved the decision to participate in EMU after a referendum; Denmark reserved for its self the decision on whether or not to participate in EMU. However the non-participating States are bound by the rules on economic policy and the multi-lateral surveillance mechanisms outlined below. The Delors Committee had proposed that the first stage of EMU should start on July 1, 1990 and this involved the use of increased surveillance and coordination of the monetary and economic policies of the Member States using the existing EC Treaty procedures and implementing what was to be the forerunner of the open method of co-ordination now used widely in the Lisbon Process. However the implementation of EMU sailed close to the wind: the Treaty of Maastricht came into operation in November 1993 the second stage of EMU beginning on January 1, 1994.

[26] In 1995 the Member States decided to call the ecu the euro, displayed as the sign €.

based on the close coordination of the Member States' economic policies, on the internal market and on the definition of common objectives, and conducted in accordance with the principle of an open market economy with free competition."[27]

This principle is repeated in art.98 EC *(art.120 TFEU)*. Thus the Member States have conceded their decision-making autonomy in monetary policy, one of the most important areas of macro-economic policy making. The introduction of this clause has raised questions of the nature of the social dimension to European integration and how far State intervention in the economy can be compatible with art.4 EC (Szyszczak, 2007).

Article 4(2) EC provides that the activities of the Member States and the Community shall include the irrevocable fixing of exchange rates leading to the introduction of a single currency as well as the definition of a single monetary and exchange rate policy. The primary objective is the maintenance of price stability and support of the Community's general economic policies. Article 4(3) EC provides Guidelines in the form of: stable prices, sound public finances and monetary conditions and a sustainable balance of payments.

Articles 98–104 EC *(arts 120–126 TFEU)* address economic policy. Article 99 EC states that the Member States are to regard their economic policies as a common concern and shall co-ordinate the policies within the Council. The Maastricht Treaty imposed constraints on the Member States' fiscal management prohibiting certain kinds of government financing[28] and imposing strict limits on public spending in the form of public sector borrowing. The latter is scrutinised the by the Commission and the Council as part of the

---

[27] After much public debate in the summer of 2007, art.4 EC was moved away from the basic Principles of the EC to form *art.119 TFEU* under *Title VII Economic and Monetary Policy*: "For the purposes set out in Article 3 of the Treaty on European Union, the activities of the Member States and the Union shall include, as provided in the Treaties, the adoption of an economic policy which is based on the close co-ordination of member States' economic policies, on the internal market and on the definition of common objectives, and conducted in accordance with the principle of an open market economy with free competition."

[28] There are three rules: no monetary financing, no privileged access and no bail-out. art.101 EC prohibits the ECB and national central banks from providing credit to the governments or to buy government bonds, art.102 EC does not allow the adoption of any Community or national measure other than measures aimed at safety and soundness of the financial sector, which would give the government preferential access to the credit of the commercial banking sector as well as precluding the assumption of liabilities of the government sector of one member States by another Member State.

multilateral surveillance procedure set out in art.99 EC. Article 104 EC imposes specific limits (set the same as the convergence criteria for membership of the single currency in art.121(1) EC) on the Member States' reliance upon deficit financing. The enforcement of these provisions is in the hands of the Council. In 1997 the Member States adopted, by means of a Resolution, the Stability and Growth Pact which obliges the Member States to pursue a fiscal policy resulting in the mid-term budgetary position remaining close to a balance or in surplus. The Economic and Financial Affairs Council (ECOFIN) monitors the Member States' programmes (which include also the programmes of the member States who are not in the Euro-zone). The surveillance mechanisms lack any real enforcement, remaining discretionary in the hands of the Commission, and the Council (Hodson and Maher, 2004; Louis, (2006).[29]

Finally monetary policy is addressed through the creation of a European Monetary Institute (EMI) in art.117 EC.[30] The EMI had to specify the regulatory, organisational and logistical framework for the creation of the ESCB. Member States were obliged to ensure that their own central banks were independent[31] and to treat their exchange rate policies as a matter of common interest.[32] The Member States had to work towards meeting a set of convergence criteria as a condition precedent for the adoption of a single currency. The convergence criteria are set out in art.21(1) EC and in a Protocol attached to the TEU:

(i) the achievement of a high degree of price stability. Judged by an average rate of inflation, over a one year period prior to the examination, which does not exceed by more than 1.5 per cent the average of the three best performing States;

(ii) the sustainability of the government's financial position. This is defined as the avoidance of an excessive government budgetary deficit: an annual budget deficit of less than 3 per cent of GDP, and an overall public debt ratio of not more than 60 per cent of GDP;

---

[29] Case 27/04 *Commission v Council* [2004] E.C.R. I-4829. Council Report to the European Council, *Improving the Implementation of the Stability and Growth Pact* (March 20, 2005), Annex II of the Conclusions of the Brussels European Council Meeting, March 22–23, 2005.

[30] This was the forerunner to the European Central Bank (ECB) established under the third stage of EMU (Andenas et al, 1997; Louis, 2004).

[31] Arts 109 and 116(5) EC.

[32] Art.124 EC.

(iii)  the observance of the normal fluctuation margins provided by the ERM for at least two years without severe tensions and without devaluation against the currency of any other Member State; and

(iv)  the durability of convergence achieved by the Member State as reflected in long term interest rates, defined as over a period of one year prior to the examination, the Member State has had an average nominal long-term interest rate that does not exceed by more than 2 per cent that of the best three performing Member States in terms of price stability.

The third stage of EMU was managed through art.121 EC and according to the EC Treaty was to start no later than January 1, 1999. The Commission and the EMI reported to the Council on the progress of the Member States towards EMU, examining the extent to which the Member States had created independent central banks, whether the convergence criteria had been met. The Council acted by QMV on the Commission's recommendations, looking for a majority of the Member States to meet the criteria to move forward into a single currency,[33] and finally set a date for the start of the third stage of EMU.[34] Before the date of July 1, 1998 the Council had to decide which Member States met the conditions for the adoption of a single currency. The Council, meeting as the Heads of State or Government, was thus obliged to repeat the whole exercise set out in art.21(1) and (2) EC of examining if the Member States met the convergence criteria but did not have to examine if a majority of the Member States did so.

After the decision was made to move to the third stage of EMU the ECB was created and the EMI wound up. The ECB has legal personality and has an Executive Board and a Governing Council. The ECB belongs to the ESCB. The independence of the ECB is set out in art.108 EC which states that it shall not take any instructions from Community Institutions.[35] The ECB has the power to make Regulations, Recommendations, Opinions and take Decisions.[36] Under art.110(3) EC the ECB has the power to fine or impose

---

[33] This was not without controversy see F. Snyder above fn 22 at pp.457–463, with allegations that some Member States had "cooked the books".

[34] Art.121(3) EC. If the Council could not agree a date art.121(4) EC stated that the third stage was deemed to start on January 1, 1999.

[35] However it is not immune from investigation by OLAF: Case C-11/00 *Commission v ECB* [2003] E.C.R. I-7147.

[36] These measures have the same meanings and consequences as in art.249 EC for the other EU Institutions.

periodic penalty payments on undertakings for failure to comply with ECB Regulations and Decisions.

Neither the ECB nor the ESCB have the management of the exchange rate of the euro included within their objectives. The management of the exchange rates between the euro and non-eurozone currencies is a matter for common concern (art.24(2) EC) and there has been a voluntary "ERM II" in place since January 1, 1999.[37] The relationship between the euro and non-EU currencies is split between the ECB and the Council in art.111 EC (Zilioli and Selmayr, 1999).

The ECB must be consulted on any Community act within its fields of competence and also by national authorities in relation to any draft legislative provisions within its competence. It has the exclusive right to issue banknotes within the EC. The ECB has, however, turned out to be one of the least democratically account-able Institutions of the EU (Gormley and de Haan, 1996; Amtenbrink, 1999). An Economic and Financial Committee was also established at the start of the third stage of EMU. Its tasks are set out in art.114 (2) EC.

The Council fixed the conversion rates for the Member States eligible to enter the single currency and on January 1, 2002 the new euro banknotes and coins were introduced with the national currencies withdrawn from circulation. To date there are 15 Member States who belong to the eurozone.[38]

After the Treaty of Lisbon 2007 the new *TEU* states that as part of the Union's objectives "The Union shall establish an economic and monetary union whose currency is the euro" *(art.2(4) TEU)*. Under art.3 9 (c) the Union shall have exclusive competence for the monetary policy of the Member States whose currency is the euro. The new *art.5 TFEU* state that the Member States shall co-ordinate their economic policies within the Union. The Council shall adopt broad guidelines for these policies. A new policy is the creation of the "Euro Group" in *arts 136–138 TFEU and Protocol No. 3 on the Euro Group*. This policy is for the Member States in the single currency and is intended to co-ordinate the economic guidelines and budgetary discipline of these States. The President of the Euro Group will be appointed by the members of the group by qualified majority for a period of two and a half years.

---

[37] Resolution of the European Council on the establishment of an exchange rate mechanism in the third stage of economic and monetary union, OJ 1997 C 236/5.

[38] Although erstwhile travellers will know that the euro is an acceptable international currency outside of the Eurozone!

# 9: Horizontal or Flanking Policies: the Social Dimension to Integration

## SUMMARY

9.1   **Anti-discrimination Policies**

9.2   **Social Policy and the European Employment Strategy**

9.3   **Environment**

9.4   **Economic and Social Cohesion**

9.5   **Consumer Policy**

9.6   **Cultural Policy**

9.7   **Sport**

9.8   **Youth**


Since the 1970s the EU has struggled to find a "social" identity for itself (Shaw, Hunt and Wallace, 2007). The EEC Treaty was negotiated and drafted quickly (Collins, 1983). It was a highly non-interventionist, market-orientated legal document and therefore social policy issues received scant attention in the original Treaty of Rome (EEC) 1957. It was an issue of economic and political debate as to whether the functioning of the Common Market necessitated intervention in the social sphere. The EEC Treaty assumed that the raising of living standards and social progress would be automatic by-products of economic integration. There were only two references to social policy in the Principles of the EEC: art.3 (c) EEC advocated the abolition of obstacles leading towards the free movement of persons and art.3(i) committed the Common Market towards the creation of a Social Fund. Title III of the original EEC Treaty contained a Title on Social Policy but with the exception of the equal pay for equal work provision contained in what was art.119 EEC the provisions were exhortatory. Subsequent case law gave these provisions a teleological role.[1]

---

[1] Case 43/75 *Defrenne v Sabena (No.2)* [1976] E.C.R. 455, para.15; Case 126/86 *Zaera v Instituto Nacionale de la Seguridad Social* [1987] E.C.R. 3697, para.14. Nielsen and Szyszczak, 1997.

A turning point in the direction of European integration is often traced to the Declaration of the Heads of State or Government in Paris 1972, the eve of the first enlargement of the EEC. The Declaration states that the Heads of State or Government:

". . . attached as much importance to vigorous action in the social field as to the achievement of economic union . . . it is essential to ensure the increased involvement of labour and management in the economic and social decisions of the Community."

An ambitious Social Action Plan 1974–1976 was drawn up[2] but was difficult to implement because of the lack of a clear legal base for social policy measures, alongside economic problems. Academics have different explanations for the motivation to involve a social dimension to European integration. Lodge (1978) argues that economic and fiscal crises, unemployment and persistent imbalances between the Member States were contributing factors to the commitment towards greater social intervention, whereas Shanks (1977) argues that the political upheavals of the 1960s led to greater questioning of economic and political policy, with individual politicians (such as the then west German Chancellor Brandt) emphasising the need to paint a "human face" on European integration. Also, the Court began to emphasis the social dimension to European integration:

". . . Article 119 EEC forms part of the social objectives of the Community, which is not merely an economic union but at the same time intended, by common action, to ensure social progress and seek the constant improvement of the living and working conditions [of the peoples of Europe]."[3]

The Fontainebleau Summit of 1984 created the Adonnino Committee whose remit was to propose measures which were designed to strengthen the image of the EU.[4] The lack of a firm legal base to create a social dimension to the economic dimension of

---

[2] OJ 1974 C 13/1; *Bulletin of the EC*, Supp.2/74, 8.
[3] Case 43/75 *Defrenne v Sabena (No.2)* [1976] E.C.R. 455, para.10.
[4] Commission of the European Communities, *A People's Europe, Reports from the ad hoc committee,* COM (84) 446 Final, para.5.9.

European integration resulted in a fragmented and ad hoc approach to introducing flanking or horizontal policies to support the core policies and the fundamental four economic freedoms. Scharpf (2002) describes the focus upon economic integration at the expense of social policy as a "constitutional asymmetry". Over time social policy issues have emerged in law and policy-making as part of the "spill-over" of the economic integration project. Their development often follows similar patterns of using soft governance techniques, especially through Action Plans, and a reluctance to give the EU competence to harmonise national laws. The justifications for widening the ambit of the integration project into the social policy arena range from efficiency arguments, to reasons related to redistributive grounds, to the modern ideas of social solidarity, citizenship and fundamental rights. However, even today having accepted a role for social policies in the EU, disagreements persist on what *kind* of social policies should the EU pursue and what are the aims behind these policies (Maduro, 2000).

The EU has a fragmented competence to address social policy issues. Yet, as various horizontal and flanking policies have emerged we discover that, as with the CAP, they have had a major impact on substantive law principles, the evolution of EU procedural rules and the general principles of Community law. Article 2 EC sets as one of the tasks of the Community the promotion of "a high level of employment and of social protection, equality between men and women . . . a high level of protection and improvement of the quality of life, and economic and social cohesion and solidarity among Member States." The specific legal bases for legislative competence are found in Title XIX, arts 174–176 EC (*Title XIX, arts 174–176 TFEU* (Environment), Title XVII arts 158–162 EC (*Title XVII, renamed Economic, Social and Territorial Cohesion, arts 174–178 TFEU)* (Economic and Social Cohesion), Title XI arts 136–145 EC (*Title IX, arts 151–161 TFEU) (Social Policy*), and Education, Vocational Training and Youth art.149–159 EC (*Title XI, renamed Education, Vocational Training and Sport, arts 165–166)*.

The maturity of the Internal Market and the interest in using competition law has led to a number of challenges to social services normally provided by the State but now provided in competitive markets. For example, EU law may apply to healthcare services even though there is no legislative competence within the EC Treaty for the EU to regulate this sector. This in turn may have de-stabilising effects on national healthcare systems because the EU does not have the capacity to re-regulate the gaps which appear as a result of individual litigation.[5] To counteract this, the Member States use the open method of co-ordination to iron out differences between the Member States and manage the "exchange" of patients between the Member States.

## 9.1 Anti-Discrimination Policies

Gender equality in the limited form of equal pay for equal work was included in the original Treaty of Rome 1957. Article 119 EEC (now art.141 EC, *art.157 TFEU*) was included as a labour market provision to prevent States which did not have an equality clause from gaining a competitive advantage over States such as France, which did have equality provisions. The landmark case of *Defrenne v Sabena*[6] led to a new raft of secondary legislation expanding the gender equality concept.[7] Equally important was the fact that art.119 EEC was held to be capable of both vertical and horizontal direct effect opening the way for national courts to be the forum for equality issues, backed by rulings from the Court of Justice (Hoskyns, 1996; Alter and Vargas, 2000). The Court also recognised that the principle of equality was one of the general principles of Community law and a foundation principle of the EU.[8]

---

[5] Hervey and McHale 2004; Ross, 2007. Similarly the economic dimension of other areas such as sport may be regulated by the free movement and competition rules even though Sport has only recently been added to the *TFEU* as a result of the Treaty of Lisbon 2007 (Szyszczak, 2007; Weatherill, 2007).

[6] Case 43/75 *Defrenne v Sabena (No.2)* [1976] E.C.R. 455.

[7] The legislative initiatives of the 1970s relied upon unanimity voting in the Council and therefore were ad hoc, containing various exemptions, for example differences relating to pension ages, issues of social security. The legislation was consolidated in a recasting directive (European Parliament and Council dir.2006/113 of December 13, 2004, OJ 2004 L373/37) (Burrows and Robinson, 2007). However the EU also made use of various forms of soft law as well as gender mainstreaming through EU policies. *Framework Strategy of Gender Equality* (2001–2005); *Roadmap for Equality Between Men and Women* COM (2006) 92. See Pollack and Hafner-Burton 2000; Stratigaki 2005.

[8] Case C-381/99 *Brunnhofer v Bank der Osterreichischen Postsparkasse* [2001] E.C.R. I-4961, para.28. More recently the Court has applied the principle of equality to a horizontal situation in an age discrimination/fixed-term work issue: Case C-144/04 *Mangold v Helm* [2005] E.C.R. I-9981. This is a controversial move which has been criticised by A.G. Mazak in Case C-411/05 *Palacios de la Villa v Cortefiel Services SA* judgment of October 16, 2007 and A.G. Geelhoed in Case C-13/05 *Sonia Chacon v Eurest Colectivdades SA* [2006] E.C.R. I-6467. The Court may take the opportunity to comment on *Mangold* in Case C-427/06 *Bartsch v BSH Bosch und Siemens Hausgerate Alterfursorge GmbH*, pending. See also Opinion of A.G. Poiares

Discrimination and equality issues were included in other aspects of social and labour law, for example, legislation on part-time work, pregnancy and maternity protection, health and safety issues,

The growing recognition of other forms of anti-discrimination legislation at the international, regional and national level, alongside calls for greater recognition of fundamental rights in Community law led the EU to recognise a wider range of anti-discrimination grounds in art.13 EC (*art.19 TFEU*)[9] introduced by the Treaty of Amsterdam 1997. Article 13 EC provides a new legal base for secondary legislation and to date two directives have been adopted.[10] The directives have been introduced in a piecemeal manner in the Member States and the Commission has initiated a number of infringement actions against the Member States (Bell, 2008). To date only nine art.234 EC references have been made from the national courts[11] and case law suggests that not all grounds of non-discrimination are equal[12] and a hierarchy of protected rights is emerging (Howard, 2006; Waddington and Bell, 2001; De Búrca, 2006).

The principle of non-discrimination is now seen in human (or fundamental rights) clauses found in the Charter of Fundamental Rights signed in Nice in 2001 (now revised and signed on December 12, 2007). Article 20 guarantees equality before the law. Article 21 provides a non-exhaustive list of grounds of anti-discrimination. The Charter also addresses cultural, religious and linguistic diversity. *Article 2 TEU* states that:

> *"The Union is founded on the values of respect for human dignity, freedom, democracy, equality, the rule of law and respect for human rights, including the rights of persons belonging to*

Maduro in Case C-303/06 *Coleman v Attridge Law and Steve Law*, January 31, 2008, para.11 and compare Case C-227/04 *Lindorfer v Council*, judgment of September 11, 2007.

[9] The grounds are: sex, racial, or ethnic origin, religion or belief, disability age and sexual orientation (Bell, 2002)

[10] Dir.2000/43/EC, OJ L 180/22 which is a racial equality directive, prohibiting discrimination on grounds of racial or ethnic origin, not only in the labour market but also in housing, healthcare and education; and dir.2000/78/EC, OJ L 303/16 which is a general employment equality directive prohibiting discrimination on grounds of religion or belief, disability, age and sexual orientation.

[11] Only one reference has been made concerning race discrimination: Case C-54/07 *Centrum voor gelijkheid van kansen en voor racismebestrijding*, Opinion of A.G. Poiares Maduro, March 12, 2008.

[12] See Case C-13/05 *Chacón Navas* [2006] E.C.R. I-6467. But cf: the Opinion of A.G. Poiares Maduro in Case C-303/06 *Coleman v Attridge Law and Steve Law*, January 31, 2008.

*minorities. These values are common to the Member States in a society in which pluralism, non-discrimination, tolerance, justice, solidarity and equality between men and women prevail."*

This is complemented by *Article 10 TFEU*:

*"In defining and implementing its policies and activities, the Union shall aim to combat discrimination based on sex, racial or ethnic origin, religion or belief, disability, age or sexual orientation."*

On December 20, 2006 the Council adopted a regulation[13] establishing a European Institute for Gender Equality. On February 15, 2007, the Council adopted reg.168/2007/EC[14] establishing a European Union Agency for Fundamental Rights (FRA) which was launched on March 1, 2007 in Vienna. The FRA replaces, and builds on the work of, the European Monitoring Centre on Racism and Xenophobia. It will have three key functions: to collect information and data; provide advice to the European Union and its Member States and promote dialogue with civil society to raise public awareness of fundamental rights.

## 9.2 Social Policy and the European Employment Strategy

Article 117 EEC stated that the "Member States agree upon the need to promote improved working conditions and an improved standard of living for workers". It was generally thought that European integration would result in an automatic increase in wealth within the Member States and this would be reflected in a higher standard of living. The Member States were reluctant to grant any harmonisation powers to the EU, in either the employment or the social welfare field. Again the catalyst for EU intervention was the 1972 Paris Summit Declaration which led to the 1974 Social Action Programme. This programme contained two strands relating to employment law: employment protection and worker participation. However, as with the equality programme the original EEC Treaty did not provides a sound legislative base on which to build an employment law programme, relying upon (the pre-Amsterdam)

---

[13] Reg.1922/2006, OJ 2006 L 403/9.
[14] OJ 2007 L 53/1.

Articles 100 and 235 EC, both of which required unanimity voting in the Council. The UK was at the forefront of opposing EU competence in this area (Hepple, 1987). Thus beyond health and safety measures,[15] the employment protection programme was limited to directives on redundancy, transfer of undertakings and insolvency.

The SEA 1986 introduced a new legal base in art.118a EC which facilitated the adoption of a number of measures related to health and safety legislation. The SEA 1986 also introduced the idea of involving the social partners (representatives of employers and workers) in the policy making process.[16] Perhaps the most significant piece of legislation adopted was the Working Time Directive.[17] Other measures included a Young Workers' Directive[18] and a Directive on Atypical Workers.[19]

In 1989 11 of the 12 Member States[20] agreed upon a "Social Charter" (Charter of Fundamental Social Rights for Workers) which created a list of basic employment and social rights recognised in international agreements and in the Member States. This did not have a legally binding force and has been neglected over the years.[21]

Few firm legislative measures were accepted after the Treaty of Maastricht 1991 which attempted to circumvent the UK veto on social and employment policy proposals by annexing a Social Chapter as a Social Policy Agreement and Protocol 14 allowing the eleven Member States, using the Social Partners, to proceed with proposals without the UK.[22] Even after the UK "opted in" to the

---

[15] Council dir.93/104/EC, OJ 1993 L307/18. Even in relation to health and safety issues the UK government abstained from voting, and then, challenged the competence of the EU to enact health and safety legislation: the challenge to the Working Time Directive in Case C-84/94 *United Kingdom v Council* [1996] E.C.R. I-5755.

[16] However, it was not until 1991, as part of the negotiations on the Treaty of Maastricht 1991, that the model for choosing who should represent the social partners was fully developed, and even then created problems on the issue of non-representation: Case T-135/96 *UEAPME v Council* [1998] E.C.R. II-2335. Council Decision 2003/174/EC OJ 2003 L 70/31 established a Tripartite Social Summit for Growth and Employment, formalising the annual summit which developed. (*art.152 TFEU*).

[17] Council dir.93/104, OJ 1993 L307/18, later amended by European Parliament and Council dir.2000/34, OJ 2000 L295/41, consolidated by European parliament and Council dir.2003/88, OJ 2003 L299/9.

[18] Council dir.94/33, OJ 1994 L216/12.

[19] Council dir.91/383 OJ 1991 L206/19.

[20] The UK abstained, but interestingly posted reports to the Commission under the Action Plan which accompanied the Charter COM (89) 568.

[21] Cf. the reference to the Charter by A.G. Kokott in Case C-313/02 *Wippel* [2004] E.C.R. I-9483 (Opinion of May 18, 2004); Case C-341/05 *Laval*, judgment of December 18, 2007.

[22] Smismans, 2007. Of significance were Council dir.94/45 on European Works Councils, OJ 1994 L254/64 and Council dir.94/34 on Parental leave OJ 1996 L145/4.

Social Policy Agreement in 1997 few legislative measures were agreed with the focus continuing upon soft law agreements.

The Treaty of Amsterdam 1997 was a watershed in the development of social policy and employment measures (Szyszczak, 2000). Alongside the new art.13 EC creating the modern antidiscrimination legal base, new arts 136–139 EC created, for the first time, a broad legal base for employment law measures recognising the Social Partners as institutional actors in the process. The measures reflect individual employment law rights, for example, Parental Leave, Part-Time Work and Fixed–term Work, sectoral initiatives,[23] and Framework Agreements.[24] Collective labour law measures are problematic. The worker participation proposals were scattered across employment and company law harmonisation measures. It took many years before agreement could be reached on such measures. However, significantly after the Treaty of Amsterdam 1997 the EU has adopted a wider range of employment law measures, with use made of Framework Agreements drawn up by the Social Partners and many measures addressing issues of collective labour law,[25] an area of employment law hitherto seemingly impervious to EU intervention.

In 1994 the Essen Summit focused policy attention on EU unemployment (Szyszczak, 2000). This led to the inclusion of an Employment Strategy in arts 125–130 EC introduced by the Treaty of Amsterdam 1997. The aim of this strategy is to set a series of common goals with the aim of achieving full employment, quality and productivity at work and cohesion and inclusion, leaving the Member States to implement the goals through individual national programmes. A cycle of reporting and monitoring was put in place to allow for the setting of indicators, benchmarking, exchange of best practice and peer review, with the Council adopting Recommendations for the Member States. The EES was a central policy in the Lisbon Strategy where the EU committed itself to become the most dynamic, knowledge-driven society by the year 2010 (Ashiagbor, 2006). In 2002 the EES was coordinated with the economic policy co-ordinating mechanisms of the Broad Economic Policy Guidelines, working around a three-year cycle. By the year

---

[23] Council dir.1999/63 on the Agreement on the Organisation of Working Time for Sea-farers, OJ 1999 L167/63; Agreement on the Organisation of Working Time of Mobile Workers in Civil Aviation, OJ 2000 L 302/57.

[24] Framework Agreement on Telework, 2002; Framework Agreement on Work-Related Stress, 2004.

[25] See, for example, Council dir.2002/14 OJ 2002 L80/29 establishing a general framework for informing and consulting employees.

2005 it became clear that the Lisbon Strategy was not on course to achieve the ambitious goals set and the Strategy was re-worked with a new momentum.

The Treaty of Lisbon 2007 clarifies the role of social policy by stating that social policy will be an area of shared competence between the Union and the member States *(art.4(b) TFEU)*. The Union has a duty to take measures to ensure the coordination of the employment policies of the Member states *(art.5(2) TFEU* and it may take initiatives to ensure co-ordination of the social policies of the member states *(art.5 (3) TFEU)*. *Article 152 TFEU* introduces a specific reference to the Social Partners, the social dialogue and the Tripartite Summit. *Article 153(3) TFEU* amends art.137 (3) EC by extending the competence of the Social Partners to Council Decisions codifying agreements reached under art.139 EC *(art.155 TFEU)*. In areas covered by co-ordination and monitoring in art.140 EC, *art.156 TFEU* the Commission's possible actions are clarified as relating in particular to: "initiatives aiming at the establishment of guidelines and indicators, the organisation of exchange of best practice, and the preparation of the necessary elements for periodic monitoring and evaluation". Declaration 31 on art.156 TFEU confirms that the policies described in *art.156 TFEU* fall within the competence of the Member States. From the UK perspective the most controversial aspect of the Treaty of Lisbon 2007 is the "red line" drawn in measures relating to social security for migrant workers, which is discussed in Chapter 5. Under art.42 EC such measures are adopted by unanimity voting in the Council but move to qualified voting after the Treaty of Lisbon. The UK introduced an "emergency brake" procedure whereby any proposal may be referred to the European Council if the Member State believes the measure will affect important aspects of its social security system *(Article 48 TFEU)*.

## 9.3 Environment

The beginning of a *coherent* EU environmental *policy*[26] is usually traced back to the Paris Summit of 1972 when the Heads of State or Government committed the EU to developing the social dimension

---

[26] Prior to this the then EEC had adopted *ad hoc* legislation which had an environmental dimension, for example, Council dir.67/548 on the classification, packaging and labelling of dangerous substances, OJ 1967 L196/1.

of economic integration.[27] The fact that environmental concerns were an EU social issue is reflected in the external pressures to recognise environmental concerns as an aspect of international cooperation, starting with the 1972 UN Conference on the Human Environment in Stockholm. From 1973 onwards a series on Environmental Action Plans were drawn up.[28] It was not until the Single European Act 1986 that a clear legal base for an environmental policy for the EU was introduced.[29] This coincided with the Court declaring that environmental protection was "one of the Community's essential objectives".[30] The 1980s saw a new pace to addressing environmental issues both within, and outside of, the EU and a growing advocacy for environmental concerns (Chalmers, 1985, 1999; Jans and Vedder, 2008). The new environment policy relied upon subsidiarity but also introduced a mainstreaming or integration principle, which has been adopted in other horizontal policies of the EU (Dhondt, 2003).[31]

The legal base for an EU environmental policy is art.175 EC (*art.192 TFEU*) which allows for the adoption of the Action Plans and legislation.[32] Article 176 EC allows the Member States to maintain or introduce more stringent measures than the measures at EU level under art.175 EC. Article 6 EC (art.11 *TFEU*) introduced by the Treaty of Amsterdam 1997, creates a constitutional mainstreaming principle that environmental protection requirements must be mainstreamed into the definition and implementation of all Community policies, in particular with a view to promoting sustainable development (Hans and Scott, 2003).[33] This mainstreaming idea is see also in art.37 of the CFR.

The choice of the correct legal base for environmental measures has always been a controversial aspect of litigation in the EU. The harmonisation of the way in which harmful products are placed on

---

[27] Bulletin EC 10-1972.

[28] The most recent is the *Sixth Environmental Plan* which covers the period 2002–2012. COM (2001) 31 Final.

[29] Prior to this art.94 EC and art.308 EC were used as the legal base for environmental measures (Jacobs, 2006).

[30] Case 240/83 *Procureur de la République v ADBHU* [1985] E.C.R. 531.

[31] Art.159 EC (regional policy), art.151(4) EC (culture), art.152(1) (public health), art.153(2) (consumer protection), art.157(3) (industrial policy), art.178 EC (development cooperation).

[32] Legislation is usually adopted using the co-decision procedure except for areas covered by art.175(2) EC which include measures of a fiscal nature and measures affecting town and country planning.

[33] This has been implemented by soft law processes, most notably the Cardiff Process from 1998 which requires the different sectors to develop appropriate environmental strategies.

the market relates to the free movement of goods and therefore such measures may fall within the competence of the Internal Market legal base, art.95 EC (*art.114 TFEU*).[34] However, if the effects of a measure have only an incidental effect on the functioning of the Internal Market then art.175 EC is the more appropriate legal base.[35] In *Commission v Council*[36] the Court was asked to what extent art.175 EC could be used as a legal base to harmonise national criminal law. Using Title VI of the TEU (arts 29 and 34(2)(b)TEU) the Council adopted a Framework Decision 2003/80 on the protection of the environment through criminal law. (Comte and Krämer, 2004). The Commission challenged the legal base of the measure. The Court found that the main purpose of the measure was the protection of the environment and *not* the harmonisation of criminal law and art.175 EC was the correct legal base for the measure. In *Commission v Council*[37] the Commission sought annulment of Council Framework Decision 2005/667[38] which aimed to strengthen the criminal law framework for the enforcement of pollution caused by ships. The Court held that when criminal penalties are essential to combat serious offences against the environment a measure can fall within Community competence under art.175 EC. But art.175 EC does not provide a legal base to determine the *level* and *type* of criminal penalties. This requires legislation under the third pillar. It is likely that this kind of conflict will be minimised when the Treaty of Lisbon 2007 comes into force because the ordinary legislative procedure will be used for environmental and criminal law.

Article 95(4) and (5) EC allow a Member State to maintain or introduce national rules derogating from a harmonisation measure taken within the framework of the Internal Market. This is an exception to the principle of uniform application of EU law and the unity of the market and therefore is interpreted narrowly and is subject to the principle of proportionality.[39] It is for the Member State raising

---

[34] Case C-300/89 *Commission v Council* [1991] E.C.R. I-2867.
[35] Case 45/86 *Commission v Council* [1987] E.C.R. 1493, para.11; Case C-300/89 *Commission v Council* [1991] E.C.R. I-2867, para.10, Case C-268/94 *Portugal v Council* [1996] E.C.R. I-6177, para.22; Case C-176/03 *Commission v Council* [2005] E.C.R. I-7879, para.45.
[36] Case C-176/03 *Commission v Council* [2005] E.C.R. I-7879. Note the Commission later proposed a directive on the protection of the environment using criminal law: COM (2007) 51 final.
[37] Case C-440/05, judgment of October 23, 2007.
[38] OJ 2005 L255/164.
[39] For example a Member State cannot say it merely wants stricter environmental legislation: Case C-439/05P *Land Oberösterreich und Österreich v Commission*,

the derogation to show that the conditions have been met (Sadeleer, 2007).[40] Although arts 95(4) and (5) EC apply to all Internal Market measures the sector of the environment is the area in which they are invoked most often.

A new dimension to EU environmental policy was introduced at the European Council in Gothenburg 2001. This was the *Sustainable Development Strategy* which added an environmental dimension to the Lisbon Process.[41] *The EU Sixth Action Programme (2002–2010) Environment 2010: Our Future, Our Choice* aims to implement this new strand of the Lisbon Agenda but it has been criticised for being too strategic without having clear and attainable objectives and time frames, focusing upon co-operation and agreement and less on centralised EU enforcement. This dimension may be challenged by changes in the Treaty of Lisbon 2007 which links sustainable energy resources to the environmental policy.

The European Community is a signatory to the UN Framework Convention on Climate Change and to the Kyoto Protocol. Under art.4 of the Kyoto Protocol the parties may take the option of electing to fulfil their commitments jointly and the European Council agreed to share the burden of reducing greenhouse gas emissions by creating what is known as the "European Bubble".[42] The Kyoto Protocol Regime is a mixed agreement under which the

judgment of September 13, 2007. A Member State cannot use art.95(3) EC to address a general environmental danger: Case T-182/06 *Netherlands v Commission*, judgment of June 27, 2007.

[40] Case T-182/06 *Netherlands v Commission*, judgment of June 27, 2007.

[41] Commission Communication, *A Sustainable Future for a Better World: A European Strategy for Sustainable Development* COM (2001) 264; *The Sixth Action Programme (2002–2012) Environment 2010 Our Future, Our Choice* COM (2001) 31 final.

[42] Council Decision 2002/358/EC of April 25, 2002 concerning the approval on behalf of the European Community of the Kyoto Protocol to the United Nations Framework Convention on Climate Change and the Joint Fulfilment of Commitments Thereunder. See also Dir.2003/87/EC of the European Parliament and of the Council of October 13, 2003 establishing a scheme for greenhouse gas emission allowance trading within the Community and amending Council dir.96/61/EC. This sets up a Community scheme for greenhouse gas emission allowance trading in order to reduce such emissions. Each Member State must develop a national plan for the allocation of greenhouse gas emission allowances ("NAP"), in accordance with certain criteria set out in the directive. The NAP must state the total quantity of allowances that the Member State intends to allocate and how it proposes to allocate them. The first NAP, for the three-year period beginning on January 1, 2005, had to be published and notified to the Commission by March 31, 2004 at the latest. Under the directive, the Commission has three months to reject a NAP, in whole or in part, if it is incompatible with the criteria laid down by the directive. All amendments made to the NAP by the Member State must be approved by the Commission. See Case T-374/04 *Germany v Commission*, judgment of November 7, 2007.

European Community and its Member States have shared competence and are jointly liable. Under arts 5.1 and 5.4 of the Protocol Member States within the European Bubble which do not meet their individual reduction commitments will only be responsible if the group as a whole fails to achieve its combined level of emission reductions. But in practice the main responsibility for taking policies lies with the Member States with any measures taken at the European Community level constituting a useful complement to national initiatives.[43] The EU sees itself as a leader in the post-Kyoto environmental policy arena.

The Treaty of Lisbon 2007 states that environmental policy shall continue to be an area of shared competence between the Union and the Member States (*art.4(2)(e) TFEU*). The Treaty introduces climate change into the basic Treaties for the first tome stating that Union policy should contribute to the pursuit of a number of objectives, one of which will be the promotion of measures at the international level to promote climate change (*art.191(1) TFEU*). The EU sees itself at the forefront of the post-Kyoto international debate.

The Treaty of Lisbon also promotes energy issues as a prime focus of EU policy. Climate change is linked to a new article which will allow Union action to promote energy efficiency and energy saving and introduce the development of new and renewable sources of energy (*art.194 TFEU*) to create:

"*. . . a spirit of solidarity between the Member States*, to:

(a)   *ensure the functioning of the energy market;*
(b)   *ensure security of energy supply in the Union;*
(c)   *promote energy efficiency and energy saving and the development of new and renewable forms of energy; and*
(d)   *promote the interconnection of energy networks.*"

The Commission has suggested a policy, similar to the European Bubble, for greenhouse gas emission whereby Europe will collectively reduce greenhouse gases emissions and move towards greater use of renewable energy by the year 2020. This is known as the "20 20 by 2020" Plan. The Commission has set targets of reducing energy consumption by 20 per cent and obtaining 20 per cent of Europe's energy from renewable sources. However introducing measures related to climate change may create "legal base" or

---

[43] *Communication from the Commission to the Council and the European Parliament— Preparing for Implementation of the Kyoto Protocol*, COM (1999) 239 final.

"competence" problems. The Commission argues that the legal bases of arts 174 and 175 EC can be used but some measures may be subject to shared Community-Member State competence involving different voting procedures under art.175 EC. Measures affecting the choice of energy supplies will be subject to unanimous voting in the Council. It may be that other legal bases are necessary, for example the use of agricultural policy (art.37 EC), fiscal policy (art.93 EC, transport policy (art.71 EC), internal market (art.95 EC) or trade policy (art.133 EC).

Other provisions on solidarity and on civil protection are relevant to the environment, particularly the consequences of terrorist attacks and natural and "man-made" disasters (*art.222 TFEU and art.196 TFEU*).

The Treaty of Lisbon 2007 introduces a passerelle clause to instigate procedural changes to decision-making relating to sensitive national environmental matters.[44] The Council, acting unanimously, may change these types of measures to the ordinary legislative procedure (*art.192(2)TFEU*), allowing the European Parliament a greater role in environmental decision-making.

The majority of cases relating to the EU environmental provisions are infringement actions,[45] which now include follow-on fines.[46] In *Commission v Ireland* [47] the Court ruled that the Member States are required to ensure that the appropriate measures are taken, including administrative action or criminal proceedings against persons who have failed to comply with Community law. In another case against Ireland involving 12 factual infringements of the Waste Framework Directive 91/869 the Court ruled that in principle the Commission is entitled to deduce from a series of individual infringements that there is a general practice of non-compliance and non-enforcement within a Member State (Wennerås, 2006, 2007).[48]

---

[44] For example, planning laws, quantitative management of water resources (but not including waste management), a Member State's choice of different energy resources.

[45] Hattan, 2003. The Commission has prioritised non-transposition cases over non-application infringements: Commission, *Communication Implementing Community Environmental Law*, COM (96) 5000.

[46] Case C-387/97 *Commission v Greece* [2000] E.C.R. I-5047; Case C-278/01 *Commission v Spain* [2003] E.C.R. I-14141; Case C-304/02 *Commission v France* [2005] E.C.R. I-6263. *Commission Communication Application of Article 228 of the EC Treaty*, SEC (2005) 1658 final, 3.

[47] Case C-317/02, November 18, 2004.

[48] A general practice of non-compliance must be consistent and general and not confined to only part of the territory of the Member State: Case C-441/02 *Commission v Germany* [2006] E.C.R. I-3449, para.50; Case C-248/05 *Commission v Ireland*, judgment of October 25, 2007.

The Commission may demand that individual infringements are remedied but also the public authorities change their enforcement policies.

An important issue for the development of policy and the enforcement of environmental law is ownership of the interest in protecting environmental issues and this creates problems in the EU, for example, in showing standing to challenge Community measures.[49] The Aarhus Convention on Access to Environmental Information, Public Participation in Decision-Making and Access to Justice in Environmental Matters established a set of rights[50] which are now found in EU directives.[51] Additional new forms of governance and enforcement have emerged, for example, the IMPEL which is an informal network of national environmental authorities designed to create a resource base to exchange information, best practice. However, the implementation of the Aarhus principles varies between the Member States and Obradovic (2007) has called for the streamlining of the EU requirements across the Member States.

As a result of the legislative programme and the Court's case law a number of principles have evolved to underpin the environmental policy. The most important principle is the "Preventive Principle", which is the idea that prevention of environmental damage should be foremost in EU and Member State policy. Examples of this principle are seen in legislation, for example, the Packaging and Waste directive[52] which aims to reduce packaging and increase recycling of materials and directives which aim to control the disposal of goods, for example, the End of Life Vehicles and Waste Electrical and Electronic Equipment Directive.[53] The Environmental Impact Assessment programme contains the Strategic Environmental Assessment Directive[54] which in turn has been the basis of many

---

[49] Case T-585/93 *Stichting Greenpeace Council v Commission* [1995] E.C.R. II-2205; Case C-321/95P *Stichting Greenpeace v Commission* [1998] E.C.R. I-1651. Elefthedias (2007)

[50] It is organised around three pillars: first pillar, the right of everyone to receive environmental information held by public authorities (this includes information on the state of the environment); second pillar, the right to participate in environmental decision-making, enabling environmental ngos and the affected public to comment on plans, proposals projects affecting the environment; third pillar, the right to review procedures to challenge public decisions that have been made without respecting the rights contained in the first two pillars, or environmental law.

[51] See also reg.367/2006 on the Application of the provisions of the Aarhus Convention to Community Institutions and Bodies, OJ 2006 L264/13.

[52] Council dir.94/62, OJ 1994 L365/10.

[53] Kroepelian, 2000.

[54] European Parliament and Council dir.2001/42, OJ 2001 197/30.

infringement actions against the Member States.[55] Another principle underpinning environmental law is the "Proximity Principle" which is the idea that environmental damage should be corrected at source. Interestingly this principle developed through the free movement of goods case law in spite of the fact that art.30 EC does not contain a justification based upon environmental grounds. In the *Wallonian Waste*[56] case a challenge was made to the ban imposed by the Wallonian region of Belgium on the transport of a number of products, including non-hazardous waste. It was argued that the ban was a hindrance to free trade and discriminated against national and foreign goods. The Court found that there was no discrimination in the ban and therefore no infringement of art.28 EC.

In contrast the *Preussen Elecktra*[57] case concerned both the Internal Market and the State Aid rules. The case concerned a German law that placed an obligation on energy providers to source a proportion of their supplies from local renewable energy installations. The German utility companies opposed the feed-in schemes developed in Germany from 1998–2000, and one way of challenging them was to claim that the feed-in schemes were contrary to the EU State Aid and free movement rules. The Court held that there was no State Aid present in the German scheme, because consumers paid for the electricity and therefore there was no transfer of State funds which benefited individual firms. On the Internal Market rules the Court appears to indicate support for policies which promote renewable energy. The Court found that there *was* discrimination but that the German measure could be justified on environmental grounds. The Court's reasoning in the case can be criticised because art.30 EC (which is the basis for derogations from the free movement provisions) does not contain an explicit protection of the environment provision. A derogation which satisfies the principle of proportionality can be found in the clause which refers to measures which protect the health and life of humans, animals and plants. Under the *Cassis* principle, the protection of the environment has become one of the accepted mandatory requirements,[58] but the *Cassis* principle should, strictu sensu, apply only to indistinctly applicable measures. The Opinion of A.G. Jacobs casts some light on the problem. He argued that by limiting the ground of protection of the environment to indistinctly applicable measures:

---

[55] See for example, Case 486/04 *Commission v Italy* [2006] E.C.R. I-11025.
[56] Case C-2/90 *Commission v Belgium* [1992] E.C.R. I-4431.
[57] Case C-379/98 *Preussen Elektra v Schleswang* [2001] E.C.R. I-2099.
[58] Case 302/86 *Commission v Denmark* [1988] E.C.R. 4607.

". . . national measures for the protection of the environment are inherently liable to differentiate on the basis of the nature and origin of the cause of harm, and are therefore liable to be found to be discriminatory, precisely because they are based on such accepted principles as 'environmental damage should as a priority be rectified at source' (Article 130r(2) EC). Where such measures necessarily have a discriminatory impact of that kind, the possibility that they may be justified should not be excluded."

The Court's ruling left unanswered the effect of the German trade of green electricity to other Member States since the buying-in obligation was limited to green electricity produced in Germany. Was this an import-restriction? Germany justified the scheme as increasing the supply security from national renewable sources, arguing this is a justifiable derogation in free movement of goods. It also referred to art.6 EC that environmental protection is a goal in all Community policies, including trade between Member States.

A third environmental principle is the "polluter pays" principle. This was set out in a Communication from the Commission in 1975[59]:

". . . natural or legal persons governed by public or private law who are responsible for pollution must pay the costs of such measures as are necessary to eliminate that pollution or to reduce it so as to comply with the standards or equivalent measures which enable quality objectives to be met or, where there are no such objectives, so as to comply with the standards or equivalent measures laid down by the public authorities."

The principle has been adopted by the Court[60] and is also seen in EU legislation.[61] Advocate General Kokott found that it was

---

[59] Council Recommendation of March 3, 1975 regarding cost allocation and action by public authorities on environmental matters.

[60] See Case C-293/97 *R v Secretary of State Ex p. Standley and Metson* [1999] E.C.R. I-8033, paras 93–95 where the Court explains that there are two dimensions to the "polluter pays" principle: ". . . it must be understood as requiring the person who causes the pollution, and that person alone, to bear not only the costs of remedying the pollution, but also those arising from the implementation of a policy of prevention. It can therefore be applied in different ways. Thus, it may be applied either after the event or preventatively before the harm occurs".

[61] See European Parliament and Council dir.2004/35 on environmental liability with regard to the prevention and remedying of environmental damage, OJ 2004 L143/56. See Betlem and Brans, 2005.

possible to limit the Community concept of the "polluter pays" principle by reference to international Conventions. In an action brought by the Breton Commune of Mesquer against the Total Group for the clean-up costs of one of its tankers which had sunk off the French coast,[62] the Advocate General pointed out that International Liability Convention 1969 precludes a claim for compensation against anyone other than the owner of a ship unless the damage was caused intentionally or recklessly. Thus it was permissible for France to limit the scope of liability in this way and yet its law to be compatible with the Community "polluter pays" principle. The Advocate General also found that France could limit the amount of compensation payable under the International Convention of December 18, 1971 on the Establishment of an International Fund for Compensation for Oil Pollution Damage. The rationale for this Convention, which has be ratified by many of the Member States, is that the Contracting Parties accept that there are risks in the transport of oil by sea and that some of these risks should be borne from public funds.

The "Precautionary Principle" was introduced by the TEU (the Maastricht Treaty), having already found expression in international law.[63] However, it is a complicated controversial concept involving risk analysis: risk assessment, risk management and risk communication.[64] Each analysis is not free from political intervention[65] or scientific uncertainty.[66]

A newer principle is the mainstreaming[67] or "Integration Principle" as set out in art.6 EC:

". . . environmental protection requirements must be integrated into the definition and implementation of all

---

[62] Case C-188/07 *Commune de Mesquer v Total France SA and Total International Ltd.,* Opinion of March 13, 2008.

[63] The 1992 Rio Declaration defined the principle as: "Where there are threats of serious irreversible damage, lack of full scientific certainty shall not be used as a reason for postponing cost-effective measures to prevent environmental degradation."

[64] Commission, *Communication on the Precautionary Principle* (COM (2000) 1.

[65] See, for example, Case C-180/96 *United Kingdom v Commission* [1998] E.C.R. I-2265; Case T-13/99 *Pfizer Animal Health v Council* [2002] E.C.R. II-3305; Case T-70/99 *Alpharma v Council* [2002] E.C.R. II-3495.

[66] Lee, 2005:98; Lenschow, 2002.

[67] See Case C-513/99 *Concordia Bus Finland v City of Helsinki* [2002] E.C.R. I-7213 where art.6 EC was applied to procurement criteria; Case T-210/02 *British Aggregates v Commission* [2006] E.C.R. II- environmental concerns applied in the state aid field; Case T-13/99 *Pfizer* [2002] E.C.R. II-3305 the application of the precautionary principle to the agriculture sector.

Community policies and activities . . ., in particular with a view to promoting sustainable development."

The aim of this principle, which is also a policy, is to create an integration strategy which sees the economic, social and environmental aspects of EU development as mutually reinforcing. This is an acknowledgment of the underlying tensions inherent with the modern integration process, of balancing competing interests and values, explained by A.G. Léger in *R v Secretary of State for the Environment, Transport and the Regions Ex p. First Corporate Shipping Ltd*[68]:

"The concept "sustainable development" does not mean that the interests of the environment must necessarily and systematically prevail over the interests defended in the context of the other policies pursued by the Community in accordance with Article 3 of the EC Treaty. On the contrary, it emphasises the necessary balance between various interests which sometimes clash, but which must be reconciled."

These tensions were played out in the use of the justifications to the four freedoms, particularly the balancing of arts 28 and 30 EC with the use of the principles of subsidiarity and proportionality.[69] A central policy in this new strategy has been managing the effects of climate change and more recently a sustainable energy policy for the EU (Szyszczak, 2008).

## 9.4 Economic and Social Cohesion

It was recognised in 1957 that the benefits derived from economic integration would not be evenly balanced across the EU. For example, the reliance upon the four economic freedoms to create a unified market was dependent upon economic actors and economic activity taking place across borders. Thus the mobile, educationally well-trained and qualified workforce would benefit from migration and certain regions of the EU would be attractive for inward investment of finance, jobs and people. Other regions of the EU would also be on the periphery of integration with a tendency towards

---

[68] Case C-371/98 [2000] E.C.R. I-9235.
[69] Case 302/86 *Commission v Denmark (Danish Bottles)* [1988] E.C.R. 4607.

under-development. The recent enlargement of the EU, bringing in a number of central and eastern European States with low per capita GDP has accentuated the problems created by European integration processes. The original EEC Treaty was committed in the Preamble to reduce the differences existing between the various regions and backwardness of the less favoured regions. A European Social Fund was created in art.123 EEC to facilitate the mobility of workers and the Agricultural Fund provided guidance and guarantees for the farming sector. In 1975 the European Regional and Development Fund was created to correct regional in-balances. However it was not until the SEA 1986 that a Community regional policy was officially given Treaty status. A new Title on "Economic and Social Cohesion" was introduced in arts 158 EC *(art.174 TFEU)* (Allen, 2000; Scott, 1995; Evans, 1999).

The current programme covers the period 2007–2013 and focuses upon three priorities. The first is the Convergence objective aimed at developing the least developed Member States and regions by improving the conditions for growth and employment. The second objective addresses Regional Competitiveness and Employment and the third objective addresses European Territorial Cooperation.

The programme relies upon secondary legislation and soft law and does not create legally enforceable individual rights; the European Courts have been reluctant to allow third parties, for example, environmental groups or ngos to be granted standing to challenge decisions taken under the economic and social cohesion programmes.[70]

The 1974 SAP addressed social exclusion and poverty and this led to a series of Anti-Poverty Programmes.[71] In 1989 the Council adopted a Resolution on combating social exclusion[72] recognising that combating social exclusion was an important tool in building the social dimension of the Internal Market. The Commission was asked to study and report on the measures taken by the member States to combat social exclusion and in 1990 a research and monitoring Observatory was established and the European Anti-Poverty Network was funded by the Commission. However some Member States (notably Germany the UK) opposed the increase in EU competence in this area arguing that it should not go beyond a

---

[70] Case T-461/93 *An Taisce and WWF( UK)* v *Commission* [1994] E.C.R. II-711, on appeal case C-325/94P [1996] E.C.R. I-3727; Case C-321/95P *Stichting Greenpeace Council v EC Commission* [1998] E.C.R. I-1651; Case C-417/04P *Regione Siciliana v Commission* [2006] E.C.R. I-3831.

[71] Council Decision 75/458, OJ 1975 L1999/34; Council Decision 85/8, OJ 1985 L2/24; Council Decision 89/457, OJ 1989 L224/10.

[72] OJ 1989 C 277/0.

research co-ordination role. The Council failed to adopt a fourth Anti-Poverty programme in 1993 and the Court held that the Commission could not fund further anti-poverty projects without an Anti-Poverty Programme in place.[73] It was not until the Treaty of Amsterdam 1997 introduced arts 136 and 137 EC (*arts 151 and 152 TFEU*) that EU competence was fully realised. However, social inclusion policies have taken shape mainly through the open method of co-ordination.[74] Article 34(4) of the Charter of Fundamental Rights of the European Union states that:

"in order to combat social exclusion and poverty, the Union recognises and respects the right to social and housing assistance so as to ensure a decent existence for all those who lack sufficient resources, in accordance with the rules laid down by Union law and national laws and practices."

In the Treaty of Lisbon 2007 *Title XVII* is renamed *Economic, Social and Territorial Cohesion. Article 174 TFEU* includes reference to rural regions affected by industrial transition and regions which suffer from severe and permanent natural or demographic handicaps, for example, the northernmost regions with low population density, island, cross-border and mountain regions.

## 9.5 Consumer Policy

Consumer policy was mentioned in the 1972 Paris Summit. In 1975 the Council adopted a Resolution on Consumer Protection and Information Policy (OJ 1975 C92/1) which set out priorities for the EU relating to the protection of health, the safety and economic interests of consumers, the right of redress, the right to information and education and the right to representation. This Resolution proved to be the forerunner of the later EC Treaty base, introduced by the TEU (Treaty of Maastricht 1991) which is now found in art.153 EC (Article *TFEU*).

Until the clear consumer policy legal base was introduced the EU relied upon arts 94 and 95 EC and the jurisprudence emerging from the free movement of goods and services provisions of the EC

---

[73] Case C-106/96 *United Kingdom supported by Germany, the Council and Denmark v Commission* [1998] E.C.R. I-2729.

[74] Szyszczak (2005).

Treaty. Indeed the extent to which the EU had a "consumer policy" was largely as a by-product of the functioning of the Common Market (Stuyck, 2000; Bourgoigine, 1998).[75] Now the EU has legislative competence to act in the promotion of interests of consumers and of ensuring a high level of consumer protection (Nebbia, 2007). Additionally the Member States may supplement the EU legislation with their own legislation setting higher standards provided that it is notified to the Commission.

A Consumer policy has thus developed following trends found elsewhere in the social dimension of the EU of developing Action Plans[76] to specific legislation from a protective perspective, to framework directives on general policies to modern concerns over food safety[77] supplemented by soft law governance techniques (Howells and Wilhelmsson, 2003). Consumer policy occupies a wide range of issues: access to justice, consumer credit, consumer health, food safety, financial services, the information society, advertising, product safety, sale of goods, services of general economic interest e-commerce and unfair contract terms and the harmonisation of private law.[78] However, the definition of a consumer in Community law is limited to the protection of consumers as private individuals.[79]

The Treaty of Lisbon 2007 states that consumer protection shall be an area of shared competence (*art.49 (f) TFEU*) and *art.12 TFEU* gives the existing art.153(2) EC greater prominence.

## 9.6 Cultural Policy

A Cultural Policy for the EU developed through ECJ jurisprudence through cases where the Member States attempted to argue that measures which hindered the free movement provisions were justi-

---

[75] See also the Commission's *Consumer Protection Programme 2007–2013* COM (2007) 99, pp.4 and 5: "The internal market remains the fundamental context for consumer policy. Consumer policy is also key to improving the functioning of the internal market. The 2004 and 2007 enlargements of the internal market have brought specific new challenges." Cf. Howells and Wilhelmsson, 2003; Davies, 2005.

[76] The current Action Programme 2007–2013 can be found at: OJ 2006 L404/39.

[77] *White Paper on Food Safety,* COM (1999) 719.

[78] The Commission issued a Green Paper on the Consumer Acquis 2007, COM (2006) 744 final inviting stakeholders to comment on how the fragmented consumer law of the EU could be brought together in a systematic horizontal approach. See Heiderhoff and Kenny, 2007.

[79] Case C-361/89 *Criminal Proceedings Against Patrice di Pinto* [1991] E.C.R. I-1189; Case C-46/96 *Bayerische Hypoteken und Welchselbank AG v Dientzinger* [1998] E.C.R. I-1199.

fied in protecting national cultural heritage issues.[80] It has now materialised into a more specific policy with a role to play in developing Citizenship ideas (Craufurd-Smith, 2004, 2007; Sassatelli, (2007). The TEU added as one of the activities of the Community "a flowering of the cultures of the Member States". Article 151 EC (*art.167(5) TFEU*) gives the Community competence to "contribute to the flowering of the cultures of the member States, while respecting their national and regional diversity and at the same time bringing the common cultural heritage to the fore." The focus of this policy is to improve the knowledge and dissemination of European history and culture; the conservation and safeguarding of cultural heritage of European significance, noncommercial cultural exchanges; artistic and literary creation including the audio-visual sector. These policy themes are problematic, especially as the EU enlarges and have been criticised for neglecting the true diversity of the EU, especially in the recognition of minority cultures which are not visible in national cultures.[81] Culture is mainstreamed into all Community policies through art.151(5) EC although art.151(5) EC explicitly excludes the harmonisation of national policies.

The Treaty of Lisbon 2007 makes a small but significant change in *art.167(5) TFEU* by allowing the Council to take decisions by QMV rather than unanimity voting, thus removing the national veto.

## 9.7 Sport

Sport was not included within the competence of the EEC in the original Treaty of Rome 1957. In the 1950s sport was viewed as an amateur activity and not a significant economic activity. Sport as a regulatory issue has been brought to the attention of the EU as a result of individual litigation, a proactive response from the Commission and the lobbying of political actors, using primarily the vehicle of the European Parliament. In recent years the latent regulatory space offered by EU law has been used to tackle regulatory activity using the free movement and competition rules. This in turn has provoked a reaction from the professional bodies that see their

---

[80] Joined Cases 60 and 61/84 *Cinéthèque SA v Fédération Nationale des Cinémas Francais* [1985] E.C.R. 2605; Case C-379/87 *Groener v Minister for Education* [1989] E.C.R. I-53967; Case C-154/89 *Commission v France* [1991] E.C.R. I-659.
[81] Barber, (2002).

autonomy chipped away by this opportunistic litigation. The *Bosman*[82] ruling was a turning point in the EU policy towards sport and subsequent litigation has drawn upon the free movement and the competition law provisions of the EC Treaty as a way of challenging the autonomy of the regulatory bodies in sport.[83]

Lobbyists and the Institutions of the EU have drawn upon EC Treaty provisions which may be of relevance to sport issues. For example, art.149 EC which addresses "Education, Vocational Training and Youth" was used as the legal base to designate 2004 as the "European Year of Education through Sport". Article 151 EC, addressing Public Health, was used as the EU legal base for policy on anti-doping.[84] Through soft law processes the Commission and the European Parliament have created the notion of a "European Model of Sport" which does not operate under same conditions as other industries. Several European Parliament Reports addressed how sport could play a role in the European integration but the Commission was the main driver in addressing sport from a regulatory perspective, using its competence and powers in the field of competition policy.

The Treaty of Amsterdam 1997 included a weak, non-binding Declaration on Sport, Declaration No.29:

"The conference emphasises the social significance of sport, in particular its role in forging identity and bringing people together. The conference therefore calls on the bodies of the European Union to listen to sports associations when important questions affecting sport are at issue. In this connection, special consideration should be given to the particular characteristics of amateur sport."

The Commission issued a Consultation Document, *The European Model of Sport* and *The Helsinki Report*.[85] The European Council responded to *The Helsinki Report* in the Presidency Conclusions of Santa Maria da Feira, June 2000 in which:

---

[82] Case C-415/93 [1995] E.C.R. I-4921.

[83] Case 36/74 *Koch and Walrave v ICU* [1974] E.C.R. 1405; Case C-415/93 *Bosman* [1995] E.C.R. I-4921; Case C-519/04P *Meca-Medina v Commission* [2006] E.C.R. I-6991; Szyszczak, 2007.

[84] Discussed in Case T-313/02 *David Meca-Medina and Igor Majcen v Commission* [2004] E.C.R. II-3291.

[85] COM (1999) 644 final of December 10, 1999.

"the European Council requests the Commission and the Council to take account of the specific characteristics of sport in Europe and its social function in managing common policies."

The Treaty of Nice 2000 did not address the issue of sport as a new competence for the EU. Instead, the Nice Presidency Conclusion adopted a, *Declaration on the Specific Characteristics of Sport and Its Social Function in Europe, of which account should be taken in Implementing Common Policies.* This Declaration emphasises that the Community acting under various Treaty provisions:

"should take account of the social, educational, and cultural functions inherent in sport and making it special, in order that the code of ethics and the solidarity essential to the preservation of the social role may be respected and nurtured".

A Commission White Paper[86] was followed by the inclusion of Sport in *Title XI Education, Vocational Training, Youth and Sport TFEU. Article 165 (1) TFEU* states that:

"*The Union shall contribute to the promotion of European sporting issues, while taking account of the specific nature of sport, its structures based on voluntary activity and its social and educational function.*"

*Article 165(2) TFEU* states that Union action shall be aimed at:

"*developing the European dimension n sport, by promoting fairness and openness in sporting competitions and cooperation between bodies responsible for sports, and by protecting the physical and moral integrity of sportsmen and sportswomen, especially young sportsmen and sportswomen.*".

## 9.8 Youth

The inclusion of a policy on "Youth" in *art.165(2) TFEU* has the aim of encouraging participation of young people in the democratic

---

[86] COM (2007) 391.

life of Europe. Under *art.3(3) TEU* the Union shall promote the rights of the child. This policy will feed into other horizontal policies of the Union, for example, adequate social protection, the fight against social exclusion, a high level of training and the fight against discrimination based on age, sex, race or ethnic origin, religion or belief, disability and sexual orientation (*arts 9 and 10 TFEU*). The Council will be able to adopt Recommendations in the field of vocational training (*art.166(4) TFEU*).

# 10: The European Union and its Relations with the Outside World

## SUMMARY

## 10.1 Introduction

Walter Hallstein, the first Commission President stated that "one reason for creating the European Community was to enable Europe to play its full part in world affairs". (Hallstein, 1962:79). Hallstein's argument was based upon the view that it was vital for the European Community to speak with one voice and to act as one in its economic relations with the outside world. The defining characteristic of the EEC's and latterly EU's foreign policy has been an attempt to simultaneously foster political stability and economic development in neighbouring regions thereby contributing to conflict prevention.

In January 2007 the EU became an economic and political union of 27 Member States which together account for over 20 per cent of total global trade in goods. Despite the eastward enlargements that have taken place since 2004 the EU cannot ignore the wider world.

For internal policies to function, for example immigration and asylum, the EU requires the co-operation of its neighbours and has accordingly developed political and economic strategies such as the Neighbourhood Policy through which it co-operates with third countries situated on the EU's borders. The EU has recognised the necessity of a common approach towards its relations with third countries since its inception. Initially, such co-operation was economic in character in the form of the Common Commercial Policy (CCP), but since the Maastricht Treaty the co-operation has broadened to encompass political collaboration.

The Common Foreign and Security Policy (CFSP), the so-called second pillar of the EU provides the framework for the EU's political relations with third countries. It also provides a Treaty structure for limited military co-operation between the Member States. The EU's political relations with its neighbours and many developing countries are predominantly based upon a principle of reciprocity. The EU provides economic assistance in return for administrative, political and human rights reforms (Smith, 2001). For example, since 2003 the EU's Neighbourhood Strategy[1] seeks to develop a partnership with European, North African and Mediterranean States. In return these States commit to address jointly with the EU problems such as illegal immigration, organised crime and human rights abuses, with the EU providing economic and technical assistance.

The Neighbourhood Strategy has two underlying objectives. Firstly, it seeks to minimise the economic and social disparities between the EU and its neighbours. Secondly, it forms part of a much broader EU objective to develop an ethical foreign policy by bringing together economic objectives and EU norms on political and administrative reform and human rights in one coherent policy.[2] The protection of human rights is not only a foundation for the EU itself, (art.6 (1) TEU) and an objective of development co-operation, but also an aim of the CFSP (art.11 TEU). For example in the EC—India Agreement on Scientific and Technical Co-operation[3] there is a clear interaction between commercial objectives and the political objectives of the EU. It can be said that through its external relations

---

[1] COM(2003) 104 final *Communication from the Commission to the Council and the European Parliament Wider Europe—Neighbourhood: A New Framework for Relations With Our Eastern and Southern Neighbours.*

[2] See further K. Smith 'The EU Human Rights and Realtions with Third Countries: Foreign Policy with an Ethical Dimension', in K. Smith and M. Light (eds) *Ethics and Foreign Policy* (Cambridge: CUP, 2001).

[3] OJ 2001 C 304, 16.

policy the EU seeks to export an EU standard of human rights norms.

To achieve its foreign policy objectives the EU has drawn upon the experiences of its own integration model building economic and political partnerships with third countries. Firstly, the EU has created an extensive network of bilateral international agreements which, since 1995, have all included a clause which allows for the suspension of the agreement if human rights and democratic principles are not respected (Horng, 2003). Secondly, the EU has established a variety of financial assistance programmes for third countries. The purpose of these programmes is to support and promote economic development, improve administrative organisation and capacity, strengthen democracy and promote the rule of law.[4] Perhaps the most successful examples of such assistance can be seen in the Europe Association Agreements which provided the framework for relations between the EU and the 2004 and 2007 Accession States.

Thirdly, the EU is involved in fostering regional integration across the globe. The African Caribbean and Pacific Countries (ACP) partnership with the EU was signed in 2000. Through the ACP-EU Partnership Agreement the EU is providing expertise and know-how to ACP countries on how to pursue closer regional co-operation and it can be said that the EU is "exporting" elements of its own integration model. Fourthly, the EU has pursued the multilateral liberalisation of global trade. Trade liberalisation is intended to bring economic benefits to the EU, but it is also part of a broader strategy to foster the integration of developing countries in the world economy. For example, in 2001 the Council introduced a regulation whereby developing countries which respect international social and environmental standards would benefit from the EU's scheme of generalised tariff preferences for a period of three years.[5]

A coherent external relations policy remains an important political priority for the EU to complement the EU's commercial relations with third countries. The Common Commercial Policy (CCP) which governs EU external trade policy is regulated by the EC Treaty and creates a single coherent economic policy towards third countries in relation to taxes, custom duties and the operation of trade relations. These relations are subject to the agreements of

---

[4] This includes the PHARE, and TACIS programmes.
[5] Council reg.2501/2001EC of December 10, 2001 applying a scheme of generalised tariff preferences for the period from January 1, 2002 to December 31, 2004, OJ L 346.

World Trade Organisation (WTO) to which the EU is a signatory in addition to the Member States. The chapter will consider the competence of the EU to enter into international agreements such as the WTO, together with their status in the EU's legal order, the operation of the CCP and how this compliments the Internal Market. The chapter will also examine the interaction between the CCP and the political objectives of the EU's external policy under the CFSP. To begin with it is necessary to consider how, why and to what extent the EU has acquired legal competence and capacity, to act on behalf of the Member States in commercial matters.

## 10.2 The EU's Treaty-Making Capacity

The original EEC Treaty included clear provisions on the conclusion of international agreements between the Community and third countries or international organisations. Since the Treaty of Amsterdam the EU has, under art.24 TEU, limited capacity to conclude international agreements in the implementation of the CFSP and of police and judicial co-operation in criminal matters under Pillar 3.

Competence is not just restricted to the question of whether the EU has the power to act. It also raises wider, but related, questions of what legal capacity the EU has and what is the role of the legislative Institutions undertake. It is through the CCP that the EU has its most obvious presence in international relations. Article 281 EC provides that the EC has legal personality and thereby the capacity to make binding agreements on behalf of the EU. The exercise of this legal personality is subject to express or implied powers being granted to act in a particular policy area. In its external relations the EC has a capacity to create contractual relations with third countries over all objectives that are set out in the EC Treaty (de Zwaan, 1999:77). This was confirmed by the ECJ in the judgment of *Costa v ENEL*. The Court stated that:

"By contrast with ordinary international treaties, the EEC Treaty has created its own legal system ... By creating a Community of unlimited duration, having its own institutions, its own personality, its own legal capacity, and capacity of representation on the international plane and, more particularly, real powers stemming from a limitation of sovereignty or a transfer of powers from the states to the Community, the

Member States have limited their sovereign rights, albeit within limited fields and have thus created a body of law which binds both their nationals and themselves."

By contrast, the Member States have not granted similar legal personality to the EU in relation to activities under the CFSP. The post-Amsterdam art.24 TEU has granted the EU some limited treaty-making powers and under this provision the Council is entitled to conclude international agreements in the implementation of the CFSP. Sari argues that art.24 TEU is unclear as to the legal position of the Council and has failed to clarify on whose behalf the Council concludes such agreements (Sari, 2008:75). This has given rise to conflicting interpretations of what capacity the Council acts in when it concludes such agreements. Commentators have offered two differing opinions on this with Monar (1997:427), Cremona (1998:70) and Dashwood (1999) suggesting that the Council acts as an agent on behalf of the Member States, with art.24 TEU granting the EU de facto international legal personality through which it can sign binding legally agreements on behalf of the EU Member States and the Council act on behalf of the EU as a separate legal entity. According to this view, the purpose of art.24 TEU is to lay down a procedure for the collective conclusion of international agreements by the Member States.

By contrast Langrish (1997:13) has suggested that under art.24 TEU the Council acts on behalf of the EU as a separate legal entity which has the power to make treaties and is therefore recognised as an independent subject of international law. Sari suggests that neither while both arguments are legitimate neither has been able to fully rebut the other. The Constitutional Treaty addressed the uncertainty of art.24 TEU and proposed that explicit legal personality be granted to the EU (Sari, 2008:76). This has been retained in the Treaty of Lisbon 2007 (*art.47 TEU*) which states that the EU will have legal personality.

There are four types of international agreements involving the EU and the Member States which can be identified:

1.  international agreements concluded by the EC in areas of exclusive competence and without the involvement of the Member States;

2.  international agreements concluded by the EU in Pillar 2 or Pillar 3 matters without the participation of the Member States;

3.  international agreements concluded by the EU/EC together with the Member States in areas of shared competence; and

4.  international agreements where competence rests solely with the Member States.

The procedures for negotiating agreements where the EC has traditionally had competence, for example, trade policy, differs from that used by the EU to negotiate international agreements covering the CFSP. For traditional Community agreements the Commission acts as negotiator but to commence any negotiations the Commission must be authorised by the Council of Ministers. It is also the Council which concludes any international agreements which result from the negotiations and the Council will usually act by qualified majority. Unanimity will only be required where the corresponding internal policy area requires Council unanimity or in the conclusion of Association Agreements.

For second and third pillar agreements the rules differ from the traditional Community practice and arise from the inter-governmental nature of these policy areas. Such agreements are negotiated by the Presidency of the Council of Ministers with assistance from the Commission where necessary. The Council authorises the Presidency to commence negotiations and agreements are concluded with the Council acting unanimously on a recommendation from the Presidency.

The precise scope of the Community's external competence has been the subject of much dispute between the Commission and the Council. Generally, the Commission has taken an expansive interpretation of its role and the Court has acknowledged[6] that the Community has the authority to conclude international agreements either because of an express power that is granted within the Treaty or from implicit powers arising from the Treaty provisions. In *Opinion 1/76*[7] the Court stated that the Community is authorised to enter in to international agreements where concluding an international objective is necessary for the attainment of a specific Treaty objective and there are no internal rules that have been adopted through secondary legislation.[8]

---

[6] Case 22/70 *Commission v Council* [1971] E.C.R. 263.

[7] *Opinion 1/76* [1977] E.C.R. 741.

[8] Though the Court has narrowed the impact of Opinion 1/76 in subsequent pronouncements; see the discussion of Opinion 1/94 (*Competence of the Community to Conclude International Agreements Concerning Services and the Protection of Intellectual Property*) [1994] E.C.R. I-5267 discussed below.

The Court has adopted a principle of parallelism between internal and external Community competences confirming exclusive Community competence in the latter when it is granted in the former. The majority of international agreements cover policy areas where competence is shared between the Community and the Member States. Such "mixed agreements" require both the consent of each individual Member State in addition to the formal approval by the Community. With respect to the negotiation, conclusion and implementation of such mixed agreements the Court has stated that the Community and Member States are obliged to co-operate closely.[9]

## 10.3 Competence and the Common Commercial Policy

In the field of commercial policy competence is derived from arts 131–134 EC. Article 133 EC grants express competence to develop a "common commercial policy" based on "uniform principles". The provision does not expand upon what the aims and objectives of the common policy should be. The purpose of the CCP is to complement the external aspect of the EU's customs union by providing a single uniform policy in other aspects of international trade, for example, export policy and trade liberalisation.

The CCP is controversial, not only because of the exclusive powers granted by art.133 EC, but also because of the qualified majority decision-making procedure it uses. Together with the procedures in art.300 EC, the EC utilises both autonomous and contractual legislative instruments in the conclusion of CCP agreements. Under art.300 EC the agreements are negotiated by the Commission and concluded by the Council pursuant to the procedures set out in art.300 (1)–(6) EC. Article 300 (7) EC provides that:

"[a]greements concluded under the conditions set out in this Article shall be binding on the institutions of the Community and on the Member States."

In the context of the CCP autonomous instruments invariably take the form of regulations because of the need for direct implementation by the relevant customs authorities within the Member States.

---

[9] See *Opinion 1/78* (*Natural Rubber Agreement*) [1979] E.C.R. 2871, paras 34–36 and *Opinion 1/94* [1994] E.C.R. I-5267.

One such example is reg.2603/69/EEC[10] which regulates Common Rules for Exports. Additionally, measures which are specifically targeted at a particular product, such as anti-dumping duties or protectionist measures also come within the scope of art.133 EC. The introduction of anti-dumping regulations has led to significant litigation before the Court under art.230 EC. Individuals affected by such measures challenge their validity through judicial review on the basis that these regulations affect their legitimate expectations.[11] The Court has stated that procedural propriety is essential, both in the legislative and enforcement processes, and consequently will declare invalid a measure which does not meet expected standards.

Contractual instruments include treaties or other international agreements. Under the CCP art.300 EC grants the Commission powers to negotiate the agreement, but the final decision is reserved for the Council. Article 300 EC merely provides the procedural mechanism through which agreements are made and a substantive provision must have a clear legal base to demonstrate external competence, for example art.133 EC. Through Decision 94/800EC[12] the Council concluded that the WTO Agreement that provides a partial framework of the CCP, but it must be noted that the entire WTO Agreement is not within the scope of the CCP. Some aspects of the WTO, such as the Trade Related Aspects of Intellectual Property Rights (TRIPs) agreement (TRIPs), are referred to as mixed agreements because competence is shared with Member States. Shared competence between the EU and Member States has led to tension as to the precise scope of art.281 EC and how mixed agreements should be enforced.

In *France v Commission*[13] the Court dismissed an action brought by France for annulment of the act which had been used by the Commission to conclude an agreement with the US. This act created Guidelines intended to improve regulatory competition between the EU and the US and to promote transparency towards third parties in relation to technical rules concerning goods covered by the WTO/TBT agreement. The French government argued that the Commission had concluded a binding international agreement when the conclusion of such an act is normally within the exclusive competence of the Council under art.300 EC. The Commission

---

[10] OJ 1969 L 324, 34.

[11] See Joined Cases 113 and 118/77 *Japanese Ball Bearings* [1979] E.C.R. I-1185.

[12] OJ 1994 L 336, 1.

[13] Case C-233/02 *Commission v France* [2004] E.C.R. I-2759.

argued that the guidelines were not binding and therefore the Commission had competence to adopt them.

The Court rejected the French government's argument, but also issued a warning to the Commission. The fact that the Guidelines were non-binding was not sufficient to confer competence upon the Commission to adopt them. Account must be taken of the division of powers and the institutional balance established by the Treaty in the field in question:

"... determining the conditions under which a measure may be adopted requires the division of powers and the institutional balance established by the Treaty in the field of the common commercial policy to be duly taken into account, since in this case the measure seeks to reduce the risk of conflict related to the existence of technical barriers to trade in goods."[14]

The Court further stated, at para.42, that the intention of the parties must be the "decisive criterion for the purpose of determining whether or not the Guidelines are binding." The Court reached the conclusion that the Guidelines had no binding force and therefore are not logically concerned by art.300 EC.

In the framework of the WTO the situation with respect to the division of powers between the Community and its Member States was less clear. The multilateral agreements of the WTO now encompasses the General Agreement on Tariffs and Trade (GATT), the General Agreement on Trade in Services GATS, and for the first time agreement over certain protection of intellectual property rights through the TRIPs Agreement. The TRIPs Agreement is groundbreaking because it covers several aspects of trade, particularly the granting of patents for, amongst other things, pharmaceutical products. The WTO contributes to the protection of intellectual property and the corresponding commitments made by the Member States have led to some standardisation through EU law of national laws in specific fields. One such example is dir.98/44[15] EC which provides legal protection for Biotechnological developments.

The impact of TRIPs has been to necessitate a closer co-ordination of EU intellectual property policy which inevitably results in increased competence for the EU. This has already generated litigation in which the ECJ has examined the scope of TRIPs

---

[14] Case C-233/02 *Commission v France* [2004] E.C.R. I-2759, at para.40.
[15] OJ 1998 L213, 1.

and its application to intellectual property protection in the EU.[16] More generally, the Commission has published proposals for a European Patent Directive[17] and the necessary changes to allow the ECJ competence to hear cases relating to disputes in intellectual property have already been introduced by the Nice Treaty in art.229A EC. This is a preparatory Act and creates a legal base to allow the Council, acting unanimously, to adopt provisions to confer jurisdiction on the ECJ in disputes relating to industrial property rights. This provision will apply primarily to disputes between private individuals concerning the future Community Patent.

Decision 94/800 on the WTO signalled the conclusion of many years of negotiation between the EU and its world trading partners. Through this Decision the EU participates in a more liberalised word-trading regime. Though the WTO is a mixed agreement, the ECJ has stated that in those circumstances where competence is transferred to the EU, and the criteria for direct effect are satisfied, these provisions of the WTO will be enforceable within the Member States.[18]

During the 1970s the ECJ sought to develop a clearer concept of the CCP based on the needs of the Community within the changing international context. The CCP had to react and adapt to changing circumstances of world trade and in particular globalisation. The primary step was to move towards multilateral, rather than bilateral trade negotiations, through which the EU had a single commercial policy towards all third countries. For an effective CCP the ECJ identified that the EU must have exclusive competence to act on behalf of all Member States. Exclusive competence is derived from the Treaty and covers both the CCP and the Common Agricultural Policy (CAP) and the signing of Association Agreements. Exclusive competence must be distinguished from concurrent competence to which the principle of subsidiarity applies. In practice the effect of granting exclusive competence to the EU means that Member States lose the right to regulate in that particular policy area. This differs from concurrent competence where the presumption remains that Member States will retain the right to legislate. Member States will only lose this right when the Community has satisfied certain criteria which demonstrate the benefits of action at the supra-national level.

---

[16] See *Opinion 1/94* [1994] E.C.R. I-5267.
[17] COM(2000) 412 final.
[18] Case 181/73 *Haegmann* [1974] E.C.R. 449.

In *Opinion 1/75*[19] the ECJ stated that the objective of the CCP in art.133 EC arises:

"[i]n the context of the operation of the Common Market. . .with which the particular interests of Member States must endeavour to adapt to each other."

The ECJ viewed the provisions of art.133 (1)–(4) EC as being incompatible with the exercise of concurrent powers by Member States. The ECJ's justification for this is that without exclusive competence, economic integration and the reciprocity and mutual trust that is required for the EU to function would be undermined. McGoldrick (1997:70) does not consider these arguments as being particularly persuasive and points out that exclusive competence is not the norm in Community decision-making. Furthermore he argues that the presence of concurrent competence per se does not undermine integration. According to McGoldrick, such judgments demonstrate the integrationist interpretation of supremacy which the ECJ has applied.

## 10.4 Mixed Agreements

A mixed agreement is one to which both the EU and one or more of the Member States is a party because there is shared competence between the Member States and the EU. Mixed agreements are significant from a legal perspective because the Treaty includes a number of policy areas where there is a degree of shared competence and this raises questions of whether regulation falls within the domain of the EU or the Member States.

Even though the Community is granted exclusive competence in the CCP the Court has recognised that in certain circumstances, particularly where Member States are required to contribute financially, that capacity will be shared. In *Opinion 1/78*[20] the ECJ held that the CCP governed an international agreement designed to regulate the world market in natural rubber. Despite this, the ECJ also acknowledged that in this instance there would be shared competence because the agreement required Member States to individually contribute to the financing of natural rubber reserves. The question of financing the surplus rubber was important to the Court's

---

[19] *Opinion 1/75* (*OECD Local Cost Standard*) [1975] E.C.R. 1355.
[20] *Opinion 1/78* (*Natural Rubber Agreement*) [1979] E.C.R. 2871.

reasoning, though this factor did not detract from the Court's overall expansive view of art.133 EC and exclusive competence (Koutrakos, 2002:26).

McGoldrick (1997:85) criticises *Opinion 1/78* and argues that on the Court's logic the financing should have come from the Community and not the Member States, thereby making the matter one of exclusive Community competence. For McGoldrick, the Court's conclusions are inconsistent with the reasoning of the Court in *Opinion 1/75*. Eeckhout distinguishes these judgments on the basis that in *Opinion 1/75* the Member States were required to refrain from taking any action, whereas on the facts at issue in *Opinion 1/78* the positive act of expenditure justified the judgment.[21] Despite this academic disagreement regarding the consistency of these two cases, both judicial Opinions are consistent on the crucial point of the importance of exclusive competence to achieve the objectives of the CCP.

An area of dispute, even prior to the EU's signing of the WTO relates to the question of competence for the protection of intellectual property rights. The dispute was magnified in the light of the TRIPs agreement. According to Dörmer (2000:28) TRIPs represents a new challenge to EU law, especially the EU's external relations policy and the relationship of EU law, international convention law and the legal systems of the individual EU Member States. In *Parfums Christian Dior SA*[22] the ECJ considered how EU law, national law and international conventions operate in the protection of intellectual property rights. This case allowed the ECJ an opportunity to analyse the application of EU law in the light of the WTO Agreements, and explore questions relating to the jurisdiction of the Court and the direct effect of the TRIPs Agreement.

The complexity of the situation relating to mixed agreements such as TRIPs originated with the Court's initial statement in relation to TRIPs, in *Opinion 1/94*.[23] The Commission sought the opinion of the ECJ on the competence of the EU to conclude the Agreement establishing the WTO, and in particular GATS and TRIPs. The ECJ concluded that the Institutions and its Member States were jointly competent to conclude the TRIPs Agreement, as only certain

---

[21] Eeckhout, P., *External Relations of the European Union, Legal and Constitutional Foundations* (Oxford: OUP, 2004) at 18.

[22] Joined Cases C-390 and 392/98 *Parfums Christian Dior SA v Tuk Consultancy BV* [2000] E.C.R. I-11307.

[23] *Opinion 1/94 (Competence of the Community to Conclude International Agreements Concerning Services and the Protection of Intellectual Property)* [1994] E.C.R. I-5267.

aspects of TRIPs, such as trade marks, came within the exclusive competence of the EU. Other aspects of intellectual property, for example, the protection of patents, remained within the domain of the Member States. The Court's view in Opinion 1/94 is important, not least because it adopted a narrower interpretation to the exclusive external powers doctrine by comparison to that stated by the Court in Opinion 1/76. It will be recalled that here the Court stated that the Community is authorised to enter in to international agreements where concluding an international objective is necessary for the attainment of a specific Treaty objective, even if there is an absence of internal rules. Following Opinion 1/94 this exclusive power is restricted only to situations where the Treaty objectives cannot be attained through the introduction of autonomous internal rules. Consequently, the Court has held that the Community can only claim the exclusive external powers doctrine recognised in Opinion 1/76 on condition that internal and external action are inextricably linked and that the Treaty objective cannot be achieved through the exercise of internal power alone.

The Court's Opinion was disappointing for the Commission because it prevented the simple extension of the traditional Community method to "new" trade areas. Instead, following *Opinion 1/94* competence for the regulation of intellectual property is shared between the Community and Member States and this may lead to uncertainty as to where the actual boundaries of Community competence are and what this means for the operation of TRIPs.

In *Parfums Christian Dior*[24] the issue concerned an action commenced in the Dutch court by Dior, the proprietor of different trademarks for perfumes, against Tuk BV. Dior alleged that Tuk BV had infringed its trademark rights by selling perfumes bearing those marks when they had not been put on the market in the European Economic Area (EEA). The Dutch court considered that the proceedings raised the question of the direct effect of art.50(6) of TRIPs and made a preliminary reference to the ECJ under art.234 EC. The Dutch court was seeking guidance on whether art.50(6) of the TRIPs Agreement is to be interpreted as having direct effect in the sense that the legal consequences set out therein take effect even in the absence of any corresponding provision of national law?

As to the Dutch court's query over its jurisdiction, the ECJ ruled that:

"[w]here the judicial authorities of the Member States are called upon to order provisional measures for the protection of

---

[24] Case C-300/98 [2000] E.C.R. I-11307.

intellectual property rights falling within the scope of TRIPs and a case is brought before the Court of Justice in accordance with the provisions of the Treaty, in particular Article [234] thereof, the Court of Justice has jurisdiction to interpret Article 50 of TRIPs." (para.40)

On the question of direct effect, the Court held that the provisions of TRIPs are:

"[n]ot such as to create rights upon which individuals may rely directly before the courts by virtue of Community law" (para.44).

In its judgment, the ECJ qualified this statement by reference to a field of intellectual property to which TRIPs applies and in respect of which the EU has acquired competence and legislated. One such area is trademarks, through which reg.40/94 has established the concept of the Community Trademark. As the EU has exclusive competence in relation to trademarks, national courts are required to apply rules relating to the protection of trademarks as far as possible in light of the wording and purpose of art.50 of TRIPs. According to Koutrakos (2000:43), the objective of this is to ensure uniformity of application of EU law within the Member States and in such cases references to the ECJ under art.234 EC are permissible.

Alternatively, in a field of intellectual property in respect of which the EU has *not* yet legislated and which consequently falls within the exclusive competence of the Member States, protective measures adopted by the national courts do *not* fall within the scope of EU law. Accordingly, EU law neither requires nor forbids that the legal order of a Member State should accord to individuals the right to rely directly on the rule laid down by art.50 of TRIPs with the effect that an art.234 EC reference is not possible.

## 10.5 Completion of the CCP

Cremona (1990:283) points out that the removal of internal barriers to trade took place far more quickly than the completion of the CCP. *Opinions 1/75* and *1/78,* have raised controversy as to their scope of application, with any increase in Community competence signalling an inevitable decrease in powers for the Member States. For an effective CCP it was necessary to bridge the gap between internal and external trade. In particular the EU had to find a mechanism through which the protectionist instincts of Member States could be overcome. The CCP can only function if all Member States adopt a uniform view to customs duties from third countries in the same way they have agreed to their abolition for wholly internal trade. The concern for some Member States is illustrated by this simple example. If Member State A operates a quota system with regard to goods imported from a non-EU country, then Member State B, which does not operate such quotas, could import the goods from outside the EU and transport them to Member State A. Member State A could not, under Internal Market principles, prevent the import of these goods which were already in lawful circulation.

This concern is addressed by art.134 EC which governs so called "indirect imports". Under the Treaty of Rome 1957 the import of goods in to the Community allowed Member States to preserve and enforce quotas on imports from third countries and reg.288/82 contained a list of approved quotas. Under art.134 EC and reg.288/82 a Member State could control indirect imports, and this effectively provided an exception to the principle of uniformity with regard to imports. The Court approved this action in its judgment in *Dockenwolcke v Procureur de Républic*[25] but when on to qualify this by stating that only those quotas which did not breach the Treaty, and had been approved by the Community, would be acceptable. As the CCP lies within exclusive competence any deviation required prior approval.

In 1994 the Member States agreed reg.3289/94[26] for common rules for imports in to the EU. This regulation applies to products imported in to the EU and is based upon a principle of free trade. Contained within the regulation is a list of permitted safeguards which do not originate from the Member States and reflect the list of permitted safeguards agreed by the parties to the WTO, including the EU.

The scope of the CCP was debated by the Member States at the 1996 IGC. Although the Commission wanted an extension to its powers to apply to economic matters more generally the Member States rejected this. The Commission proposed an explicit extension of the CCP to trade in services, intellectual property and foreign investment thereby restricting shared competence. The Commission argued that such an extension was logical because the purpose of this extension of competence was to avoid the complications

---

[25] Case 41/76 *Dockenwolcke v Procureur de République* [1976] E.C.R. 1921.
[26] OJ 1994 L 349, 85.

inherent to situations of shared competence and would guarantee a consistent and effective policy in the field of external trade relations. The Commission's proposals met with resistance from all Member States and in particular France and a compromise was reached in the form of a new para.5 which was added to art.133 EC by the Treaty of Amsterdam. This allowed for the possible future extension of the CCP to cover international negotiations and agreements on services and intellectual property (in so far as they are not already within the CCP) by means of a unanimous Council decision.

The compromise reached at Amsterdam led to the inclusion of a new para.5 in art.133 EC which allowed for the possible future extension of the CCP to cover international negotiations on intellectual property and services insofar as these were not already covered by the CCP. Cremona (2000:12) criticised the re-drafting of art.133 (5) EC for failing to provide for a full constitutional procedure that would include each national parliament. Article 133 (5) EC merely requires a unanimous decision of the Council and even excluded the European Parliament. This suggests that internal constraints to procedurally amend the Treaty and extend EU competence are required. The ECJ recognised this through it judgments in relation to the application of TRIPs.

In *Opinion 1/94* the ECJ examined the issue of exclusive and non-exclusive competence within specific areas of the CCP and stated there were limits to EU competence. The Court held that the TRIPs agreement did not fall within the exclusive competence of the EU, either through art.133 EC or more general Treaty bases such as arts 95 or 308 EC. On the issue of intellectual property and services, the ECJ stated in *Opinion 1/94* that those areas which were already within the scope of the CCP, such as the protection of trademarks, would continue to be governed by the principles in art.133 (1)–(4) on the basis of exclusive competence. This was confirmed by the ECJ in *Hermès International v FHT Marketing.*[27] Conversely if the agreement related to intellectual property and services which came within the scope of art.133 (5) EC, for example, patents, then in such circumstances, the Member States would retain competence, provided that the agreement did not breach EU law.[28] *Opinion 1/94* therefore reinforces the ECJ's cautionary approach to the question of shared competence and mixed agreements with regard to the CCP which the ECJ first raised in *Opinion 1/75*. The Court suggested that amendments, of the type subsequently included in the Amsterdam

---

[27] See Case C-53/96 *Hermès International v FHT Marketing* [1998] E.C.R. I-3603.
[28] See for example *Parfums Christian Dior*.

Treaty, were required to art.133 EC if the EU was to acquire increased competence.

A further extension of the CCP took place, not by means of Council Decision as provided for in the Amsterdam Treaty, but by further Treaty amendment. The negotiations leading to the Treaty of Nice in December 2000 resulted in a complex amendment to art.133 EC. Under the amended art.133(5):

> Paragraphs 1 to 4 shall also apply to the negotiation and conclusion of agreements in the fields of trade in services and the commercial aspects of intellectual property, insofar as those agreements are not covered by the said paragraphs and without prejudice to paragraph 6.

Paragraphs 1 to 4 of art.133 EC include the concept of uniform principles, provisions on decision-making for the negotiation and conclusion of agreements, and (by virtue of Court of Justice case law) the principle of exclusivity. But the Treaty also places limits upon this power. Both the decision-making process and the exclusivity of Community competence in these new areas have been heavily qualified by the remainder of para.5 and para.6.

The Treaty of Nice 2001, in amending art.133 EC, for the first time clearly separates the CCP from the doctrine of exclusivity. In the fields of services and intellectual property different types of exclusive and non-exclusive competence apply. Firstly, those aspects of services and intellectual property which had already been held by the Court of Justice in *Opinion 1/94* to fall within the CCP will continue to be governed by art.133 (1)–(4) EC and exclusivity will apply. Secondly, for agreements relating to services and intellectual property and falling within art.133(5) EC, that paragraph makes it clear that the Member States will retain competence to conclude their own agreements with third countries and international organisations, "insofar as such agreements comply with Community law and other relevant international agreements." Thus, competence will be shared. Third, para.6 defines a further category of agreement to which a specific form of shared competence applies; these agreements, covering inter alia trade in cultural and audio-visual services, must be concluded jointly by both the Community and the Member States. Action by the Community alone is not be possible.

The amendments to art.133 EC by the Treaty of Nice reflect the views stated by the Court in *Opinion 1/94* and have divided expressly the CCP in to those areas within and those outside the exclusive competence of the EU. Following the reasoning of the judgments in

*Hermès* and *Dior* it would appear that if the there is a link between the spheres of competence, for example the protection of the Community Trademark in national courts, then TRIPs would be applicable. Where such a link was lacking, because of an absence of harmonising legislation, such as in disputes covering the protection of patents, TRIPs would not be applicable and the matter could not be referred to the ECJ under art.234 EC (Koutrakis, 2002:37). For Cremona the judgments in *Hermès* and *Dior* demonstrate the interest of the ECJ to maintain the unity of international representation of the Community. These cases also suggest a need for unity between the EU and the Member States in the determination of the EU's international obligations. This unity is achieved by *not* insisting on an all-embracing exclusivity of EU powers in areas where there is shared competence. According to Cremona (2000:29) the judgments of *Hermès* and *Dior* exhibit judicial self-restraint by not going beyond those areas where the EU has already legislated.

The Treaty of Lisbon 2007 extends the competence of the EU under the CCP and simplifies the complicated provisions of art.133 EC. *Article 3 TFEU* states that that the Union shall "exclusive competence in the common commercial policy". *Article 207 TFEU* provides that the Commission shall negotiate on behalf of the EU and that the Council will approve and conclude agreements by qualified majority. This broadly mirrors those provisions which under the Nice provisions are agreed by qualified majority.

As for agreements which cover intellectual property rights and the trade in services Council unanimity is required. The major development to the CCP in the Treaty of Lisbon comes in removal of the current derogation found in art.133 (6) EC which stated that agreements relating to trade in cultural and audiovisual services are subject to shared competence. The Treaty of Lisbon brings these areas and agreements for trade in social, education and health services within the scope of the exclusive EU competence but makes the approval subject to Council unanimity.[29] This requirement of unanimity reflects a concern, expressed by France since the Amsterdam Treaty, that cultural and linguistic diversity in the EU should be protected.

Article 207 (6) TFEU confirms that the exercise of exclusive competence will have no effect on the allocation of competences between the EU and the Member States. The primary effect of this will be that action taken externally will *not* extend the EU's internal

---

[29] *Art.207 (4) TFEU.*

exclusive competence, thereby leaving Member States to regulate certain external agreements themselves.

The Lisbon Treaty expresses more broadly the aims and principles of the CCP and the EU's external relations policy more generally. *Article 206 TFEU* states that "Union development cooperation policy shall have as its primary objective the reduction and, in the long term, the eradication of poverty. The Union shall take account of the objectives of development cooperation in the policies that it implements which are likely to affect developing countries." This suggests that the CCP is connected to the EU's other foreign policy objectives and is an integral part of the EU's attempts to create an ethical external relations agenda.

The logical conclusion of the transfer of exclusive competence to the EU in the CCP is that as the EU represents all Member States, it will enter in to agreements on *behalf* of those Member States. The primary issue raised by granting the EU competence to negotiate international agreements is what status are such agreements afforded in EU law. The principle of supremacy of EU law provides only for the supremacy of EU law and not international agreements. For such agreements to function there is a requirement of mutual trust between the EU and third countries necessitating a mechanism through which they are brought within the scope of the EU law. The position of such international agreements within the EU's legal order will now be considered.

# 10.6 The Status of International Agreements in EC Law

One consequence of exclusive EU competence in the CCP is that it has led to the EU negotiating international agreements with third countries on behalf of the Member States. One example is the WTO. The primary issue this raises is what legal status is granted to such international agreements within the EU, and in particular how has the ECJ viewed the EU's obligations with regard to these agreements? The WTO, and previously GATT, has raised questions not only in relation to Treaty base issues and competence of the CCP, but also to what extent, if any, do such agreements create enforceable rights within the Member States?

According to the Court in *Haegmann*[30] international agreements which are signed by the Community become:

---

[30] See fn. 20 above. See also Case C-239/03 *Commission v France* [2004] E.C.R. I-9325.

"[a]n integral part of Community law and may, in certain circumstances, have direct effect within the legal systems of the Member States."

The EU contracts with third countries in several ways with the two most common being agreements made directly between the EU and a third country, or an agreement which is made jointly between the EU, the Member States and a third country. Agreements made between the EU and third countries can be in the form of Association Agreements as seen in the pre-accession strategy that led up to the 2004 and 2007 enlargements. These Association Agreements provide the legal basis for bilateral relations between these countries and the EU. The EU had already established similar Association Agreements with Turkey (1963), Malta (1970) and Cyprus (1972). In the case of Turkey, a Customs Union entered into force in December 1995.

Article 310 EC provides for the conclusion of Association Agreements and other agreements between the EU and third countries. Article 300 EC states that such agreements:

"[s]hall be binding on the institutions of the Community and the Member States."

In *Gloszczuk*[31] the ECJ confirmed that Association Agreements can have direct effect within the Member States with the consequence that third country nationals may exercise the rights contained within the Agreements (Bogusz, 2002:275). In *Hauptzollamt Mainz v CA Kupferberg*,[32] which concerned the pre-accession Association Agreement with Portugal, the ECJ stated that such agreements must have direct effect to ensure uniformity of application within the Member States thereby recognising the relevance of such Association Agreements to the operation of the Internal Market.

---

[31] Joined Cases C-63/99, C-257/99 and C-235/99 *The Queen v Secretary of State for the Home Department Ex p. Wieslaw Gloszczuk and Elzbieta Gloszczuk*; *The Queen v Secretary of State for the Home Department Ex p. Julius Barkoci and Marcel Malik*; *The Queen v Secretary of State for the Home Department Ex p. Eleonora Ivanova Kondova* [2001] E.C.R. I-6369.
[32] Case 104/81 [1982] E.C.R. 3641.

## 10.7 Direct Effect of International Agreements

The criteria for direct effect have been considered in the context of Community legislation. To give rise to rights which can be enforced in national courts, a measure must first satisfy the criteria laid down by the Court in *Van Gend en Loos*. In particular this requires a measure to be precise and unconditional. With regard to international agreements this can be problematic and the Court has held that an agreement will have direct effect where the objectives of that agreement are the same as those of the EU.[33] In *International Fruit*, the Court considered the status of GATT, which the founding six Member States had signed individually prior to the agreement of the Treaty of Rome. The Court was of the opinion that while the GATT was intended to bind the EEC, the Agreement gave some degree of flexibility to Member States and contained a procedure that could allow them to vary, or even withdraw, from the Agreement. The Court's reasoning reflects a lack of reciprocity and legal certainty, especially in the event of signatories being in dispute. It also acknowledges that agreements such as GATT, and even the WTO, are based upon diplomacy rather than seeking to create legal rights.

By contrast in *Haupzollmat Mainz v Kupferberg* the Court held that certain provisions of a free trade agreement between the EEC and Portugal would have direct effect where they had a uniform impact across the Community. With regard to such agreements the Court has regularly stated that they do not have direct effect, as their primary objective is not to assist in the creation of the single market. For the Court, the defining feature in *Kupferberg* was that Portugal was seeking Community membership. Consequently, the free trade agreement fell within the objective of creating a single market, of which Portugal would eventually become a member.

The position of international agreements in EU law has proved a problematic issue for the Court and the status of GATT in particular gave rise to contentious litigation. Judgments such as *International Fruit* and *Kupferberg*, and the different status the Court awarded to GATT and free trade agreements respectively have been the subject of much criticism. In *Germany v Council (Bananas)*[34] the Court was asked to consider the legality of a Regulation which established the common organisation of banana markets in favour of African, Caribbean and Pacific (ACP) growers closely attached to French, Spanish and Portuguese importers. This was to the detriment of a

---

[33] Cases 21-24/72 *International Fruit* [1972] E.C.R. 1219.
[34] Case C-280/93 *Germany v Council (Bananas)* [1994] E.C.R. I-4737.

third country, mostly US-owned, growers established in Central America and from where German importers had enjoyed a regime of tariff-free imports. The regulation, on the one hand, set up a system of assistance to ACP-banana producers, and on the other established quotas and tariffs for third country bananas with a view to restricting their import or making them more costly to consumers. There is no doubt that the regulation hit German importers particularly hard. They were de facto banned or severely restricted from importing third country bananas at the preferential tariffs which had made them particularly popular with German consumers. Prior to this point there had been little or no restrictions on such imports.

Germany challenged the regulation through the judicial review procedure in art.230 EC and argued that the regulation was in breach of the GATT rules. The Court rejected this argument and held that it is not generally open to Member States to challenge Community law by relying on the GATT rules. The Court held[35] that the GATT rules do not have direct effect and that individuals could not rely on them before national courts. The Court did state that this would not be the case where the adoption of measures implementing obligations assumed within the context of the GATT is in issue or where a Community measure refers expressly to specific provisions of GATT. In such cases the Court held that it must review the legality of the Community measure in the light of the GATT rules.

As part of the WTO, a new GATT agreement was signed which included an increased number of binding provisions and the establishment of a quasi-judicial Dispute Settlement Understanding procedure to resolve differences between contracting parties. In such circumstances the ECJ felt that conditions existed, which had not done so previously, under which GATT could bind the EU. The Court stopped short of stating that that it had direct effect. The *Bananas* judgment was controversial and led to significant debate as to whether the arguments hitherto applied by the ECJ to the question of the direct effect of GATT should be applied to the new GATT agreement within the WTO. In the light of the improved quasi-judicial system to resolve disputes and the ECJ's acknowledgement in the *Bananas* judgment that GATT *may* prevail over EU law in limited circumstances, would there not now be a more convincing argument to extend direct effect to the WTO agreements generally?

This issue was addressed by the Court in *Portugal v Council*.[36] In this case Portugal challenged a Council Decision, which concluded

---

[35] Case C-280/93 *Germany v Council (Bananas)* [1994] E.C.R. I-4737, paras 103–112.
[36] Case C-149/96 *Portugal v Council* [1999] E.C.R. I-8395.

various agreements on textiles with India and Pakistan, arguing that they breached the WTO agreements including GATT. The ECJ acknowledged the developments in the WTO but concluded that these changes did not suffice to grant direct effect. The Court stated[37]:

"[h]aving regard to their nature and structure, the WTO agreements are not in principle among the rules in the light of which the Court is to review the legality of measures adopted by the Community institutions."

For the Court the WTO still lacked certainty and contained a degree of diversity, in particular with regard to application and enforcement of the agreements by the contracting parties. The agreements still operated to a large extent on mutual trust and the quasi-judicial dispute resolution procedure was not sufficiently formal to ensure consistency of application. The underlying assumption of the Court's judgment is that WTO law lacks unconditional mandatory force, and an identifiable notion of reciprocity. In *Léon Van Parys NV*[38] the Court points out that the WTO agreements are not in principle among the rules which the Court must take into account when reviewing the legality of measures adopted by the Community institutions. It is only where the Community has intended to implement a particular obligation assumed in the context of the WTO, or where the Community measure refers expressly to particular provisions of the WTO agreements, that it is for the Court to review the legality of a Community measure in light of the WTO rules.

This judgment follows the Courts reasoning in *Portugal v Council* in which the Court did not deviate from its view which it first expressed in *International Fruit*. That is WTO law (previously GATT) cannot be relied on to review the legality of acts of the EU. Setting out a two-part reasoning, the Court first denied that the WTO Dispute Settlement Understanding itself obliges the EU to implement rulings by making them directly enforceable. Secondly, the Court denied the possibility of doing so autonomously. The Court upheld its judgment in the *Bananas* case regarding the limited exceptions to this rule, including the possibility that WTO provisions can serve as a benchmark for reviewing Community acts taken to implement WTO Agreements. As a result of the *Portugal v Council*

---

[37] Case C-149/96 *Portugal v Council* [1999] E.C.R. I-8395, para. 47.
[38] Case C-377/02 *Léon Van Parys NV v Belgisch Interventie- en Restitutiebureau* [2005] E.C.R. I-1465.

judgment there remains a degree of dissatisfaction with the status of the WTO in EU law and with the status of international agreements in EU law more generally. Direct effect is central to ensuring the uniform application of EU law but the principle and the conditions required to satisfy it, do not readily apply to international agreements which are often vague and leave significant discretion in the hands of contracting parties. The Court will apply an "interpretative obligation" whereby EU legislative measures will, as far as possible be interpreted to give effect to WTO rules. By contrast, individual Member States, who have granted the EU competence to negotiate the WTO, remain impotent and cannot use the principles of the WTO to challenge the legality of EU acts.

## 10.8 Common Foreign and Security Policy and EU External Relations

*Origins of the political co-operation in foreign affairs*

The TEU introduced the pillar structure to the EU and with it the Common Foreign and Security Pillar through which the EU has sought to become a more prominent entity in international relations. Political co-ordination of foreign policies at the European level was not a new idea at Maastricht with the Member States having already established in 1970 a loose framework of co-ordination between foreign ministers to discuss traditional foreign policy topics.[39] This co-ordination was known as European Political Co-operation (EPC) and initially operated outside the Treaty. EPC received a legal basis in the Single European Act 1986[40] and was transformed in to the CFSP at Maastricht.

The objective of the CFSP is to galvanise EU action and works on the basis that Member States share similar strategic foreign policy objectives. This political co-operation in foreign affairs compliments the economic co-operation of the CCP. Unlike the CCP, the CFSP has had a chequered history, with Member States lacking agreement on several major foreign policy issues. One identifiable reason for this is that the CCP has a single policy arising from legislative provisions which are enforced by the Court. By contrast the CFSP is

---

[39] This mechanism was based upon a network of correspondents in the Ministries of Foreign Affairs who would keep in regular contact.
[40] Art.30 SEA 1986.

based upon inter-governmental co-operation that seeks a common policy which has not always been attainable with decisions being taken by unanimity in the Council. An inter-governmental decision-making process was insisted upon by both France and the UK at Maastricht with the European Council taking charge of the task of defining the principles and guidelines of the CFSP.[41]

It is evident that this inter-governmental approach, which was not favoured by Germany and the Benelux countries, has hindered decision-making under the CFSP. For example, the EU's response to the disintegration of the former Yugoslavia in the mid 1990s, or the lack of political agreement over the war in Iraq demonstrates that on key policy decisions the EU has not been able to arrive at a consensus. The absence of agreement is not altogether surprising and it must be emphasised that the agreement of the CFSP pillar at Maastricht merely provided the legal framework within which the EU could establish a common policy and did *not* create a common foreign and security policy. Koutrakos identifies a tension inherent in developing a collective model of foreign policy in which the Member States wish to rule out encroachment into their dominant role as the ultimate authority. This paradox has resulted in the CFSP being written in such a way as to highlight the policy's limitations, the problems of which, he argues, became evident in the Union's difficulties in coping with the break-up of Yugoslavia (Kotrakos, 2006: 386).

## Decision-making under the CFSP

The CFSP is based upon inter-governmental cooperation and not on legislative action which characterises the EC pillar. The powers of the Council are set out in art.13 TEU which requires the Council to ensure the unity, consistency and effectiveness of EU action. By art.12 TEU Member States adopt joint actions, decide on common strategies, adopt joint positions and seek to create a political consensus on foreign and security policy. Article 12 TEU contains a mix of formal legal instruments and informal co-operation which Member States may use in the CFSP. The Council is the primary Institution and is responsible for execution of the CFSP objectives found in art.11 TEU which reflects the inter-governmental nature of the co-operation. Unlike the EC Community method of decision-making which encompasses the Council, European Parliament and the Commission and is based upon a clear division of powers and responsibility, the CFSP is dominated by the Council. Furthermore

---

[41] Art.23 (1) TEU.

the Court has no jurisdiction over the CFSP. Under art.18 TEU it is the Presidency of the Council that represents the EU in CFSP matters and is assisted by a High Representative for the common foreign and security policy. The latter provides a degree of continuity to policy and negotiations through the six-monthly Presidency rotation.

The Constitutional Treaty proposed that EU's foreign policy High Representative and the Commissioner for External Relations would be merged into a single EU "Foreign Minister", who was able to speak for the Union on those subjects where EU countries agree a common line. This proposal for an EU "Foreign Minister" was unpopular amongst the Member States and while the Treaty of Lisbon Treaty retains the merger of the two posts, the job title of "Foreign Minister" is changed. Following the Treaty of Lisbon the EU's foreign policy chief will be referred to as the "High Representative of the Union for Foreign Affairs and Security Policy" who will preside over the Foreign Affairs Council (*art.18 TEU*).

Decision-making under the CFSP is defined by art.23 TEU. All decisions must be taken unanimously. An abstention by a Member State will not prevent the adoption of a decision, but the exercise of a Member States' veto will. Eeckhout (2004:411) describes this "constructive abstention" as being unique in EU decision-making and reflects the position that unanimous agreement cannot always be reached. Unlike the Community method of decision-making, the veto has been retained because of the sensitive and political nature of the co-operation. Post-Nice some limited qualified majority voting has been introduced under art.23 (2) TEU and applies to the agreement of joint actions or common positions or when such agreements are being implemented. It will also apply to the appointment of any special EU representatives for the CFSP. The voting rights allocated for use of qualified majority voting are the same as those in art.205 EC and used in the co-decision process. Given the difficulty of arriving at unanimous agreements one issue considered by the Convention on the Future of Europe was the extension of qualified majority voting to decision-making more generally under the CFSP, which was resisted by both the UK and France Eeckhout points out the EU adopted no joint actions or common positions with regard to the war in Iraq because of the requirement for unanimity (Eeckhout, 2004:412).

The Commission has a peripheral role in the execution of the CFSP. Article 27 TEU requires it to be "fully associated" with the work of the CFSP and art.18 TEU requires the Commission to be 'fully associated' with the work programme of the Presidency in the CFSP. Of greater value is art.22 TEU which enables the Commission to refer to the Council any question relating to the CFSP. The Commission has produced Communications outlining strategies for the CFSP, for example in relation to human rights and external relations. In this context the CFSP should be viewed as part of the EU's wider external relations objectives together with the CCP. In the CCP the Commission takes the lead and negotiates on behalf of the Member States, for example, the WTO or bilateral trade agreements. It is through these bilateral trade agreements that human rights are mainstreamed by linking trade and/or developmental aid to improved standards of human rights protection. Though peripheral to CFSP decision-making per se, it can be argued that the Commission adopts an important role to ensure that wider EU objectives are attained and co-ordinated through both CCP and the CFSP policies.

Under art.21 TEU the European Parliament is confined to a mere consultative role and has a right to be kept "regularly informed" of progress in the CFSP. Even the consultation is restricted to general questions of policy rather than specific decisions and this reinforces the inter-governmental nature of the co-operation. The Parliament does pay close attention to the CFSP, in particular to human rights issues. It will regularly present to the Council opinions and reports which the Council will invariably incorporate in to negotiations with third countries.

## The Court of Justice and the CFSP

In complete contrast to the EC pillar, the Court is largely excluded from jurisdiction over the CFSP as described in art.46 TEU. For a Union founded on the rule of law, the exclusion of the CFSP from the Court's jurisdiction is questionable and arguably one that undermines the principles the Union seeks to defend. Denza (2002:337) explains the background to this seemingly anomalous position as being based partly on the concerns of some Member States, notably the UK, over the Court's integrationist approach under the EC Pillar and their desire to ensure that Member State competence in foreign affairs would not be eroded by expansive rulings of the Court. Moreover, even without these concerns she argues that judicial control over CFSP instruments is not essential.

Denza highlights that measures under the CFSP are firstly, short-term nature and that the lack of a legal framework and absence of mutual legal obligations makes it difficult to review. Secondly, she argues that the Court has considered international relations within the context of the CCP, which has a different objective to the CFSP. Denza contends that Member States did not want principles of exclusive competence, applied by the Court to the CCP, to be applied to the CFSP. Moreover, the insistence on a common rather than single foreign and security policy, combined with the need for rapid resolution of differences means that the conditions for dispute resolution through the Courts does not really exist (Denza, 2002: 312). However, this does not mean that the Court has no role in relation to EU external relations.

Wessels (2000:1151) identifies that for those foreign and security policy elements that sit within the EC Pillar, the Court may exercise its full range of jurisdiction. Article 47 TEU protects the Court's right to ensure that the acquis communautaire is respected in the functioning of the CFSP.[42] For example, in the *Airport Transit Visas* case,[43] the Court reviewed a measure adopted under the Third Pillar (and in the light of the subject matter considered several CFSP Pillar issues) to determine whether it affected the EC. This broad approach to reviewing pillar activities was confirmed in the judgment of the Grand Chamber of the Court in the *Environmental Crimes* judgment,[44] where the matter at stake was the EC's ability to impose criminal penalties for environmental offences. Although in principle criminal law and criminal procedures were not Community competences, the Court held that this principle:

"does not prevent the Community legislature, when the application of effective, proportionate and dissuasive criminal penalties by the competent national authorities is an essential measure for combating serious environmental offences, from taking measures which relate to the criminal law of the Member States which it considers necessary in order to ensure that the rules which it lays down on environmental protection are fully effective".[45]

The *Airport Transit Visas* and *Environmental Crimes* cases show that Community competence cannot be marginalised by a political decision to adopt measures using non-Community law instruments. Although the CFSP may cover all aspects of foreign and security policy, Eeckhout argues that where the EC Treaty confers powers for

---

[42] This obligation similarly applies to Pillar 3 and PJCCM.
[43] Case C-170/96 *Commission v Council* [1998] E.C.R. I-2763.
[44] Case C-176/03 *Commission v Council* [2005] E.C.R. I-7879.
[45] Case C-176/03 *Commission v Council* [2005] E.C.R. I-7879 at para.48.

a specific form of external relations, those specific powers take precedence as a form of lex specialis (Eeckhout, 2004:151). The judgments further confirm that, despite art.46 TEU, the Court sits at the heart of a unified system of rules that underpin the EU's foreign policy efforts (Trybus, 2007:253). The Court has also ruled on the boundary between EC trade policy and CFSP in relation to goods having both military and civilian application, so-called "dual-use" goods. In *Richardt,* the Court allowed Member States to impose restrictions on the export of dual-use goods, observing that art.30 EC allowed restrictions based on the protection of public security, which could include both domestic and international security.[46] The judgment indicated that the public security argument would not give Member States free-reign to deviate from EC law, a point that was subsequently confirmed in *Centro-Com*.[47] Here the ECJ held that:

"while it is for Member States to adopt measures for foreign and security policy in the exercise of their national competence, those measures must nevertheless respect the provisions adopted by the Community in the field of common commercial policy".[48]

Despite UK fears about an expansionist and integrationist Court, the Court has hitherto respected the limits of its jurisdiction and not examined the substance of actions against the CFSP where these were seeking to establish liability for loss resulting from inclusion on a list of terrorist organisations[49] or of annulment proceedings.[50] This deference to the substantive choices made by the EU Institutions about the effectiveness of CSFP actions was evident in the *Bosphorus* judgment discussed in Chapter 3.[51] Here it will be recalled that the Court justified its judgment to uphold the sanctions as to do otherwise, "would jeopardise the effectiveness of the

---

[46] Case C-367/89 *Criminal Proceedings against Aimé Richardt* [1991] E.C.R. I-4621.

[47] Case C-124/95 *The Queen Ex p. Centro-Com Srl v HM Treasury and Bank of England* [1997] E.C.R. I-8.

[48] Case C-124/95 *The Queen Ex p. Centro-Com Srl v HM Treasury and Bank of England* [1997] E.C.R. I-8. at para.27.

[49] Case C-354/04P *Gestoras Pro Amnistia v Council* [2007] E.C.R. I-1579. See also Case C-355/04P *Segi v Council* [2007] E.C.R. I-1657.

[50] Case T-349/99 *Miskovic against Council* [2000] OJ C 79/35 and Case T-350/99 *Karic against Council* [2000] OJ C 79/36 (both removed from the Register).

[51] Case C-84/95 *Bosphorus Hava Yollari Turzim v Minister for Transport, Energy and Communications* [1996] E.C.R. I-3953. A similar approach was also adopted in Case C-177/95 *Ebony Maritime SA and Loten Navigation Co Ltd v Prefetto della Provincia di Brindisi* [1997] E.C.R. I-1111.

strengthening of sanctions" against the former Yugoslavia and that this justified the "negative consequences, even of a substantial nature" for non-absolute fundamental rights.[52] Similar conclusions were reached by the CFI in *Kadi*[53] and *Yusuf*,[54] where art.308 EC, combined with arts 301 and 60 EC, was used controversially by the Community to implement, via a regulation,[55] a CFSP measure to target sanctions against specific individuals with no link to the State (Garbagnati-Ketvel, 2006:111; Tomuschat, 2006:537).

In *Kadi*, Mr Kadi brought an action for annulment of the Council regulation before the Court of First Instance, arguing that the Council lacked competence to adopt the regulation and that the regulation breached several of his fundamental rights, notably the right to property and the right to a fair hearing. The CFI rejected Mr Kadi's claim and upheld the regulation. In so doing the CFI ruled that the Community Courts had only limited jurisdiction to review the regulation in question given that the Member States were required to comply with the UN Security Council resolutions by the terms of the UN Charter, an international treaty which took precedence over Community law.

On appeal to the Court of Justice A.G. Maduro suggests that the Court set aside the judgment of the CFI and annul the contested regulation insofar as it concerns Mr Kadi.[56] In particular, the Advocate General took the view that the CFI erred in finding that the Community Courts had only limited jurisdiction to review the regulation. The Advocate General argues that it is the Community Courts that determine the effect of international obligations within the Community legal order by reference to conditions set by Community law. In particular the Advocate General noted that the relationship between international law and the Community legal order is governed by the Community legal order itself and that international law can only take effect under the conditions prescribed by the constitutional principles of the Community. Foremost of these

---

[52] Judgment of the Court in *Bosphorus* at paras 18 and 26.
[53] Case T-315/01 *Kadi v Council and Commission* [2005] E.C.R. II-3649 (on appeal in Case C-402/05P).
[54] Case T-306/01 *Yusuf v Council and Commission* [2005] E.C.R. II-3533 (on appeal in Case C-415/05P).
[55] Council reg.(EC) No. 881/2002 of May 27, 2002 imposing certain specific restrictive measures directed against certain persons and entities associated with Osama bin Laden, the Al-Qaeda network and the Taliban, and repealing reg.(EC) No. 467/2001 (OJ 2002 L 139).
[56] C-402/05 *Yassin Abdullah Kadi v Council of the European Union and Commission of the European Communities*, Opinion of A.G. Maduro January 16, 2008.

principles is that the Community is based on respect for fundamental rights and the rule of law.

The Advocate General also rejected the view of the CFI that judicial review would be inappropriate in this case given the "political" nature of the matter in question. In the view of A.G. Maduro, the claim that a measure is necessary for the maintenance of international peace and security cannot operate so as to silence the general principles of Community law and deprive individuals of their fundamental rights. On the contrary, the Advocate General argues that when the risks to public security are believed to be extraordinarily high and the pressure to take measures that disregard individual rights is particularly strong, it is the duty of the courts to uphold the rule of law with increased vigilance.

Advocate General Maduro addresses directly the conflict that on occasion exists between international law obligations and the fundamental principles of Community law. In particular the Advocate General is of the opinion that the EU cannot dispense with judicial review proceedings when implementing the UN Security Council resolutions. In so doing, the resulting absence of any possibility of an applicant in Mr Kadi's position to seek an independent review of the implementing EU measure which infringes his fundamental rights. For A.G. Maduro this cannot be permitted in an EU based on the rule of law and the regulation should be annulled in relation to Mr Kadi's position.

## 10.9 EU External Relations and the Protection of Fundamental Rights

In the light of the focus of the CFSP on promoting human rights the Court may seek to benchmark the EU's decisions under the CFSP to ensure that they do not breach the fundamental rights principles contained within the Charter. Menéndez (2002:485), considering this similar development (first proposed within the Constitutional Treaty), argues that the Charter should have a positive impact upon the pursuit of a common foreign policy. Article 11 TEU sets out the objectives of the CFSP and includes a commitment to safeguard the values and interests and independence of the EU within the framework of the UN Charter. Article 11 TEU also includes the objective to develop and consolidate democracy and respect for fundamental rights and freedoms, suggesting that EU seeks to "export" its values to third countries. This commitment to promoting human rights beyond its borders reflects more generally the EU's increased human rights discourse since the Maastricht Treaty. Article 6 TEU states that:

"The Union is founded on the principles of liberty, democracy, respect for human rights and fundamental freedoms and the rule of law, principles which are common to the Member States."

This policy of promoting democracy and fundamental rights which the EU pursued rigorously following the collapse of the Berlin Wall in 1989 formed an integral aspect of the social, political and economic changes which the countries of Central and Eastern Europe adopted prior to EU Accession in 2004. In the decade leading to Accession the EU signed Association Agreements with all applicant States which contained prominent human rights clauses. Additionally, regular Country Reports produced from 1997 by the Commission evaluated the progress of Accession States towards complying with acquis communitaire. These reports considered not only progress towards economic transformation, but also progress of the Accession States towards improved human rights protection, the combating of corruption and improvement of administrative capacity. Consequently, in 15 years the political and economic systems of these countries were transformed, with economic assistance and ultimately EU membership being conditional on meeting EU norms of human rights. This "carrot and stick" approach to external relations is an integral strategy of EU external relations policies generally whereby economic assistance is linked to improved standards of human rights.

Denza (2002:86) has described art.11 TEU as containing principles rather than operational objectives, with the CFSP being less precise than common policies under the EC Treaty. For Denza (2002:96) this lack of specificity distinguishes the "common" policy of the CFSP from the "single" policy that characterises decisions of the EC. This identifies one reason why progress on the CFSP has remained slow. For example, attempts to create closer military co-operation between the Member States, as provided for by art.17 TEU, have proved limited. One reason for this is that Member States cannot agree on the objectives of a common policy and how this will co-exist with the responsibilities that many Member States have towards NATO. Furthermore, closer military co-operation creates difficulties for some Member States which feel that this may compromise their status of neutrality. The Nice Treaty strengthened the "security" dimension of the CFSP to form the European Security and Defence Policy (ESDP) and this development has been viewed as creating a military alliance within the EU. However, this perception of EU military co-operation endangering neutrality can be identified as one reason why Irish citizens initially voted against the Nice Treaty in the April 2001 referendum.

The progress towards "common" objectives under the CFSP, where inter-governmental decision-making is characterised by the retention of the veto by Member States, has proved more difficult to achieve than "single" economic policies under the co-decision process of the EC pillar. According to Eeckhout (2004:143), the slow pace of development of the CFSP should not overshadow positive aspects which have taken place since Maastricht. In addition to the very fact that co-operation exists, Eeckhout argues that through art.11 TEU certain core values of the EU have been constitutionalised. In particular the commitment in art.11 TEU to "develop and consolidate democracy" and "respect for fundamental rights and freedoms" has, according to Eeckhout, created a "sophisticated human rights policy" which is a core component of the CFSP.

The promotion of human rights has been a distinct characteristic of the EU's external relations strategy. A strong commitment to human rights in art.6 TEU is a foundation of the EU, so it is not all surprising that the EU seeks to promote human rights through its external policies, for example through the use of development co-operation as provided for by art.177 (2) EC and reg.975/1999. Regulation 975/1999 introduces the European Initiative for Democracy and Human Rights (EIDHR). This regulation lays down the requirements for the implementation of development co-operation actions. The objective of these actions is to contribute to the development and consolidation of democracy and the rule of law and to that of respecting human rights and fundamental freedoms.

The Commission's action in the field of external relations is guided by compliance with the rights and principles contained in the EU Charter of Fundamental Rights and a European Council Resolution of June 29, 1991. This states that respect for human rights, the rule of law and the existence of political institutions which are effective, accountable and enjoy democratic legitimacy are the basis for equitable development. In 2001 the Commission expanded upon these objectives and published a Communication[57]

---

[57] COM (2001) 252 final, *Communication From the Commission to the Council and the European Parliament the European Union's Role in Promoting Human Rights and Democratisation in Third Countries.*

which considered what role the EU should undertake with regard to promoting human rights beyond its borders. The Communication stated[58]:

> "The basis for European Union action is clear. The European Union seeks to uphold the universality and indivisibility of human rights—civil, political, economic, social and cultural. . ."

The Communication identified three areas where the Commission can act effectively in the context of external relations and human rights. Firstly, it suggests that the EU can promote coherent and consistent policies in support of human rights and democratisation. This applies both to coherence between, in particular, the CCP and the CFSP. It also relates to the promotion of consistent and complementary action by the EU and Member States through the promotion and mainstreaming of human rights within development co-operation and other economic assistance.

Secondly the Communication states that by attributing a higher priority on human rights and democratisation in the EU's relations with third countries and taking a more pro-active approach, the EU can take a world lead in promoting fundamental rights. The Commission identifies that by using the opportunities offered by political dialogue, the CCP and external economic assistance, the EU can exert effective pressure particularly in circumstances when broader world opinion, expressed through the UN, remains divided. For example, in the case of Zimbabwe the EU has acted to implement economic sanctions despite the absence of a UN resolution.[59] This demonstrates that the CFSP objectives operate alongside the CCP and external trade policy of the EC Pillar. Thirdly, the Communication suggests that the EU needs to adopt a more strategic approach to the EIDHR and matching aid and technical assistance programmes and projects in the field with EU commitments on human rights and democracy.

To promote human rights and democratisation objectives in external relations, the EU draws on a wide-range of instruments. These derive from the EU's commitment to protect fundamental rights as reaffirmed by the Charter. Some methods constitute tradi-

---

[58] COM (2001) 252 final, *Communication From the Commission to the Council and the European Parliament the European Union's Role in Promoting Human Rights and Democratisation in Third Countries,* at p.3.

[59] Common Position 2002/145/CFSP OJ L 2002 50/1.

tional diplomacy and foreign policy, such as demarches (political acts) and interventions in UN Fora, and trade sanctions. Others include financial co-operation instruments and bilateral dialogue as complimentary mechanisms. Some are more innovative, and potentially underused, namely Community instruments in policy areas such the environment, trade, the information society and immigration, which have the scope to include human rights and democratisation objectives. The EU's Neighbourhood Strategy is one such example of this type of co-operation which addresses, inter alia, immigration issues with third countries and provides financial support to counteract illegal immigration and social problems. This assistance is provided on the proviso that recipient countries give increased considerations to human rights reforms.

The EU's external relations policy continues to pursue an ethical agenda of democratisation, improved human rights and humanitarian assistance. Though economic considerations remain central to external relations through the CCP, these economic relations have become progressively influenced by the EU's desire to export EU values and norms. Consequently, trade agreements, such as the EC-India Agreement have mainstreamed EU human rights values and demonstrate the interaction between commercial relations and the EU's development policy, and the broader political objectives of improved human rights protection which the EU has set. The EU has still to create a real CFSP and it is unlikely, given the different strategic priorities of 27 Member States that it will fully succeed in doing so. Despite this the EU has, at the very least, established a set of principles which guide its relations with third countries. These principles, based upon the respect for fundamental rights and the rule of law as prerequisites for economic interaction, are contributing to the creation a joined up external relations policy which, following the Treaty of Lisbon, will remain divided between the pillars.

# Bibliography

Albors-Llorens, A. (2007) "The Principle of State Liability in EC Law and the Supreme Courts of the Member States" 66 *Cambridge Law Journal*, 270.

Allen, D., (2000) "Cohesion and the Structural Funds: Transfers and Trade Offs" in Wallace, H. and Wallace, W., (eds), *Policy-Making in the European Union* (Oxford: OUP 4th ed)

Alter, K. and Vargas, K. (2000) "Explaining Variation in the Use of European Litigation Strategies: European Community Law and British Gender Equality Policy" 33 *Comparative Political Studies* 452

Amato, G. (1997) *Antitrust and the Bounds of Power* (Oxford: Hart).

Amtenbrink, F., (1999) *The Democratic Accountability of Central Banks: a Comparative Study of the European Central Bank* (Oxford: Hart).

Andenas, M., Gormley, L., Hadjiemmanuil, C., and Harden, I., (eds), (1977) *European Economic and Monetary Union: the Institutional Framework* (London: Kluwer).

Areeda, P. (1999) "Essential Facilities: An Epithet in Need of Limiting Principles" 58 *Antitrust Law Journal* 841.

Armour, J (2005) "Who Should Make Corporate Law? EC Legislation Versus Regulatory Competition" 58 *Current Legal Problems* 369.

Armstrong, K. (2002) "Mutual Recognition" in C. Barnard and J. Scott (eds), *The Law of the Single Market: Unpacking the Premises* (Oxford: Hart).

Armstrong, K., and Kilpatrick, C. (2007) "Law, Governance, or New Governance? The Changing Open Method of Co-ordination" 13 *Colombia Journal of European Law* 649.

Arnull, A. (2006) *The European Union and its Court of Justice* (Oxford: OUP).

Arnull, A. (2004) "Editorial" 29 *European Law Review* 288.

Arnull, A. (2001) "Private Applicants Since *Cordoniu*" 38 *Common Market Law Review* 1.

Arnull, A. (1999) 'Judicial Architecture or Judicial Folly? The Challenge Facing the European Union' 24 *European Law Review* 516.

Arnull, A., Dashwood, A., Ross, M., Wyatt, D. (2000) *Wyatt and Dashwood's European Union Law* (London: Sweet and Maxwell).

Ashiagbor, D. (2005) *The European Employment Strategy: Labour Market Regulation and New Governance* (Oxford: OUP).

Avgerinos, Y. (2003) "The Need and the Rationale for a European Securities Regulator" in Andenas, M. and Avgerinos, Y., (eds) *Financial Markets in Europe: Towards a Single Regulator?* (The Hague: Kluwer).

Bantekas, I. (2007) "The Principle of Mutual Recognition in EU Criminal Law" 32 *European Law Review* 365.

Baquero Cruz, J. (2002) *Between Competition and Free Movement* (Oxford: Hart).

Barber, N.W. (2002) "Citizenship, Nationalism and the European Union" 27 *European Law Review* 241.

Barnard, C. (2001) "Fitting the Pieces into the Goods and Services Jigsaw?" 26 *European Law Review* 35.

Barrett, G., (2003) "Family Matters: European Community Law and Third Country Family Members", 40 *Common Market Law Review* 369.

Bartosch, A. "The Relationship Between Public Procurement an State Aid Surveillance—the Toughest Standard Applies?" (2002) 39 *Common Market Law Review* 551.

Bavasso, A. (2004) "Electronic Communications: A New Paradigm For European Regulation" 41 *Common Market Law Review* 87.

Bell, M., (2002) *Anti-Discrimination Law in the EU* (Oxford: OUP)

Bell, M., (2008) "The Implementation of European Antidiscrimination Directives: Converging Towards A Common Model?" 79 *The Political Quarterly* 36.

Bercusson, B. (2007) "The Trade Union Movement and the European Union: Judgment Day" 13 *European Law Journal* 279.

Bloom, M. "The US and EU Move Towards Substantial Antitrust Convergence on Consumer Welfare Based Enforcement" (2005) 19 *Antitrust* 18.

Bishop, W. (1981) "Price Discrimination under Article 86 : Political Economy in the European Court" 66 *Modern Law Review* 282.

Bogusz, B. (2004) "Modes of Governance for an EU Immigration Policy—What Role for the Open Method of Co-ordination" in B. Bogusz *et. al.* (eds.) *Irregular Migration and Human Rights* (The Hague: Brill/Kluwer).

Bogusz, B. (2002) "Regulating the Right of Establishment For Accession State Nationals: Reinforcing the Buffer Zone or Improving Labour Market Flexibility?" (2002) *European Law Review* 272.

Burnley, R., (2007) "Conglomorate Mergers" in Amato, G., and Ehlermann, C-D., *EC Competition Law. A Critical Assessment* (Oxford: Hart).

Burrows, N. and Robinson, M. (2007) "An Assessment of the Recast Equality Laws" 13 *European Law Journal* 186.

Cardwell, M. (2004) *The European Model of Agriculture* (Oxford: OUP).

Cardwell, M. and Rodgers, C., (2006) "Reforming the WTO Legal Order for Agricultural Trade: Issues for European Regional Policy in the Doha Round" 55 *International and Comparative Law Quarterly* 805.

Carrerra, S. (2005) 'What Does Free Movement Mean in an Enlarged EU'? 11 *European Law Journal* 699.

Chalmers, D., (1985) "Environmental Protection and the Single Market: An Unsustainable Development. Does the EC Treaty Need a Title on the Environment?" 1 *Legal Issues of European Integration* 65.

Chalmers, D. (1998) *European Union Law ( Volume 1 ) Law and EU Government* (Dartmouth: Ashgate).

Chalmers, D. "Inhabitants in the Field of EC Environmental Law" in Craig, P. and De Búrca, G. (eds), *The Evolution of EU Law* (Oxford, OUP, 1999).

Chalmers, D., (2005) 'Risk, Anxiety and the European Mediation of the Politics of Life.' 30 *European Law Review* 649.

Close, G. (1978) "Harmonisation of Laws: Use or Abuse of the Powers Under the EEC Treaty?" 3 *European Law Review* 461.

Collins, D. (1983) "Social Policy" in Lodge, J., (ed) *Institutions and Policies of the European Community* (London, Frances Pinter).

Competition Law Forum Article 82 Review Group, (2005) 1 *European Competition Law Journal.*

Comte, F. and Krämer, L. (eds) (2004) *Environmental Crime in Europe: Rules of Sanctions* (Groningen, Europa Law Publishing).

Coppell, J. and O'Neill, A. (1992) "The European Court of Justice: Taking Rights Seriously" 29 *Common Market Law Review* 669.

Craig, P (1993) "Francovich, Remedies and the Scope of Damages Liability" 109 *Law Quarterly Review* 595.

Craig, P. (1991) "United Kingdom Sovereignty after Factortame"11 *Yearbook of European Law* 221.

Craig, P. (1997) "Directives, Direct Effect, Indirect Effect and the Construction of National Legislation" 22 *European Law Review* 519.

Craig, P. (1999) "The Nature of the Community: Integration, Democracy and Legitimacy" in P. Craig and G. De Búrca (eds) *The Evolution of EU Law* (Oxford: OUP).

Craig, P. (2002) "The Evolution of the Single Market" in C. Barnard and J. Scott (eds) *The Law of the Single European Market* (Hart, Oxford) 1.

Craig, P. and De Búrca, G. (2003) *EU Law Text, Cases and Materials* (Oxford: OUP).

Craufurd-Smith, R. (2004) "Community Intervention in the Cultural Field: Continuity or Change?" in Craufurd-Smith, R. (ed.) *Culture and European Union Law* (Oxford: OUP).

Craufurd-Smith, R. (ed.) (2004) *Culture and European Union Law* (Oxford: OUP).

Craufurd-Smith, R., (2007) "From Heritage Conservation to European Identity: Article 151 and the Multifaceted Nature of Community Cultural Policy" 32 *European Law Review* 48.

Cremona, M. (1990) "The Completion of the Internal Market and the Incomplete Commercial Policy of the European Community" 15 *European Law Review* 283.

Cremona, M (1998) 'The European Union as an International Actor: The Issues of Flexibility and Linkage' 3 *European Foreign Affairs Review* 67.

Cremona, M. (2000) "EC External Commercial Policy after Amsterdam: Authority and Interpretation within Interconnected Legal Orders" in J. Weiler (ed.) *Towards a Common Law of International Trade? The EU, the WTO and the NAFTA* (Oxford: OUP).

Curtin, D. (1993) "The Constitutional Structure of the Union: A Europe of Bits and Pieces" 30 *Common Market Law Review* 17.

Curtin, D. and Meijers, J. (1995) "The Principle of Open Government in Schengen and the European Union: Democratic Retrogression" 32 *Common Market Law Review* 391.

Cygan, A. (2000) "Defining a Sufficiently Serious Breach of Community Law—the House of Lords Casts its Nets in to the Waters" 25 *European Law Review* 117.

Cygan, A. (2003) "Protecting the Interests of Civil Society in Community Decision-Making—The Limits of Article 230 EC" 52 *International Comparative Law Quarterly* 995.

Cygan, A. (2004) "European Union Immigration Policy after Enlargement—Building the New Europe or the New Iron Curtain?" in B. Bogusz *et al.* (eds), *Irregular Migration and Human Rights: Theoretical, European and International Perspectives* (The Hague: Brill/Kluwer) 239.

Dashwood, A. (1999) "External Relations of the Amsterdam Treaty" in O'Keeffe, D. and Twomey, P. (eds) *Legal Issue of the Amsterdam Treaty* (Oxford: Hart Publishing).

Dashwood, A., (2007) "Reducing Direct Effect to Absurdity" in Barnard, C., (ed) 9 *Cambridge Yearbook of European Law* 2006–7, 81.

Davies, G., (2003) *Nationality Discrimination in the European Internal Market* (The Hague: Kluwer).

Davies, G. (2004) "Community Law and National Health Systems in the Light of Muller-Fauré" 67 *Modern Law Review* 97.

Davies, G. (2005) "Can Selling Arrangements Be Harmonised?" 30 *European Law Review* 371.

Davies, G. (2007) "The Services Directive: Extending the Country of Origin Principle and Reforming Public Administration" 32 *European Law Review* 232.

De Búrca, G. and Scott,. J., (eds) (2005) *New Governance, Law and Constitutionalism* (Oxford: Hart).

De Búrca, G. (2006) "EU Race Discrimination Law: A Hybrid Model?" in De Búrca, G. and Scott, J. *Law and New Governance in the EU and US* (Oxford: Hart).

De Witte, B., (2006a) "Non-market Values in Internal Market Legislation" in Nic Shuibhne, N., (ed) *Regulating the Internal Market* (Edward Elgar: Cheltenham).

De Witte, B. (2006b) "Setting the Scene—How Did Services Get to Bolkestein and Why? *The Mitchell Working Paper Series, Europa Institute Working.* University of Edinburgh, available at: *http://www.law.ed.ac.uk/mitchellworkingpapers/papers.aspx* [Accessed April 14, 2008]

de Zwaan, J.W. (1999) "The Legal Personality of the European Communities" *Netherlands Yearbook of International Law* 75.

Deakin, S. (1999) "Two Types of Regulatory Competition: Competitive Federalism versus Reflexive Harmonisation. A Law and Economics Perspective on Centros" 2 *Cambridge Yearbook of European Legal Studies* 231.

Dehousse, R. (1998) "European Institutional Architecture After Amsterdam: Parliamentary System Or Regulatory Structure?" 35 *Common Market Law Review* 595.

Denza, E. (2002) *The Intergovernmental Policies of the EU* (Oxford: OUP).

Devroe, W. (1997) "Privatizations and Community Law: Neutrality versus Policy" 34 *Common Market Law Review* 267.

Dhondt, N., (2003) *Integration of Environmental Protection Into Other EC Policies* (Groningen, Europa Law Pub.)

Doherty, (2001) "Just What Are Essential Facilities?" 38 *Common Market Law Review* 397.

Dörmer, S. (2000) "Dispute Settlement and New Developments Within the Framework of TRIPs—An Interim Review" 31 *International Review of Industrial Property and Copyright Law* 1.

Douglas-Scott, S. (2002) *Constitutional Law of the European Union* (London: Longman).

Edwards, V. (1999) *EC Company Law* (Oxford: OUP).

Eeckhout, P. (2004) *External Relations of the European Union, Legal and Constitutional Foundations* (Oxford: OUP).

Egan, M. (2001) *Constructing a European Market* (Oxford: OUP).

Ehlermann, C-D. (1992) "The Contribution of EC Competition Policy to the Single Market" 29 *Common Market Law Review* 257.

Eleftheriadis, P. (2007) "Environmental Rights in the European Legal Order" 27 *Yearbook of European Law*.

Ellis, E. (ed) (1999) *The Principle of Proportionality in the Laws of Europe* (Oxford: OUP).

Enchelmaier, S. (2003) "The Awkward Selling of a Good Idea, or a Traditionalist Interpretation of *Keck*" (2003) 20 *Yearbook of European Law* 249.

Evans, A., (1999) *The EU Structural Funds* (Oxford: OUP).

Evans, A., (2003) "Evolutionary Problems of EU Law: The Case of the Union Funds" 30 *Legal Issues of European Integration* 201.

Flynn, L. (2002) "Coming of Age: The Free Movement of Capital Case Law 1993–2002 (2002) 39 *Common Market Law Review* 773.

Fox, E., (2003) "We Protect Competition, You Protect Competitors" *World Competition Law and Economics Review* 149.

Fox, E. (2006) "Monopolization, Abuse of Dominance, and the Indeterminancy of Economics: The US/E.U. Divide" *Utah Law Review* 724.

Furse, M., (2007) *The Law of Merger Control in the EC and the UK* (Hart: Oxford).

Friend, M. (2004) "State Guarantees as State Aid: Some Practical Difficulties" in Biondi, A. *et al.* (eds), *The Law of State Aid in the European Union,* (Oxford: OUP).

Garbagnati Ketvel, M-G, (2006) 'The Jurisdiction of the European Court of Justice in Respect of the Common Foreign and Security Policy' 66 *International Comparative Law Quarterly* 77

Gerber, D. (1998) *Law and Competition in Twentieth Century Europe: Protecting Prometheus* (Oxford: Clarendon Press).

Gerber, D. (2003) "The European Commission's GE/Honeywell Decision: US Responses and Their Implications" 1 *Journal of Comparative Law* 87.

Gerstenberg, O., (2002) "Expanding the Constitution beyond the Court: The Case of Euro-Constitutionalism" 8 *European Law Journal* 172.

Golynker, O. (2006) *Ubiquitous Citizens of Europe: The Paradigm of Partial Migration* (Antwerp: Intersentia).

Gormley, L. and de Haan, J. "The Democratic Deficit of the European Central Bank" (1996) 21 *ELRev* 95.

Gormley, L. (2008) "Silver Threads Among the Gold . . . 50 Years of the Free Movement of Goods" *Fordham International Law Journal*, forthcoming.

Graham, C. and Smith, F. (eds.) (2004) *Competition Law and the New Economy* (Oxford: Hart).

Gravells, N. (1991) "Effective Protection of Community Law Rights: Temporary Disapplication of an Act of Parliament" *Public Law* 180.

Hahn, H. (1998) "The Stability and Growth Pact for European and Monetary Union: Compliance with Deficit Limit as a Constant Legal Duty" 35 *Common Market Law Review* 77.

Halstein, W. (1962) *United Europe, Challenge and Opportunity* (Cambridge, Massachusetts: Harvard University Press).

Harding, C. (2000) "The Identity of European Law: Mapping Out the European Legal Space" 6 *European Law Journal* 128.

Harlow, C. (1996) "Francovich and the Problem of the Disobedient State" 2 *European Law Journal* 199.

Harlow, C. (2002) "Public Law and Popular Justice" 65 *Modern Law Review* 1.

Harm, S. (2002) "Delegation of Regulatory Powers to Private Parties under EC Competition Law: Towards a Procedural Public Interest Test" 39 *Common Market Law Review* 31.

Hartley, T. (1998) *Foundations of European Community Law* (Oxford: OUP).

Hartley, T. (2001) "The Constitutional Foundation of the European Union" 117 Law *Quarterly Review* 225.

Hattan, E., (2003) "The Implementation of EU Environmental Law" (2003) 15 *Journal of Environmental Law* 273.

Hatzopolous, V. (2002) "*Killing* National Health Insurance System but *Healing* Patients? The European Market for Healthcare Services After the Judgments of the ECJ in *Vanbraekel* and *Peerbooms*" 39 *Common Market Law Review* 683.

Hatzopoulos, V. (2008) "With or Without You. . . Judging Politically in the Field of Area of Freedom, Security and Justice" 33 *European Law Review* 44.

Hepple, B. (1987) "The Crisis in EEC Labour Law" 18 *Industrial Law Journal* 129.

Heiderhoff, B and Kenny, M. (2007) "The Commission's 2007 Green Paper on the Consumer Acquis: Deliberate Deliberation?" 32 *European Law Review* 740.

Hervey, T. and McHale, J. (2004) *Health Law and the European Union* (Cambridge, CUP).

Hervey, T. (2006–7) "The Current Legal Framework on the Right to Seek Health Care Abroad in the European Union" 9 *Cambridge Yearbook of European Legal Studies* 261.

Hodson, D. and Maher, I., (2004) "Soft Law and Sanctions: Economic Policy Coordination and Reform of the Stability and Growth pact" 11 *Journal of European Public Policy* 798.

Hodson, D., and Maher, I. (2005) "The Open Method as a New Mode of Governance: The Case of Soft Economic Policy Co-ordination" 11 *European Law Journal* 343.

Hoskyns, C., (1996) *Integrating Gender—Women, Law and Politics in the European Union* (London: Verso).

Howard, E. (2006) "The Case for a Considered Hierarchy of Discrimination Grounds in EU Law" 13 *Maastricht Journal of European and Comparative Law* 445.

Howells, G. and Wilhelmsson, T., (2003) "EC Consumer Law: Has it Come of Age?" 28 *European Law Review* 370.

Howells, G., and Weatherill, S. (2005) *Consumer Protection Law* (Aldershott: Ashgate, 2nd ed).

House of Lords, HL 106 (2002–3) *The Future of Europe: Constitutional Treaty—Articles 33–37 (The Democratic Life of the Union)* (London: HMSO).

Jacobs, F.G. (2004) 'Recent and ongoing measures to improve the efficiency of the European Court of Justice', 29 *European Law Review*, 823.

Jacobs, F. (2006) "The Role of the European Court of Justice in the Protection of the Environment" 18 *Journal of Environmental Law* 185.

Jans, J., (1997) "The Effect in National Legal Systems of the Prohibition of Discrimination on Grounds of Age as a General Principle of Community Law" 34 *Legal Issues of European Integration* 53

Jans, J. and Scott, J. "The Convention on the Future of Europe: an Environmental Perspective" (2003) 15 *Journal of Environmental Law* 323.

Jans, J. and Vedder, H. (2008) *European Environmental Law* (Groningen, Europa Law Pub.)

Joerges, C. and Vos, E. (eds), (1999) *EU Committees: Social Regulation, Law and Politics* (Oxford: Hart).

Joerges, C. (1999) "Bureaucratic Nightmare, Technocratic Regime and the Dream of Good Transnational Governance" in Joerges, C. and Vos, E. (eds), *EU Committees: Social Regulation, Law and Politics* (Oxford: Hart).

Jong, de, H., (1966–67) "Concentration in the Common Market: a Comment on a Memorandum of the EEC Commission 4 *Common Market Law Review* 166.

Kingston, S. (2006–07) "The Boundaries of Sovereignty: The ECJ's Controversial Role Applying Internal Market Law to Direct Tax Measures" 9 *CYELS* 287.

Kokkoris, I. (2005) "SLC v Dominance" 26 *European Competition Law Review* 37.

Kosior, K. (2005) "New Stakeholders in the Common Agricultural policy: A Real Burden to Reform Processes in the Enlarged European Union?" 11 *European Law Journal* 566.

Kostakopoulou, D. (2007) "The Area of Freedom, Security and Justice and the European Union's Constitutional Dialogue" in Barnard, C. (ed) *The Fundamentals of EU Law Revisited* (Oxford; OUP).

Koutrakos, P. (2002) "The Interpretation of Mixed Agreements under the Preliminary Reference Procedure" 7 *European Foreign Affairs Review* 25.

Krajewski, M. and Farley, M., (2004) "Limited Competition in National Health Sytems and the Application of Competition Law: the *AOK Bundesverband Case*" 29 *European Law Review* 842.

Krajewski, M., and Farley, M., (2007) "Non-economic Activities in Upstream and Downstream Markets and the Scope of Competition Law after *FENIN*" 32 *European Law Review* 111.

Kroepelian, K., (2000) "Extended Producer Responsibility—New Legal Structures for Improved Ecological Self-Organisation in Europe?" 9 *Review of European Community and International Environmental Law* 165.

Kühn, K-U. and Caffara, C. (2005) "Economic Theories of Bundling and their Policy Implications in Abuse Cases An Assessment in the Light of the Microsoft Case" 1 *European Competition Law Journal*.

Kurzer, P. (2001) *Markets and Moral Regulation, Cultural Change in the European Union* (Cambridge: CUP).

Langrish, S. (1998) "The Treaty of Amsterdam: Selected Highlights" 23 *European Law Review* 3.

Lasok, D. and Bridge, J. (1991) *Law and Institutions of the European Community* (London: Butterworths).

Lavranos, N. (2005) 'The New Specialised Courts Within the European Judicial System', 30 *European Law Review* 261.

Laenaerts, K., (1994) "The Principle of Subsidiarity and the Environment in the European Union: Keeping the Balance of Federalism" 17 *Fordham International Law Journal* 846

Laenaerts, K. (2003) "Interlocking Legal Orders in the European Union and Comparative Law" 52 *International Comparative Law Quarterly* 873.

Laenarts, K. (2007) 'The Rule of Law and the Coherence of the Judicial System in the European Union' (2007) 44 *Common Market Law Review* 1652.

Laenarts K. and Courhaut, T. (2006) 'Of Birds and Hedges: The Role of Primacy in Invoking Norms of EU Law' 31 *European Law Review* 287.

Lenschow, A. (2002) "New Regulatory Approaches in 'Greening' EU Policies" 8.1. *European Law Journal* 19.

Lenz, M, Sif Tynes, D, Young, L. (2000) "Horizontal What? Back to Basics" 25 *European Law Review* 509.

Lohse, E. (2007) "Fundamental Freedoms and Private Actors" 13 *European Public Law* 159.

Louis, J-V., (2004) "The Economic and Monetary Union: Law and Institutions" 41 *Common Market Law Review* 575.

Louis, J-V., (2006) "The Review of the Stability and Growth Pact" 43 *Common Market Law Review* 85.

Maduro, M. (1998) *We.the Court: The European Court of Justice and the Economic Constitution* (Oxford: Hart).

Maduro, Poiares, M. (2000a) "The Scope of European Remedies: The Case of Purely Internal Situations and Reverse Discrimination" in Kilpatrick, C. *et al.* (eds), *The Future of Remedies in Europe* (Oxford: Hart).

Maduro Poiares, M., (2000b) "Europe's Social Self: The Sickness Unto Death" in Shaw, J., (ed) *Social Law and Policy in an Evolving European Union* (Oxford: Hart).

Moloney, N. (2003) "New Frontiers in EC Capital Markets Law: From Market Construction to Market Regulation" 40 *Common Market Law Review* 809.

Maloney, N., (2007) "Innovation and Risk in EC Financial Markets Regulation; New Instruments of Financial Market Intervention and the Committee of European Securities Regulators" 32 *European Law Review* 627.

McGee, A and Weatherill, S. (1990) "The Evolution of the Single Market—Harmonisation or Liberalisation" 53 *Modern Law Review* 578.

McGoldrick, D. (1997) *International Relations Law of the European Union* (London: Longman).

McMahon, J. (2007) *The Common Agricultural Policy* (Oxford: OUP).

Menéndez, A.J. (2002) "Chartering Europe: Legal Status and Policy Implications of the Charter of Fundamental Rights of the European Union" 40 *Journal of Common Market Studies* 471.

Millns, S. and Aziz, M. (2005) (eds), *Values in the Constitution of Europe* (Dartmouth: Ashgate).

Monar, J. (1997) "The European Union's Foreign Affairs System after the Treaty of Amsterdam: A "Strengthened Capacity for External Action?" 2 *European Foreign Affairs Review* 413.

Monnet, J. (1978) *Memoirs* (New York: Doubleday & Co. Inc).

Monti, G. (2002) "Article 81 EC and Public Policy" 39 *Common Market Law Review* 1057.

Monti, G., (2007) "Merger Defences, Efficiency, Failing Firms and Industrial Policy" in Amato, G., and Ehlermann, C-D., (eds) *EC Competition Law. A Critical Assessment* (Oxford: Hart).

Mortelmans, K. (2001) "Towards Convergence in the Application of the Rules on Free Movement and On Competition" 38 *Common Market Law Review* 613.

Nagy, Istvan, C., (2007) "Refusal To Deal and the Doctrine of Essential Facilities in US and EC Competition Law: A Comparative Perspective and a Proposal for a Workable Analytical Framework" 32 *European Law Review* 664.

Nassimpian, D. (2007) "And We Keep on Meeting: (de)fragmenting State Liability, 32 *European Law Review* 819.

Nebbia, P., *Unfair Terms in European Law: A Study in EC and Comparative Law* (Oxford: Hart).

Nielsen, R. and Szyszczak, E., (1997) *The Social Dimension of the European Union* (Handelshojskolens Forlag,: Copenhagen).

Newdick, C., "Citizenship, Free Movement and Healthcare: Cementing Individual Rights by Corroding Social Solidarity?" 43 *Common Market Law Review* 1645.

Nichol, J. (1984) "The Luxembourg Compromise" 23 *Journal of Common Market Studies* 35.

Nicolaides, P. (2005) "Markets and Words: the Distortive Effect of Government Pronouncements" *European Competition Law Review* 119.

Obradovic, D. (2007) "EC Rules on Public Participation in Environmental Decision-Making at the European and National levels" 32 *European Law Review* 839.

O'Neill, A. (1994) *Decision of the European Court of Justice and their National Implications* (London: Butterworths).

Odudo, O, (2001) "Interpreting Article 81(1): object as subjective intention" 26 *European Law Review* 60.

Odudo, O. (2006) *The Boundaries of EC Competition Law: The Scope of Article 81* (Oxford: OUP).

Oliver, P. and Roth, W-H. (2004) "The Internal Market and the Four Freedoms" 41 *Common Market Law Review* 407.

Ortino, M. (2007) The Role and Functioning of Mutual Recognition in the European Market of Financial Services" 56 *International and Comparative Law Quarterly* 309.

Peers, S. (2002) "Free Movement of Capital: Learning Lessons or Slipping on Spilt Milk?" in C. Barnard and J. Scott. (eds) *The Law of the Single European Market: Unpacking the Premises* (Oxford: Hart).

Peers,. S. (2004) "Mutual Recognition and Criminal Law in the European Union: Has the Council Got It Wrong?" 41 *Common Market Law Review* 5.

Pescatore, P. (1983) "The Doctrine of 'Direct Effect: An Infant Disease of Community Law" 8 *European Law Review* 155.

Pescatore, P. (1987) "Some Critical Remarks on the Single European Act" 24 *Common Market Law Review* 9.

Pisani-Ferry, J. (2006) "Only One Bed For Two Dreams: A Critical Retrospective on the Debate Over the Governance of the Euro Area" 22 *Journal of Common Market Studies* 823.

Radaelli, C. (2003) "The Code of Conduct Against Harmful Tax Competition: Open Method of Co-ordination in Disguise?" 81. *Public Administration* 513.

Rasmussen, H. (1988) "Between Self-Restraint and Activism: a Judicial Policy for the European Court" 13 *European Law Review* 28.

Rasmussen, H. (2000) 'Remedying the Crumbling EC Judicial System' 37 *Common Market Law Review* 1071.

Reich, N. (1994) "The 'November Revolution' of the European Court of Justice: *Keck, Meng and Audi* revisited" 31 *Common Market Law Review* 459.

Reich, N., (2007) "Free Movement vs Social Rights in an Enlarged Union: The *Laval* and *Viking* Case Before the ECJ" available at: http://digitalcommons.law.umaryland.edu/cgi/viewcontent.cgi? article=1000&context=soceuro [Accessed April 14, 2008]

Ritter, C. (2006) 'Purely Internal Situations, Reverse Discrimination, *Guimont, Dzodzi* and Article 234' 31 *European Law Review* 790.

Ross, M. (1993) "Beyond *Francovich*" 56 *Modern Law Review* 55.

Ross, M., (2006) 'Effectiveness in the European Legal Order(s): Beyond Supremacy to Constitutional Proportionality' 31 *European Law Review* 476–498.

Ross, M., (2007) "Promoting Solidarity: From Public Services to a European Model of Competition?" 44 *Common Market Law Review* 1057.

Ruffert, M. (2007) Case C-173/03, *Traghetti del Mediterraneo SpA In Liquidation v Italian*, 44 *Common Market Law Review*, 479.

Sadeleer, de N., (2003) "Procedures for Derogations from the Principle of Approximation of Laws under Article 95 EC" 40 *Common Market Law Review* 889.

Sadeleer, N. de., (2006) "The Precautionary Principle in European Community Health and Environmental Law" 12 *European Law Journal* 139.

Sadeleer, N. de (ed) (2007) *Implementing the Precautionary Principle: Approaches from the Nordic Countries, EU and USA* (London: Earthscan).

Sari, A. (2008) 'The Conclusion of International Agreements by the European Union in the Context of the ESDP' 57 *International Comparative Law Quarterly* 53.

Sassatelli, M. (2007), "The Arts, The State and the EU: Cultural Policy in the Making of Europe" 51 *Social Analysis* 28.

Sauter, W. (1997) *Competition Law and Industrial Policy in the EU* (Oxford: Clarendon Press).

Schäfaer, A., (2006) "A Form of Governance? Comparing the Open Method of Co-ordination to Multilateral Surveillance by the IMF and the OECD" 13 *Journal of European Public Policy* 70.

Scharpf, F. (1999) *Governing in Europe: Effective and Democratic?* (Oxford: OUP).

Scharpf, F. (2002) "The European Social Model: Coping With the Challenges of Diversity" 40 *Journal of Common Market Studies* 645.

Schön, W. (2005) "Playing Different Games? Regulatory Competition in Tax and Company Law Compared" 42 *Common Market Law Review* 331.

Schon, W., "Special Charges: A Gap in European Competition Law" (2006) *European State Aid Law* 5.

Schmitter, P. (2000) *How to Democratize the European Union . . . and Why Bother?* (Maryland: Lantham).

Scott, A., (2006) National Champions and the Two-Thirds Rule in Merger Control" Available at: *http://www.ccp.uea.ac.uk/publicfiles/ workingpapers/CCP06-6.pdf* [Accessed April 14, 2008]

Scott, J. (1995) *Development Dilemmas in the European Community: Rethinking Regional Development Policy* (Oxford, OUP).

Senden, L. (2004) *Soft Law in European Community Law* (Oxford: Hart).

Shackleton, M. (2000) "The Politics of Co-decision" 38 *Journal of Common Market Studies* 325.

Shapiro, M (1999) "The European Court of Justice' in P. Craig and G. De Búrca (eds) *The Evolution of EU Law* (Oxford: OUP).

Shaw, J., Hunt, J. and Wallace, C. (2007) *Economic and Social Law of the European* Union Basingstoke, Macmillan).

Shuibhne, Nic, N. (2002) "Free Movement of Persons and the Wholly Internal Rule: Time to Move On?" 39 *Common Market Law Review* 731.

Shuibhne, Nic, N. (ed.) (2005) *Regulating the Internal Market* (Edward Elgar: Cheltenham).

Smismans, S. (2007) "The European Social Dialogue Between Constitutional and Labour Law" 32 *European Law Review* 341.

Smith, K.E., (2001) 'The EU, Human Rights and Relations with Third Countries: Foreign Policy with an Ethical Dimension' in Smith, K. and Light, M. (eds) *Ethics and Foreign Policy* (Cambridge: CUP).

Snell, J. (2002) *Goods and Services in EC Law. A Study of the Relationship Between the Freedoms* (Oxford: Oxford University Press).

Snell, J. (2004) "And Then There Were Two: Products and Citizens in Community Law" in Tridimas, T. and Nebbia, P. (eds), *European Union Law for the Twenty-First Century: Volume II* (Oxford: Hart Publishing).

Snell, J. (2005) "Economic Aims as Justification for Restrictions on Free Movement" in A. Schrauwen (ed.), *Rule of Reason; Rethinking another Classic of EC Legal Doctrine* (Groningen: Europa Law Publishing).

Snyder, F. (1999) "EMU Revisited: Are We Making a Constitution? What Constitution Are We Making?" in Craig, P. and De Búrca, G. (eds) *The Evolution of EU Law* (Oxford: OUP).

Soames, T. and Maudhuit, S. (2005) "Changes in Merger Control: Part 1 and II" 26 *European Competition Law Review* 57 and 75.

Soriano, L. (2003) "How Proportionate Should Anti-Competitive State Intervention Be?" 28 *European Law Review* 112.

Statigaki, M., (2005) "Gender Mainstreaming vs Positive Action. An Ongoing Conflict in EU Gender Equality Policy" 12 *European Journal of Women's Studies* 165.

Steiner, J. (1992) "Drawing the Line: Uses and Abuses of Article 30" 29 *Common Market Law Review* 749.

Stuyck, J. (2000), "European Consumer Law After the Treaty of Amsterdam: Consumer Policy In Or Beyond the Internal Market" 37 *Common Market Law Review* 367.

Szyszczak, E. (1996) "Making Europe More Relevant to its Citizens: Effective Judicial Process" 21 *European Law Review* 351.

Szyszczak, E, (2000) *EC Labour Law* (Harrow: Longman).

Szyszczak, E. (1994) "Social Policy: A Happy Ending or a Reworking of the Fairy Tale?" in O'Keeffe, D. and Twomey, P. (eds) *Legal Issues of the Maastricht Treaty* 313.

Szyszczak, E. (2000) "A Fundamental Right To Trade?" in Economides, K. *et al.* (eds) *Fundamental Values* (Oxford: Hart).

Szyszczak, E. (2000) "The Evolving European Employment Strategy" in Shaw, J. (ed) *Social Law and Policy in an Evolving European Union* (Oxford: Hart).

Szyszczak, E. (2001) "The New Paradigm for Social Policy: A Virtuous Circle?" *Common Market Law Review* 1125.

Szyszczak, E. (2002) "Golden Shares and Market Governance" 29 *Legal Issues of Economic Integration* 35.

Szyszczak, E. (2003) "Social Policy in the Post-Nice Era" in A. Arnull and D. Wincott, (eds), *Accountability and Legitimacy in the European Union* (Oxford: OUP).

Szyszczak, E. (2004) "Regularising Regular Migration in the EU" in *Irregular Migration and Human Rights* B. Bogusz *et al.* (eds), (The Hague: Kluwer, Brill).

Szyszczak, E. (2004) "State Intervention in the Market" in Tridimas, T. and Nebbia, P. (eds.), *EU Law for the 21st Century: Rethinking the New Legal Order. volume 2* (Oxford, Hart).

Szyszczak, E. (2005) "The Regulation of Competition" in N. Nic. Shuibhne (ed.), *The Regulation of the Internal Market* (Cheltenham: Edward Elgar).

Szyszczak, E. (2005) "Experimental Governance: The Open Method of Co-ordination" 12 *European Law Journal* 486.

Szyszczak, E. (2007) *The Regulation of the State in Competitive Markets in the European Union* (Oxford: Hart).

Szyszczak, (2007) "Is Sport Special?" in Bogusz, B., Cygan, A. and Szyszczak, E. (eds) (Cheltenham, Edward Elgar).

Szyszczak, E. (2008) "Lisbon, Moscow, Kyoto: Joining the Dots" *Fordham Environmental Law Review,* forthcoming.

Temple Lang, J. (1997) "The Duties of National Courts under Community Constitutional Law" 22 *European Law Review* 3.

Tomkins, A. (1999) "Responsibility and Resignation in the European Commission" 62 *Modern Law Review* 744.

Tomuschat, C., Case T-30601, Ahmed Ali Yusuf and Al Barakaat International Foundation v. Council and Commission; Case T-31501, Yassin Abdullah Kadi v. Council and Commission (2006) 43 *Common Market Law Review* 537.

Townley, C., (2007) "Undertakings. The Concept of an "Undertaking": The Boundaries of the Corporation—A Discussion of Agency, Employees, Subsidiaries" Amato, G., and Ehlermann, C-D. (eds) *EC Competition Law. A Critical Assessment* (Oxford: Hart).

Trepte, P., (2007) *Public Procurement in the European Union* (Oxford, OUP, 2nd ed)

Tridimas, T. (1994) "Horizontal Effect of Directives: a Missed Opportunity?" 19 *European Law Review* 621.

Tridimas, T. (1996) "The Court of Justice and Judicial Activism" 21 *European Law Review* 187.

Tridimas, T. (2003) "Knocking on Heaven's Door: Fragmentation, Efficiency and Defiance in the Preliminary Rulings Procedure" 40 *Common Market Law Review* 9.

Trubeck, D. and Trubeck, L., (2005) "Hard and Soft Law in the Construction of Social Europe: The Role of the Open Method of Co-ordination" (2005) 11 *European Law Journal* 343.

Trybus, M., (2007) 'The Vision of the European Defence Community and a Common Defence for the European Union' in Trybus, M. and White, N. (eds). *European Security Law* (Oxford: OUP).

Usher, J. (2002) *EC Agricultural Law* (Oxford: OUP).

Usher, J. (2003) "Direct and Individual Concern—an Effective Remedy or a Conventional Solution?' 29 *European Law Review* 300.

Usher, J. (2005) "Monetary Movements and the Internal Market" in Nic Shuibhne, N. (ed) *Regulating the Internal Market* (Edward Elgar, Cheltenham).

Van den Bogaert, S. (2002) "Horizontality" in Barnard, C. and Scott, J. (eds), *The Law of the Single Market* (Oxford: Hart).

Van der Mei, A. P (2002) "Cross-border Access to Health Care Within the European Union: Some Reflections on Geraets-Smit and Peerbooms and Vanbraekel" 9 *Maastricht Journal* 189.

Van Gerven, W. (1996) "Bridging the Unbridgeable: Community and National Tort Laws After Francovich and Brasserie" 45 *International Comparative Law Quarterly* 507.

Wade, W. (1996) "Sovereignty—Revolution or Evolution" 112 *Law Quarterly Review,* 568.

Waddington, L., and Bell, M. (2001) "More Equal than Others: Distinguishing European Union Equality Directives" 38 *Common Market Law Review* 587.

Wathelet, M. (2001) "The Influence of Free Movement of Persons, Services and Capital on National Direct Taxation" 20 *Yearbook of European Law* 1.

Weatherill, S. (1995) "Playing Safe: the United Kingdom's Implementation of the New Approach Directive" in T. Daintith, (ed.) *Implementing EC Law in the UK: Structures for Indirect Rule* (Chichester: Wiley).

Weatherill, S. (2000) "New Strategies for Managing the EC's Internal Market" 53 *Current Legal Problems* 595.

Weatherill, S., (2001) 'Breach of Directives and Breach of Contract' 26 *European Law Review* 177.

Weatherill, S. (2002) "Pre-emption, Harmonisation and the Distribution of Competence to Regulate the Internal Market" in C. Barnard and J. Scott (eds), *The Law of the Single Market: Unpacking the Premises* (Oxford: Hart).

Weatherill, S. (2004) "Why Harmonise?" in T. Tridimas and P. Nebbia (eds.) *Challenges for EU Law in the 21st Century. Volume I* (Oxford: Hart).

Weatherill, S. (2005) "Better Competence Monitoring" 30 *European Law Review* 23.

Weatherill, S. (2005) *EC Consumer Law and Policy* (Edward Elgar: Cheltenham).

Weiler, J. (1999) "The Constitution of the Common Market Place: Text and Context in the Evolution of the Free Movement of Goods" in Craig, P. and De Búrca, (eds), *The Evolution of EU Law* (Oxford: OUP).

Weiler, J. (1999) *The Constitution of Europe* (Cambridge: CUP).

Wennerås, P. (2006) "A New Dawn for the Commission Under Articles 226 and 228 EC: General and Persistent (GAP) Infringements, Lump Sums and Penalty Payments 45 *Common Market Law Review* 31.

Wessels, R., (2000) The Inside Looking Out: Consistency and Delimitation in EU External Relations 37 *Common Market Law Review* at 1151–1152.

Westlake, M. (1998) "The European Parliament's Emerging Powers of Appointment" 36 *Journal of Common Market Studies* 434.

Wright, K. (2007) "Perfect Symmetry? *Impala v Commission* and Standard of Proof in Mergers 32 *European Law Review* 408.

White, R. (2004) *Workers, Establishment, and Services in the European Union* (Oxford: OUP).

Wils, W. (2003) "Should Private Antitrust Enforcement Be Encouraged in Europe?" 26(3) *World Competition* 473.

Winter, J. (1972) "Direct Effect and Direct Applicability: Two Distinct and Different Concepts in Community law" 9 *Common Market Law Review* 42.

Wouters, J. (2000) "European Company Law: *Quo Vadis?*" 37 *Common Market Law Review* 257.

Wurmest, W. (2007) "The Reform of Article 82 EC in the Light of the "Economic Approach" in Drexl, J., et al (eds) *Article 82 EC: New Interpretation, New Enforcement Mechanisms?* (Berlin/ Heidelberg: Springer).

Wymeersh, E. (2005) "The Future of Financial Regulation and Supervision in Europe" 42 *Common Market Law Review* 987.

Zeitlin, J., Pochet, P and Magnusson, L. (eds), (2005) *The Open Method of Coordination in Action: The European Employment and Social Inclusion Strategies* (Brussels: P.I.E.–Peter Lang).

Zilioli, C. and Selmayr, M. (1999) "The External Relations of the Euro Area: Legal Aspects" 36 *Common Market Law Review* 273.

# Index